New Zealand English

Its Origins and Evolution

New Zealand English – at just 150 years old – is one of the newest varieties of English, and is unique in that its full history and development are documented in extensive audio recordings. The rich corpus of spoken language provided by New Zealand's 'Mobile Disc Recording Unit' has provided insight into how the earliest New Zealand-born settlers spoke, and consequently, how this new variety of English developed.

On the basis of these recordings, this book examines and analyses the extensive linguistic changes New Zealand English has undergone since it was first spoken in the 1850s. The authors, all experts in phonetics and sociolinguistics, use the data to test previous explanations for new dialect formation, and to challenge current claims about the nature of language change.

The first ever corpus-based study of the evolution of New Zealand English, this book will be welcomed by all those interested in phonetics, sociolinguistics, historical linguistics and dialectology.

STUDIES IN ENGLISH LANGUAGE

New Zealand English

Its Origins and Evolution

STUDIES IN ENGLISH LANGUAGE

The aim of this series is to provide a framework for original work on the English language. All are based securely on empirical research, and represent theoretical and descriptive contributions to our knowledge of notional varieties of English, both written and spoken. The series will cover a broad range of topics in English grammar, vocabulary, discourse, and pragmatics, and is aimed at an international readership.

Already published

Christian Mair
Infinitival complement clauses in English: a study of syntax in discourse

Charles F. Meyer
Apposition in contemporary English

Jan Firbas
Functional sentence perspective in written and spoken communication

Izchak M. Schlesinger
Cognitive space and linguistic case

Katie Wales
Personal pronouns in present-day English

Laura Wright
The development of standard English, 1300–1800: theories, descriptions, conflicts

Charles F. Meyer
English Corpus Linguistics: theory and practice

Stephen J. Nagle and Sara. L. Sanders (eds.)
English in the southern United States

Anne Curzan
Gender shifts in the history of English

Kingsley Bolton
Chinese Englishes

Irma Taavitsainen and Päivi Pahta (eds.)
Medical and Scientific Writing in Late Medieval English

Forthcoming

Raymond Hickey (ed.)
Legacies of Colonial English

New Zealand English
Its Origins and Evolution

ELIZABETH GORDON
University of Canterbury, New Zealand

LYLE CAMPBELL
University of Canterbury, New Zealand

JENNIFER HAY
University of Canterbury, New Zealand

MARGARET MACLAGAN
University of Canterbury, New Zealand

ANDREA SUDBURY
Kings College London

PETER TRUDGILL
University of Fribourg

PUBLISHED BY THE PRESS SYNDICATE OF THE UNIVERSITY OF CAMBRIDGE
The Pitt Building, Trumpington Street, Cambridge, United Kingdom

CAMBRIDGE UNIVERSITY PRESS
The Edinburgh Building, Cambridge, CB2 2RU, UK
40 West 20th Street, New York, NY 10011–4211, USA
477 Williamstown Road, Port Melbourne, VIC 3207, Australia
Ruiz de Alarcón 13, 28014 Madrid, Spain
Dock House, The Waterfront, Cape Town 8001, South Africa

http://www.cambridge.org

First published 2004
Reprinted 2005

Printed in the United Kingdom at the University Press, Cambridge

Typeface EhrhardtMT 10/12 pt. *System* $\LaTeX 2_\varepsilon$ [TB]

A catalogue record for this book is available from the British Library

Library of Congress Cataloguing in Publication data
New Zealand English : its origins and evolution / Elizabeth Gordon . . . [et al.].
p. cm. – (Studies in English language)
Includes bibliographical references and index.
ISBN 0-521-64292-2
1. English language – New Zealand. 2. English language – Variation – New Zealand.
3. English language – Spoken English – New Zealand. I. Gordon, Elizabeth. II. Series.
PE3602.N495 2004
427′.993 – dc22 2003055395

ISBN 0 521 64292 2 hardback

Contents

Figures

Tables

Tables in Appendix 2

Acknowledgements

A large number of people have been involved in the preparation of data, research, and writing of this book. In 1989, the University of Canterbury purchased the Mobile Disc Recording Unit archive, and Elizabeth Gordon began work on the recordings in 1990; she was joined by Gillian Lewis in 1993 and Leigh Nurkka in 1994. The Origins of New Zealand English Project (ONZE) was established in 1996 with funding from the New Zealand Public Good Science Fund. At that time, the team was Elizabeth Gordon, Gillian Lewis, Margaret Maclagan, Lyle Campbell, and Peter Trudgill, assisted by Leigh Nurkka, Chris Bartlett, and Sandra Quick. In 2000, Andrea Sudbury and Jennifer Hay joined the team as post-doctoral fellows.

Project managers (without whom this project could not have gone ahead) were Gillian Lewis (1996–9), Stacey Nicholas (1999–2001), and Rachel Rowlands (2001–3). They were responsible for, among other things, the day-to-day running of the project, the organisation of research workers, and, at times, the quest for funding. Emma Parnell of the Linguistics Department also assisted in the administration of financial expenditures.

Acquisition of data: Jim Sullivan, former Chief Archivist of Radio New Zealand Sound Archives, first made us aware of the Mobile Unit recordings; Stephen Riley, of Radio New Zealand Sound Archives in Timaru, organised the copying of the data.

Preparation of data, organisation of recorded material, and transcription: Gillian Lewis and Leigh Nurkka carried out much of this work in the first years of the project. Other research assistants were Chris Bartlett, Te Kahurangi Blake, Tim Brown, Siobhan Buckingham, Jeremy Carstairs-McCarthy, Michelle Dawe, Dianne Dwyer, Charlotte Gordon, Margaret Gordon, David Joseph, Diana Looser, David Maclagan, Wendy Nuthall, Karrie Schreier, Chris Tait, and Nathan Welham.

Technical assistance was given by Bruce Russell and Geeta Jatania of Radio New Zealand Sound Archives, and Mike Clayton from the Information Technology Department at the University of Canterbury.

The database was designed and organised by Gillian Lewis, Chris Bartlett, Jennifer Hay, Stacey Nicholas, and Rachel Rowlands.

Acoustic analysis was the responsibility of Margaret Maclagan who was assisted by David Maclagan, Jennifer Hay, and Chris Bartlett.

Identifying the British historical antecedents of the variables of early New Zealand English was carried out by Peter Trudgill, assisted by Margaret Maclagan and Lyle Campbell.

Research into early written records was done by Elizabeth Gordon, who received advice and assistance from Colin McGeorge and the librarians at the University of Canterbury, the Alexander Turnbull Library Wellington, and the Christchurch Public Library.

The historical research was the responsibility of Elizabeth Gordon. The main historical advisor to the project was Jenny Murray, who carried out the research on the case-study towns, and also gave advice and assisted with the text as a whole. Jock Phillips, former Chief Historian of the Department of Internal Affairs, gave permission to use the historical material and figures on the website http://www.nzhistory.net.nz/gallery/brit-nz/. This material was taken from a major project on the New Zealand immigrants from Britain and Ireland undertaken by the History Group funded by the New Zealand Foundation for Research Science and Technology. (It will be published in book form.) Sandra Quick, involved with historical research in the early part of the ONZE project, went to the towns visited by the Mobile Unit, looking for local sources of genealogical and historical information in museums, libraries, and so on. She also interviewed relatives of some of those interviewed in the 1940s. Nicola Woods, post-doctoral fellow at the University of Canterbury (1993–4), also visited some Otago towns and interviewed members of several generations of the families in the Mobile Unit archive. John Gordon gave advice for some of the historical discussion.

Statistical analysis was carried out by Jennifer Hay and Margaret Maclagan. John Pilkington also gave advice.

Genealogical searches were carried out by Sandra Quick and Louise Buckingham at the Department of Justice Registry of Births, Deaths, and Marriages in Lower Hutt. We are grateful to E. J. Rowland, Deputy Registrar-General, for allowing us free access to these records.

Preservation of the ONZE data has been carried out with the technical advice of Bruce Russell and Mike Clayton; Chris Tait transferred the data from audio and DAT tapes to CD-R. Max Broadbent and Jeff Palmer arranged for all the ONZE data to be held in the Macmillan Brown Library of the University of Canterbury.

Chris Bartlett assisted with the review of the literature in Chapter 4.

Information about the operations of the Mobile Unit was collected by Sandra Quick and Mike Clayton, who recorded an interview with Ash Lewis, technician on one of the Mobile Unit tours.

The project has been greatly assisted by academic visitors to the University of Canterbury. Daniel Schreier, the Marsden post-doctoral fellow for 2002, was actively involved with ONZE project discussions and gave excellent advice. James and Lesley Milroy's suggestions for studying present-day New Zealand English were adopted for the Canterbury Corpus of New Zealand English. William Labov gave invaluable advice about organising the ONZE project, and suggested methods of analysis. Other visitors to the project who gave assistance and advice were Walt Wolfram, Dennis Preston, Jenny Cheshire, Jean Hannah, John Rickford, Gunnel Melchors, Jack Chambers, Barbara Horvath, and David Gough. Two longer-term visitors to the ONZE project were Erwin la Cruz from the University of the Andes in Venezuela and Yutai Watanabe of Hosei University, Japan. Other scholars who have given input to the project were Ray Hickey, David Britain, and Roger Lass.

The ONZE project was supported by research grants from the University of Canterbury (Grants: U2007, U6456, U6207, U6261, U6318), the Macmillan Brown Bequest, the New Zealand Public Good Science Fund (UOC 607), The Royal Society of New Zealand Marsden Fund (M1039), the New Zealand Lotteries Board Fund (Grant E4834), and the Canterbury History Foundation (for data preservation).

The editing of the book was the work of Gillian Lewis, assisted by Anna Cull and Margaret Maclagan. Tony Trewinnard is to be thanked for producing the maps.

We also thank students from the Linguistics Department at the University of Canterbury who served as listeners for evaluating the accents of some of the Mobile Unit speakers. And, finally, we thank all our other colleagues who, from time to time, offered informal input, as well as moral and intellectual support.

Finally, we gratefully acknowledge the Mobile Unit interviewees and their descendants, without whom this project would not have been possible.

Abbreviations

AJHR	*Appendices to the Journal of the House of Representatives*
Mobile Unit	Mobile Disc Recording Unit, 1946–8
NZBS	New Zealand Broadcasting Service
nzhistory.net	http://www.nzhistory.net.nz/gallery/brit-nz/
ONZE	Origins of New Zealand English project, University of Canterbury
SED	Survey of English Dialects 1962–71

Abbreviations used on the Maps (Appendix 3)

Ellis	Ellis 1889
Lowman	Lowman's data, reported in Kurath & Lowman 1970
Thomas	Thomas 1994
Trudgill	Trudgill 1999d
Wright	Wright 1905

Symbols used

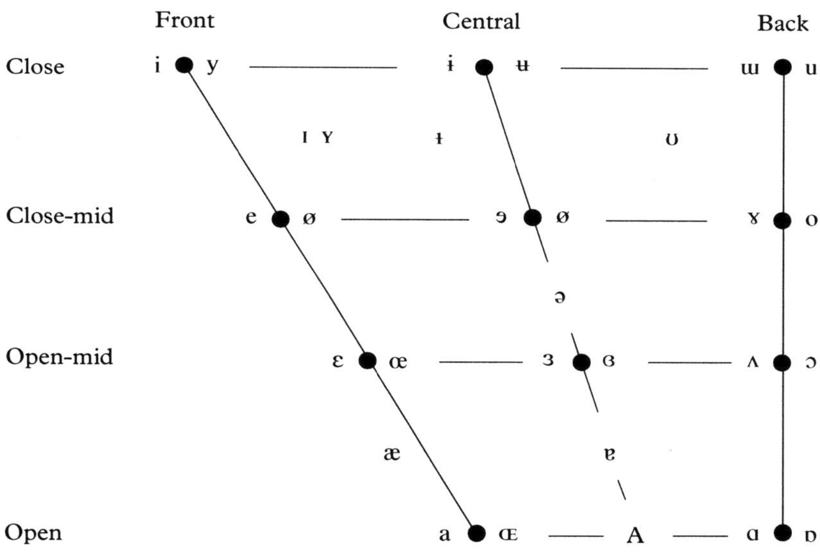

Where symbols appear in pairs, the one to the right represents a rounded vowel.

Other symbols

Consonants:
[ŋ] voiced velar nasal
[ɾ] voiced alveolar tap
[ɹ] voiced alveolar approximant
[r] voiced alveolar trill
[ɻ] retroflex approximant
[θ] voiceless dental fricative
[ʃ] voiceless postalveolar fricative
[ʍ] voiceless labial-velar fricative

Diacritics:
[a̝] raised
[a̞] lowered
[a̟] fronted
[a̠] retracted
[ḁ] devoiced
[ä] centralised
[ɫ] velarised – 'dark /l/', velarised alveolar lateral approximant

1 Introduction

> Sad to relate, one far too often hears the young generation talk with a twang that horrifies the ear of anyone used to good English . . . This twang is worse in Australia than in New Zealand but it is gaining ground here and ought to be strenuously eradicated by school teachers, for it does not sound nice, and robs sweet girlish lips of all their poesy.
>
> (Herz 1912: 352)

1 Introduction

In 1862 Richard Cotter and his wife Frances travelled with their family to New Zealand. They had left County Cork in Ireland and moved first to the goldfields in Ballarat in Australia, where two of their children were born. From there they moved across the Tasman Sea, still in search of gold, and settled in Arrowtown, in the South Island of New Zealand, where another eight children were born. The Cotter family story is a familiar one from the New Zealand goldfields of the 1860s and 70s. What makes it unusual is that one of these children, Annie, born in Arrowtown in 1877, was recorded in 1948 by the Mobile Disc Recording Unit set up by the New Zealand National Broadcasting Service (NZBS) to collect oral histories and musical recordings from the provinces. In her recording, the seventy-one-year-old Annie Cotter, now Mrs Hamilton, tells of her family's experiences as the first European settlers in the district, and of her life as a child and young woman in Arrowtown. Her interview was carried out in the same house in which she had been born. At the beginning of the recording she sounds nervous, but soon she relaxes and talks easily for over an hour. Her language has now been studied intensively, with both auditory and acoustic analyses of her pronunciation. Her recording, together with many others like it, is an invaluable resource for the study of the origins and development of New Zealand English, providing linguistic information about speakers born as early as the 1850s.

Previously, it was believed impossible to study the origins of new varieties of English directly for lack of data from the era in which they developed. Scholars approached the task indirectly, for example, extrapolating from present-day New Zealand English (Trudgill 1986b) and from earlier written comments (Gordon 1983a, 1998) what New Zealand English may have been like in previous generations. The limitations of such approaches were obvious and have always been recognised. However, with the rich corpus of spoken language provided by the Mobile Disc Recording Unit (henceforth 'Mobile Unit'), it is possible to find out how the earliest New Zealand-born European settlers spoke and, consequently, how a whole new variety of English developed on the opposite side of the world from the British Isles, 12,000 miles away. The speech of Mrs Annie Hamilton, who lived in Arrowtown all her life, is helping to provide answers to some of the most interesting and crucial questions about language change, and about the birth of a new variety of English. The recording of her speech and that of many other remarkable old New Zealanders provide the basis for the findings reported in this book.

Using a variety of sources – namely: historical documentation; shipping records; biographies and family histories; town histories and museum collections; information from official birth, death, and marriage records; parish and school archives; and information provided by the present-day descendants of the people recorded in the 1940s – it is now possible to reconstruct the backgrounds and lives of the Mobile Unit speakers. When this historical and social information is combined with the linguistic evidence derived from the analysis of the recordings, the results enable us to investigate the earliest forms of New Zealand English and to offer possible explanations for why New Zealand English is as it is today; why, for example, some features of the original British dialects were retained and others were lost, and whether there are social explanations for some linguistic developments. The results provide insights into the actual processes of language change and the formation of new dialects in general; they also allow us to evaluate a number of approaches that are used by linguists to explain new dialect formation, and provide the basis for clarifying and testing some general claims about how languages change in sociolinguistic settings.

Chapter 2 sets the stage and provides the context for the research findings reported in this book. In it, we survey the previous research on New Zealand English and provide a brief orientation to principal traits of modern New Zealand pronunciation. The history of the settlement of New Zealand is essential to understanding how New Zealand English developed, and this is presented in Chapter 3. Chapter 4 lays out the various explanations that have been proposed for the origins of New Zealand English. Chapter 5 explains the research methodology and the manner in which the research is reported in this book. Chapter 6 is perhaps the core of the book. In it, we present the findings on the linguistic variables most significant in the study of New Zealand English, using the speech of the Mobile Unit informants. For each variable we consider its antecedents in British Isles' varieties of English, the commentaries found in written records in New Zealand, and the results of our auditory and acoustic analyses of the Mobile

Unit recordings. In Chapter 7 we return to the various proposed explanations for the origin of New Zealand English and evaluate them on the basis of the findings presented in Chapter 6. We show that some of the proposals are simply not supported by the data and should be abandoned; however, other approaches are consistent with our findings and these are discussed in detail. Finally, in Chapter 8, we consider the findings on New Zealand English from the point of view of their implications for several major claims concerning language change in sociolinguistic settings in general. These include claims concerning the role that gender plays in linguistic change, the real-time investigation of linguistic change and whether adults change their basic language later in life, vowel shifts and mergers, the semantic conditioning of sound change and lexical diffusion, and whether speakers' motives to identify with different groups can impact change.

2 The Mobile Recording Unit

The original idea of a mobile recording unit that would travel around rural New Zealand came from the Director of Broadcasting, James Shelley. Shelley had been Professor of Education at Canterbury University College and, in the 1930s, had promoted rural education, sending tutors out to country areas in a van that also doubled as a mobile library. When Shelley became the Director of Broadcasting in New Zealand in 1936, he extended his vision to the use of radio, which he saw as a way of enhancing community spirit and encouraging democracy (Carter 1993: 206).

A mobile broadcasting unit was first used during World War II. Messages and greetings from soldiers and nursing staff abroad were sent home to New Zealand and broadcast to an enthusiastic audience (Hall 1980: 129–36). The success of this venture encouraged the NZBS after the war, with Shelley's support, to commission a Mobile Disc Recording Unit to travel around New Zealand. It had the aim of 'getting in touch with [musical] talent outside the cities, of reaching people in country towns and districts, and making known to New Zealanders in general how life is lived in their own country' (Fowler, *NZ Listener*, 6 February 1948). Over a period of two years, dozens of amateur choirs, pipe bands, brass bands, string orchestras of various sizes, and a host of solo singing performances were recorded on location. The unit also interviewed elderly people and recorded a number of Maori, recording Maori songs, chants, and prayers.[1] Music was the priority, but the quality of most musical recordings was found to be disappointing (Hall 1980: 152). The recordings of interviews, on the other hand, proved much more successful, and the programmes that were later broadcast, containing town histories told by way of the reminiscences of local 'old-timers', were extremely popular.

[1] Geoff Haggett notes that: 'One of the strong points on the tour was to get as much early historical Maori information as we could' (cited in Downes and Harcourt 1976: 133).

The Mobile Unit was, in fact, a large van, originally one of the mobile control towers of the New Zealand Air Force. The two heavy disc-recorders mounted inside were designed and built by the NZBS Engineering Section and were able to withstand the vibrations of New Zealand's rough country roads. Because the unit was often parked on uneven ground, the van had a hydraulic jack mounted on each corner and two spirit levels inside the cab to show if it was level. The microphones could be connected to long cables, enabling the interviews to be conducted inside people's homes, on their farms, or in the town hall, while the van was parked nearby.

The Mobile Unit made three tours: two in the North Island and one in the South Island. The first, in late 1946, went to Wanganui and New Plymouth, two provincial centres on the west coast of the North Island, along with several rural settlements in the Taranaki district (see Map 1, Appendix 3). As stated, the main purpose originally was to collect music, and only a small number of interviews (19) were recorded on this first tour. The second tour, in 1947, visited towns and rural communities in the Waikato and Thames Valley districts in the North Island. Encouraged by the very positive response of the public to the oral histories in the Taranaki broadcasts, more effort was now put into collecting interviews; 55 interviews were recorded (*NZ Listener*, 25 March 1948). The third tour ran from September to November 1948, around Otago, a large province in the South Island, where celebrations were underway to mark the centenary of the founding of its provincial centre, Dunedin. In the Otago tour, the oral histories were of paramount importance, and 127 interviews were recorded.

Hall, in the *History of Broadcasting in New Zealand*, suggests 'the mobile units came too late and too soon' (1980: 152). They came too late because the pool of pioneer reminiscences was diminishing, and too soon because tape was already beginning to replace acetate as the medium of recording. The Mobile Unit was cumbersome, the recording equipment heavy, and the tours were expensive. Yet its importance must not be overlooked – before acetate discs, there was no way of retaining radio broadcasts for posterity, or pre-recording material for later broadcast (Day 1994: 250–1). But in the end, new technology meant the end of the Mobile Unit.

The large acetate discs were stored in the New Zealand Radio Archives, with an index and description of material recorded, although much of this was difficult or impossible to read after some decades had passed. Due to the interest from linguists, preservation copies were first made on audiocassette as late as 1989.

3 ONZE

The Origins of New Zealand English project (ONZE) was formally established in 1996, with funding from the New Zealand Public Good Science Fund. Its primary data, the Mobile Unit recordings that are the basis of this book, had been acquired by the University of Canterbury in 1989[2] from the Radio New Zealand Archives, and the first analyses of a few speakers began in 1992. The first publications based on these data relied on the limited number of speakers who had been analysed to that time (see, for example, Trudgill et al. 1998).

The project continued to be funded in 1998 by a University of Canterbury research grant, and from 1999 to 2003 by a Marsden Grant from the Royal Society of New Zealand. Analysis of the Mobile Unit data has continued up to the present. Research on other periods of New Zealand English has also been carried out as part of the ONZE project, including: (1) the transcription and analyses of recordings of over 100 speakers born in what we have dubbed the Intermediate Period (1891–1930) (the majority born 1900–20); (2) the analyses of World War II recordings from the Radio New Zealand archives consisting of (usually short) recorded messages sent home to New Zealand by approximately 300 military personnel while overseas; (3) the analysis of variables from over 400 informants from the Canterbury Corpus of New Zealand informants born 1930–80, the speakers having been selected according to a quota sample representing both sexes, two age groups, and an upper and lower socioeconomic class. Some results from these other corpora have been published,[3] though much remains to be done with these data sets.

In the following chapters, we report the findings of our analysis of the Mobile Unit recordings and, in so doing, contribute both to explaining the origin and development of New Zealand English and, we hope, to the sociolinguistic study of language change in general.

[2] At the first New Zealand Oral History Conference in 1986 at Victoria University, Wellington, when Elizabeth Gordon commented on the lack of recorded evidence of nineteenth-century New Zealand speech, she was approached by Jim Sullivan, then Director of the Radio New Zealand Archives, who told her about the Mobile Unit recordings held in the archives in Timaru, South Canterbury.

[3] See Gordon and Maclagan 2000, 2001; M. Maclagan 1998, 2000; Maclagan and Gordon 1996a, 1996b, 1998, 1999, 2000; Maclagan et al. 1999.

2 Overview and background

In no other country was the speech of the children so good as it was in New Zealand . . . constant vigilance was the price to be paid for keeping the well of English undefiled in New Zealand.

(Mr John Caughley, Director of Education, cited in 'English Undefiled: Is there an NZ accent?', *The Press*, 5 February 1925)

There is not enough difference between the environments of the Englishman and the New Zealander to produce the existing difference in pronunciation. It should evidently be the teacher's aim to stay the process, and if possible restore to the New Zealand speech the culture it has unfortunately lost. We must, therefore examine the faults one by one and enumerate the definite sounds of English that the colonial ear has failed to catch and reproduce.

(Mr E. W. Andrews, 'New Zealand English', *The Triad*, 10 August 1910)

1 Overview of the study of New Zealand English

The English spoken in New Zealand has been the subject of comments since the early European settlers first began to notice new words and words being used in new ways. For example, in 1863 Samuel Butler (who later wrote the book *Erewhon*) wrote *A First Year in Canterbury Settlement*. Here he commented on several things: the use of the Aboriginal word *coo-ee* [which] 'corresponds to our English Hoy! Halloa!'; the change in the meaning of the word *bush* in New Zealand; the use of the expression *to go eyes out*, meaning to go fast; and the advantages of a *hiphole* when sleeping on the hard ground (quoted in Turner 1966: 43, 56, 177).

Observations about early New Zealand pronunciation were made largely by educationalists and others who had no linguistic training and whose aims were primarily prescriptive and critical rather than descriptive (most appeared rather late, in the 1880s). Later writers, in the 1930s and 1940s (Arnold Wall, Sidney Baker, and J. A. W. Bennett), also provided observations about features of New Zealand speech, but still with a prescriptive purpose, and it was not until the 1960s that New Zealand speech began to be treated more systematically as a variety in its own right. The 1980s marked a considerable change in the study of New Zealand English, with both overseas interest (Trudgill and Hannah 1982; Wells 1982) and local research. Tony Deverson's (1988) comprehensive bibliography of published work on New Zealand English contained 159 items (not including specialised glossaries); of these, 85, slightly more than half, were published in the years 1980–7. Since then, studies of various aspects of New Zealand English have continued to appear at a remarkable rate. Now New Zealand English is taught and researched in New Zealand universities and is a topic in the English syllabus for senior school students.

In this chronological overview we concentrate on the writings on New Zealand speech up to the mid-1980s, since these are relevant to our study but are not as readily accessible as more recently published material.

1.1 Nineteenth-century comments on New Zealand speech

As mentioned, the first reported comments on spoken New Zealand English appear in the 1880s and the originators of these comments were usually educationalists concerned with evaluating the speech of school children. There are two main published sources of information in this period, the reports of New Zealand school inspectors and comments by Samuel McBurney, both of which we discuss briefly.

1.1.1 Reports of New Zealand school inspectors. Every year from 1880 onwards, New Zealand school inspectors were required to submit annual reports about the pupils and teachers they were evaluating, and these were published in the Appendices to the *Journal of the House of Representatives* (or *AJHR*). From time to time some of the inspectors commented on the pronunciation of the children whose reading and recitation they were examining and these reports have been a fruitful source of early observation of spoken English in New Zealand (see Gordon 1983a, 1983b, 1991, 1994, 1998; Gordon and Deverson 1989; Gordon and Abell 1990). Until about 1900 the inspectors wrote favourably of the school children's 'correct pronunciation', which was free from 'marked accents or provincialisms' (Gordon 1983a: 35). Because they were concerned with making an evaluation of what they heard, the inspectors also noted features they felt should be eradicated. Two features in particular received frequent comment: h-dropping and the pronunciation of words that end in '-ing' with word-final /n/ instead of /ŋ/ (Gordon 1983a: 33–4). Gordon concludes that in the school inspectors' reports prior to 1900 'there was almost no reference at all to anything that suggests a distinctive New Zealand variety [of English]' (1983a: 33). Several of the specific observations from this period are presented in Chapter 6 alongside the variables to which they relate.

1.1.2 Observations of Samuel McBurney. In 1887 Samuel McBurney made the first known attempt to apply phonetics to the study of English pronunciation in

New Zealand. McBurney, a Scot, was a visiting singing teacher and school principal engaged in examining singing classes in Australasian schools (see Turner 1967: 84–5). On the sea journey to Australia he had taught himself phonetic transcription by reading Melville Bell's *Visible Speech* and A. J. Ellis's *Pronunciation for Singers* (Ellis 1889: 248), so he was able to provide a more formal phonetic description of the speech of the children in schools he visited. Such description, which is lacking from the school inspectors' reports, is one reason why McBurney's work has been described as 'the earliest trustworthy account of New Zealand English pronunciation' (Bauer 1994: 391, after Turner 1967: 84 and Wall 1939: 8). Another reason is because McBurney's observations are based on data he collected from different regions of New Zealand; Ellis records that McBurney's method was

> to take a number of test words, and record the pron[unciation] in glossic [a phonetic transcription system], and then mark by symbols whether these were general, in the majority or minority, about half, or sporadic. In some cases he . . . even found it expedient to separate the habits of boys and girls in schools. (Ellis 1889: 237)[1]

McBurney wrote a summary article for the Christchurch newspaper, *The Press*, in October 1887 (reprinted in Turner 1967) and also forwarded his data to the dialectologist Alexander Ellis, who published a full account of McBurney's findings in his major work on English dialects (Ellis 1889: 236–48). Specific details of his findings are incorporated in Chapter 6 of this book. McBurney summarised his observations on colonial pronunciation, remarking that it is inexplicable 'why there should be a general tendency, as there undoubtedly is in Australia, to a Cockney pronunciation' (1887: 5). Although he claimed there were seven phonological features of 'modern Cockney' in Australasian English,[2] McBurney indicated that all but one (word-final '-ing' as /n/ rather than /ŋ/) are relatively infrequently heard in New Zealand (1887: 5). He concluded that there was 'another type' of English in New Zealand, but added that the variety was 'difficult to define' (McBurney 1887: 5). This comment and his data tables suggest that there was a high degree of variability to be heard in the New Zealand towns he visited. McBurney's findings have until recently been the main source of information on nineteenth-century English in New Zealand.

1.1.3 Charles Baeyertz and The Triad*: 1893–1915.* *The Triad* was one of New Zealand's most famous early periodicals, edited and published by Charles

[1] Gordon and Abell (1990: 35) caution that McBurney commented on some features of colonial pronunciation only after they had been brought to his attention, which is perhaps why Trudgill et al. (2000b: 119) consider that McBurney is 'not a particularly reliable witness'. Furthermore, it is not possible to assess his ability as a phonetician.

[2] See our comments on this claim in Chapters 4 and 7.

Baeyertz, a third-generation Australian who came to New Zealand in 1892. It was dedicated to music, art, science, and literature, and later also reported on current events. It appeared in New Zealand from 1893 until 1915, when it moved to Australia where it continued until 1927. *The Triad* rapidly achieved popularity in New Zealand; by 1897 circulation reportedly reached 10,000, and it was said in 1919 that *The Triad* was found 'in every club, hotel and reading-room' (Baughen 2002).

Baeyertz was a notable polyglot, speaking several languages fluently, including Maori. He lived in Dunedin where he taught modern languages, Greek and Latin, also elocution, music, singing and 'other vicious habits'. In *The Triad* he frequently commented, sometimes caustically and abusively, about the enunciation of singers and actors, and his trenchant comments about 'mispronunciations' are a useful guide to early New Zealand speech. For example, when writing about the singing of the psalm at the All Saints church in Nelson, he complained: 'The congregation sang it in three different keys and the variety is not always charming. "Lord keep us safe this night" sounded like "Lord kee-e-e pus syfe the snight", and yet they say there is no accent in New Zealand' (September 1895). Readers of *The Triad* were told that 'children who did not speak well could not appreciate good poetry' (July 1910) and were assured that the New Zealand accent itself was responsible for 'minor throat and nasal disorders' (August 1910). In addition, Baeyertz was very critical of people (usually women) who tried to produce 'genteel' pronunciation:

> Rather hopelessly, I have again to raise my voice in protest against these distressing . . . affectations. Recently a lady rang me on the 'phone. I asked for her number, she told me 'nayne, fayve, fayve.' I think such affectations, as these are worse or viler than what we are beginning to execrate as the Australian accent. 'May' for *my*, 'bay' for *by*, 'cray' for *cry* – the revolting idiocy of it all! (August 1912)

Baeyertz regularly published the comments of others on the subject of New Zealand pronunciation. A good example is an article (10 August 1910) which gives an account of a speech on 'New Zealand English' by E. W. Andrews, of Napier Boys' High School. The title 'New Zealand English' itself is notable because it indicates that the changes in pronunciation were significant enough for people to talk about a national language variety:

> Lest . . . I may appear to speak rather too comprehensively, let me at once acknowledge that very many New Zealanders born and bred do speak the King's English with propriety and euphony; there is nothing to distinguish their speech from that of a highly cultured Englishman in England . . . I am merely just now observing that a dialect, and that not a defensible one, is gradually becoming fixed in the Dominion among the children and younger adults. (E. W. Andrews quoted in *The Triad*, August 1910: 37)

Andrews saw this dialect as homogeneous:

> In New Zealand the dialect is not a matter of locality and occupation, not even of social position nor education. You hear the same peculiarities wherever you go; the university graduate has the same faulty vowels as the bushman. (1910: 37)

He then goes on to 'enumerate the definite sounds of English that the colonial has failed to catch and reproduce' and suggests that one of the reasons for the emergence of the 'new dialect' is the existence of a large number of different dialects in New Zealand:

> [I]f a New Zealand child hears his language pronounced differently by his parents, his clergyman, his friends, his teacher, his inspectors, he will probably acquire a new and ugly polyglot speech of his own, reproducing the laziest and most slipshod methods of the others, without adding to the world's stock a language representing any truly local individuality. (Andrews, in *The Triad*, August 1910: 39)

1.2 Reports on the developing New Zealand English variety: 1900–1935

The school inspectors' reports continued to appear in *AJHR*, and from 1900 onwards their views concerning the pronunciation of school children were almost always negative. (A number of their comments on specific variables are given in Chapter 6.) Similarly negative comments appeared in submissions to the 1912 Cohen Commission on Education in New Zealand (*AJHR* E12, 1912: 1–744). Others in the education system commented on the rise of 'impurities' in the children's speech and their reports were published in the *New Zealand Journal of Education* (1899–1918), which became *National Education* in 1919, and later in *The New Zealand Education Gazette* (1921–present). Margaret Batterham's (1993) study of the language used by these writers shows that much of it is in the form of metaphor, involving among other things, *disease*, 'an incurable disease', *filth*, 'vile, muddy, a blot on our national life', *crime*, 'the blood of the language on their hands', *wickedness*, 'evil sounding, despairing depths', *degeneracy*, 'corrupt, slovenly, unspeakably bad', and *damage*, 'mangled, twisted and debauched' (Batterham1993: 5–24). Educationalists increasingly deplored the pronunciation of unstressed /ɪ/ and the closing diphthongs /ai/, /ei/, /ou/, and /au/ (Gordon 1994: 6; see commentary in Chapter 6). Although these features of pronunciation attracted the most comment, a number of others were also criticized (see Andrews' comments above).

After 1900, favourable comments on school children's pronunciation were rare (Gordon 1983a: 35). Shortly after this time, speech lessons in schools were proposed as a corrective measure but they had little effect (Gordon and Deverson 1989: 43–50; Gordon and Abell 1990: 28–31). The educationalists' negative attitudes towards New Zealand English continued, as Harry Orsman recalls:

> I had looked forward to reading a copy of a thesis completed in 1930 by J. W. Shaw, a lecturer in English at Auckland Teachers' Training College . . . The thesis *New Zealand speech – a study in development and tendency* was . . . rejected as an unsuitable topic by the University of Auckland Department of Education, and was then destroyed by its disappointed author. (Orsman 1995: 12, fn. 2)

While the main object of criticism was the speech of children, said by the school inspectors and others to be badly influenced by 'the home and the street', there were also adverse comments about New Zealanders who tried to emulate upper-class British speech, a variety the New Zealand writer A. R. D. Fairburn (1947) named 'colonial-genteel'. One of the members of the Cohen Commission on Education in 1912 complained, 'What hope is there for change when we find two of the principals of the largest secondary schools in New Zealand in giving evidence, using these expressions: "taim-table" for "time-table", "may own" for "my own", "faive" for "five", "gairls" for "girls"' (*AJHR* E-12, 1912: 637).

1.3 The characterisation of New Zealand English: 1936–1965

In the years 1936 to 1965 the first significant studies to give a sense of the character of New Zealand English appeared. Arnold Wall, the single most important figure in this period, published his first book on English pronunciation *The Mother Tongue in New Zealand* in 1936, and in 1966 a number of key works appeared that marked a significant advance on what had already been published.

Three writers in this period – Arnold Wall, Sidney Baker and J.A.W. Bennett – identified salient features of New Zealand English, but for the most part they did not attempt to give a comprehensive description of the phonological system, nor did they employ the data-collection methods developed by nineteenth-century European dialectologists. However, their observations provide valuable information on what they saw as the defining characteristics of New Zealand English.

1.3.1 Arnold Wall (1936–1966). Wall is the main source of information on New Zealand English in the early to mid-twentieth century (Wall 1936, 1939, 1951a, 1958, 1959, 1964, 1966). He was an Englishman who moved to New Zealand in 1899 to take up a position in the English Department at what was then Canterbury University College in Christchurch. In a talk entitled, 'The way I have come', broadcast in 1951, he noted changes in New Zealand pronunciation between 1910 and 1930 as the accent developed (Wall 1951b). After he retired as Professor of English in 1931, he began publishing his observations, initially writing newspaper columns (collected in Wall 1958, 1964) and giving weekly broadcast talks designed to explain to listeners where New Zealand English diverged from Standard English. Wall can be described as a prescriptivist, since his primary intention was to teach people the 'correct' way to pronounce words (e.g. Wall 1936, 1939). He acknowledged the influence of the famous English phonetician Daniel Jones in his recommendations of 'good' and 'bad' pronunciations. Even though he claimed he did not want to 'criticize New Zealand speech unkindly' (especially because of his young students 'whose speech left much to be desired yet died gloriously at Gallipoli') (Wall 1939: preface, n.p.), he nevertheless made value judgements about the language:

> This book is designed for use by residents in New Zealand who wish to speak 'good' English, or 'standard' English, as spoken by the 'best' speakers in the old land; it is not intended for those who wish to develop a new dialect of English in this country, nor for those who openly say that they care nothing for standards or authorities but mean to pronounce English words as they please. (Wall 1939: 1)

Wall noted many features of New Zealand English pronunciation, although he labelled them 'essential faults in New Zealand speech' (1939: 15) and 'prevalent errors in New Zealand pronunciation' (1939: 16). Some of his descriptions of these features are quoted in Chapter 6. He was of the opinion that 'in most cases, where a sound varies from the standard in New Zealand speech, it is simply Cockney' (1936: 136) and noted that some New Zealanders 'speak English as correctly and with as pure an accent as the best speakers in the Old Land', but that 'about eighty percent of the population, at a rough guess, speaks English with a more or less marked London, or "Cockney," accent' (1939: 8). Wall says his own speech was modified in the direction of Cockney when he was a schoolboy living in London (1951b), so his judgements are based on his memories from his childhood.

Wall continued writing columns on New Zealand English for *The Press* and the *New Zealand Listener* for a number of years and in 1958 published a collection of them (Wall 1958); its title *The Queen's English* indicates that his intention was still to correct 'errors' in New Zealand English. In the following year, an expanded version of his earlier work on New Zealand English (Wall 1939) was published (Wall 1959). He added comments on the correct pronunciation of about a hundred lexical items, but did not update his discussion of the features of New Zealand English pronunciation. However, in Wall 1964, he did add a significant new piece of information: in a section entitled '*Uz Ut*', he indicates that the centralisation of /ɪ/ had spread to all stressed positions. In 1939 he had noted that /ɪ/ was centralised in unstressed positions and before /l/ (e.g. in Wall 1939: 16). He transcribed *is it* as [ɪz ət]) and in Wall (1951a) he noted that the pronunciation had spread to monosyllabic words: 'Monosyllables having the short *i* are similarly pronounced [i.e. centralised], *ut uzz, uzzn't ut* (it is, isn't it), and such words as "did"' (Wall 1951a: 91). Wall's feelings on this development were characteristically prescriptive:

> Some, if not all dialects of Scottish and Anglo-Irish exhibit this same peculiarity, but I should not attribute the New Zealand 'i' to the influence of either of those dialects – no, I should make it due to original sin. Why 'sin'? Well, it is sheer laziness, a reluctance to make a very slight effort and I make bold to call that a sin in the everyday, not the biblical, sense. (Wall 1964: 138)

1.3.2 Sidney Baker (1941). At around the same time that Wall published his first books on New Zealand English, Sidney Baker (1912–76) investigated Australasian speech. Baker, born and educated in New Zealand, published several books on Australian English (e.g. 1941a, 1947, 1959) and one book on New Zealand English, *New Zealand Slang* (1941b), which was 'concerned with telling something of our indigenous colloquial speech, of the extraordinary colour of it, of our habits of speech, and in what ways they differ from the English language of England' (1941b: 8). As its title indicates, the book is largely devoted to the discussion of slang terms, but the final chapter gives Baker's impressions of New Zealand pronunciation. He noted that he undertook 'several years of close study of the subject, during which [he took] many tests of speech in New Zealand, Australia, and England' (1941b: 93) but he gives no clues about his methodology. However, the implication is that he carried out some kind of formal investigation, in contrast to Wall's indirect observations.

Baker focused on what he called the 'general characteristics' of New Zealand English in order to make his work easier for his readers to understand (1941b: 103). He noted that New Zealand English is characterised by: 'a tendency to diphthongise short vowels'; 'a general sharpening [= shortening] of vowel values'; 'a strong tendency to give the various vowels in a word the same value; an equalization of stress'; 'rapidity of speech'; and 'a much longer word-grouping than in English speech' (1941b: 103–4). Perhaps one of the most interesting points is that Baker claimed direct influence of Maori (particularly via placenames) on New Zealand English pronunciation as the reason for a number of the distinctive features of the latter.

Although Baker referred to Wall's prescriptiveness and claimed that he himself was 'concerned as far as humanly possible only with presenting the facts' (1941b: 94), he also evaluated the New Zealand English accent. He noted 'the emergence of (i) an educated and (ii) a vulgar New Zealand speech, the former being clear, decisive, and pleasant, though tending to sharp nasalization' (1941b: 104), by implication suggesting that the 'vulgar' speech was perhaps not so pleasant. Baker also commented that the diphthong /au/ is commonly nasalised and remarked that it 'is probably the only seriously unpleasant sound to be found in common use' (1941b: 102) in New Zealand English. In his book *New Zealand Slang*, he also made the remark: 'More nonsense has been spoken and written and there is generally more misinformed opinion about pronunciation in this country than about our indigenous slang – which is saying a lot' (Baker 1941b: 93).

1.3.3 J. A. W. Bennett (1943). Jack Bennett was a New Zealand medievalist, working in Queen's College, Oxford, in England, who published just one article on New Zealand English (in *American Speech*, 1943). He pointed out the general lack of information on New Zealand English:

> There has been little attempt to give a picture of English as it is spoken (and written) in New Zealand: partly because any such survey involves a form of self-criticism which it is especially difficult for a native of a small and comparatively isolated community to undertake, lacking as he does adequate standards of comparison; partly because few visitors, even when qualified for such a study, stay long enough to make it. (Bennett 1943: 69)

The aim of Bennett's article is stated as being 'to indicate some of the modifications which so-called Standard British English has undergone in the dominion furthest removed from Britain' (Bennett 1943: 70). Most of the article consists of a discussion of the distinctive vocabulary of New Zealand English, particularly slang items, probably because it was written for an American audience and comparisons could be made more readily between New Zealand English and American English by considering lexical items. As a result, he perhaps overstated the degree of American influence on New Zealand English.

Bennett discussed just a few phonological features of New Zealand English that he claimed were very noticeable and widespread (1943: 70). These are: fronted /a/, the fronted and raised first element of the diphthong /au/, the diphthongisation of /u/, the pronunciation of word-final /ɪ/ (e.g. in *fifty*) as [i] (see '*happ*Y-tensing', Chapter 6), and the retention of aspirated *wh* (e.g. /hw/ in *which*). There is no attempt to give a systematic treatment of the complete phonemic system.

1.4 Overseas interest in New Zealand English

During World War II there was some interest in New Zealand English. The US Army included information mainly on New Zealand English vocabulary items in its guide for soldiers, *A Short Guide to New Zealand* (United States War and Navy Departments 1944, excerpts reprinted in *New Zealand English Newsletter* 5, 1991: 42–4), and also described New Zealand English as sounding 'a bit like English Cockney to American ears, although it really isn't' (1944: 34). Three key features of New Zealand English pronunciation are highlighted, namely the shifting of the diphthongs /au/, /ei/, and /ai/.

Mario Pei's (1946) *The World's Chief Languages* included a brief section of only one-and-a-half pages, mainly on New Zealand English vocabulary. The only reference to pronunciation is the (erroneous) claim that 'intonation and pronunciation, while distinctive, are closer to American than British' (Pei 1946: 76).

In *New Zealand: Pacific Pioneer*, about New Zealand in general, Philip Soljak (1946) included a brief section on language (reprinted in *New Zealand English*

Newsletter 5, 1991: 42–4). As in the other overseas reports from this time, most of the overview of New Zealand English deals with vocabulary. However, Soljak made a few general statements about New Zealand English pronunciation, noting features such as: the tendency to 'speak rapidly, reducing pitch or rhythm to an even monotone'; the 'clipped' syllables; and the 'flattened or shortened vowels', the sole example given of the latter being the shortening of /i/ to [ɪ] as in 'New Zilland' (Soljak 1946: 118).

Eric Partridge and J. W. Clark's (1951) *British and American English since 1900* includes brief contributions by Wall and Orsman on New Zealand English, classified as a sub-type of British English. Wall noted a few general tendencies in New Zealand English, including just six features of pronunciation that had 'developed rapidly during the last fifty years' (Wall 1951a: 91), while Orsman's contribution focused on distinctive vocabulary items, listing a few random slang terms, and commenting that the 'American invasion' of the war years 'left little lasting impression on the language' (Orsman 1951: 94). This book is notable because local experts were invited to contribute first-hand knowledge of the features of New Zealand English.

The final example of information on New Zealand English in overseas publications from this period is G. L. Brook's *English Dialects* (1963). He included a brief summary of New Zealand English, and noted 'New Zealand has often been called the most British of the Dominions' (1963: 134). He also emphasised the close relationship between New Zealand English and Australian English. He claimed:

> Since many New Zealanders both aim at speaking like Englishmen and succeed in doing so, it is possible in speaking of New Zealand pronunciation only to indicate some tendencies which are fairly widespread in New Zealand, without suggesting that the pronunciations indicated are invariable. (Brook 1963: 134)

Six features of New Zealand English pronunciation – an apparently random list – are mentioned.

In summary, the overseas reports on New Zealand English that appeared in the years 1940–65 were sparse and sometimes not accurate. They each chose different features in order to describe New Zealand English pronunciation and in some places contradicted each other, particularly in their assessments of the relationships between New Zealand English and both British and American English.

1.5 Advances in the study of New Zealand English: 1966–1984

The year 1966 was significant for the study of New Zealand English. That year a number of items appeared in print that marked a notable step forward from what had been published up until that point. One item in particular was indicative of the growing interest in New Zealand English: a bibliography of previous work on New Zealand English (Coleridge 1966), published for the benefit of teachers. Further evidence of the interest in New Zealand English at this time is the re-publication of McBurney's newspaper article of 1887 in Turner 1967. It seems likely that the main impetus came from advances in research on Australian English, particularly the landmark study *The Speech of Australian Adolescents* by Mitchell and Delbridge (1965). Around this time, 'plans for a survey of New Zealand English [were] beginning to be discussed' (Turner 1966: 213) but this turned out to be premature. Nevertheless, the quality of work on New Zealand English improved in this period as more linguists became involved.

L. G. Kelly was a New Zealander who had a post at Laval University in Canada as a graduate fellow carrying out research in language teaching. In 1966 he published a paper on New Zealand English pronunciation in *The Canadian Journal of Linguistics*. The source of his information is not stated, although it is possible that his paper was based on course work he carried out when in New Zealand. Its main contribution to the development of the study of New Zealand English is the inclusion of a complete vowel quadrilateral diagram showing the location of general New Zealand English vowels, along with detailed discussion of the individual vowel phonemes. However, some of the details were incorrect, given what was already known about New Zealand English then. In particular, Kelly claimed that New Zealand English /e/ (e.g. in *bed*) is lowered to the point where it overlaps with raised versions of /æ/; he claims that 'extreme forms' of /e/ and /æ/ 'can often be found in the same speaker, so that the two vowels become identical' (Kelly 1966: 80–1).[3] New Zealand English /e/, however, is normally characterised as being raised when compared with other English varieties, though /æ/ is also raised (but also distinct from /e/; see Chapter 6). Kelly's paper is noteworthy in that it attempts to give a systematic overview of New Zealand English pronunciation, but the errors indicate that there were still gaps in knowledge, perhaps as a result of the lack of fieldwork and actual data-based studies.

In 1966 L. F. Brosnahan, Professor of English Language at Victoria University Wellington, published a systematic, if small-scale, data-based study investigating the allophones of /l/ in the speech of a 'few adult educated native speakers' of New Zealand English (1966: 230). Even though his sample was very small, he states, 'the main features of the description . . . probably have fairly wide applicability to educated New Zealand English' (1966: 230). The paper is significant because it reports actual data, a method that was not to become the norm in the field of New Zealand English studies for another twenty years.

1.5.1 George Turner (1966–1972). George Turner is a pivotal figure in the evolution of New Zealand English studies. He was one of the first linguists to investigate

[3] This merger is not characteristic of New Zealand English, although it can be observed before /l/.

the variety. Like the work of most of those who wrote before him, his publications on the topic are based on personal observations rather than data. What sets him apart from most earlier writers is that his overviews of New Zealand English pronunciation in particular were systematic, thorough, and detailed.

In *The English Language in Australia and New Zealand* (Turner 1966), he discussed Australian English and then noted where New Zealand English diverged from it. He justified this procedure as follows:

> But though New Zealand has had to be specifically mentioned often, and many details have applied to one of the two countries alone, a great deal is shared and, so far as language is concerned, the term *Australasian* could well be revived to refer to a single variety of English with two major subdivisions. (Turner 1966: 164)

The treatment of pronunciation in Turner (1966) is comprehensive. There is a systematic discussion of voice quality, speech rhythm, stress, intonation, all the vowels and diphthongs of Broad Australian English (and of Educated Australian English and New Zealand English where they differ), and the consonants which Turner considered to be the 'few genuinely current deviations from RP pronunciation' (1966: 105), including the post-vocalic /r/ in the Southland variety of New Zealand English. The vowels and diphthongs of RP form the framework for his overview of those of Broad Australian English. These two varieties are contrasted because they are at 'two ends of a cline' (1966: 96). He considered Educated Australian English and New Zealand English to be 'nearer to the English end' of the cline (1966: 96) and he discussed points where they differ from Broad Australian English. Turner also considered variation in Australian and New Zealand English. However, most of this discussion focuses on New Zealand English vocabulary; that is, New Zealand English is treated as a regional variety of Australasian English.

Turner also arranged for the re-publication of McBurney's (1887) article from *The Press*, to which he added a few comments concerning the source of the article and something of McBurney's background (Turner 1967). In 1970 he published a paper solely on New Zealand English, which appeared along with a reprint of Bennett (1943) in a collection of papers on Australasian English (Ramson 1970). Bennett's paper was re-published without significant modifications after nearly thirty years, simply because there had been very little work of note on New Zealand English in the interim. There is a parallel here in the re-publication in 1959 of Wall's (1939) *New Zealand English*, with no additional information on pronunciation, even though it was an 'updated' edition. Turner 1970 is essentially a condensed version of the information on New Zealand English in Turner 1966, again with most of the discussion focused on vocabulary items. As far as the study of New Zealand English is concerned, Turner 1966 can be considered to be a summary of the state of the art at the time, extended by Turner's own numerous observations.

1.5.2 Studies of pronunciation: defining New Zealand English (1973–1982)

1.5.2.1 Peter Hawkins. Although most of the discussion to this point has centred on pronunciation, the material on New Zealand English published prior to the early 1970s deals primarily with its distinctive vocabulary. Peter Hawkins, an Englishman teaching at Victoria University in Wellington, cited this focus on vocabulary as a key reason for his deciding to study New Zealand English pronunciation: 'Lexical . . . features which are characteristic of New Zealand usage . . . are, however, few in number and may be relatively infrequent in occurrence; what characterises a speaker as a New Zealander is not his use of particular lexical items so much as his accent, the study of which has hitherto been rather neglected' (Hawkins 1973b: 1).

Turner (1966, 1970) had outlined the features of New Zealand English pronunciation in the context of an overview of broad Australian English, but Hawkins aimed to give a more thorough description of the New Zealand English, noting that:

> I am assuming that there is such a thing as 'a N.Z. accent'. I have mentioned elsewhere [Hawkins 1973b]: (a) that there is a characteristically New Zealand pronunciation; (b) that this accent can vary along a continuum from 'broad' to 'modified', rather as Turner (1966) suggests for Australian English; (c) that the 'modified' end approximates RP, which is regarded by New Zealanders as the standard accent even though it is used only rarely; and (d) that there is relatively little regional variation of any significance within New Zealand. (Hawkins 1973a: 18, fn. 5)

Hawkins noted differences between New Zealand English and RP, including: New Zealand English's use of long /i/ word-finally in the *city* group of words; the status of /ə/, which he claims is merged with /ɪ/ in New Zealand English, thereby giving New Zealand English one less phoneme in comparison with RP; the status of the centring diphthongs, especially /ʊə/ which exists in RP as a 'somewhat marginal phoneme' and which 'New Zealand has just about got rid of altogether' (1973b: 5); the possibility that *ear* and *air* are merging in New Zealand English; the effect of /l/ on preceding vowels and also the vocalization of /l/ in broad New Zealand English (see Chapter 6 for details). Hawkins (1973b) also devised a phonemic transcription system for New Zealand English in which he proposes that transcription systems based on RP are not ideally suited for use in describing New Zealand English because of key differences between the two varieties. He concluded:

> The characteristics of New Zealand English have much in common with Australian English and with popular urban London accents (not Cockney, not RP, but something between). I believe that these three accents are not just different from RP, but are in the forefront of historical change in English sound patterns . . . So we may hazard a guess that the standard, RP, in a hundred years time will sound rather like New Zealand English

> today . . . Let me conclude, however, by dipping into my crystal ball and pulling out one more prophecy: the changes currently taking place in the diphthongs [of New Zealand English] strongly suggest that the Great English Vowel Shift . . . is happening all over again, in exactly the same way. (Hawkins 1973b: 7)

The notion of a new Great Vowel Shift in New Zealand English is further discussed by Maclagan (1975), Bauer (1979, 1982), Matthews (1981), and Trudgill (1986b); also see Chapter 8.

1.5.2.2 Margaret Maclagan. Phonetician Margaret Maclagan (1975) discussed semantics, lexis, syntax, morphology, phonology, and phonetics in a brief overview of New Zealand English. She concluded that New Zealand English 'differs most markedly from the received pronunciation of Great Britain at the phonetic level' (1975: 10). In order to give a clearer sense of the New Zealand English vowel system, she presented vowel quadrilateral diagrams of general and broad New Zealand English, based on auditory impressions. Maclagan's (1982) study of New Zealand English pronunciation marked a significant advance on what had come before; her aim 'was to provide acoustic data so that more informed analyses can be made of New Zealand English' (1982: 20). Maclagan's methodology in this paper was much more rigorous than that of any earlier work, but did not deal with social characteristics of the sample (other than a male/female distinction). Maclagan chose 50 speakers (25 males and 25 females), recorded them pronouncing 'the New Zealand vowels in an /h_d/ frame [the standard for acoustic analysis of vowels] in the phrase "Please say X again"' (1982: 20), and then analysed the data acoustically. She provided a detailed account of general New Zealand English vowels, diphthongs, and the effect of post-vocalic /l/ on preceding vowels. She also compared the results with her earlier auditory analysis (Maclagan 1975) and concluded, 'it can be seen that the auditory analysis underestimated the extent of the New Zealand vowel movements. In particular, /ɪ/, /ʊ/ and /u/ are centralised much more and /e/ and /ɔ/ are raised much higher than the auditory analysis indicated' (1982: 22). Where possible, she compared the results with acoustic analyses of Australian English and RP, and so was able to discuss New Zealand English pronunciation with a great degree of precision.

1.5.3 Renewed overseas interest in New Zealand English. The rise in interest in New Zealand English within New Zealand from the mid-1960s, as outlined so far, was followed by renewed interest in New Zealand English abroad. World Englishes were attracting more attention (e.g. Trudgill and Hannah 1982; Wells 1982; Lass 1987), and it is in that context that accounts of New Zealand English appeared in overseas publications. The first of these is Northcote-Bade 1976, written for a German readership, which covers much the same ground as Turner 1966, Hawkins 1973a, and Maclagan 1975, although in condensed form, intended as an introduction to New Zealand English.

Eagleson 1982 is somewhat similar to Turner 1966, with some updated material, focusing on the distinctive lexicon of Australian English and New Zealand English. His discussion of pronunciation uses RP for comparison purposes and he only describes features where Australian and New Zealand English differ substantially from RP. Australian English is treated in much more detail than New Zealand English – the vast majority of the examples are Australian. This is an approach often taken in overviews that discuss the two varieties together, partly because of the relative lack of research on New Zealand English. Eagleson himself refers to Mitchell and Delbridge's (1965) landmark study of Australian English pronunciation and notes that there is no study of the New Zealand accent equal to it in comprehensiveness (Eagleson 1982).

Trudgill and Hannah (1982) also place New Zealand English alongside Australian English; both are treated together as a single standard variety: 'AusNZEng', though in the third edition in 1994, the two varieties are discussed separately. A systematic description of the phonetic differences between Broad Australian English and RP is given, but as in Eagleson 1982, New Zealand English pronunciation is discussed only at points where it tends to differ from Australian English. The main features of New Zealand English identified in previous studies are also noted by Trudgill and Hannah (1982); these include the height of the front vowels, centralisation of /ɪ/, the merger of /ɪə /~/eə/, and retention of /ʍ/. A small number of grammatical features of New Zealand English, particularly aspects of the auxiliary system, are also discussed. On the whole, Trudgill and Hannah 1982 is a notable step forward in the characterisation of New Zealand English in overseas publications because of the level of detail reported.

The most comprehensive overview of New Zealand English pronunciation from this period is in John Wells' *Accents of English* (1982). Although Wells comments on the similarity of New Zealand English and Australian English, he nevertheless treats New Zealand English on its own terms. He gives a systematic description of the New Zealand English vowel system, noting in particular the centralisation of /ɪ/, the (near-)merger of /ɪə/ and /eə/, and the effects of /l/ on preceding vowels. Wells also notes variation in accents along a range from Cultivated to Broad, and that apart from the Southland variety of New Zealand English there is no regional variation (1982: 605–6). The primary source of his information was Hawkins 1973a, which was also notable for the depth in which it treated New Zealand English (see 1.5.2.1 above). The account of New Zealand English pronunciation in Wells 1982 is thus the most comprehensive of those given in overseas publications during this time period.[4]

[4] There was also significant New Zealand student research in the period 1973–82. Prescriptivism in works reporting New Zealand English was giving way to linguistic description. New Zealand English was now being taught in some universities – notably by Colin Bowley at the University of Auckland, Elizabeth Gordon and Margaret Maclagan at the University of Canterbury, and by Janet Holmes and Laurie Bauer at Victoria University in Wellington. At the University of

1.6 The modern period – the mid-1980s

The study of New Zealand English gained in vitality in the mid-1980s. Before then, nearly every study of New Zealand English was based on the personal impressions of the writers themselves. After the mid-1980s, the importance of using research data in reporting its characteristics was recognised. Two examples of rigorous data-based research from 1985 were Gordon and Maclagan's study of the *ear/air* merger in Christchurch schoolchildren and Bayard's research into social class and language change in New Zealand English (1985, 1987).

Also notable from this time is Bauer's (1986) 'state of the art' paper on phonetics and phonology. He set out the situation for the study of New Zealand English at that time as he saw it:

> During the past few years a number of major works have appeared in which international varieties of English are discussed and compared from various points of view . . . Works of this nature seem to strike problems when it comes to the discussion of New Zealand English (NZE), and particularly the pronunciation of NZE, for a number of reasons. Firstly, many of the easily available sources are extremely sketchy in the material they provide on NZE. Secondly, most of the available sources describe NZE simply as a variant of Australian English. Thirdly, much of the available material is either out of date or of uncertain accuracy. (Bauer 1986: 225)

Bauer's stated aim in the paper, therefore, is to present an overview of New Zealand English phonetics and phonology. He suggests that it is easy to talk about New Zealand English in terms of the ways that it differs from RP because the phonemic systems of the two varieties are very similar and because RP is the overt (but not covert) prestige standard (even though RP is seldom heard in New Zealand). He comments on New Zealand English's closeness to Australian English, possibly a result of the influence of Australian English on New Zealand English and states that New Zealand English is geographically homogeneous except for Southland /r/. He also refers to Maori English and the existence of social variation (citing Bayard 1985) and notes that Mitchell and Delbridge's (1965) three strata (Cultivated, General, and Broad Australian English) have generally been assumed to apply to New Zealand English as well. In his description of vowels, Bauer gives a comprehensive survey of the complete vowel system of New Zealand English, citing earlier evidence and providing the evidence of acoustic analyses to support the description.

The 1980s also mark the beginning of the investigations into the origins of New Zealand English when Elizabeth Gordon began her search for commentary on

Auckland, student research into New Zealand English included Moira Hall's (1976) acoustic study of Maori and Pakeha (New Zealanders of European descent) adults in Northland and Ingrid Huygen's attitudinal study carried out in 1979 (Huygens and Vaughan 1983), and at the University of Canterbury two significant studies were Mary Durkin's (1972) investigation of the speech of West Coast schoolchildren and Marcia Abell's (1980) attitudinal study of Christchurch teenagers.

New Zealand pronunciation in early written records (see Gordon 1983a, 1983b, 1991, 1994).

Overviews of New Zealand English also appeared in the 1980s, although they largely consisted either of brief summaries of research carried out in a wide range of topic areas (e.g., Gordon 1982; Kuiper 1987) or of more detailed accounts of research findings in the field of sociolinguistics (e.g., Meyerhoff 1987; Holmes and Bell 1990; Bell and Holmes 1991; Holmes, Bell, and Boyce 1991).

1.7 The modern period – 1990s to the present

Recent and ongoing research on New Zealand English covers a wide range of topics. Here we mention only a few of the most significant studies of the past fifteen years.

The large-scale Wellington Social Dialect Survey at Victoria University of Wellington (also known as the 'Porirua Project') analysed the speech of seventy-five adults, collected according to a speaker quota sample balanced for age, sex, and social class, and including Maori speakers (Holmes, Bell, and Boyce 1991). This corpus provided the data for various studies, including intonation (Britain 1992; Britain and Newman 1992), and a number of studies of individual variables (see Bell 1997a, 1997b; Holmes 1994, 1995a, 1995b, 1995c, 1996, 1997b; Bell and Holmes 1992; Holmes and Bell 1992, 1994, 1996). The Origins of New Zealand English project (ONZE) at the University of Canterbury, though with antecedents from the earlier work of Elizabeth Gordon and Margaret Maclagan, began in earnest after receiving significant funding from 1996 (Lewis 1996); its findings are reported in this book. Nicola Woods, a postdoctoral fellow at the University of Canterbury, also wrote on early New Zealand English (Woods 1997, 2000a, 2000b, 2001). From 1994 onwards data were also collected for the Canterbury Corpus (Maclagan and Gordon 1999); by 2002 this collection contained word-list and casual-speech data representing nearly 400 speakers. At the University of Otago in Dunedin, Donn Bayard continued to carry out data-based research on phonological variants, language and social class, and attitudes to language variation (Bayard 1990a, 1990b, 1991a, 1991b, 1991c, 1995b; Bayard and Bartlett 1996; Bayard et al. 2001; see also http://www.otago.ac.nz/anthropology/Linguistic/Accents.html).

1.8 New Zealand English in schools

By the mid-1980s the subject of New Zealand English was part of the syllabus in New Zealand secondary schools and Gordon and Deverson's (1985) *New Zealand English* was written for this purpose. In 1998 a revised and extended version *New Zealand English and English in New Zealand* was accompanied by an audiotape containing examples of variation in New Zealand English for use in secondary schools. *English in the New Zealand Curriculum* (New Zealand Ministry of Education 1994), which sets out the national English curriculum states, 'Attention should be given to the distinctive varieties of New Zealand English' (p. 11). In *Exploring Language: A Handbook for Teachers* published by the New Zealand Ministry of Education (1996) to support the English curriculum objectives, there is a section on New Zealand English pronunciation.

2 Modern New Zealand English

2.1 Introduction

In order to help the reader appreciate the information obtained from the speakers in the Mobile Unit Archive presented in Chapter 6, we first present a brief outline of the pronunciation of New Zealand English today. This is the end-point, as it were, of changes set in motion when the parents of the Mobile Unit speakers settled in New Zealand. Although the majority of New Zealanders speak general New Zealand English, which is the basis for the description provided here,[5] New Zealand English at the start of the twenty-first century is of course not a completely unified whole. Four major factors contribute to the variation we observe within New Zealand English: the age, sex, social class, and ethnicity of the speakers. These factors are not unique to this variety, but contribute to variation within all languages (see, e.g., Labov 1994, 2001).

2.2 Variation in New Zealand English today

In New Zealand English, variation due to age can be seen with sound changes in progress. Younger speakers usually produce more innovative or advanced (in terms of the change underway) variants of these sounds than do older speakers. Younger speakers, for example, produce more tokens of raised DRESS vowels than older speakers, and fewer tokens of [ʍ] than older speakers (see Maclagan 2000).

As in other varieties of English, variation due to sex works in two ways in New Zealand English. Women are both more conservative and more innovative than

[5] Following the Australian practice started by Mitchell and Delbridge (1965), writers often refer to Cultivated, General, and Broad New Zealand English. Our experience indicates that, over time, fewer speakers use Cultivated and Broad New Zealand English and proportionally more use General New Zealand English (see Gordon and Maclagan 1989 and Gordon and Trudgill forthcoming for New Zealand English and Horvath 1985: 91 for a parallel trend in Australian English). In this section, we will use *general New Zealand English* to refer to the pronunciation of the majority of New Zealanders and use it as the basis for discussion in this chapter. We compare general New Zealand English both with more conservative and more innovative New Zealand pronunciations. In this discussion, we do not consider ethnically accented New Zealand English, which is usually described as Maori English or Maori Accented English (see Bell 2000; Benton 1991; Holmes 1997b).

men (see Labov 1994 for examples). Where phonemes have stigmatised as well as non-stigmatised variants, women produce fewer tokens of the stigmatised forms. Women, for example, produce fewer examples of the diphthong of the MOUTH class of words with [ɛə] than men do in modern New Zealand English. Where sound changes in progress are not stigmatised (usually because they are below the level of consciousness) women produce more tokens of the more innovative variants. Women thus produce more raised DRESS and TRAP tokens than do men (see Maclagan, Gordon and Lewis 1999; Woods 1997; see Chapter 6).

Analysing variation due to social class is complicated because New Zealanders do not readily acknowledge a class system parallel, for example, to that of Britain. Further, researchers in New Zealand do not easily agree on a methodology for dividing speakers into social-class groupings. For New Zealand we use a model based on occupation and education. The revised Elley-Irving scale (Elley and Irving 1985; New Zealand Ministry of Education 1990) divides census occupations into six bands, with band 1 being the highest; to this we add an educational classification that is also divided into six bands. Children and young adults are rated according to whichever parent's occupational and educational level is higher. (See Maclagan, Gordon, and Lewis 1999; see Gregersen and Pedersen 1991 for a similar way of assessing social class.) For the description of New Zealand English presented here, we will use two social-class divisions: a higher social class, which we refer to as *middle class*, and a lower social class, which we refer to as *working class*.

2.3 The vowel system of general New Zealand English

Speakers of modern New Zealand English have seventeen or eighteen vowel phonemes, depending on the extent to which they merge the centring diphthongs of the NEAR and SQUARE lexical sets (see section 2.3.3 below). Many researchers have commented on the pronunciation of New Zealand English, usually basing their conclusions on auditory analysis (see Batterham 1995, 2000; Bauer 1986; Bell 1997a, 1997b; Maclagan, Gordon, and Lewis 1999; Trudgill, Gordon, and Lewis 1998). We present here acoustic data that supports the basic thrust of the auditory analyses.

2.3.1 Monophthongs. Vowel plots for the eleven monophthongs for male and female speakers of general New Zealand English are presented in Figure 2.1. The data are not normalised. These plots are based on data from fifty young adult speakers aged approximately 20 years. They were born around 1960 – just over one hundred years after the birth of the oldest generation of Mobile Unit speakers (see Maclagan 1982). All were judged to speak a general variety of New Zealand English and all were middle class.

These vowel plots show features that characterise New Zealand English, namely:

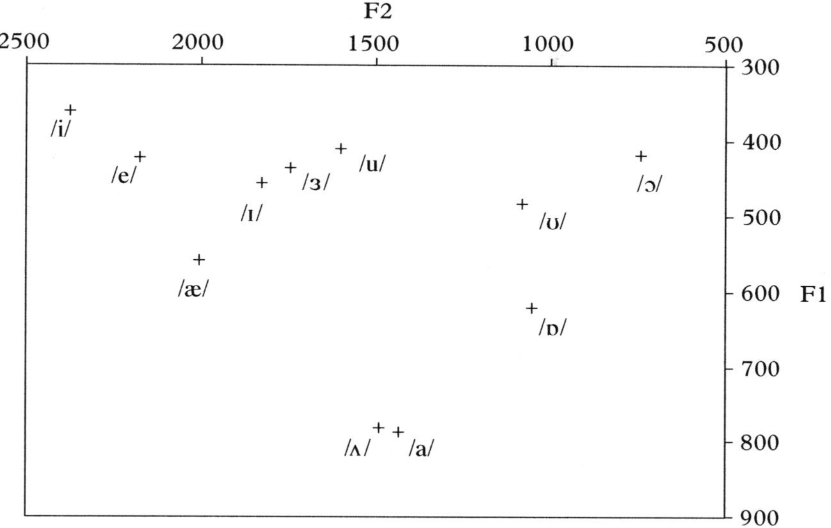

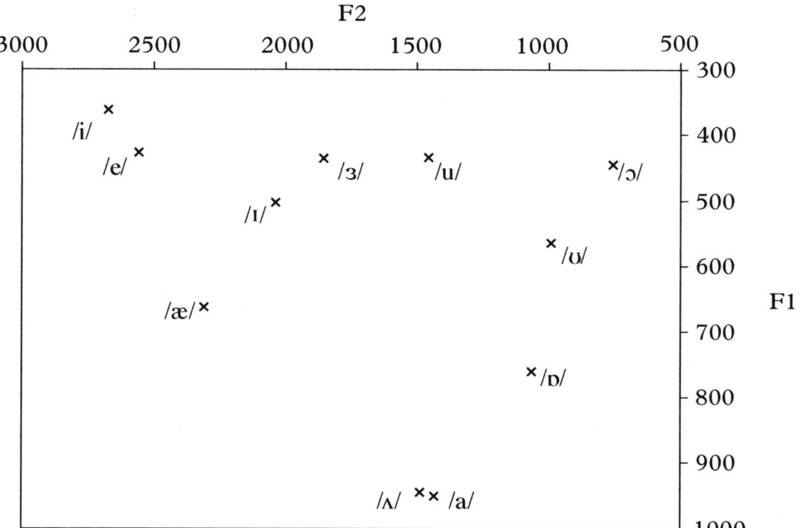

Figure 2.1 The monophthongs of modern New Zealand English, non-normalised

- the raised front vowels, DRESS [e̝] and TRAP [ɛ̝]
- the centralised and lowered KIT vowel [ɘ] or lower
- the fronted START vowel [a̟ː ~ ɐ̟ː] and the fronted and lowered STRUT vowel [a̟ ~ ɐ̟]. For New Zealand English, START and STRUT are distinguished only by length. (Note that the non-IPA symbol [ᴀ] is sometimes used in this book instead of [ɐ̟]. Both represent a central open vowel.)
- the centralised GOOSE vowel [ʉ]
- the raised and fronted NURSE vowel [ø̝]. Because NURSE is rounded in New Zealand English, and because lip rounding lowers formant frequency, NURSE may be articulated even farther forward than Figure 2.1 would indicate. The transcription, [ø̝], reflects this.
- the raised back vowels, THOUGHT [ö̝] and LOT [ɔ̝̈]. Although it does not show up in Figure 2.1, THOUGHT in New Zealand English often has an off-glide, [ü̝ə] or [ö̝ə], even in closed syllables.
- Because the unstressed vowel is not included, the vowel plots do not show the merger of KIT and schwa (the lexical set of *commA*) which occurs in unstressed syllables in New Zealand English.

A recent acoustic analysis of New Zealand English by Watson, Harrington, and Evans (1998), based on twenty-one speakers, shows similar patterns to Figure 2.1. The major difference is that GOOSE is somewhat more fronted in Watson et al. 1998 than in Figure 2.1, being relatively more fronted than START for the females as well as the males.

More advanced pronunciations of the New Zealand English vowels will show DRESS and TRAP raised still further to [i̞] and [e̞] respectively; KIT lowered towards STRUT, [ə] or [ɜ]; and GOOSE and NURSE fronted still more, but will not differ from what is shown here with regard to LOT and THOUGHT. Advanced examples of FLEECE and GOOSE may have on-glides, with the on-glide for GOOSE being very pronounced for speakers of broad New Zealand English so that it is almost [əʉ] and can be mistaken for GOAT. Except for the diphthongisation of FLEECE and GOOSE, none of the characteristically New Zealand English pronunciations of the monophthongs is stigmatised within New Zealand. The more advanced pronunciations are therefore heard most from younger speakers, and from females (both middle class and working class) as well as males. More conservative speakers may not centralise KIT or GOOSE as much as most general New Zealand English speakers do (using [ɪ̟] and [u̟] respectively), but even the most conservative speakers, such as older women from higher social classes, will produce relatively close variants of both DRESS [e̞] and TRAP [ɛ̞] (see Maclagan, Gordon, and Lewis 1999).

2.3.2 Closing diphthongs. Vowel plots for the closing diphthongs for male and female speakers of general New Zealand English are shown in Figure 2.2. Again these data are based on the speakers born around 1960 (Maclagan 1982) and again

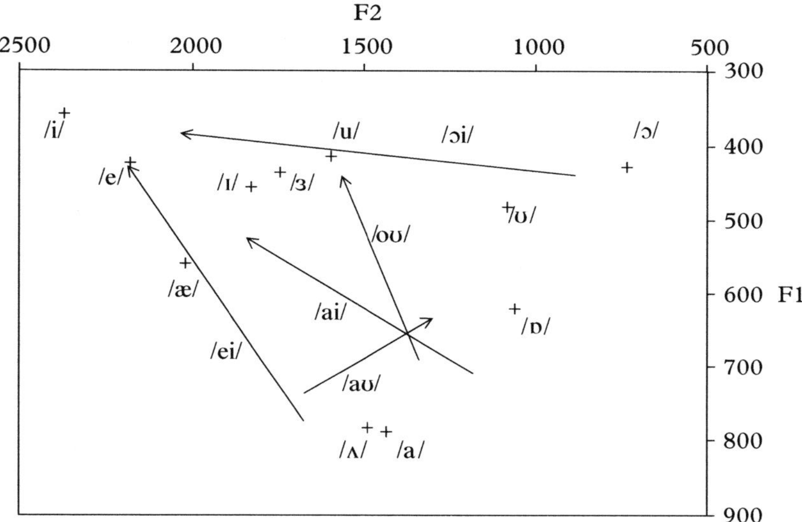

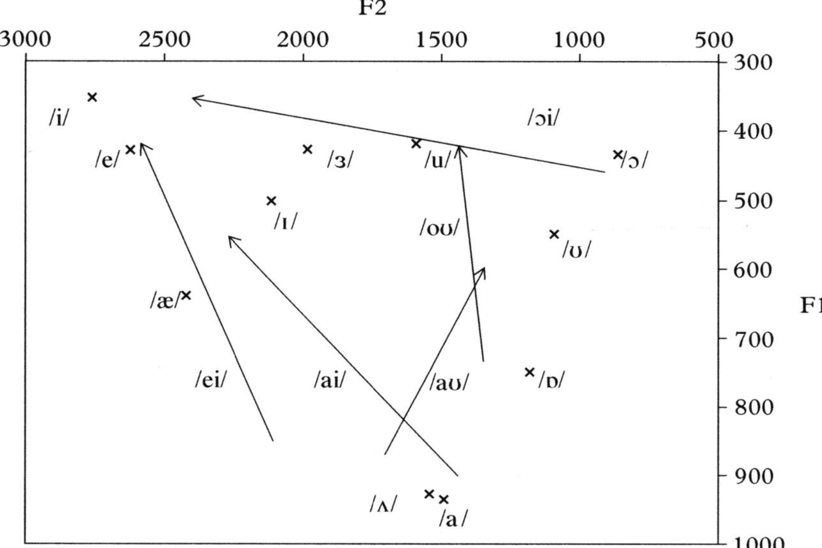

Figure 2.2 The closing diphthongs of modern New Zealand English, non-normalised

similar patterns are shown for the closing diphthongs in Watson, Harrington, and Evans (1998).

- FACE starts at a relatively open point between TRAP and STRUT, producing a relatively long glide, [ɐe].
- PRICE starts from an open back position, between LOT and START for the men, and close to START for the women. More conservative variants are [ɑe] and more advanced variants are [ɔ̞ë].
- MOUTH starts from a fronted position below TRAP for the men and close to STRUT for the women. More conservative versions of MOUTH are [æʊ] and more advanced variants are [ɛə].
- GOAT starts from a central, relatively open position above STRUT for the men and closer to LOT for the women. Its pronunciation ranges from [ɜʊ] to [ɐʉ].
- CHOICE starts back and close, near to THOUGHT for both men and women, [o̝i̞].

Four of the closing diphthongs make a clear closing movement: CHOICE moves towards FLEECE; PRICE and FACE move towards DRESS; GOAT moves towards GOOSE. However, while MOUTH moves towards FOOT for the women, it shows very little closing movement for the men, hardly progressing past the central area. Auditorily, the second element of MOUTH is now often COMMA rather than FOOT (see Maclagan, Gordon, and Lewis 1999), so that MOUTH is becoming a centring diphthong rather than a closing one. Since the data presented in Figure 2.2 were recorded in 1979, middle-class men now usually start MOUTH above TRAP, and even middle-class women start it just below TRAP (see Maclagan, Gordon, and Lewis 1999).

All the closing diphthongs except CHOICE show both diphthong shifting and glide weakening as defined by Wells (1982) and discussed in Chapter 6. *Diphthong shift* refers to continuing processes in recent stages of the Great Vowel Shift whereby the closing diphthongs FACE, PRICE, MOUTH and GOAT, are acquiring first elements that are increasingly removed from their second elements, for example /au/ [ɑʊ → aʊ], /ai/ [ai → ɑi], and so on. *Glide weakening* would appear to be a continuation of this ongoing change. It is a kind of catching-up process whereby the second element of the diphthong compensates for diphthong shift by moving to a position where it more closely approaches the first, thereby once again reducing the distance between them: for example, PRICE /ai/ [ɑi → ɑɛ], MOUTH /au/ [æʊ → æə].

More advanced examples of New Zealand English closing diphthongs display greater diphthong shifting and glide weakening, and more conservative examples display less. Advanced pronunciations of FACE, PRICE, MOUTH, and GOAT are stigmatised in New Zealand; they are avoided by middle-class speakers, especially women, and produced by working-class speakers, especially males (see Maclagan, Gordon, and Lewis 1999).

Advanced pronunciations of MOUTH and PRICE have been noticed in New Zealand for a long time. Around 1900, school inspectors criticised the 'colonial twang' of school children, complaining about their pronunciation of 'house' as 'heouse' (Mr Augustus Heine, acting headmaster of Wellington College, *AJHR* E-12, 1912: 624, and see further comments quoted in Chapter 6).

2.3.3 Centring diphthongs. The phonemic system of the New Zealand English monophthongs and closing diphthongs does not differ from that of RP. With the centring diphthongs, New Zealand English enters a class of its own because of the ongoing merger of NEAR and SQUARE. Originally, English had a balanced set of centring diphthongs, /ɪə, ɛə, ɔə, ʊə/ (see O'Connor 1973) but /ɔə/ as an independent phoneme is now rare in RP and other forms of English (O'Connor 1973: 171) so that Wells does not even provide a key word for /ɔə/. A realisation of [o̞ə] for THOUGHT is common in New Zealand English, but /ɔə/ as a separate phoneme is not part of the New Zealand English phonemic system.

CURE is becoming increasingly rare in New Zealand English, with speakers realising CURE words with [o̞] or [ʉə] and implicitly assigning them to other phonemes. When *tour* for example, is pronounced as [to̞], it is reassigned to the THOUGHT phoneme. When it is pronounced as [tʉə], it becomes a disyllable – GOOSE plus schwa.

The main point of interest in the New Zealand English vowel phonological system is the merger of NEAR and SQUARE (see Gordon and Maclagan 1989; Holmes and Bell 1992; Maclagan and Gordon 1996a; Gordon and Maclagan 2001; Batterham 2000). While there has been consensus that the centring diphthongs are merging, there has been discussion about whether they are merging on the closer (NEAR) or the more open member (SQUARE) of the pair. Holmes and Bell (1992) considered that they were merging on the more open phoneme, while Fromkin et al. (1984), Batterham (1995, 2000), and Gordon and Maclagan (2001, see also Maclagan and Gordon 1996a) considered that the merger was towards the closer phoneme. Figure 2.3 shows the centring diphthongs NEAR and SQUARE, based on the data from the speakers born about 1960 (Maclagan 1982). The women in this group still make a slight difference between members of the pair, with NEAR starting closer to FLEECE, and SQUARE starting closer to DRESS, but the extent of the merger between NEAR and SQUARE is particularly apparent in the speech of the men.

In other varieties of English, NEAR starts close to the position of KIT or FLEECE, and SQUARE starts close to the position of DRESS (O'Connor 1973: 170, 171). Acoustic analysis of four Mobile Unit speakers born around 1900 shows them following this traditional pattern (see Watson, Maclagan, and Harrington 2000): three of the speakers have NEAR starting close to their FLEECE vowels and SQUARE starting close to their DRESS vowels, with FLEECE and DRESS considerably more separated than for modern New Zealand English. The fourth speaker, Miss Bannatyne, born 1899, sounds more like a modern New Zealand speaker than the other three do – her KIT vowel is starting to centralise and

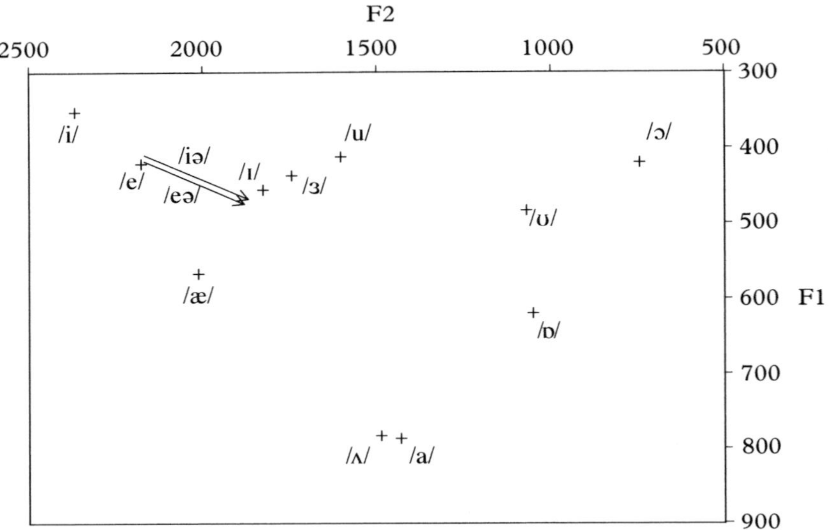

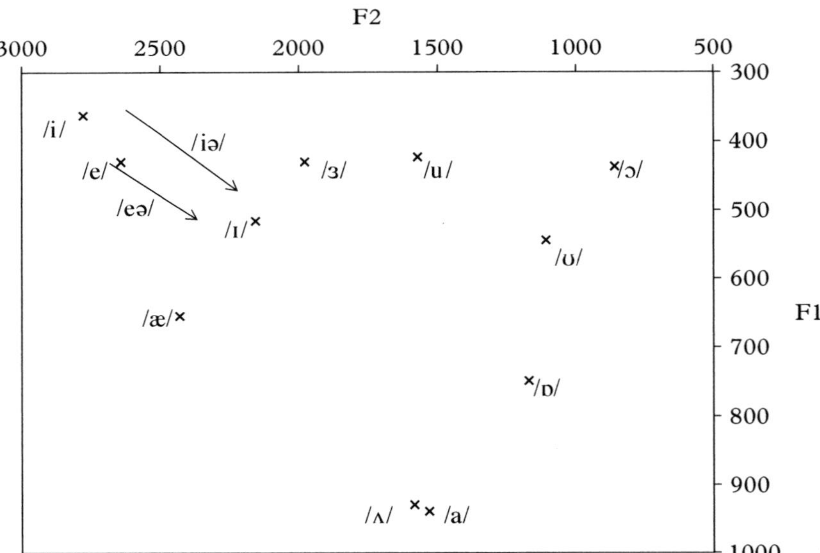

Figure 2.3 NEAR and SQUARE in modern New Zealand English, non-normalised

her DRESS vowel has raised so that it is higher than KIT. Miss Bannatyne still has some separation between NEAR and SQUARE, but the onset of SQUARE has raised so that it is starting above DRESS and closer to FLEECE. In this respect, Miss Bannatyne's speech more resembles the pattern we find for modern New Zealand English speakers.

We carried out a longitudinal study of the NEAR/SQUARE merger in New Zealand English, recording over one hundred fourteen-year-old school children every five years from 1983 (see Gordon and Maclagan 1985; Gordon and Maclagan 1989; Maclagan and Gordon 1996a; Gordon and Maclagan 2001). In 1983, most of the speakers were variable in their use of the centring diphthongs, not using [ɪə] or [e̞ə] consistently for either NEAR or SQUARE. By 1998, there had been a clear movement towards a close starting point for both diphthongs for all speakers. Only one speaker out of the 120 recorded in 1998 used the traditional distinctions between NEAR and SQUARE at each opportunity. Other speakers occasionally used a more open start for a diphthong, but overwhelmingly the speakers born in 1984 and recorded in 1998 realised NEAR and SQUARE with a close onset.

A possible explanation of the NEAR/SQUARE merger is the close pronunciation of DRESS, one of the most noticeable characteristics of modern New Zealand English. The vowel spaces for FLEECE and DRESS overlap to a large degree, and for many speakers the main difference between the two vowels is length. There is anecdotal evidence of misunderstandings of New Zealand English FLEECE and DRESS vowels – did the speaker mean *beast* or *best* in the utterance 'She brought out the [bi̞st] in him'? As FLEECE and DRESS are so similar to each other and so high in the mouth, it no longer makes sense to try to work out which one is the starting point of the merged centring diphthongs. Watson, Maclagan, and Harrington (2000) suggest that the vowel area for the merged NEAR/SQUARE onset vowels is situated between the areas of the original NEAR and SQUARE vowels (based on Watson, Harrington, and Evans 1998). Acoustic analysis of the school children that we studied suggests that the articulation of NEAR and SQUARE is as high as that of FLEECE and DRESS, with the vowel areas of NEAR, SQUARE, and FLEECE all contained within the larger area of DRESS (see Maclagan and Gordon 2000).

Most modern New Zealand English speakers thus use only one of the traditional centring diphthongs, the merged NEAR/SQUARE. However, many of these speakers, especially younger speakers, produce MOUTH with a central unrounded second element [æə] or [ɛə]. Speakers who merge NEAR and SQUARE and produce MOUTH with central unrounded second elements are moving towards again having two front centring diphthongs – the close NEAR/SQUARE and the open MOUTH. Examples of intrusive /r/ following MOUTH in phrases like *now and again* pronounced [næə ɹ ən əgen] provide confirmation of the shift of MOUTH from a back closing diphthong to a centring diphthong. As indicated above, THOUGHT is also often now realised with an off glide, again creating a (back) centring diphthong.

2.4 *Consonants*

The consonant system of New Zealand English is not remarkable in itself; what are interesting are the changes that are currently happening. Modern New Zealand English is an /h/-full variety (but see Bell and Holmes 1992 for a different perspective) and, apart from a small area in the south of the South Island, it is non-rhotic (Bartlett 1992). Like English English, syllable final stops tend to be glottalised (see Wells 1982: 260), and like General American English, intervocalic /t/ tends to be tapped or flapped (see Holmes 1994; Wells 1982: 248). In this section we comment on the features characteristic of New Zealand English consonants, making reference to the modern data collected in the Canterbury Corpus (see Maclagan and Gordon 1999; Maclagan 2000; Gordon and Maclagan 2000). The issues considered are: the contrast between /w/ and /hw/, post-vocalic /l/, h-dropping, t-flapping, affrication of /tr/ and /dr/, and TH-fronting.

2.4.1 /w/ and /hw/. The distinction between the initial consonants in *witch* and *which* is a feature of Scottish and Irish English, and is found in some other regional varieties of English (see Wells 1982). Historical information about /hw/, together with its usage by the Mobile Unit speakers is given in Chapter 6. From analysis of the data in the Canterbury Corpus, it is clear that the /w/~/hw/ distinction is now only found among older middle-class speakers; but even among older middle-class women, who tend to be the most conservative speakers, less than half make a distinction when they read a word list (Maclagan 2000; Gordon and Maclagan 2000), and fewer still make one in their interview or casual speech. For younger New Zealand speakers, *which* and *witch* are identical (see also Bauer 1986).

2.4.2 *Post-vocalic /l/*

2.4.2.1 l-vocalisation. In 1995 a writer in *The Press* newspaper in Christchurch reported seeing a notice offering 'warnuts for sale' (10 February 1995). Similarly, the letters 'AW MINE' on a car number plate in Christchurch indicate the prevalence of l-vocalisation in New Zealand English. Traditionally there are two variants of /l/ in English: clear /l/ which appears at the beginning of words, *look*, *long*, and between vowels, *silly*, *failing*; and dark (velarised) /l/ which appears in final positions, *ball*, *doll*, and before consonants, *milk*, *child*. In New Zealand English the dark /l/ is becoming vocalised which means that effectively it is being replaced by the vowel in FOOT. The /l/ phoneme is not being lost; rather it is being realised differently. Many people find it very difficult to hear the difference between a dark /l/ and a vocalised /l/, and vocalising /l/ does not lead to misidentifications between words.

This change is not unique to New Zealand and there are indications that it can sometimes be heard in RP (Wells 1994: 202). Barbara Horvath from Sydney University has been carrying out research into l-vocalisation in different countries

(Horvath and Horvath 2001). Her current findings are that New Zealand English is ahead of Australian English in percentage of l-vocalisation, and from our analysis of the Canterbury Corpus there is good evidence that it is increasing. When reading twenty words from a list, only older middle-class women continue to use dark /l/ more than 50% of the time, whereas younger working-class males vocalise /l/ over 70% of the time (see Maclagan 2000; Gordon and Maclagan 2000). Reading words in a list is a very formal (and artificial) linguistic exercise so we would expect even more l-vocalisation in everyday speech. There is a steady increase in l-vocalisation from the more conservative older middle-class women to the more innovative younger working-class men, indicating that l-vocalisation is a change from below, that is, a change being led by lower-class speakers (see Labov 1990, 1994), which will probably continue to increase in New Zealand English.

2.4.2.2 Changes in vowel pronunciations before /l/. Students doing phonemic transcriptions of New Zealand English have great difficulty choosing appropriate symbols for the vowel sounds in words containing post-vocalic /l/. This is because, as well as being vocalised itself, post-vocalic /l/ also affects the pronunciation of preceding vowels, causing them to be realised in a more back or open manner, so that some vowel contrasts are neutralised before /l/.

Canterbury Corpus data show that several vowel contrasts can be neutralised before dark /l/: DRESS and TRAP can be almost identical so that *Ellen* and *Alan* or *elementary* and *alimentary* sound the same – students called *Ellen*, *Alan* or *Helen* report that they all respond when [æ̞lən] is called out; LOT, GOAT, and STRUT are pronounced so that there is little if any difference between *doll*, *dole*, and *dull*; KIT, FOOT, THOUGHT, and GOOSE become very similar, so that *fill*, *full*, *fall*, and *fool* are difficult to distinguish; and because the GOOSE vowel is retracted before /l/ rather than being central, the main difference between *full* and *fool* is now length.

2.4.3 h-dropping. The amount of h-dropping occurring in contemporary New Zealand English has been questioned. Trudgill (1986b) characterises New Zealand English as 'devoid of h-dropping' (1986b: 138) and Wells (1982) does not even mention it in his discussion of the variety, whereas he does mention variable h-dropping in Australian English. Bell and Holmes (1992) report up to 30% h-dropping for some groups of speakers in their sample, but they did not remove all grammatical words starting with /h/. Like other varieties of English, New Zealand English drops /h/ in unstressed grammatical words in utterances like *John said to ˈgive it to him* (where ˈ marks the stressed syllable). A small minority of speakers in the Canterbury Corpus, especially working-class speakers, will use h-dropping in stressed grammatical words (though it has to be noted that phrases like *Come here!* are almost universally pronounced without the /h/). However, for most speakers the /h/ is retained when grammatical words are stressed – *John said to give it to*ˈ /hɪm/, and /h/ is almost never dropped from lexical words, whatever their stress. There is also no evidence of h-dropping in New Zealand English in the 'prestige' set of words including *humour*, *hospital*, *humble*, *hotel*, *herb* (see D. Maclagan 1998; Phillipps 1984).

2.4.4 t-flapping. New Zealand English uses glottal reinforcement for syllable final stops, but tends not to use glottal stops in intervocalic position. By contrast, the flapping or voicing of intervocalic /t/ in words like *city* and *letter* has probably occurred for a long time in working-class New Zealand speech. Recent research suggests that it is becoming more widespread. Holmes (1994) found up to 80% intervocalic /t/-flapping in the casual speech of younger male working-class speakers. In the Canterbury Corpus speakers read the words *city*, *letter*, *scatter*, *better*, *batter* and *Peter*. There is a sharp stylistic difference between the formal speech of word-list reading, when there were relatively few flaps, and casual speech, where every group used flaps relatively freely (with the exception of the older middle-class women who still used them sparingly) (see Maclagan 2000; Gordon and Maclagan 2000).

2.4.5 Affrication of /tr, dr, str/. In New Zealand English /tr/ has always been pronounced with friction in the /r/. Recently speakers in New Zealand, together with speakers of English elsewhere, have begun to use more friction in /tr/ clusters so that the production sounds more like [tʃɹ̥] and *tree* sounds like '*chree*' (see Bauer 1986). This is called 'affrication' because it is making the /tr/ cluster more like the affricate. The word list for the Canterbury Corpus contains the words *street*, *train*, *tree*, and *dream* to test for /tr/ affrication. Words with /tr/ clusters are so far showing the greatest degree of affrication (with up to 80% of younger male speakers saying '*chree*'), followed by words with /dr/, while those with /str/ are showing least affrication. At present the change seems to be being led by younger speakers irrespective of social class (see Maclagan 2000; Gordon and Maclagan 2000).

2.4.6 TH-fronting. 'TH-fronting' is the term being used by some sociolinguists to refer to the substitution of /f/ and /v/ for /θ/ and /ð/ in words like *something* and *nothing*, *mother* and *father*. This is becoming increasingly frequent in casual speech in New Zealand English but has not yet been the subject of letters of complaint. So far its prevalence has not exceeded 5% in the more formal style of the Canterbury Corpus word list (Maclagan 2000). It is used more by the younger working-class speakers and also by the older working-class males. The word *with* may be one of the key words in the spread of th-fronting. Because there is already variation in its pronunciations, /wɪθ/ or /wɪð/, the additional pronunciations /wɪf/ or /wɪv/ are not so immediately noticeable. There is evidence of speakers (including some who are middle class) who have th-fronting only on *with* (see Campbell and Gordon 1996). Like the NEAR/SQUARE merger, th-fronting is a change from below.

3 Summary

This summary of the research carried out into New Zealand English and its current pronunciation provides the background against which to evaluate the data provided by the Mobile Unit speakers presented in Chapter 6 below. As the speakers from the Mobile Unit are presented, we will demonstrate how the great variety found in their pronunciations was levelled and shaped into the relative homogeneity of New Zealand English pronunciation today.

3 The historical background

> Whenever by choice or fate men set out on journeys across the earth they drag the burden of their past with them as a snail drags its shell. No matter how ardent the adventurer or how inescapable the exile, ghosts of the past lurk at the back of the voyager's mind to bemuse him.
>
> (Sidney Baker 1947: 13)

1 Introduction

The origins and development of New Zealand English are, quite obviously, intimately intertwined with the history of immigration to New Zealand. In this chapter, therefore, we survey the European settlement history of New Zealand and its relation to the development of New Zealand English. As will be seen in Chapters 6 and 7, historical factors, in particular population figures and places of origin, are important to any consideration of how new dialects develop. If we are to consider concepts such as the 'founder effect' (Mufwene 1996), 'First Effective Settlement doctrine' (Zelinsky 1992: 13; Labov 2001: 45), 'swamping' (Lass 1990), or processes involved in 'koinéisation' (Trudgill 1986b) in relation to New Zealand English (see Chapter 7), then specific historical information is needed.

2 Historical background: the immigrants

The investigation of the origins and evolution of New Zealand English requires an understanding of both sociolinguistics and history. The connections between language, history, and social setting are important and complex. In order to establish the origins and development of New Zealand English it is necessary to know the parentage of the earliest New Zealand-born Anglophones – where their families came from, and by what route these immigrants travelled to New Zealand. Clearly, most of the early settlers came from the British Isles, but to understand their dialectal background, more precise information is needed about their regional origins in England, Scotland, Ireland, or Wales. The

Australian connection is also important, because although a much smaller proportion of immigrants were Australian born, many who came from other places had either lived in Australia or spent time there before arriving in New Zealand, which also means that some of their children were born there (see Chapters 4 and 7).

Unfortunately, as New Zealand historians are well aware, there is a serious lack of historical data on the origins of the early immigrants. In what Simpson (1997: 8) has described as 'a breath-taking act of official vandalism', in 1972 the New Zealand Department of Statistics destroyed all the nineteenth-century returned questionnaires that had been collected since the beginning of comprehensive census-taking in 1857, and which reported the original birthplaces of much of the New Zealand population. For early immigration figures, scholars have had to use other sources, such as shipping records, knowing full well that the place of a person's embarkation was not necessarily the same as that person's place of birth or even residence. Up to 1873, the United Kingdom's Colonial and Land Commissioners made annual reports about the numbers of individuals leaving the various ports in the British Isles, but they did not provide any information about the national origin of those immigrants (Akenson 1990: 21). In particular, so few ships went directly from Irish ports to New Zealand that the shipping records for many Irish immigrants show an English or Scottish port of embarkation (Akenson 1990: 21).[1]

Care must also be taken with terminology. Akenson (1990: 7) points out that it is not always clear from early reports what is meant by terms such as 'British' and 'English'. In the late nineteenth century, people from Wales were sometimes described as 'English'. In New Zealand, a person described as 'English' may have, indeed, been a person of English extraction or just someone who was not Maori or Asian or from continental Europe – someone labelled 'British' may have come directly from the British Isles or be a third generation New Zealander whose family originally came from the British Isles. Some reports use 'Irish' for all migrants from Ireland, while others restrict it to those Irish who were Catholic; northern Irish were frequently referred to as 'Scottish', given their historical background and Presbyterian religion (Ray Hickey, personal communication, 2002).

Given the importance of immigration information for New Zealand history, historians are now in the process of reconstructing the evidence by studying the history of individual early settlers. Recent in-depth analyses of death registers, sponsored by the New Zealand government, as well as shipping records and military records, provide the clearest information at the present time (http://www.nzhistory.net.nz/gallery/brit-nz/; hereafter nzhistory.net 2002). In a comparable way, the ONZE project reconstructs the language of early

[1] Belfast in the north and Cork (Port of Cobh) in the extreme south were the only ports from which the Irish set sail for far-off destinations; people from Dublin (either originally or passing through) went to Liverpool for overseas destinations (Ray Hickey, personal communication, 2002).

New Zealanders of European origin from a painstakingly detailed investigation of the speech of individuals.

The historical complexities involving early settlement are paralleled by the complexities in the social context. The early settlement of New Zealand was not socially homogeneous. Moreover, in some places the population was relatively stable; in others it was constantly changing. In some places the population came primarily from one specific area of the British Isles; in other places it came from several different areas. The Mobile Unit data include people both from remote areas and from larger towns on busy transport routes. People from many occupations, from different social classes, and from both town and country were interviewed. In some ways, the material collected by the Mobile Unit reflects the social and linguistic variation found throughout New Zealand, but we should not make sweeping generalisations on the basis of these data. If instead of visiting Otago and the Waikato, for example, the Mobile Unit had visited Auckland and Canterbury, we might have had different results for the North and South Islands. We are limited by the data available to us.

In the end, in spite of varied origins, social circumstances, and historical events, we know that in a relatively short period of time very different individuals were beginning to develop common linguistic traits in their language, so that by the end of the nineteenth century, complaints began to surface about people all over New Zealand with 'twangy pronunciations', 'poor enunciation', and 'something akin to Austral English' (see Chapter 2 for details).

2.1 The early history and settlement of New Zealand

In comparison to the rest of the world, the settlement history of New Zealand is a recent one. Though the exact date remains a point of discussion, the Polynesian ancestors of the Maori arrived in New Zealand some centuries ahead of the first Europeans. The first European settlers arrived in New Zealand by the 1790s, and for the next fifty years there were isolated enclaves settled by Europeans which were essentially rather unruly and ungoverned outposts of the Australian colony of New South Wales (with Sydney as its capital city). In Sinclair's (1991) *A History of New Zealand*, the chapter describing this period is headed 'Australian Colony'. A trickle of British people entered the country, mainly from Australia – traders, missionaries, sealers, whalers, and escaped convicts. These men – the population was almost entirely male – carried out enterprises from their bases in Sydney. The largest European New Zealand settlement at the time was Kororareka (later called Russell) in the northern Bay of Islands; there were a few smaller coastal settlements, and in the south there was a fluctuating population of whalers and sealers. Apart from these, the European population was scattered along the coasts, with the men often living with local Maori in mutual dependence, supplying the Maori with guns and receiving food and shelter in return (Owens 1992: 50).

By 1839 there were thought to be about 2,000 non-Maori living in New Zealand (Owens 1992: 50), although the number who had lived there temporarily was much larger (nzhistory.net 2002). Up to now, the British government had no legal power to deal with British subjects in New Zealand and had shown little inclination to acquire another colonial possession. However, by this time the activities of 'land-sharks' and other predators from Australia were becoming so blatant, many people, including traders and missionaries, were calling upon the British government to intervene to control the situation. Eventually, Captain William Hobson was sent to negotiate a treaty with the Maori for all or some of New Zealand. On 6 February 1840, representatives of the British government and about fifty Maori chiefs signed the Treaty of Waitangi; there were more Maori signatories over the next few months, bringing the total number to over 500. This gave New Zealand a rudimentary British colonial administration which, in theory, was to govern both Maori and pakeha (the Maori term for New Zealanders of European descent), but which had very limited power in the early years. From the British point of view, this is when Britain gained sovereignty over the whole country.

2.2 *1840 onwards – the beginnings of significant settlement*

From 1840 onwards, the European population of New Zealand grew at a remarkable rate. By 1858, Europeans outnumbered Maori by a ratio of 59,000 non-Maori to 56,000 Maori. (European diseases had already significantly reduced the Maori population, and it continued to decrease throughout the nineteenth century.) By 1872, the European population had reached 256,000, and by 1881 it was half a million, with the number born in the colony at 250,000 (Belich 1996: 278). Also, by the mid-1880s, the number of locally born New Zealanders exceeded that of immigrants: the 1886 census shows that by then 52% of the non-Maori population[2] was born in New Zealand (Graham 1992: 112).

These figures give some idea of the enormous change that occurred with European migration to New Zealand, a movement that was part of the greater diaspora from the British Isles and Europe, whereby people moved to the United States, Canada, Australia, South Africa, and New Zealand, seeking countries with temperate climates and economic opportunities (Baines 1991). New Zealand differed from the other destinations in one important respect – it was the most distant of the colonial destinations. The journey could take between three and six months, and for most of those on assisted passages[3] it was a one-way ticket. The reasons why people undertook such a journey were various. Some were enticed by the well-organised advertising campaigns of the New Zealand Company, a land speculation organisation whose purpose was to settle the new colony with British people (and money). Their propaganda bore little semblance to reality, but prospective immigrants in Britain were not to know this. As Belich tells us:

[2] Census figures given in this chapter are always exclusive of Maori.

[3] Assisted passages were subsidised (later, usually by the government).

> The earliest New Zealand Company literature described the precipitous hills of Wellington as undulating plains, perfect for grapevines, wheat and olives – 'the rain but seldom falls during the day'. The Hutt river was said to be as broad as the Thames, and navigable for 80 miles into the interior instead of the actual six. (Belich 1996: 281)

Some immigrants arrived as part of a 'chain migration'. A son might come first, then two years later his parents and other siblings would join him. Others came in 'clump migration', whereby groups of people from the same village would later follow a village member who had sent back encouraging reports of the new land. There were also 'remittance men', sent as far from Britain as possible for some unacceptable behaviour, and paid a remittance by their families to stay away. 'Step migration' was also very common, where immigrants moved from one British colony to another, eventually ending up in New Zealand. More British Isles migrants to New Zealand came via Australia than directly from the British Isles, which may well have had an impact on the formation of New Zealand English (see Chapters 4 and 6). Whatever the individual reasons, there was an overriding belief that travelling to this distant land would enable people to 'better themselves'.

2.2.1 Periods of settlement

2.2.1.1 1840–1852: The NZ Company, Australian, and military immigrants. In this period, the largest number of immigrants came on assisted passage to the five New Zealand Company settlements established between 1840 and 1852. The first group of settlers arrived in Wellington in late January 1840, a few days before the Treaty of Waitangi was signed. A year later, planned settlements were established at Nelson and New Plymouth. These settlements were designed and promoted in Britain as compact settlements representing the stratification of British society without the top and bottom levels. In reality, they were basically instruments of land speculation by the New Zealand Company under the direction of Edward Gibbon Wakefield; they are sometimes known as Wakefield settlements. They were not instant successes and proved to be poor business propositions. Wakefield then shrewdly managed to persuade the Free Church of Scotland and the Church of England to set up denominational settlements. The first Presbyterians set out in the *Mayflower* for Otago in 1848, and two years later, in 1850, the Canterbury Association established the settlement of Canterbury, destined in the eyes of its founder, John Robert Godley, to be 'English, Anglo-Catholic [i.e. high Anglican], and Conservative' (Sinclair 1991: 92).

Wanganui, one of the towns visited by the Mobile Unit, was founded in 1841, one year after New Zealand became a British colony, as an offshoot of the New Zealand Company's first settlement in Wellington. Mrs Cameron, one of the speakers recorded by the Mobile Unit, talks about her father bringing the Wakefields (probably the nephew and brother of Edward Gibbon Wakefield) up the Wanganui river and negotiating the sale of land with Maori there.

The five Wakefield settlements, together with the unplanned and haphazard settlement of Auckland, were the basis of the six provinces into which New Zealand was divided by the Constitution Act of 1852, which gave the country representative government, and by 1856 New Zealand had attained a considerable degree of self-government. The provinces achieved a high degree of independent local government and were responsible for their own immigration, appointing immigration officers who travelled to the British Isles to recruit more immigrants.

The early Wakefield settlements struggled, some more than others, and depended on the goodwill of the local Maori and on capital injections from Britain. Stability was to come only later, through the production of such commodities as wool, wheat, and, in some areas, gold. The immigration schemes based on Wakefield's principles brought 15,612 settlers to New Zealand (Sinclair 1991: 99). Originally, in the planned settlements, there were attempts to control the social mix and nature of the colonists, but these attempts soon proved ineffectual.

While the planned settlements provided the largest number of immigrants in this period, there was also a flow of free migrants, including a significant number with Irish backgrounds. Many of these came from Australia and made up a large part of the population of Auckland, which lacked the attempted social controls of the other settlements.[4]

A third source of immigrants in this period was the military. Armed clashes between Maori and settlers in the Cooks Strait and in Northland developed into what is known as the Northern War of 1845–6. This led to a build-up of imperial troops from the mid-1840s, 700 of whom were later discharged and remained as settlers (King 1981: 33). Other military immigrants were from the Royal New Zealand Fencibles, established to give military protection to the area south of Auckland, and through them, over 2,500 men, women, and children came to New Zealand.

2.2.1.2 1853–1870: The gold rush and the New Zealand Wars. In 1850 there were estimated to be 22,000 Europeans in New Zealand (Borrie 1987: 204). Auckland, a garrison town, which until 1865 was the capital of New Zealand, had reached nearly 12,000 by 1854 (Sinclair 1991: 100). However, by 1870, the European population had increased to 250,000, partly through the efforts of individual provinces which provided assistance with fares and, in Auckland, grants of land of 40 acres. This was a more than tenfold population increase in twenty years.

[4] While the overall number of Irish immigrants was roughly comparable to that of settlers from Scotland, there were no planned settlements of predominantly Irish immigrants such as those that were established with the ideal of maintaining and improving English and Scottish religious and cultural foundations. This may have contributed to Irish dialects having less impact in the development of New Zealand English (Ray Hickey, personal communication, 2002).

The planned settlements struggled for survival and were looking for ways to secure economic stability. The discovery of gold in Otago in May 1861 was immediately followed by a huge influx of hopeful, but often transient, immigrants. In December 1860, the population of Otago was estimated at 12,000; in the next twelve months it increased to 30,000, and by 1863 it had reached a total of 79,000 (a sixfold increase in just two years). At one stage, immigrants were arriving at the Port of Otago at the rate of a thousand per day (Page 1956: 64–5). In 1863 the gross migration to New Zealand was 45,730 people, the largest annual figure in New Zealand's history to that point (nzhistory.net 2002). Compared with other goldrushes, in Victoria (Australia), Alaska, California, and South Africa, the volume of gold discovered in New Zealand was quite small, but the social and economic impact on the country was great. Gold secured the permanent viability of many of the settlements, especially in the South Island. It extinguished any idea of settlements based on Wakefield's principles of social planning, and people now came to New Zealand from all over the world. They came in large numbers from Australia, and this included considerable numbers of Irish Catholics, a group the original planners had tried to exclude. There was certainly no attempt to respect notions such as the idea that Canterbury might be a Church of England/English settlement and Otago a Free Church/Scottish one.

The Mobile Unit visited Arrowtown, a goldmining town in Otago, where most of those interviewed talked about the goldmining days, as they did in Thames, also a goldmining town, on the Coromandel peninsula in the North Island. In fact, all the speakers from Thames had some connection with mining, either through their fathers or their own employment.

Most of the Maori population lived in the North Island. Oliver (1960: 81) states that at the end of the 1850s there were fewer than 75,000 Europeans in New Zealand and 55,000 Maori. However all but 2,000 of those Maori lived in the North Island, where there were only 34,000 Europeans. The 1860s were a period of conflict in the North Island between certain Maori tribes and Europeans, a conflict now referred to as the 'New Zealand Wars'. By the middle of the 1860s there were more than 10,000 imperial troops and 2,000 recruited from Australia, together with 10,000 local soldiers in New Zealand. The soldiers were promised land, and eventually over 2,000 men took their discharge in New Zealand. In addition, there were over 6,000 military settlers in the Auckland areas (nzhistory.net 2002). The New Zealand Wars were conclusive in that, during the 1860s, the government of New Zealand, with the support of the British army, was able to exert its control over most of the North Island.

The Mobile Unit travelled around townships in the Waikato, and interviewed people in Hamilton, Cambridge, Ngaruawahia, and Te Awamutu, towns that came into being as military settlements set up by the government during the New Zealand Wars of the 1860s. The fathers of the Mobile Unit speakers from the Waikato were all associated in some way with the military in the New Zealand Wars. The fathers of Samuel Temple, Frank Bertram, and Mrs Emily Cruikshank, for example, were members of the Forest Rangers, a voluntary corps of militia. The fathers of Frances Rigby, James Hill, and Jack Little came from the Otago goldfields to join the militia in the Waikato. The Waikato Mobile Unit speakers all describe similar patterns of settlement for their families, whereby their fathers served in the militia (usually one of the Waikato regiments) and then received grants of land to farm.

2.2.1.3 1871–1880: Government-assisted immigration. New Zealand had responsible self-government starting in 1852; by the 1870s, it had its own army, banks, and merchant houses, education through chartered universities, and, in 1877, a system of compulsory state primary education. This period is associated with Julius Vogel, the colonial treasurer and instigator of the great public works schemes, who borrowed large sums of money from Britain to finance huge land purchases in order to undertake public works such as the building of roads and railways, and to stimulate immigration.

After 1876, the provincial governments were abolished and immigration was managed by the central government in New Zealand. Agents of the New Zealand government went to Britain to recruit assisted immigrants and some 100,000 (93% from the UK) were brought to New Zealand in the 1870s. The year 1874 saw over 32,000 assisted migrants and the highest level of annual net migration ever (nzhistory.net 2002). There were anxieties about having extensive Irish immigration to New Zealand, but a quota system that was put in place to prevent this proved impossible to enforce. Akenson (1990: 15) goes on to explain that the government was never fully committed to restricting the Irish, partly because there was a shortage of women in the colony, and single Irish women were more prepared to emigrate than their counterparts in Scotland, England, or Wales.

2.2.1.4 1881–1900: Depression. In the 1880s and early 1890s, New Zealand suffered from a long economic depression which made it a less attractive destination for immigrants. The policy of giving assisted passages came under question and the numbers were reduced during the 1880s, with the last small group of assisted immigrants arriving in 1891. At the same time, the economy of Victoria, Australia (with its biggest centre, Melbourne) was booming and a large number of people left New Zealand to move there. In 1888 there was a net population decline of over 9,000 (nzhistory.net 2002). The New Zealand economy began to improve around the turn of the century, with a consequent increase again in the number of immigrants arriving.

2.3 *Where did the migrants come from?*

Though, as mentioned, it is difficult to determine the precise origins of early settlers, we can get a general idea of the immediate origin of many in the period of planned settlement (1840–52). For example, with the first settlement of Wellington by the New Zealand Company, there was one ship from Glasgow, but all the rest of the people brought out on the company's ships came from London and the counties nearby (Sutch 1966: 12). Not everyone on those ships was necessarily born and raised in places around or within London, but it is highly likely that many were. Taranaki was colonised at first by the Plymouth Company, which brought six ships from Devon and Cornwall between 1841 and 1843. Otago was settled predominantly by Scots, and Canterbury predominantly by people from Southern England. Unlike the other provinces, Auckland was settled in a haphazard way, with very rapid growth. Its early population included Maori, British troops, and ninety boys sent out from Parkhurst (on the Isle of Wight) in England. According to Sinclair (1991: 100), by 1851 Auckland's population was 31% Irish (compared with only 2% in Wellington) and over half of its population came from Australia. Sinclair quotes William Fox (from Wellington) who thought Auckland 'a mere section of the town of Sydney transplanted' (Sinclair 1991: 100).

From the census figures of 1871, it is clear that the vast majority of migrants in New Zealand came from the British Isles. Of the migrant population of New Zealand, the English formed the largest ethnic group (51%). However, the Scots, who made up 10% of the population of the British Isles, constituted 27.3% of the migrants in New Zealand, concentrated in Otago and Southland, but also found elsewhere throughout the country. The Irish, who in 1871 made up 18.8% of the UK population, constituted about 22% of the New Zealand migrant population. As previously mentioned, the Welsh were often conflated with the English in official records but, even allowing for this, the Welsh were under-represented among immigrants to New Zealand; perhaps because of their lack of proximity in the UK to major ports such as London and Glasgow (nzhistory.net 2000). These percentages (51% English, 27.3% Scottish, 22% Irish) are no doubt important to the formation of New Zealand English, and this relative make-up of the migrant population is often cited in studies of the history of New Zealand English. Nevertheless, as we will see, there is much more involved than these simple proportions.

For one thing, labels can conceal a large amount of variation and complexity within national boundaries. This can be seen, for example, in Hearn's (2000) study of the Irish in Auckland from 1840 to 1860:

> The inflow appears to have had five components: first a Roman Catholic stream, originating largely in Leinster and Munster and coming predominantly from farming and labouring backgrounds, with a smaller and similar flow from Ulster; second, an Anglo-Irish stream, originating particularly in Leinster, professing allegiance to the Church of Ireland and coming largely from farming, white collar and 'other' backgrounds; third, a smaller stream, also originating largely from Ulster, professing allegiance to the Church of Ireland and coming in particular from farming backgrounds; fourth, a smaller stream, also from Ulster and from farming backgrounds but professing allegiance to the Presbyterian Church; and fifth, a small stream whose members professed allegiance to the Church of Ireland and who originated largely in three counties of Munster, namely Cork, Limerick and Tipperary. (Hearn 2000: 60)

Table 3.1 *Birthplace of overseas-born in 1881* (NZ *Census 1881: 191*)

	Number	%
England	119,224	45.0
Scotland	52,753	19.9
Ireland	49,363	18.6
Australian Colonies	17,277	6.5
Wales	1,963	0.7
British North America and other British Possessions	4,014	1.5
China	5,033	1.9
Germany	4,819	1.8
Sweden, Norway, and Denmark	4,734	1.8
Other countries of Europe	3,160	1.2
USA	841	0.3
Others (unspecified)	2,023	0.8

Belich also makes the point that people's regional origins were often suppressed in the interests of 'fitting in' and that some groups were seen as more likely to fit in:

> New Zealand was to be more British than Britain in the sense that English, Scots and Welsh were to mix more. The linchpin prophets heavily criticised the attempt to keep Otago exclusively Scottish, and applauded its partial failure as much as Otago Pioneers bemoaned it. They saw the mingling of the British people as desirable. (Belich 1996: 303)

Table 3.1 shows the birthplaces of the immigrants in New Zealand in 1881, that is about half of the total non-Maori population of New Zealand. When we look at migration to New Zealand, we also need to bear in mind that if we take the long- and short-term migrants as a single group, in most, though not all, years the number of migrants who came directly to New Zealand from the British Isles was less than the number of migrants who came from Australia. The migrants from Australia included those who were Australian born, but far more were originally from the British Isles, who spent some time in Australia before arriving in New Zealand (Akenson 1990: 20–1, see Chapter 7). Akenson suggests that this is not surprising because until 1883 there was no direct steamship communication between New Zealand and the British Isles, even though, earlier than this, some sailing ships had come directly. He also points out that, even after this, it was still advisable for those migrants without connections or prearranged employment in the colonies to first travel to Australia and then seek out information about opportunities before finally settling in either Australia or New Zealand (Akenson 1990: 21).

Table 3.2 *Regional origins of the English immigrants (Taken from http://www.nzhistory.net.nz/gallery/brit-nz/english.htm)*

	London (%)	South-east (%)	South-west (%)	Lancashire (%)
UK Census 1871	15.5	10.6	8.3	12.4
New Zealand:				
1840–52	14.9	21.1	23.0	5.3
NZ Company 1839–50	25.9	20.8	26.4	3.4
Auckland 1840–52	20.1	17.2	21.8	?
1853–70	17.3	12.7	16.2	8.6
Miners – Otago 1853–70	7.8	8.5	36.8	9.4
1871–80	15.8	15.1	18.7	4.7
1881–1914	18.8	12.9	12.2	11.6

2.3.1 Regional origins of the English immigrants. Table 3.2[5] shows the regional origins of the English migrants to New Zealand and also provides the regional proportions taken from UK census information.

Emigration was unevenly distributed, with some areas of the British Isles contributing large numbers of emigrants, others none. The West Country (Devon and Cornwall) had a strong tradition of emigration, seen in the settlement of Taranaki by the Plymouth Company in 1841–3 (named for the major seaport

[5] Tables 3.2, 3.3 and 3.4 are derived from a forthcoming book on British and Irish immigration to New Zealand and are used with permission.

in Devon). The counties of the south-west, especially Cornwall, were over-represented among the immigrants because of the migration of miners after the collapse of the tin-mining industry there in the 1840s. (Other immigrants came from areas where there was no defined pattern of emigration, such as from Surrey.) Belich (1996: 319) suggests that the Scottish and Irish immigrants in New Zealand tended to come from counties that were close to but not actually in the major urban centres – for example, from areas around but not in Glasgow, Edinburgh, Belfast, and Dublin. It is possible that this also applies in England to areas such as Surrey, Essex, and Kent – near but not in London, and good sources of agricultural workers.

Table 3.2 shows the high proportion of immigrants from the south of England. London was an important birthplace for immigrants to New Zealand, but the percentage of Londoners among the immigrants was about the same as the percentage of Londoners in England as a whole. Many people, particularly in the 1840s, came from the counties surrounding London,[6] especially from Kent. The numbers from the south-west remained consistently high until 1880, with over twice as many coming to New Zealand as were represented by their proportion of the population of England. Pickens' (1977) research into the birthplaces of nineteenth-century Canterbury migrants – an area with a very high percentage of English immigrants – demonstrates that they came from the West Country counties of Cornwall, Devon, and Somerset, the South Midland counties of Oxfordshire and Gloucestershire, and the London hinterland counties of Surrey, Essex, and Kent. Arnold's (1981) investigations also show that these areas were important sources of migrants. Charlotte Macdonald's book, *A Woman of Good Character*, an account of single women who were immigrant settlers in nineteenth-century New Zealand, gives London as the main recruiting centre for single women, though, as she explains, many of these women were already mobile and had originally moved to London from country areas (Macdonald 1990: 45). After London, the second largest group of women immigrants came from the south-west of England and the third largest group came from Sussex, Surrey, Kent, Hampshire, and Berkshire (p. 54). The more industrial areas of the north-west, including Lancashire, did not contribute many immigrants to New Zealand until the end of the nineteenth century.

The predominance of immigrants from the south of England is reflected in the Mobile Unit archive of early New Zealand-born speakers. Of ninety-five speakers analysed auditorially, only one, Mr Temple, whose father came from Lancashire and mother from Cheshire, has the Northern England phonological feature where the FOOT vowel is used in the lexical sets of both FOOT and STRUT (see Chapter 6). This feature is diagnostic of Northern England (north /lʊv/; south /lʌv/). The overwhelming influence of the south, and especially of London and the south-east, is evident in the findings of the ONZE project

[6] This included Essex, Hertfordshire, Kent, Surrey, Sussex, plus parts of Bedfordshire, Berkshire, and Buckinghamshire (Wells 1982: 335).

Table 3.3 *Regional origins of the Scots immigrants (Taken from http://www.nzhistory.net.nz/gallery/brit-nz/scotshtm)*

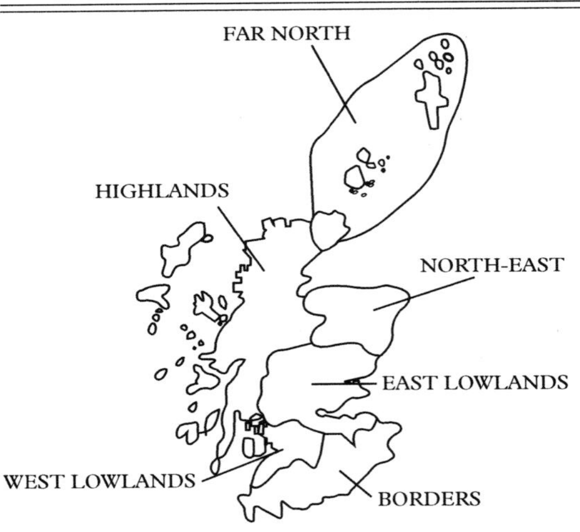

	Far North (%)	Highlands (%)	North-east (%)	East Lowlands (%)	West Lowlands (%)	Borders (%)
UK Census 1871	3.1	8.5	11.7	31.5	37.1	8.1
New Zealand:						
1842–52	6.1	10.3	7.9	36.2	36.2	3.3
1853–70	5.9	16.0	10.2	32.7	26.5	8.6
1871–80	12.6	10.4	9.7	25.5	32.8	9.0
1881–1915	3.6	8.8	11.9	31.2	38.0	6.7

and in the traits of modern New Zealand English, both of which predominantly exhibit traits characteristic of the English of the south-east of England (see Chapters 4 and 6).

2.3.2 Regional origins of the Scots immigrants. Table 3.3 shows the regions from which the Scots immigrants came and it can be seen that the migrants to New Zealand constituted a cross-section of the Scots as a whole. Most of the Scottish population lived in the Lowlands, and most of Scottish migrants to New Zealand (more than 60%) also came from this area. There were also a surprising number of migrants from the far north of Scotland, especially from the Shetland Islands. Some 13.8% of the Scottish miners who came from the Shetland Islands went to Westland (on the west coast of the South Island) and 6.2% to Otago. Among the miners generally there was a high proportion from the Scottish Highlands (18.5%), but this proportion drops in comparison to Scottish immigration overall (nzhistory.net 2002).

In modern New Zealand English, it is difficult to discern a significant Scottish influence, though clearly the impact of some Scottish features was felt significantly as New Zealand English developed, as revealed in the analysis of the Mobile Unit speakers (see Chapters 6 and 7; also Trudgill, Maclagan, and Lewis in press).

2.3.3 Regional origins of the Irish immigrants. According to Denoon et al. (2000: 87), the Irish comprised a quarter of white Australia in the nineteenth century and brought with them 'a heavy dose of anti-authoritarianism, Catholicism, and folklore'. The large Irish migration to Australia was in part because of the Irish famine of 1845–8. In New Zealand, the main period of settlement postdated this famine, and authorities had always opposed Irish immigration, preferring the Scots. However, although Irish migration to New Zealand was never as extensive as it was in Australia, many Irish arrived at the time of the goldrushes; significant numbers were in the North Island militia, and many more came via Australia. By 1881 they made up about 19% of the overseas-born population.

Table 3.4 shows the regional origins of the Irish immigrants to New Zealand. It shows that among the earliest Irish migrants to New Zealand (in the 1840s) many came from Leinster, but the number from there declined through the century. However, it would be misleading to interpret the Leinster figures here as meaning of Dublin origin. Many only passed through Dublin (Leinster), especially during the Great Famine, largely from western and central counties. The fact that such a large portion of the Irish immigrants to New Zealand had a farming background (see Table 3.7 in section 2.4) also shows that a Dublin, that is urban, origin should not be assumed for most of the Leinster emigrants.[7] Irish soldiers who were eventually discharged in New Zealand appear to have been recruited into the British army from in and around Dublin, though their ultimate origin may be from elsewhere in Ireland (nzhistory.net 2002).

The two areas in Ireland that contributed the largest number of migrants to New Zealand were Munster in the south-west and Ulster in the north (the areas nearest the two ports from which emigrants set sail, respectively Cobh (Cork) and Belfast). Those from Munster were almost all from a Catholic background; many came to New Zealand via Australia at the time of the goldrushes. During the 1870s, Munster Catholics took advantage of the assisted immigration scheme and nominated their relatives to join them in New Zealand. When assisted immigration ended, the numbers coming from Munster also began to decline. A significant number of the Irish immigrants came from Ulster, and this number increased over the years. Only 20–25% of the Ulster immigrants were Catholic; the New Zealand immigration authorities preferred Protestants and this is reflected in an increasing number of Ulster Presbyterians coming to New Zealand (nzhistory.net 2002). Galbraith (2000: 42) suggests that Ulster's prominence in migration to New Zealand was because of widespread contemporary stereotypes about, and prejudices against, the Irish, which caused New

[7] We are grateful to Ray Hickey for pointing this out to us.

Table 3.4 *Regional origins of the Irish immigrants (Taken from http://www.nzhistory.net.nz/gallery/brit-nz/irish.htm)*

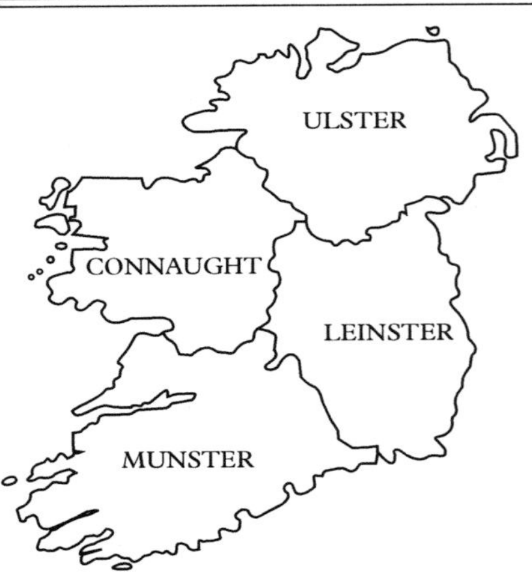

	Leinster (%)	Munster (%)	Ulster (%)	Connaught (%)
UK Census 1871	23.9	25.9	34.2	16.0
New Zealand:				
1840–52	34.1	27.8	31.7	6.3
1853–70	19.9	31.7	39.8	8.5
1871–80	16.1	34.5	42.0	9.4
1881–1915	13.8	31.5	48.4	6.3
1911–15	20.0	20.0	56.0	4.0

Zealand's immigration networks in Ireland to discriminate heavily in favour of the mainly Protestant Ulster.

As will be explained in Chapters 4 and 7, the Irish immigrants had little impact on the development of New Zealand English.[8]

2.4 *Where the migrants to New Zealand settled*

A look at the migration patterns from different parts of the British Isles in Table 3.5 shows that there were strong regional differences and concentrations within New Zealand.

[8] In contemplating the Irish input to New Zealand English, the Ulster Irish mostly had accents not consistent with the other Irish but rather mixed, being closer to Scottish varieties of English in some of their phonological features. It could be argued from a linguistic point of view, then, that the figure of 18.6%, representing the Irish proportion of immigrant population of New Zealand in 1881 (see Table 3.1), rather overestimates the input of Irish English into the formation of New Zealand English.

Table 3.5 *New Zealand locations of immigrant population, by place of birth (1871)*

	NZ (%)	Australia (%)	England (%)	Scotland (%)	Ireland (%)	Other* (%)
Auckland (67,451)	43.6	4.0	26.6	7.7	12.6	5.5
Wellington (29,790)	49.8	3.4	28.1	7.8	6.1	4.8
Taranaki (5,465)	53.8	2.6	28.5	4.4	7.8	2.9
Hawkes Bay (9,228)	37.2	2.6	29.3	7.4	10.6	8.7
Nelson (22,558)	43.9	4.3	25.1	7.4	10.6	8.7
Canterbury (58,775)	41.1	2.7	33.1	8.5	10.3	4.3
Westland (14,860)	27.5	10.8	19.2	8.9	19.0	14.6
Otago (85,113)	35.9	6.1	16.9	25.1	8.2	7.8

(**Note:* The main countries under the birthplace category 'Other' are Sweden, Norway, Germany, and China. (Adapted from McKinnon 1997: 53))

Table 3.6 *New Zealand locations of UK immigrants, by place of birth (1871) (Taken from nzhistory.net 2002)*

	England (%)	Scotland (%)	Ireland (%)
Auckland	54.9	17.0	27.2
Taranaki	69.6	9.5	20.5
Hawkes Bay	55.2	20.9	23.2
Wellington	63.5	20.0	15.4
Nelson	56.4	15.9	25.9
Marlborough	62.1	20.4	16.4
Canterbury	62.7	16.9	19.4
Westland	40.1	19.9	37.9
Otago	31.0	51.5	16.9
Southland	24.4	61.4	13.9
New Zealand	49.7	27.3	22.0

In the nineteenth century, the Wellington, New Plymouth, and Canterbury provinces were dominated by the English because of their New Zealand Company origins. Table 3.6 shows the percentages of only the English, Scottish, and Irish-born people living in the New Zealand provinces in 1871.

In the early New Zealand settlements, those who stayed in New Zealand long enough to die there were, for the most part, from a labouring, agricultural, or lower-middle-class background. The death certificates of the British and Irish immigrants give information about their fathers' occupations. Although not showing the occupations of the migrants themselves, information about their family background shown in Table 3.7 gives some indication of the social

Table 3.7 *Occupations of immigrants' fathers (Taken from nzhistory.net 2002.)*

	Agriculture (%)	Builders (%)	Pre-industrial Crafts (%)	Industrial (%)	White Collar (%)
1841–52	34.6	9.1	17.4	4.2	15.9
1853–70	37.6	8.3	21.2	2.7	12.2
1871–80	31.2	8.9	22.1	6.6	15.5
1881–90 (English)	25.9	7.9	21.9	6.6	15.5
1881–1915 (Scots)	27.2	8.9	24.5	9.8	7.4
1881–1915 (Irish)	65.2	3.9	7.2	2.8	5.5

background of the migrants; the dates refer to the year in which individuals migrated to New Zealand.

The figures show that a large proportion of the immigrants (and a very high proportion of the Irish) came from a farming background. It also shows that a considerable number of immigrants came from a background in pre-industrial crafts, such as flax-workers, blacksmiths, wheelwrights, coopers, and so on. According to nzhistory.net 2002, those with an agricultural background and those with a craft background often came from the same communities in the UK, communities where people would mix farming and traditional crafts. Migrants from Ulster, for example, combined flax-weaving and spinning with farming; those from the Shetlands combined farming and fishing. The number of migrants from an industrial background remained below 10% in the nineteenth century; there was, however, a significant number of white-collar workers.

As mentioned, the intent in the planned Wakefield settlements was to replicate a vertical slice of British society (with the top and bottom levels removed), and neither those of very high class or those of very low class came to New Zealand. Graham describes New Zealand as 'overwhelmingly a working settlers' society' (1992: 116). Sinclair suggests that poverty, or the fear of poverty, was the chief stimulus for emigration:

> The pioneers of New Zealand were not from the highest, nor were they usually from the most down-trodden sections of British society. They were people who while poor, while usually from the upper working class or lower middle class – 'the anxious classes' Wakefield called them – had lost neither enterprise nor ambition. (Sinclair 1991: 101)

The immigrant ships maintained British class distinctions. In the 1840–52 period, those who came on the Company ships paying for their own passages were known as 'colonists' and travelled as 'cabin passengers'. They amounted to about 12–14% of the total passengers. Those who were on assisted passages were referred to as 'emigrants' and travelled steerage in crowded conditions, usually lacking most forms of privacy. Sinclair points out that many of the 'colonists' did not remain in New Zealand – for example, of the early settlers in Wellington, only 85 of the original 436 remained (Sinclair 1991: 96). For the assisted emigrants, of course, there was usually no choice but to remain.

3 Historical background: colonial society

New Zealand English developed from the different varieties of English imported by the immigrants to New Zealand. Once settled, immigrants and their language were also influenced by social factors – social class, schooling, religious affiliation, transport and mobility, the later arrival of many more immigrants, the make-up of particular early settlements, and attitudes towards Britain and Australia. Gardner described the fluid nature of early New Zealand society:

> In New Zealand we are not dealing with communities established on the same ground over millennia, with age-old dialects, customs, symbols and family names. Our society has included many rising and falling towns and districts; there has been a large mobile element, and the 'stable' proportion in any given region or centre may have fallen as low as 10% or even less. This is our untidy past, a game of regional snakes and ladders, and we have to accept it. Historical community in New Zealand may mean a rather small solid core, and a large fluid overlay. (Gardner 1999: 50)

There were two significant characteristics of the early colony: (1) men outnumbered women, and (2) there were a large number of children.

3.1 Demography

In the early years of settlement, there were more males than females in the colony, and it was not until 1901 that the census showed that these had approached a normal balance. Table 3.8 gives population figures for males and females of all ages from 1864 to 1881.

Of course there was considerable variation around the country, and in some places the balance was achieved relatively early. There was a higher imbalance in country areas than in the towns. The goldfields were predominantly male, with 2.9 men to every woman (Sinclair 1986a: 67–8).

The early population of New Zealand was also predominantly a young one. Graham (1996: 71) states that about a quarter of the population in the 1840s and 1850s were children, and that there were few people over forty-five. Many children arrived with their immigrating parents. The New Zealand Company dispatched nearly 10,000 settlers to New Zealand in the 1840s, among them more

Table 3.8 *Male and female population figures, 1864–1881 (From NZ Census Reports, years stated)*

	1864	1867	1871	1874	1878	1881
Males	106,580	131,929	150,356	179,981	230,998	269,605
Females	65,578	86,739	106,037	128,533	183,414	220,328

Table 3.9 *New Zealand population aged under 15 (From NZ Census Reports, years stated)*

	Persons under 15 years of age	Percentage of total population
1864	58,369	31.7
1867	79,185	36.21
1871	101,348	36.38
1874	124,035	41.41
1878	174,968	42.22
1881	207,826	42.42
1886	238,528	41.23

children (3,800) than adult males (Denoon et al. 2000: 87). Then, of course, many children were born in New Zealand. Sinclair notes that in 1896, when 62% of the Europeans in New Zealand were New Zealand-born, only 11,600 (5%) of these were over twenty, with the remaining 330,000 native-born being under twenty-one (Sinclair 1986b: 2). Table 3.9 provides some further evidence based on census information.

Although there is no direct way of establishing family size from nineteenth-century statistics, some idea can be gained from sampling family histories and from the work of genealogists. Toynbee's study of Wellington fecundity shows that across a five-point social scale, there were 1,631 births from 220 marriages, averaging 7.4 per family. The 112 farming couples produced 900 children – or 8 per family (cited by Gardner 1999: 85).

Gardner (1999: 85) suggests that these large families were the most powerful argument for establishing a local school and/or a church, and provided the 'principal cement of colonial society'. The large families were a source of both stability and instability. On the one hand, women needed a fixed home for themselves and their children – the building-up of neighbourly networks, the requirement to be near a midwife, and the time it took to establish gardens and orchards all provided disincentives for families to move. On the other hand, even a large farm would not be able to support more than two or three sons, so younger members of the second generation had to leave home to find work or land for themselves.

3.2 Education

With so many young people in the colony, education became an important issue. At first, the provision of education was very uneven. In some of the early settlements, private schools were established, often in conjunction with the churches. In some places, the only schooling was through Sunday schools; in others it was subject to sectarian squabbles.

Before 1876, in some of the provinces there was a fee-paying system for schooling, but many parents could not afford the fees, and children were needed by their families to work for money or to assist with farm or other labour. Mr William Dufty, a Mobile Unit speaker born in Thames in 1865, describes leaving school when he was nine to go to work. As described by Campbell, the provincial system failed to meet the minimum educational needs of the colony:

> As late as 1870, not more than half the children between the ages of five and fifteen were going to school at all, and the proportion who were receiving regularly even moderately efficient instruction was very much smaller. Nelson, Otago and Canterbury were far ahead of the other provinces; in 1869 their governments spent on the average £2 10s for every child of school age as against an average of only 5s in the rest of the colony. It was said that compared with the South, the whole of the North Island was an intellectual desert. The main reason for the difference was economic. Canterbury and Otago were the wealthy provinces, with well-filled treasuries and substantial church endowments, whereas in the North Island, which had been harassed and impoverished by the Maori wars, the provincial governments were in acute financial difficulties. (Campbell 1941: 44)

The 1877 Education Act replaced the provincial educational system with a national system of free primary education. After the passing of this act, which made attendance at primary schools compulsory, popular education spread rapidly. Nevertheless, though regional disparities were reduced, they were not eliminated, and in spite of the compulsory attendance clause, truancy continued, being frequently sanctioned by the children's parents (Graham 1992: 132). By the standards of the time, the level of education in New Zealand became high. By 1886, 73% of the total population were literate and another 5% could read but not write. By 1891, 80% of New Zealand's 167,000 non-Maori children aged five to fifteen were receiving elementary education at the 1,255 public primary schools or the 281 private schools (Graham 1992: 32). Equal numbers of boys and girls attended these schools.

The introduction of free compulsory primary education meant that large numbers of children in New Zealand were now coming together for their education.

Table 3.10 *New Zealand statistics of school attendance, 1871–1886 (From Gardner 1999: 100)*

	(a): Population aged 5–14 years	(b): Number attending public schools	(c): (b) as a percentage of (a)
1871	54,771	14,953	27.30
1874	72,134	34,307	47.70
1878	105,235	62,866	59.74
1881	125,527	87,811	69.95
1886	151,685	110,644	72.95

Table 3.11 *Urban-rural distribution of non-Maori population, 1861–1891*

	1861 (%)	1871 (%)	1881 (%)	1891 (%)
Urban*	33.8	37.4	42.0	45.5
Rural	66.2	62.6	58.0	54.5

(*Urban area = over 1,000 population (Adapted from Gibson 1971: Table 22, cited in Graham 1992: 136))

The mixing of these children could have been very significant in the development of New Zealand English. Statistics of school attendance are given in Table 3.10.

3.3 Town and country

At first the differences between living in the town and living in the country were not great, though the country was characterised as being more peaceful and free from 'sights of drunkenness and vice' (Graham 1992: 137). Both town and country dwellers suffered from shortages of supplies and inadequate services (Graham 1992: 135). As time went on, these were more quickly remedied in the towns, and by the 1870s people were beginning to move from the country to the towns for better educational and work opportunities. By the 1880s the need for welfare provision in the towns was apparent, and the children there were more likely to succumb to diseases such as diphtheria, whooping cough, and typhoid fever (Graham 1992: 136). Table 3.11 shows a steady increase in the percentage of town dwellers and at the same time a decrease in the percentage of those living in the country.

3.4 Immigration

Immigrants continued to arrive throughout the nineteenth century (see section 2.2.1). The Vogel immigration policy of the 1870s had a major impact on the population. Gardner (1999) believes that there is good reason to regard the immigration of this period as the most significant event in the social history of New Zealand. By comparison, the number of Europeans who arrived in the 1840s and 1850s was relatively small, and the effect of the goldrush population was relatively localised:

> Immigration doubled the colony's population in a decade [1870–80]; it provided the right kind of workforce for development; it extended the frontiers of settlement; it confirmed the predominantly rural character of New Zealand; it strengthened the British culture in the colony; it critically eroded the natural defences of the Maori enclaves in the North Island. (Gardner 1999: 71)

3.5 Transport

Vogel's 1870 budget involved the borrowing of large sums of money to meet the chief needs of the country, which were considered to be immigration, roads, and railways. Many of the early settlements were completely isolated, and this fact is often mentioned by the speakers in the Mobile Unit archive, who describe arduous journeys by wagon, on horseback, on foot through deep mud or difficult terrain, or by boat. One speaker, Mrs King, grew up in Makarora in the Haast Pass, which in the 1860s and 1870s was accessible only by a forty-mile journey by boat up Lake Wanaka. Mrs Reid of Te Awamutu describes a four-day journey in 1860 from Auckland to Taupiri in the Waikato, by coach, horse, and Maori canoe, with two of the overnight stays in Maori whares (houses or huts). (Today, this journey takes little over an hour by car via a motorway.)

The roads and railways that were eventually built connected the scattered provinces. As Bassett et al. describe it:

> Before 1870 it was often easier to go from Auckland to Sydney than from Auckland to Wellington. There were no roads through the centre of the North Island. People travelled by coastal ships and by horseback on rough bush tracks. Railway lines were disconnected fragments reaching inland from ports. In 1874 there were only 418 kilometres of railway tracks in the whole country. (Bassett et al. 1985: 95)

3.6 Attitudinal factors

The attitude of the early settlers towards the new colony, as some have argued (see Chapter 7), may have had an influence on the development of a distinctive variety of New Zealand English. The first European settlers to New Zealand were confronted with all the problems and dangers of survival and making a living in the new land. Letters that have survived from this period bear eloquent testimony to the hardships so many endured (see Porter and Macdonald 1996). Many of the Mobile Unit speakers give graphic accounts of the difficulties of early settler life. Attitudes towards their new country ranged from total dislike to total delight. Some loathed the new country and yearned to return to Britain. For example, Louisa Rose wrote from Christchurch to her sister Constance in 1852, 'Oh how thankful I am you are safe out of this vile country; I never wish to see anybody I love come out here' (quoted in Porter and Macdonald 1996: 88). On the other hand there were those who delighted in colonial life. In 1853, Maria Richmond, who at the age of twenty-eight exchanged her middle-class life with servants in England for life in New Plymouth, where she did her own housework, wrote:

> It has just occurred to me that I have never distinctly said how much I like this country . . . you find people who don't see beauty in the place because there are no country lanes, hedges, pretty little villages with church spires dotted about . . . but how the absence of such things should blind people to the loveliness before their eyes I cannot understand . . . the thinking over this and a hundred other things of this nature is enough to make the most sluggish nature 'feel spirited'. Sometimes I am in such a state that I feel convinced that nothing short of going up Mt Egmont can properly relieve me and let off the steam. At present I only explode in the baking of ten loaves or the making of a dozen pounds of butter and the occasional scramble down a gully tearing my clothes to pieces. (Porter 1989: 56)

3.7 Social class

Colonial circumstances brought about some changes in the way a person's social background was viewed. While some early attempts had been made to replicate the British class system in New Zealand, it did not really succeed. Historians recognise the difficulties in using terms like 'social class' for this early period. McAloon suggests the following typology of class origins:

> The gentry includes all substantial landed families, including the titled. The upper middle class is larger working farmers, manufacturers, merchants, and established professionals; the lower middle class includes self-employed artisans, smaller farmers, traders, farm managers, [and] other earners. The lower class are manual wage earners. (McAloon 1996: 49)

McAloon points out (1996: 58) that in New Zealand the principal motivation for people's accumulation of wealth (and this includes all levels of wealth) was the desire to pass it on to their families. Equal treatment of all heirs was the rule, with estates being divided equally and without sons being favoured above daughters. In this way, the inheritance practices of the colonial wealthy were more like those of the British middle classes than of the British upper classes, who saw land as the basis of dynastic power, maintained under the system of primogeniture. McAloon's (1996) study of the colonial wealthy demonstrates that almost all the rich people in New Zealand were typically lower middle class and wage-earning in origin, and did very much better for themselves in the colony than they would have done at home. He writes:

> The crucial element in this upward mobility – amounting almost to an iron law – was early arrival. To be the first to take up a given landholding was to have an enormous advantage. Also important was access to capital. This was achieved either through patronage, through family networks, through one's own work, or luck. (McAloon 1996: 59)

A shortage of labour in the new colony meant that those who had domestic servants in Britain often found they had to engage in manual labour themselves. The shortage of labour also meant that manual workers could command more money and a higher degree of respect than they would have received in Britain. Those who did employ servants would often work beside them and avoided using terms like 'servant'. In 1853, on the day he landed, a member of the Canterbury Association was shocked to find that servants referred to each other as 'Mr' and 'Mrs' but to 'gentlefolk' by their surnames only (quoted in Sinclair 1991: 96). However, Belich remarks:

> Colonial life blurred class boundaries and mixed together all elements of society. Jack considered himself in many respects as good as his master. But there were still boundaries to blur and elements to mix. Master was still master, and Jack was still Jack. (Belich 1996: 321)

The family history of Mrs North (one of the Mobile Unit speakers from Te Awamutu) also shows a fluidity of class boundaries in New Zealand. Her father was the son of Baronet Knutsford and her mother (the child of a trading-ship deserter and a Maori) held high status within the Ngati Maniapoto and Ngati Ngutu tribes. However, Mrs North makes it clear that she was raised and educated as a 'white woman' and, in spite of her own Maori ancestry, makes disparaging remarks about Maori.

The ways in which people adapted to colonial life were affected by their position in society. Those higher on the social scale were less likely to adapt and more likely to follow British customs, import their clothes from Britain – even their housing was either prefabricated in Britain or built of native timbers with imported joinery (Drummond and Drummond 1967: 75). People lower down the social scale were more likely to adapt to the colonial situation in their dress, food, and leisure pursuits, and to build very simple houses entirely from local materials. It is not surprising, therefore, that those speakers recorded by the Mobile Unit who came from wealthy and privileged backgrounds do not show evidence of the early New Zealand accent, unlike people born at the same time but in poorer circumstances. For example, Miss Brenda Bell from Palmerston, in Otago, a third-generation New Zealander born in 1880, talks at length about the titled members of her family; she could be mistaken for a speaker of old fashioned RP. On the other hand, Mrs Catherine Dudley from Arrowtown, also in Otago, born in 1886 and married to a road mender, is usually identified as sounding like 'an old New Zealander' in perception tests carried out annually over many years by Elizabeth Gordon, using New Zealand university students as subjects.

This relates to the claims (see Chapter 7) that the emergence of a distinct variety of English here was motivated, at least in part, by a desire to emphasise a sense of colonial identity. There are reports from the first decades of the European settlement of New Zealand of those who were already settled distinguishing themselves from newcomers. It was a case of the 'old hands' mocking the 'new chums'. William Swainson, whose book on *New Zealand and its Colonisation* was published in London in 1859, wrote:

> A new comer is still immediately recognised: an air of conscious superiority not infrequently betrays itself in every look and gesture. But the new arrival is not long in finding his true level; for in apprehension of character the people of New Zealand are marvellously clear-sighted – quick in detecting it, and just in appreciation: no one can long pass for what he is not; and if not distinguished by some useful or agreeable quality, the new arrival soon finds his level in a modest insignificance; and many who, on landing, move confidently on with buoyant step and lofty mien, may soon be seen passing modestly along, undistinguished from the common crowd. (Swainson 1859: 230–1)

From a linguistic point of view, this desire of newcomers to fit in could be crucial to the development of a distinctive variety of language, as Turner (1966) suggested:

> When a new form of language develops, the study of that language must give a disproportionate attention to the first generation of settlers, new things are named early and new ways of speech develop from a linguistically mixed community. Later arrivals, even if numerous, are less important because they are absorbed as newcomers and learn to conform, and indeed wish to conform. (Turner 1966: 6)

(See the discussion of 'founder effect' in Chapter 7.)

3.8 Relations with Australia and Great Britain

3.8.1 Australia. The relationship between Australia and New Zealand is as complex and interesting as the relationships are between family members. New Zealanders abroad are constantly mistaken for Australians, and intense national rivalry at home has been known to change to solidarity on the other side of the world. An important claim (considered in detail in Chapters 4 and 7) is that New Zealand English owes its origin to, or was highly influenced by, Australian

English; therefore, it is important to understand the historical connections between the two countries. Arnold describes the situation as it was in 1888 most eloquently:

> Any real probing of the trans-Tasman relationship quickly throws up a curious blend of certainties and ambiguities, of subtle shifts between near and far and between shifting and emigrating, or uncertainty about one or two peoples, of interplay between strangers and brothers . . . As isolated outposts of British settlement, and common participants in the British imperial system, the seven Australasian colonies of 1888 had so much in common in terms of colonial experience, of similar or identical institutions, of common citizenship and unhampered freedom of inter-migration, that it seemed absurd to contemplate two peoples. Yet the forces that divide are also apparent; the strong contrasts in physical environment between Australia's 'haggard continent', and New Zealand's rain-drenched, wind-swept islands; the differing social and economic thrusts of metropolitan dominance in Australia and the rural/small town nature of New Zealand; the conflict of interests of primary producers working the same market places, above all, the feel of distance created by those 1200 miles of thundering ocean. (Arnold 1987: 52–3)

The histories of early European settlement in New Zealand and Australia are tightly interwoven and there was constant interchange between the two countries. For example, as early as 1861 there were 2,500 Australian-born people living in New Zealand and about 1,500 New Zealand-born people living in Australia. According to Belich (1996: 316) the two shores of the Tasman Sea were seen by some as being so closely connected that the movements of people between them were more like internal than external migration. He suggests that perhaps as many as 20% of the founding Pakeha population of New Zealand were touched by Australia in some way, whether by being born in, or bred in Australia, or by subsequent influence (Belich 1996: 316). As we have seen from the regional population differences, the influence was stronger in some parts of New Zealand than in others. It was especially strong in Auckland and in the goldmining areas of Westland, Otago, and Southland. The close relationship between the two countries can be seen in the large amount of shared lexicon. This includes everyday words such as *creek* (stream), *paddock* (field), and *gully* (deep-sided valley); and slang terms such as *crook* (ill), *sheila* (woman), and *dinkum* (genuine) (Gordon and Deverson 1998: 57). In Bauer's opinion, 'the number of words which Australia and New Zealand share – virtually to the exclusion of the rest of the English-speaking world – is astounding if the two varieties have independent origins . . . much of the shared vocabulary tends to be early vocabulary' (Bauer 1994: 427).

The seven British colonies (six in Australia, together with New Zealand) formed an early community. They were collectively described as 'Australasia' (a term invented by Charles de Brosses in the eighteenth century for the land 'au sud de l'Asie'). In addition to the constant exchange of population, there were other strong connections through organisations such as trade unions, church administration, and also mail and cable services, and jointly organised tariffs and tariff preferences.

In the 1880s, there was serious consideration given to New Zealand joining an Australian federation. In the end, New Zealand decided not to federate. The distance of ocean between the countries was thought to be too great; their trade was competitive rather than complementary; their economic circumstances were not parallel – when New Zealand was in a depression in the 1880s Australia was in a boom, but as the New Zealand economy recovered, the Australian economy collapsed. However, the main reasons that New Zealand decided to remain independent were the fear of losing political identity and nationhood, and the concern that New Zealand would not be able to deal directly with the British government (Sinclair 1986a: 118–19).

Yet New Zealanders living overseas still feel a strong affinity with Australians. The fact that the two countries have always been so close is the reason the identity of the smaller country is threatened by the larger. This can be seen in a cartoon in the *New Zealand Graphic* in 1900. Under the caption 'How we see it' is an especially ugly Australian ogre with a huge head, horns, and large grinning teeth, bearing chains on his arms, saying, 'Come into these arms'. New Zealand is portrayed as a Victorian maiden in a flowing classical gown and a feather cloak over one shoulder, sheltering a rather demure looking Maori. She replies, 'Nay, sir, those arms bear chains'.

By the 1880s, some New Zealanders had developed a sense of nationalism. Premier John Ballance attacked the idea of federating with Australia, stating, 'we might supply Australia with a few oats, but we would lose our freedom' (cited in Sinclair 1987: 94). The sense of nationalism can be seen in this speech in a parliamentary debate in 1890:

> We have been an individualised nation, and we should keep up our identity and nationality. I think we ought to have a nationality, and that New Zealand should be a country for New-Zealanders. With the wings of Great Britain over us we need look to no other country or colony for protection . . . We are here the pioneers of a great nation, and shall, no doubt have a glorious history. (Sinclair 1986a: 119)

As referred to in Gordon and Deverson 1998 (p. 29), it is possible that it was the presence of Australia that caused New Zealand to be so closely attached to Britain (in a way similar to the Canadian attachment to Britain under the shadow of the US).

Perhaps it was this desire to withstand Australian domination that is the basis of the tone of superiority that infiltrates some of the New Zealand commentary. Those who described the New Zealand pioneers as being of 'selected stock' or 'the best British' could also be making an implicit comment about the prominence of its penal colonies in Australia's history (Sinclair 1986a: 96). Sometimes the comments about Australia were overt, as when we find descriptions of the early New Zealand accent being likened to the Australian accent 'but not quite as bad' (see Chapter 4 for more detail). In 1912, one commentator discussing the New Zealand accent said, 'it fortunately has not reached the despairing depths of what we in New Zealand call "Orstreilian", but it is in grave danger of touching that point' (quoted in Gordon and Deverson 1998: 28). Here is a similar remark, from Herz (1912: 352):

> Sad to relate, one far too often hears the young generation talk with a twang that horrifies the ear of anyone used to good English . . . This twang is worse in Australia than in New Zealand but it is gaining ground here and ought to be strenuously eradicated by school teachers, for it does not sound nice, and robs sweet girlish lips of all their poesy.

3.8.2 Great Britain. The European population of New Zealand, as shown above, came from the British Isles, but by coming to New Zealand, the earliest pioneering settlers were certainly not abandoning their British roots. Their reasons for emigrating were not to put all things British behind them, but rather to make a new Britain in the South Pacific and to better themselves, but always within the context of British institutions, British law, and British religions, education, social values, and practices.

Some settlers took great comfort in the fact that they were living in a British colony and tried to make New Zealand as British as possible. Alice Lees writing from Oamaru in 1873, described her bay-windowed sitting room with English trees in the garden and ducks on the pond: '[with] everything about me feeling so English and homelike it is almost impossible to believe that we are so far away from you. One feels far more a stranger 20 miles away from England, on the French coast, than you can possibly do at this great distance in an English colony' (quoted in Porter and Macdonald 1996: 99).

By the 1860s–1870s, the New Zealand colony had established itself as a viable and secure member of the British Empire. By the 1880s there were more non-Maori New Zealand-born inhabitants than there were immigrants. The intention of these New Zealand-born pakeha was not to replicate Britain in the South Pacific, as their parents had wished and tried for; their only contact with Britain was second-hand, through the accounts and attitudes of their parents. The idea of the first generation of New Zealand-born pakeha was to establish a loyal British colony that, nevertheless, had its own character. Most of the speakers recorded by the Mobile Unit belonged to this first generation of the native-born New Zealanders who regarded themselves as distinct from the continuing stream of newcomers (sometimes called 'foreigners') from Britain. Sinclair (1986a: 107) describes a joke in the *New Zealand Graphic* (31 May 1890) in which a young New Zealand-born boy says to his father, 'Don't yer go deceiving yerself by thinking I'm a "cryin" 'cause yer licked me, for I ain't. I'm all upset at being struck by a furriner, an' not bein' able to strike back!'.

Even so, attachment to Britain remained strong. Sinclair compares the numbers of letters sent to Britain from New Zealand with letters sent from Australia. In 1866, when the population of New Zealand was 220,000, a million letters were sent to Britain, compared to the half a million sent from New South Wales with a population of 430,000 (Sinclair 1986a: 96). This stronger attachment could be accounted for by the more recent settlement, the lower proportion of Irish (as opposed to British) in New Zealand, and perhaps the fact that those of convict stock were less likely to have a romantic attitude towards the country they came from.

The ties with Britain were certainly strong for some New Zealanders, who continued to refer to Great Britain as 'home' into the second and third generation. Alan Mulgan, born in New Zealand in 1881 of Ulster parentage, in *Home: A New Zealander's Adventure* (1927), describes his feelings when, crossing the English Channel, he first caught sight of the English coastline:

> A door had been opened and England was before us – old gracious, and lovely. We could hardly speak. . . . We walked about the deck on an inner tide of full and soundless joy. A fellow passenger asked me what I thought of England. I replied, not with any trace of rudeness, I hope, that you might as well ask a man what he thought of his wife. (Mulgan 1927: 18–19)

This idealistic and sentimental view of Britain continued among those who were better educated and able to afford the sea journey 'home'. They were given an education that was centred exclusively on things British; the history and literature taught were the history and literature of England. Mulgan describes reading imported British papers: *The Boys' Own Paper*, the *Graphic*, and [*The*] *Illustrated London News*, works by Scott, Dickens, Thackeray, Tennyson, Wordsworth, and many more. 'The trend of all this literature . . . was to fix my thoughts ever on England' (Mulgan 1927: 8).

At the same time, people in New Zealand could also be critical of Britain. Sinclair reports that such criticism was much more frequent than the historical and other contemporary writings would lead us to believe (1986a: 107). He quotes the example of a children's story that appeared in the *New Zealand Graphic* in August 1890. A fantail and a tui (two New Zealand native birds) are talking to a fairy. The fantail asks the tui what she is saying. 'I think she is English', answered the tui gravely. 'At all events she talks very fast and very badly; I cannot understand what she says.' 'She looks English', said the fantail. 'She is shy and stupid, not like the New Zealanders at all' (Sinclair 1986a: 107). In contrast with the idealistic view of Britain often held by the wealthy in New Zealand (as typified in Alan Mulgan's account of his journey 'home'), among working-class New Zealanders, people from Britain were popularly known as 'Homies', a pejorative term revealing their different attitude to England.

In Chapter 7 the possible linguistic impact of attitudes on the development of New Zealand English is considered. Opinion has differed on whether, or to what extent, senses of prestige and prescriptive notions of proper English may have impacted aspects of the New Zealand variety. Many would follow Whitney's view that 'new dialects are wont to grow up among the common people, while the speech of the educated and lettered class continues to be what it has been' (1904: 44; cf. Labov 2001: 30). Others assume that even a new dialect that grows up among the ordinary people may be influenced by sentiments about the prestige standard.

Whatever New Zealanders' feelings were about Britain and the British, they were unfailingly loyal to the British crown. The British royal family were loved and admired. Copies of a phonographic record of King George V and Queen Mary giving a message to 'the children of the Empire' were distributed through New Zealand primary schools in the 1920s. It was described as 'an excellent model of standard English pronunciation, and should be used for this purpose as much as for the value of the messages conveyed' (quoted in Gordon and Deverson 1989: 48).

At the end of the nineteenth century, ties with Britain were reinforced when refrigerated shipping enabled New Zealand meat to be exported to Britain. By the beginning of the twentieth century, the earlier trade with Australia gave way to trade with Britain, and by 1930, 80% of New Zealand's exports went to Great Britain. As Sinclair describes it: 'Almost all of the country's overseas loans came from Great Britain. The pakeha culture derived from Great Britain. Most of the immigrants still came from the same place. In other words, the direction of trade and migration strengthened the imperial bonds' (1986a: 108).

4 Previous attempts to explain the origins of New Zealand English

> Why there should be a general tendency [in New Zealand], as there undoubtedly is in Australia, to a Cockney pronunciation, when there must have been a very small proportion of the emigrants from Kent, whence this dialect has lately sprung, is a mystery still to be explained.
>
> (Samuel McBurney, *The Press*, 5 October 1887)

1 Introduction

In this chapter, we survey some of the attempts to explain the origins of New Zealand English that mostly predate the research reported in this book. The various theories are treated more or less in chronological order (although in the case of the lay explanations this is not possible, since they appear throughout the years). We believe it will be helpful for the reader if we present these ideas here in order to set the scene, as it were, for the analysis of the ONZE data presented in Chapter 6.

Apart from the lay theories and the notions of possible Maori contact, the various explanations are presented here without comment or assessment; they are discussed and evaluated in Chapter 7 in the light of the analysis of the ONZE data. Because discussions of the origins of New Zealand English are closely tied to discussions on the origins of Australian English, we also survey the main proposed explanations for the origins of Australian English.

It is true that New Zealand English is now very similar to the English of London and the south-east of England, but it is also true that early immigrants spoke various different varieties, particularly, in addition to the English from southern England, Scottish and Irish varieties of English. At the same time, New Zealand English also differs from these; hence it has its own unique character. Some have interpreted the similarity of New Zealand English to the varieties of the south-east of England to mean that New Zealand English comes directly from this English dialect. This has been called a 'single-origin theory' (Bauer 1999: 287). Several have combined this opinion with a 'Cockney explanation', the belief that New Zealand English is transported Cockney (possibly via Australia).

Some see New Zealand English as coming from Australia, explaining similarities between the New Zealand and Australian varieties of English in this way – another single-origin theory. They believe that the similarities shared by New Zealand English and the London/south-east England dialects are not the result of direct transplantation, but rather came about because New Zealand English derives from Australian English, and Australian English owes so much to the London/south-east dialects of England. Some just see New Zealand English as heavily influenced by contact with the London/south-east English dialect through continued immigration over time. Others have argued that New Zealand English is not the result of transplantation of south-east English English to New Zealand nor of subsequent influence from that variety, but rather is the result of dialect mixture in a process of new-dialect formation. Approaches of this latter sort have been called 'multiple-origin theories' (Bauer 1999: 287). Some argue that some of the features shared by New Zealand English and varieties from south-eastern England are independent parallel developments.

A surprising number of the issues that confront us today when we look at explanations for the origin of New Zealand English were anticipated by Ellis (1889), and therefore it is worth quoting at length from the introductory paragraph of his section 'Australasian South Eastern':

> English colonies . . . necessarily at first speak the English which they carry with them . . . This English alters in generations, and is much interfered with by constant immigration from the mother country. And now, when education is so prominent both in the mother country and the colonies, the speech of the colonists is modified artificially, by teachers aiming at what each considers a 'good' pronunciation, and the test of this 'goodness' must necessarily be the habit of persons of 'consideration', that is, social position, first in the mother country and secondly in the colonies themselves. Now the centre of English is London, which as far as pron[unciation] is concerned, lies in the E[astern] division, and, as we have seen, is at present, at least in the middle and lower strata, distinctly modified by the habits of the Eastern Counties. The habit of speech among the educated classes in London may be looked upon as the basis of 'received speech and pron[unciation]'. It is, therefore, to be expected that the pron[unciation] of the colonies would, as a whole, tend to resemble it. On examination we find that the colonies speak generally such a form, with modifications belonging to a less artificial stratum . . . In the Australasian colonies, that is, those in Australia, Tasmania (or Van Diemen's Land) and New Zealand, there is more than a tinge of what is commonly called 'cockney' . . . On the whole, therefore, a visitor from England to Australasia finds great resemblance to the mode of speech he left behind him, and, struck by that, does not much observe the differences. (Ellis 1889: 236)

Remarkably, in this single passage, Ellis manages to raise most of the controversial issues involved in attempts to explain the origins of New Zealand English: (1) the affinity with dialects of the south-east of England and London, (2) the alleged 'cockney' connection, (3) the role of the founding population, (4) the issue of whether subsequent immigration influenced the language in the colony, and (5) the question of whether social factors (of education, class, and the prestige of external varieties) had an impact. Here and in Chapter 7, we show that all of these enter significantly into the approaches that have been taken in attempting to explain the origins of New Zealand English. Those issues raised by Ellis that are not considered in this chapter are addressed in Chapter 7.

2 Lay theories of the origins of New Zealand English

Over the years, people have asked where the New Zealand accent came from, and some have put forward decidedly fanciful suggestions. For example, the nasal quality of some Australian and New Zealand speech was said to be the result of hay fever because of all the pollen in the air (Horadge 1980: 15). In a radio talk in 1983, the Hon. Nigel Wilson Q.C. blamed what he judged 'the monotonous and dull quality of New Zealand speech' on the loss of the enjoyment of life occasioned by the 1930s Depression. He suggested both fatigue from overwork and boredom from having too little work as possible contributing factors (Radio NZ Concert Programme, 6 June 1983). A very well-known commentator has recently suggested (quite seriously) that false teeth contributed to the origins of the New Zealand accent:

> For many decades it was either a fashion or the norm for adult New Zealanders to have all their teeth out, even when there was no strong reason to do so. One result of this was a long-time caution about pronouncing anything that required too much muscular tension or energy. A fairly narrow and unmoving oral style favoured words and phrases that could be spoken without risk of dentures losing their anchor. Even when false teeth went out of fashion and people started to retain their own teeth, the upcoming generations had heard their parents' speech style and vocabulary and tended to perpetuate it. (Cryer 2002: 6)

Some of the most persistent allegations that we find in the writings of early commentators were that the New Zealand accent was the result of laziness and of children being badly influenced by the 'home and the street'. For example, in 1910, Taranaki School Inspectors W. A. Ballantyne and R. G. Whetter were of the view that:

> A large proportion of the children when they enter school have already acquired habits of slovenly speech and defective methods of breathing in connection with the organs of speech ... Intelligent and systematic practice in correct speaking will gradually overcome such common defects – the result largely of the child's surroundings outside the school. (*AJHR* E-12, 1910: 104)

Similar views were expressed by the barrister Louis Cohen in his submission to the 1912 Cohen Commission on Education:

> I think that the degradation of the spoken English in the Dominion is not more marked in one province than another, and is due mainly to carelessness, laziness, indistinct utterance and slovenliness . . . it is said that the teachers in the schools speak good English, that the good English they speak is impaired by the baneful influence of home and home life, that the parents do not speak good English and that neutralises the influence of the teacher. (*AJHR* E-12, 1912: 459–60)

For many years, educationalists recommended speech training and exercises as a way of counteracting lazy lips and tongues (Gordon and Deverson 1989). Andrew Morrison, an examiner for Trinity College, London, gave a talk during one of his visits to New Zealand, which was published as 'The New Zealand Voice' (*New Zealand Listener* 19 (491), November 1948). Here he summed up the situation in a manner typical of lay commentators of the period: 'An idle tongue, a rigid jaw, atrophied labial muscles. These will account for most of the habits and mannerisms that colour New Zealand speech' (p. 7).

Needless to say, our data provide no evidence in favour of the influence of hay fever, depression, toothlessness, degeneration, or laziness as potential causes for the New Zealand accent. These lay explanations can be abandoned; they are not considered further in this book.

3 Language contact

One idea, although not especially common, is that New Zealand English may owe something to other languages. It is sometimes asked whether Maori had an impact on the development of New Zealand English (as suggested by Baker 1941b: 103; Bauer 1994: 387; and Burchfield 1994a: 6, for example). Some have asked if languages other than Maori had any influence. The short answer is 'no', to both questions.

In the early years of the formation of New Zealand English, a number of languages other than English were present in New Zealand. Though the date of the arrival of Maori from elsewhere in Polynesia is still debated, Maori had certainly already been in New Zealand some centuries at the time of the first European colonisation. A good number of Europeans became more or less fluent in Maori, including some people recorded by the Mobile Unit (as their stories reveal).[1] Thus, while it is possible in principle that Maori could have had some impact on the pronunciation or grammar of New Zealand English, this does not appear to have happened. Maori did contribute to New Zealand English,

[1] There are reports in the written records that appear to suggest the possible existence of a Maori-English pidgin or pidgin-like language in the early nineteenth century, though nothing of this has survived, and so we know nothing of its structure or how it may have been used (see Clark 1990).

but only lexically. There are many Maori loanwords in New Zealand English – most reflect indigenous trees, such as *kauri*, *rimu*, and *totara*; indigenous birds such as *tui*, *pukeko*, *kiwi*, and *kea*; and Maori life, such as *pa* (stockaded village), *whare* (house or hut), *haka* (dance with a warlike posture), *hui* (meeting), *kumara* (sweet potato), *tangi* (mourning or lamentation associated with funerals, hence also meaning funeral), and *waka* (canoe). (For a listing of Maori loanwords in New Zealand English, see L. Bauer 1994: 402–6; W. Bauer 1995; Deverson 1985, 1991; Gordon and Deverson 1998: 65–74.) There is also an abundance of Maori placenames throughout New Zealand.

There is a distinctive form of English associated with Maori, usually called 'Maori English', or 'Maori Accented English', though also called 'bro talk' by many who use it. One of its functions is emblematic, as a marker of Maori ethnic identity. The general practice in New Zealand is to use the term 'New Zealand English' to refer to the mostly homogeneous English spoken generally across New Zealand both by pakeha and by many Maori. It is true that Maori English should probably be considered a variety of general New Zealand English, but it is usually treated separately. Thus, while Maori had no significant structural impact on the formation of general New Zealand English, this does not appear to be the case with the Maori English/Maori-accented English variety itself. Its major features are understood but it deserves much more attention; some of these features reflect Maori influence.[2] (See Bell 2000; Benton 1985, 1991; Holmes 1997a; Holmes and Ainsworth 1997; Holmes and Bell 1996; King 1993, 1995, 1999; Stubbe and Holmes 2000.) There is evidence that Maori-accented English is a relatively recent phenomenon and therefore it is not possible for it to have influenced the early formation of New Zealand English (Benton 1991).

It is also true that a number of the early British settlers in New Zealand also spoke other languages, for example, Welsh, Irish Gaelic, and Scottish Gaelic, and there were also very small numbers (especially in the goldmining towns) who spoke Chinese, German, and Scandinavian languages. The ONZE project indicates, however, that all essential (non-lexical) traits of New Zealand English come from its British English input and its own subsequent internal developments, and that it owes nothing of importance, aside from loanwords, to any other language (see Chapter 6).

The phonology of modern New Zealand English is geographically quite uniform and is entirely 'English' in origin.[3] The only exception to this uniformity is the so-called 'Southland burr' in the Southland area and parts of Otago in

[2] Some of its most salient characteristics are: relatively syllable-timed instead of stress-timed rhythm; variable non-aspiration of voiceless stops where standard English would aspirate; devoiced final /z/, much use of the particle *eh?* and of the 'high rising terminal' intonation pattern in ordinary affirmative utterances.

[3] On standard criteria, linguists find no significant regional dialect differences in most of New Zealand outside of Southland; however, lay persons routinely report their belief that people from the West Coast of the South Island talk differently, and many insist there is a difference for the Canterbury district and for Auckland (see P. Gordon 1997). The bases for these perceptions need to

the southernmost region of the South Island, characterised by its retention of rhoticity (and a few other minor features), generally assumed to be due to Scottish settlement of the region (see Chapters 3 and 6). These Southland features are, however, now mostly giving way to general New Zealand English ones (Bartlett 1992).[4]

4 The Cockney explanation

In Australia and later in New Zealand, the most common and persistent early explanation offered for the newly emerging 'colonial twang' was that it was derived from Cockney, the dialect of the London working class. Bauer (1994: 420) notes that it is common knowledge that Australasian vowels sound Cockney to British ears. As seen in the quotation at the beginning of this chapter, McBurney (1887) had asked, 'why there should be a general tendency [in New Zealand], as there undoubtedly is in Australia, to a Cockney pronunciation' (*The Press*, 5 October 1887). The editor of *The Press* (8 October 1887) responded:

> now that Mr. McBurney has raised the question of colonial pronunciation, there is one matter to which we should like to advert. We allude to the incorrectness with which colonials, and more especially young colonials, pronounce their vowels. The sounds are attenuated down from their original native breadth into something very much resembling Cockney.

Another lament about the assumed Cockney influence on the English of New Zealand noted its presumed social divisiveness:

> At a meeting of the national Council of Women in Wellington in 1898, Mrs Sievwright spoke about 'Parental Responsibility'. '. . . well-bred mothers like their children to speak English, and the Cockney-American-colonial jargon, sometimes supposed to be such, is catching, and Mrs Robinson does not therefore let her child play with Mrs Jones' children and so misunderstandings and bitterness arise, and these last are not little things'. (Sinclair 1986a: 88)

Ellis (1889: 236–7) saw the Cockney influence as pervasive throughout 'the Australasian colonies': 'in Australia, Tasmania (or Van Diemen's Land) and New Zealand, there is more than a tinge of what is commonly called "cockney"'.

Arnold Wall, Professor of English at Canterbury University College, strongly believed in the Cockney origins of New Zealand English. He had lived close to London as a child and had developed a form of Cockney speech, which he said his father took great pains to correct. In a 1951 radio broadcast called 'The way

be investigated, though at present they certainly do not seem founded on any detected segmental, phonetic, grammatical, or even many lexical differences.

[4] There is some evidence that a positive attitude towards rhoticity (of the NURSE vowel) that is associated with local identity may be tending to slow down this trend (Bartlett 1992, 2003).

I have come' he described his impressions of speech in New Zealand when he arrived in 1899 as having a 'tendency towards a rather Cockney form of speech with which I was so familiar from childhood':

> As the Canterbury settlement was only 50 years old, a large proportion of Christchurch residents were still English born and retained their English habits of speech. Both men and women of the best educated class, professional men, lawyers, the clergy and so on spoke and still speak perfect standard English. But the younger generation of New Zealand born speakers, or at any rate the great majority of them, spoke that form of English which I have already referred to as 'Enzedic' with a more or less marked Cockney trend – far less marked, however, than Australians. (Wall 1951b, cited in Gordon and Deverson 1998: 26)

Wall's opinion about how New Zealand English came about both incorporates the 'Cockney' explanation and foreshadows some modern theories of new-dialect formation:

> [A]bout eighty percent of the population, at a rough guess, speaks English with a more or less marked London or 'Cockney' accent . . . the differences between the Home and the colonial pronunciations are more clearly marked in Australia than in New Zealand. Among the pioneers, and especially among those who became the first school teachers, there was a preponderance of persons who came from London and its vicinity and spoke with what is usually called a Cockney accent. The results, when in the long run a homogeneous manner of speech had developed throughout the country, especially in the growing cities, was that this type of pronunciation prevailed, and both the various provincial dialects, the Scottish, the Irish, etc., and the more correct or standard type were more or less completely submerged. (Wall 1939: 8)

As in Australia, the Cockney explanation came to be questioned in New Zealand (see, for example, Bennett 1943: 84, and McGeorge 1984: 16), though Turner (1960: 35–7) defended the notion.

5 The 'New Zealand English as Australian' hypothesis

The assumption that New Zealand English derives from Australian English was put forward by a number of scholars in the 1980s and 1990s (see, for example, Gordon and Deverson 1985, 1998; Bauer 1994; Woods 1997; Bayard 2000). For instance, Gordon and Deverson (1985: 19) wrote, 'it seems probable that children born in New Zealand might have picked up [the] existing colonial variety of Australian speech'. Similarly, Bauer (1994: 425) wrote, 'I shall suggest that the most likely origin of New Zealand English is as an imported variety of Australian English' (see also Bauer 1994: 386), and he concludes that 'in our current state of knowledge, the hypothesis that New Zealand English is derived from Australian

English is the one which explains most about the linguistic situation in New Zealand' (Bauer 1994: 428). Indeed the striking degree of similarity between Australian and New Zealand English does beg for explanation.

The arguments offered in favour of the Australian origin of New Zealand English generally include the pervasive similarities between the two varieties (Gordon and Deverson 1998: 28; Bauer 1994); it is quite common for New Zealanders travelling abroad to be mistaken for Australians (Gordon and Deverson 1998: 18). In a letter to Elizabeth Gordon (16 October 1984), John Bernard of Macquarie University, Sydney, wrote:

> As I see it, New Zealand English is, or at least has been, closer to Australian English than many people in New Zealand care to acknowledge. Again and again I meet New Zealanders, usually of older rather than younger years, who could pass as Cultivated speakers of Australian English with no trouble at all. At the same time I am meeting more and more who certainly could not.

In New Zealand, Bauer (1994: 425) wrote that, while Australian English and New Zealand English are different, not only do outsiders sometimes conflate them, but even New Zealanders will not always notice an Australian accent. Bayard's (1995a: 107) research, using perception tests, showed that out of 559 Otago undergraduates only 39% recognised a speaker as Australian. Bayard et al. (2001: 32) found that New Zealanders typically identify other New Zealanders correctly from their speech, and Australians correctly identify other Australians; however, a surprisingly large number of New Zealanders misidentified Australian speech as that of New Zealanders, and similarly, many Australians misidentified New Zealanders as Australians from their speech.

As mentioned previously, early commentators commonly considered the two varieties the same and sometimes gave them the single name of 'Austral English'. Otago school inspectors in 1903 observed, 'our schools have been fairly free from what is erroneously styled "Austral English". It is now, however, insidiously gaining ground, and teachers should be on their guard against it' (*AJHR* E-1B, 1903: 44–5).

The general opinion in the early days was that New Zealand English was not 'quite so bad' as Australian English:

> Sad to relate, one far too often hears the young generation talk with a twang that horrifies the ear of anyone used to good English . . . This twang is worse in Australia than in New Zealand but it is gaining ground here and ought to be strenuously eradicated by school teachers, for it does not sound nice, and robs sweet girlish lips of all their poesy. (Herz 1912: 352)

> And, oh, that Australian language! Words cannot speak the intensity and badness of it . . . Slurred and gobbled consonants, vowels flattened and horribly misused. These things fell in hundreds upon one's shrinking ear. The English spoken in New Zealand is very far ahead of the English

> spoken in Australia. The Australian accent is everywhere on the side, and everywhere appalling and disfiguring. (Charles Baeyertz, *The Triad*, 10 August 1912: 52)

Similarly, Cohen commented:

> I think it is beyond controversy that the English spoken in the Dominion of New Zealand has become characteristically colonial. It fortunately has not reached the despairing depths of what we in New Zealand call 'Orstreilian', but it is in grave danger of touching that point. (*AJHR* E-12, 1912: 460)

More recent arguments for New Zealand English as a variety of Australian English are given by Bauer (1994), Gordon (1989), and Gordon and Deverson (1985, 1998).

Bauer (1994: 425–7) put forward three arguments for this hypothesis. The first is 'the overwhelming phonetic and phonological similarity of Australian and New Zealand English'. The second is the demographic evidence that there has always been a close association between the two countries, and immigration figures show large numbers of immigrants coming to New Zealand from or via Australia (for detail, see Chapter 3) – 'The influence of Australia in all walks of life is ubiquitous in New Zealand'. The third argument is the large amount of shared vocabulary:

> The number of words which Australia and New Zealand share – virtually to the exclusion of the rest of the English speaking world – is astounding if the two varieties have independent origins. The shared vocabulary is explained if New Zealand English is, in origin, a variety of Australian English.

Gordon (1989: 79) argued against the Cockney origin of New Zealand English, in favour of an Australian connection: 'It seems to me more likely that New Zealand speech came across the Tasman Sea from Australia where it developed first'. Like Bauer, she supported this view with demographic information, showing that a large number of immigrants to New Zealand came from or via Australia (again, see Chapter 3 for details). She suggested that the main influence could have come through children:

> We know that Australian English emerged before New Zealand English, and it seems to me a strong possibility that children coming from Australia, speaking this existing, antipodean variety of English, could have had a strong influence on New Zealand children. Peer-group pressure in school is a powerful force to make children conform in their speech, and this explanation would account for the rapid development of the accent among schoolchildren by the turn of the century. (Gordon 1989: 79)

Gordon and Deverson (1998: 28) suggested that children coming to New Zealand would have wanted to pick up the existing colonial variety: 'it is a common experience for "new chums" to want to sound and behave like "old chums" as soon as possible'. They also refer to the Mobile Unit speakers, where there is a similarity between the Australian and New Zealand pronunciation of some variables:

> Recordings made in the 1940s of old people who were born in New Zealand in the [19th] century show that many of them used pronunciations which today we would associate with Australians. They pronounced words like *chance*, *dance*, *Alexandra*, *Francis* with the vowel in *cat* /æ/ rather than in *cart* /a/. Their pronunciations of words like *school*, *tool* and *pool* is also different from the New Zealand pronunciation today and these words sound much more like the way Australians pronounce them today. (Gordon and Deverson 1998: 28)

6 New Zealand English as a transplanted south-east/ London dialect

Another single-origin theory (see Bauer 1994) holds that New Zealand English owes its origin to the dialect of south-east England and London (with or without the 'Cockney' claim being included). Lass (1990: 247), has made the remarkable claim which he calls 'a simple characterization which is true without exception: there is no ETE [Extraterritorial English, i.e. colonial variety of English] that is not a dialect of Southern English'[5]. Indeed, studies of New Zealand English have always favoured the notion of a general influence from the south-east of England. For example, Bauer (1994: 391) asserts, 'it is clear that New Zealand English derives from a variety of English spoken in the south-east of England' and, 'phonologically speaking, New Zealand English is a variant of the south-east England system' (p. 388).

The south-eastern traits in New Zealand English could have come about in different ways. (1) They could be from direct transportation of this dialect to New Zealand from the south-east of England along with the founding settlers or with the greater masses of later immigrants. (2) They could have come via Australia (where many of the same south-east-of-England features are found in Australian English). (3) It could be that these south-eastern dialect traits were selected in the process of new-dialect formation due to the majority of south-eastern speakers and south-eastern tokens in the input. (4) It is possible that some features even came about by independent development, in a process of drift. (5) It is also possible that they are due to multiple causation, to some or all of these possibilities working in concert. (For details, see later this chapter and Chapter 7.)

The relative impact (or lack thereof) from Irish and Scottish English varieties on New Zealand English (see Bauer 1997 for Scottish English) is considered in Chapter 7.

[5] Newfoundland is a clear exception.

7 The mixing bowl (or 'melting pot') approach

The 'mixing bowl theory' on the origins of New Zealand English has been put forward by Gordon and Deverson (1985, 1998) and Bauer (1994); it was also often cited for the origins of Australian English (see later). Gordon and Deverson (1985: 17) wrote:

> [W]hen people move from the country to a large city such as London a kind of mixture of their accents and dialects takes place creating a new urban accent. Translating this theory to newly colonised countries it could be said that a similar process takes place.

In support of this, Gordon and Deverson (1985) quote from Arnold Wall's 1951 radio broadcast:

> Living in Christchurch I would point out to my students that they could study such provincial dialects more conveniently than in any one locality at Home [England]. Among the persons employed by me as nurses, cook, and gardener and so on I had at one time or another, Yorkshire, Oxfordshire, Scottish, Welsh, Devonshire and Australian persons, all speaking their native dialect in its purity, while nearly all the younger members of such groups already spoke what is sometimes called 'Enzedic English' with great uniformity. (Wall 1951b, quoted in Gordon and Deverson 1985: 18)

Bauer (1994: 422) concluded that 'the preferred theory about the origins of Australian and New Zealand English seems to be that they arise through dialect mixture', that a new dialect arises when speakers of various different dialects of English are thrown together, as in these colonial situations. This was also Wall's (1939: 8) view (for discussions of others, see Bauer 1994; Bayard 1995a: 44–5; Gordon and Deverson 1998; Turner 1966: 10). Recent work on new-dialect formation in situations of dialect contact is in this mixing bowl tradition (see Section 8 below).

A slightly different perspective comes from Lass (1990) who is confident that the only likely outcome of dialect mixing of English varieties, regardless of the mix, is an easterly version of 'southern' English English:

> ETEs [Extraterritorial Englishes] typically grow out of multiple migrations, and each component wave tends to have a distinct regional character. But it is not normally the case that all sub-migrations contribute equally – or at all – to the character of the final product. Nor does this product necessarily reflect in any very close way the demography of the original wave, or any particular one, or even all of them put together. There is a peculiar sort of development in most cases, in which the overall profile of

> the 'finished' ETE tends to be of one regional type – southern – regardless of what types are represented in the settlement history. (Lass 1990: 267)
>
> (i) in cases of mixed input to an ETE, whatever the original demography, the output is (a) southern, and (b) more eastern than western.
>
> (ii) Whatever the size of the non-southern input, it will normally leave only unsystematic relics (e.g. odd lexical items, idioms, or minor constructions); there will rarely be large-scale structural effects (e.g. in the system of phonemic oppositions).
>
> In short, outside of Ulster . . . everything tends towards the southeast. (Lass 1990: 269)

8 New-dialect formation

New-dialect formation is generally understood to mean a process where, in a mixture of different dialects, different variants are levelled out and a single, new, focused dialect arises which is different in some ways from all the input varieties. Peter Trudgill (1986b, 1999c; Trudgill et al. 1998, 2000a, 2000b) is credited with launching modern studies of new-dialect formation. Several others have followed Trudgill's approach, sometimes with modifications (Britain 1997a, 1997b, 2002; Britain and Sudbury 2002; Hornsby 2002; Kerswill 2001; Kerswill and Williams 2000, 2002; Schreier 2001; Sudbury 2000; see also Milroy 2002). The best-known studies of new-dialect formation are of newly formed towns – particularly the new town of Milton Keynes (Kerswill 1995, 1996, 2001; Kerswill and Williams 2000; Williams and Kerswill 1999), the population of the English fens (Britain 1991, 1997a,b), and the Norwegian cases (Omdal 1977; Trudgill 1986b; Kerswill and Williams 2000: 73–4). Other recent ones are Sudbury's (2000, 2001) study of the English of the Falkland Islands and Schreier's (2001) of Tristan da Cunha English, as well as Simpson's (1996) of Telford English, plus a number of non-English cases: Burträsk in Northern Sweden (Thelander 1979), Fiji Hindi (Siegel 1985) (and Hindi elsewhere outside of India, in South Africa (Mesthrie 1993), Trinidad (Mohan 1978), and Mauritius (Domingue 1971, 1981)), and Ijsselmeer Polders in the Netherlands (Scholtmeijer 1992, 1997).

In his book *Dialects in Contact* (1986b), Trudgill set out his theory of dialect mixing and new-dialect formation. At first, in a situation where several dialects come together and large numbers of variants are present, 'interdialect' phenomena develop. By this, Trudgill means intermediate forms that are not found in any of the existing dialects, but which come into existence when people who speak different dialects accommodate one another in face-to-face interaction (cf. Britain and Trudgill 1999: 246; Trudgill 1989). In time, especially as the new town or colony begins to develop an independent identity, 'focusing' begins to take place, and the number of variants in the mixture is reduced, especially variants of 'salient' or significant features (cf. Kerswill and Williams 2002). Trudgill explains that this process is not haphazard, but will involve demographic factors taking account of the proportions of different dialect speakers present. Linguistic factors may also be involved; the reduction of variants in this focusing stage takes place through the process of 'koinéisation' (cf. Kerswill 2001). Trudgill explains 'koinéisation' as follows:

> This comprises the process of *levelling*, which involves the loss of marked and/or minority variants; and the process of *simplification*, by means of which even minority forms may be the ones to survive if they are linguistically simpler, in the technical sense, and through which even forms and distinctions in the contributory dialects may be lost. Where this occurs, *reallocation* may occur, such that variants originally from different regional dialects may in the new dialect become social-class dialect variants, stylistic variants, areal variants, or in the case of phonology, allophonic variants. (Trudgill 1986b: 126)[6]

Under the heading 'Koinéisation in Colonial English' Trudgill (1986b) discusses this theory in relation to a number of colonial varieties of English, concentrating on Australian English, but also referring to New Zealand English. In evidence of Australian English being a levelled variety, he points to the great similarity between Australian English and other southern-hemisphere Englishes, especially New Zealand English. He considers a number of possible explanations for these similarities:

1. That all southern-hemisphere varieties are simply nineteenth-century London English, plus some independent developments.
2. That the varieties descend from a mixed south-east of England variety that was formed before colonisation.
3. That the colonial varieties all continue trends already present in England but slowed down by the inhibiting influence of RP.
4. That Australians played an important role in the settlement of New Zealand.

Trudgill allows that some of all of these explanations might be relevant, but considers it more likely that the similarities 'arise from dialect mixture processes that took place' (1986b: 144).

8.1 Trudgill's new-dialect formation stages

Trudgill distinguishes three chronological stages, seen as corresponding roughly to generations in new-dialect formation (Trudgill 2001: 43; Trudgill et al. 1998: 38; cf. Britain 1997a: 41 and Kerswill and Williams 2000), and applied these stages to interpreting the formation of New Zealand English.

[6] See also Britain's (2002: 35) characterisation of levelling: '*Dialect levelling* involves a reduction of marked, socially heavily stigmatized, highly localised, or minority forms in favour of unmarked, less stereotyped, supralocal, majority variants in a dialect mix'. See also L. Milroy 2002: 7.

8.1.1 The first stage: rudimentary levelling. The first stage of new-dialect formation involves the initial contact between adult speakers of different regional and social varieties in a new location, with certain types of accommodation of speakers to one another in face-to-face interaction and thus, as a consequence, rudimentary dialect levelling. In the case of New Zealand, Trudgill estimates that this stage would have lasted until approximately 1860.

8.1.2 The second stage: (a) extreme variability. Trudgill estimates that the second stage of new-dialect formation would have lasted in New Zealand until approximately 1900. A key concept in this stage is linguistic 'diffuseness' (LePage and Tabouret-Keller 1985; Kerswill and Williams 1992: 13; see also Sudbury 2000: 45), that is, considerable heterogeneity. This variability is of three main types.

First, unlike stable situations where children normally learn to speak like their peers, in a dialect-mixture situation there may be no single peer-dialect for children to acquire, and the role of adults, especially perhaps of parents and other caretakers, will therefore be more significant than usual. As a result of having not one but several different adult linguistic models to aim at in this stage of new-dialect formation, children will select variants from different dialects and form them into new combinations (see Trudgill 1998b).

Second, people who have grown up in this type of situation are likely to vary in their own speech quite considerably, sometimes using one linguistic variant, sometimes another. This *intra*-individual variability will occur in a dialect-mixing situation to a much greater extent than in more stable, homogeneous speech communities.

Third, groups of speakers who have grown up in this type of situation are also likely to demonstrate *inter*-individual variability to a much greater extent than speakers from more stable, homogeneous speech communities.

8.1.3 The second stage: (b) further levelling. Although the inter-individual variability at the second stage is striking and considerable, it is perhaps somewhat reduced compared to what is present during the first stage when speakers of different dialects first come together in a new setting. That is, in spite of the extent of the variability in this second stage of new-dialect formation, it is possible that some further levelling may take place during this stage.

8.1.4 The third stage: focusing. It is only subsequently, then, in the third stage, that the new dialect is expected to appear as a stable, crystallised variety. This crystallisation is the result of 'focusing', a process whose effects are clear in modern New Zealand English because it is a variety with remarkably little regional variation.

9 Determinism in new-dialect formation

Trudgill argues that the new-dialect formation that results from dialect contact and dialect mixture is not a random process:

> If the British Isles varieties that went into the initial dialect mixture were roughly the same for all southern hemisphere countries, and in approximately the same proportions, then it is not surprising if the *output* of the mixture is roughly the same in each case. This is particularly likely to be so if it is true . . . that the same universal or at least widespread levelling tendencies were at work in each of the dialect contact situations. (1986b: 144)

In Trudgill et al. 2000a, this is called *determinism* in new-dialect formation and is elaborated further using data from New Zealand English. It is hypothesised that, given sufficient linguistic information about the dialects that contribute to a mixture, and given sufficient demographic information about the proportions of speakers of the different dialects, it is possible to make predictions about what the outcome of the mixture will be (p. 299). In this view, new-dialect formation is thus deterministic, and similarities between geographically separated varieties of a single language may therefore be due not to continued contact or connection between them, but to the fact that they developed from similar mixtures of similar dialects in similar proportions at similar times. Trudgill argues that the similarities between Australian, New Zealand, and the other southern-hemisphere Englishes can be explained in this way.

10 Drift

For a number of cases for which the final outcome is not well explained by the processes of new-dialect formation as described so far, Trudgill and colleagues propose 'drift' – inherited propensities for change – as a subsidiary principle (Trudgill et al. 2000b). In 1921, Sapir wrote, 'language moves down time in a current of its own making. It has a drift' (1921: 150), by which he referred to inherent or inherited tendencies in languages and language families:

> The momentum of . . . drift is often such that languages long disconnected will pass through the same or strikingly similar phases . . . The English type of plural represented by *foot: feet*, *mouse: mice* is strictly parallel to the German *Fuss: Füsse*, *Maus: Mäuse* . . . Documentary evidence shows conclusively that there could have been no plurals of this type in Primitive Germanic . . . There was evidently some general tendency or group of tendencies in early Germanic, long before English and German had developed as such, that eventually drove both of these dialects along closely parallel paths. (Sapir 1921: 172)

In Sapir's notion of drift, some of the resemblances among dialects of the same language or among related languages come about because they continue to evolve in similar directions. That is, they not only share characteristics they have inherited from a common parent, but also share a *tendency* or *propensity* to develop the same (or similar) characteristics, even after separation. Following Sapir, Trudgill et al. (2000b) argue that some similarities between geographically separated varieties of a single language may be due not to characteristics inherited directly from some parent variety, nor to continued contact between the varieties, nor even to their having derived from similar dialect mixtures (i.e. *determinism*), but to *drift*. Drift, in this view, can refer both to inherited changes already taking place when emigrants set out for the colonies, and also to independent but parallel developments that take place after the separation of dialects. For example, most of the older ONZE speakers born in New Zealand before 1870 have at least some diphthong shift (see Wells 1982: 256; also Chapter 6, Section 12), while those born after 1870 have a good deal more. Significant for Trudgill et al.'s argument is the observation that similar developments have also occurred elsewhere in the southern hemisphere (Wells 1982: 597, 614) and in the American South – what Labov (1994) calls the 'Southern Shift' (cf. Britain and Sudbury 2002: 211). Diphthong shift, then, is seen here as one of the drifts to which English has been prone and which has progressed further in the southern hemisphere than in most other varieties. Trudgill et al. claim that recently formed varieties of colonial English provide evidence of drift and demonstrate how it works. (See also the discussion in Britain and Sudbury 2002.)

In Chapter 7 the theory of drift is examined as a possible explanation for several features of New Zealand English.

11 Hypotheses for the origins of Australian English

Because, as Bauer (1994: 420) points out, discussions of the origins of New Zealand English are closely tied to discussions of the origins of Australian English – 'indeed in most cases the discussion is the same' – we need to survey proposed explanations for the origins of Australian English. As with explanations for New Zealand English, these also involve the influence of Cockney, the effects of dialect mixing, and the influence of English from south-east England.

11.1 Australian English and Cockney

The association of Australian English with Cockney was an early and constant assertion. We read in the *Australian Bulletin* 1893 of 'the twang of Cockney vulgarity – we imported it long before rabbits, sparrows, snails and other British nuisances were grafted on our budding civilisation' (cited in Gordon and Deverson 1998: 27). Ellis (1889: 237) repeated the common refrain: 'that persons who have visited Australia declare that there is a marked "cockney" element to its speech'. Brook (1963: 132) noted, 'when Englishmen describe Australian pronunciation the most frequent summing up is to say that it is like Cockney' (cf. Bernard 1969: 64).

Baker believed Cockney was first implicated in Australian English in Cunningham's (1826) report that 'the London mode of pronunciation has been duly engrafted on the colloquial dialect of our currency [i.e. Australian born] youths' (cited in Baker 1945: 432). Baker added that just as 'a large amount of London slang and cant was delivered to Australia by convicts and their caretakers . . . it would be illogical to expect that the accent of London slums and prisons should have been left behind' (ibid.). Mundy (1852) spoke of 'Sydney Cockneys' and Mossman (1852) of 'the Cockney drawl of hucksters, selling fish and fruit [which] sounds so refreshing to the ear – so thoroughly English' (both cited in Baker 1945: 433). By the 1880s and 1890s the perceived association between Australian speech and Cockney was widespread; for example, Kingslake (1891) wrote of some bush children, 'they all had the colonial accent which is almost identical with the Cockney slang' (cited in Baker 1945: 433).

Though the Cockney-origins idea was quite entrenched in Australia, by the 1930s and 1940s, some Australian writers were questioning the claim. Baker (1945: 433) wrote, 'Since no observer has been able to produce more than a few resemblances between the Australian and the Cockney accent, the allegation that Australians talk like Cockneys must be regarded as one of the popular myths to which we as a young nation are susceptible'.

Hammarström (1980: 4) offered the explanation that Australian English originated from London or the south-east of England of the late eighteenth century. In a chapter headed 'Is Australian English an early London dialect?', he compared Australian and Cockney, using Sivertsen's (1960) work on Cockney phonology; he noted that 'similarities in the vowels, particularly the diphthongs, are striking'. Turner (1960), Baker (1945), and Hammarström (1980) all examined Australian vowels in detail and showed correspondences with Cockney.

11.2 The mixing bowl theory for Australian English

Another approach to the origin of Australian English is the 'amalgamation theory' or 'mixing bowl' approach (mentioned above) – that Australian English is the result of dialect mixing. Hammarström (1980) doubted this theory: 'Australian pronunciation is too homogeneous to be an amalgam since it is not likely that the same amalgamation would have occurred in different places' (cited in Clark 1985: 370). However, the idea of a mixed origin for Australian English was supported by several other writers. Bernard (1969) described the original mixture that produced Australian English:

> It is hard to know what this mixture might have been in more than a general way – certainly a mish-mash of deracinated regional and social British dialects, with every county of the land somewhere represented among the soldiers, settlers, administrators and convicts, who made up that unpleasant first population. The convicts were by far the most numerous group until after the postulated linguistically critical first period and are especially important. (Bernard 1969: 64)

Bernard also argued that because the different Australian states were made up of similar components from Britain, this accounted for the homogeneity of Australian English:

> Each state capital attracted at its inception much the same cross section of British dialects. The deprivations and hardships which led to crime and to transportation also provided the incentives for free migration and so, whether in convict Sydney after 1788 or, say free Adelaide after 1836, the ingredients of the mixing bowl were much the same, and at different times and in different places the same process was carried out and the same end point achieved. (Bernard, in *Macquarie Dictionary* 1981: 20)

Alex G. Mitchell elaborated this view:

> There is the question of the pre-1788 origins [of Australian English]. What sort of speech was brought by the original migrants? It is very likely that many of them spoke a reduced and attenuated form of their own original dialect. The breaking down of regional dialects through enforced mobility began in London before the industrial revolution. The industrial revolution brought large numbers from the rural areas to the industrialised cities. There was a very large migration of the Irish. There is a lot of evidence of movement among working people in search of work, including difference between place of birth and place of trial in the convict indents. There was the centuries old drift towards the capital. It does not, therefore, seem appropriate to put all the dialects from England, Ireland and Scotland in the mixing with the same status. There was without much doubt a hierarchy of dialects among convict arrivals. (Mitchell 1995: 27)

Mitchell (1995: 27, quoting figures from Camm and McQuilton 1987: 201) says of the different percentages of immigrants from different areas that the 'figures suggest that in a struggle for survival some regional forms of speech would succumb more quickly than others'. He goes on to ask:

> Should we be thinking in terms of struggle for survival, not of a mixing process but one in which the peak characteristics of dialects were smoothed away and they became more alike? Survival, dominance, extinction may be a more likely model. The peak characteristics of St Giles Cockney might have gone down along with many others.
>
> We might consider a hypothesis of a threefold process:
>
> (1) Struggle for survival, dominance.
> (2) Transmission through peer group of the native born.
> (3) The wearing away of peak characteristics that would not go as far as uniformity and complete extinction.
>
> The three could well be mutually reinforcing. (Mitchell 1995: 28)

Horvath (1985: 29) offered the following overview: 'Basically there are two types of response that are given: that (i) AE [Australian English] is simply the continuation of changes already in progress in England . . . or that (ii) AE is basically London Cockney and was transported here by the first people to arrive from England'.

Whatever the disagreements about the input and the process that led to modern Australian English, there is general agreement that 'a distinctive Australian accent (or accents) must have been emerging quite early in New South Wales' (Yallop 2000: 289), and that the Australian accent is similar to those found in the south-east of England and not much like accents from other parts of England or Scotland or Ireland. Further, Yallop states, What emerges . . . at the level of segmental phonology, is the almost total system convergence between London English and Australian English. Vowel for vowel and consonant for consonant they match with only an occasional marginal difference (pp. 178–9). The same is essentially true for New Zealand English.

While the possible impact of Australian English in the formation and development of New Zealand English remains controversial, it is nevertheless an important proposed explanation that will be considered seriously in Chapter 7.

12 Conclusion

It can be seen that a number of different proposals have been put forward to attempt to explain the development of New Zealand English. We turn now to a consideration of the ONZE project, its methodology (Chapter 5) and results (Chapter 6), before returning to the question (in Chapter 7) of how New Zealand English came to be the way it is. In that chapter, we consider each of these proposed explanations in the light of the ONZE data and their analysis presented in Chapter 6 as well as other background research. We also consider other sociolinguistic theories that so far have not been applied specifically to New Zealand English and discuss them in the light of the results from the ONZE project.

5 Methodology

The most difficult step in the study of language is the first step.

(Bloomfield 1933: 21)

1 Introduction

ONZE has been (and is) an evolving project. The methodology was not completely defined when the project began, and the techniques we have used have been refined constantly throughout the course of our research. Although we knew the types of analysis we intended to carry out, some of the details only became clear after we had started. For example, at the start of the auditory perceptual analysis, only phonological features that seemed significant at the time were noted. Later we realised that we were undoubtedly missing features that may turn out to be important, and so the template described in Section 3.1 below was created in order to provide structure for this part of the analysis. At other times, the research led us down blind alleys. We were sure that the type of settlement in which the speakers lived was significant but it was a considerable time before we found the exact division that proved to be relevant. Before we realised that the significant factor was the make-up of the towns, with predominantly Scottish towns and mixed towns being significantly different, we had investigated towns that were predominantly rural or goldmining or military, only to find that this distinction was not as significant as first imagined. New information came to light during the course of the project; for example, we learnt more about the early immigrants from newly available historical material (from nzhistory.net 2002), so we could make more accurate estimates of the dialect mixtures present at the earliest stages of the development of New Zealand English. The methodology described below did not come ready-made; it developed over the course of the project. One effect of this is that the results presented here differ in some areas from preliminary results published earlier.

The net result of our evolving methodology has been a fruitful combination of three main approaches to analysis. This book therefore discusses the results of three complementary analysis techniques. We have found that the combination of these techniques has yielded important findings that any one approach alone could not have revealed.

1. A broad auditory perceptual analysis of speakers provides details about the range of variants present in the speech of different individuals, and in the corpus as a whole.
2. A detailed quantitative (token by token) auditory analysis of selected variables allows for the precise documentation of the behaviour of these variables over time, and the subtle (and sometimes not so subtle) effects of social and linguistic conditioners.
3. Acoustic analysis allows for precise and accurate analysis of individuals' entire vowel systems, and allows us to analyse variables as true continua, as opposed to imposing artificial category lines that the former two approaches require.

In order to examine the origins and development of New Zealand English, we have analysed the speech of 115 speakers from the Mobile Unit archive, 85 males and 30 females, using a combination of the above three techniques. The oldest of the speakers was born in 1851 and the youngest in 1904. Of the speakers analysed, 108 were born in New Zealand or came to New Zealand at a young age (before puberty) and the other 7 were born overseas and came to New Zealand when they were older. One was born in Australia and came to New Zealand when he was older; the other six were born in England, Scotland, and Ireland.

2 Data

The members of the Mobile unit team,[1] on first arriving in a town, would visit the mayor or the town clerk and obtain a list of people to contact who had lived in the town for a long time. Geoff Haggett described the process:

> They would say – well so and so has lived here for fifty years or seventy years – he would know what happened way back in the early days – just when they found gold or when they started cutting the road through there . . . and from that we'd get a whole list of people to see and we would make up our itinerary from that. (Haggett n.d.)

In some recordings it is possible to hear speakers advising the Mobile Unit to visit a certain place (such as the bowling club) to interview more suitable elderly people. It is clear from recordings that some speakers had been given advance notice of the recording sessions as they came equipped with books, pamphlets, or written notes. From information in the recordings it is also apparent that speakers

[1] The Mobile Unit was run by returned servicemen. Leo Fowler, the producer and officer in charge, had been a sergeant in the Pacific; the announcers, Alf Sanft and Geoff Haggett, had been army majors, and the technicians, B. H. Cosnett and R. L. Miller, had been with the broadcasting unit in North Africa and Italy (Hall 1980: 151).

were chosen because they were 'old identities' in the town and likely to be able to tell a good story.

The recordings were made in private homes, in schools or in town halls with the Mobile Unit van parked outside (see Chapter 1 for more details). The recording equipment in the van was operated by the producer and a technical assistant, and a power cable and microphone cables were run into the area where residents were being interviewed by another member of the Mobile Unit team. The producer in the van was able to communicate with the interviewer through headphones. The microphones were 44BX for recording music and an 8-ball microphone (STC no. 4021) for recording interviews. The recordings were captured on 16-inch discs made of an acetate coating on a steel or aluminium base; most of the discs could record ten to eleven minutes per side. Playing back was discouraged because the acetate was a soft material, but if discs were to be played back, a special wood-fibre needle was used (A. Lewis: 1994).

Four stages were involved in analysing the information in the Mobile Unit archive. Firstly, the Mobile Unit speakers were selected for analysis; secondly, the interviews were processed so that the information was in a useable form; thirdly background information was gathered about the speakers; and finally, the interviews were analysed.

2.1 Selection of speakers

The Mobile Unit collected spoken data on three tours between 1946 and 1948. They carried out 201 interviews, some with individuals and some with groups. The ONZE project analysed speakers from the following towns:

Tour 1 (1946)	Wanganui, Tokotea, Coromandel, Ngaruawahia, New Plymouth
Tour 2 (1947)	Morrinsville, Te Awamutu, Kirikiriroa, Thames, Te Aroha, Kawhia, Hamilton, Paeroa, Te Kowhai, Howick, Wellington, Huntly, Hamilton, Rangiaowahia, Te Aroha
Tour 3 (1948)	Kaitangata, Balclutha, Waikouaiti, Palmerston, Shag Valley, Roxburgh, Arrowtown, Milton, Naseby, Cardrona, Oamaru, Port Chalmers, Lawrence, St Bathans, Wanaka, Waipori, Queenstown, Cromwell, Alexandra

The dates of birth of the 108 New Zealand-born speakers analysed are shown in Figure 5.1. Seven additional overseas-born speakers were also analysed. Not all speakers were subject to all types of analysis; 95 received a broad auditory perceptual analysis, 59 were subject to auditory quantitative analysis, and 10 were analysed acoustically.

A full list of speakers analysed, their dates of birth, place of origin, parents' places of origin (where known), and the place where they were interviewed is in Appendix 1.

Table 5.1 *Number of speakers analysed quantitatively*

	North Island (23)		South Island (36)	
	female (7)	male (16)	female (14)	male (22)
1850s/60s	4	6	5	6
1870s	3	5	7	6
1880–1907	—	5	2	10

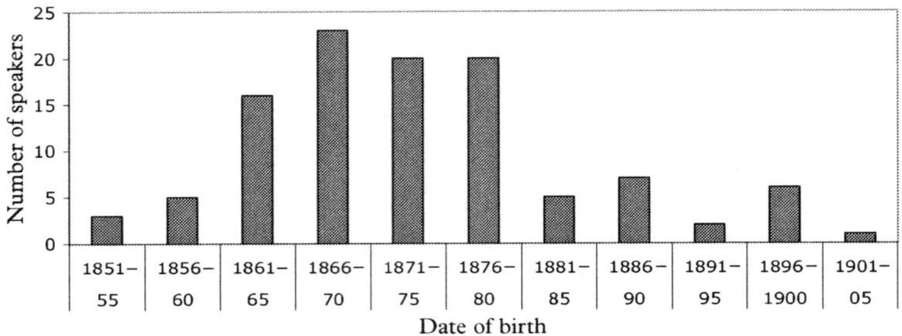

Figure 5.1 Distribution of New Zealand-born speakers analysed (Note: Different speakers received different degrees of analysis.)

The reasons for selection of speakers changed as the ONZE project progressed. The first speakers chosen for auditory perceptual analysis were selected because they were born earliest. Later, speakers were chosen for the length and quality of their recordings, with an effort made to include as many women as possible. Later selection filled obvious gaps and ensured that there was a reasonable coverage of ages and different types of settlement.

The detailed quantitative analysis made an attempt to create a stratified sample – with male and female speakers born throughout the period of the corpus, and from different regions. Due to the smaller number of females recorded, a balanced sample proved impossible. Numbers of speakers analysed quantitatively are shown in Table 5.1.

2.2 *Processing the interviews*

As mentioned, the original interviews were recorded on acetate discs – hundreds of them, as each disc only held twenty minutes or so in total. In order to avoid interrupting the flow of the interviews, the Mobile Unit technicians used a twin recording-deck: for example, they would record on side A of disc 101 until that was nearly full, then, rather than stop the interview in order to turn over the disc, would begin recording on side A of disc 102. Next they recorded on side B of disc 101 and then side B of disc 102, and so on. To add to the complexity, small spaces remaining on either side of the discs could be used to record short sections of other interviews. The first audiocassettes used by ONZE were Radio New Zealand Sound Archive copies made from of the original discs. These tapes held the contents of one disc (side A, then side B), followed by the contents of the next disc, and so on; thus, the interview material was discontinuous. Further, since some speakers were recorded by the Mobile Unit several times on different days, it was often quite a task to locate entire interviews. An early priority at ONZE was to make an accurate index of the persons recorded, showing where the interviews were located on the tapes. Later, the interviews were reconstructed and recorded continuously onto digital audiotape (DAT), and the DAT tapes were later transferred to CDs for further conservation of the original data.[2] (See Lewis 1996.)

Each interview was transcribed (see Maclagan and Gordon 1999 for the conventions used in transcription) and checked. When several speakers were interviewed in a group, because the recording quality was not always ideal, it was sometimes difficult to identify individual speakers. The transcribers also carried out historical and geographical checks for unfamiliar names of people, places, ships, or objects. The transcriptions continued to be revised throughout the project by different listeners or through the availability of new information.

2.3 *Background information*

The Mobile Unit kept a card index of recordings, as well as a book catalogue and a collection of the original recording notes. At times, these written records proved a useful source of background information for some but not all speakers, though unfortunately a large part of this material was illegible for various reasons. Some background information about the speakers could be gleaned from the recordings themselves. Systematic searches were carried out to investigate the speakers and the communities in which they lived (see Lewis 1996). The main source of genealogical information came from the New Zealand Department of Justice records on births, deaths, and marriages. Some descendants of Mobile Unit speakers were also traced and interviewed (see Woods 2000b), and relevant material was sought in local museums, libraries, and newspapers. Census data (where available) provided information about the make-up of the communities, and shipping records, also where available, were used for information about travel between New Zealand and Australia.

[2] The Mobile Unit data has now been transferred to CD-R, and master copies are held in the Macmillan Brown Library at the University of Canterbury, in Christchurch. This was made possible by a grant from the NZ Lotteries Board and the Canterbury Historical Foundation.

Databases were set up to organise the information using Reunion, a genealogical program for Macintosh computers, and FileMaker Pro. The following information was collected (where possible):

Speaker information:

- date and place of birth
- parents' date and place of birth
- number of siblings and birthplace of siblings
- date of family's arrival in New Zealand
- whether the family came to New Zealand from Australia
- where they first settled
- occupations of speaker and parents
- family's religious denomination
- speaker's schooling

Community information:

- settlement dates and patterns
- ethnic origins of early settlers
- basis for settlement, i.e. farming, goldmining, coalmining, etc.
- early churches and schools
- size of the settlement
- relative isolation of the settlement

3 Data analysis

As mentioned earlier, three different methods were used to analyse the data: auditory perceptual analysis, auditory quantitative analysis, and acoustic analysis. We were mainly interested in phonetic and phonological information about the speakers' pronunciation, however, information about lexis and syntax, especially non-standard syntax, was also collected. This book deals exclusively with phonetics and phonology.

3.1 Auditory perceptual analysis

Auditory perceptual analysis involved listening to interviews to obtain an overall evaluation of the speaker's phonetics and phonology and to listen for specific features of lexical phonology. Peter Trudgill carried out the perceptual analyses on 95 of the115 speakers reported on here.

A template was designed to record the results of the perceptual analyses. As the analyser listened to the tape of an interview, detailed notes were made on a hard copy of the template, using a narrow IPA transcription where relevant. The notes listed the pronunciations of the variables of interest, together with an indication of the relative frequencies of the various realisations found. A computer database was then set up where the templates were transcribed together with much of the background information about each speaker. Each speaker's original hard-copy data-sheets with the detailed IPA coding were kept, as well as the more codified computer analysis. Reference was regularly made to the original hard-copy analyses as we developed theories about the origins and evolution of New Zealand English. The template covered all the vowel phonemes of New Zealand English, including a category for the realisation of the unstressed vowel, consonants such as /r/ and /l/ and items of particular interest such as whether the realisations of NEAR and SQUARE were different and whether the LOT or THOUGHT vowel was used in words like *off* and *cloth*.

The database enabled us to check the number of speakers who used a particular pronunciation for a phoneme (e.g. a centralised pronunciation for KIT or an unrounded vowel in LOT) or who used a certain phoneme in a particular set of words (e.g. a long vowel in the set *off*, *across*), and to determine the variation in the pronunciation of a phoneme (e.g. the extent of post-vocalic /r/ usage).

No statistics have been conducted on the data from the auditory perceptual analysis.

3.2 *Acoustic analysis*

Acoustic analysis was carried out on a sample of ten speakers. These ten speakers were chosen to be as representative of the Mobile Unit database as possible. Five men and five women were chosen from both the North and the South Islands. They were born between 1864 and 1886 and came from a range of different settlement types. The number of speakers analysed acoustically was limited both by the time constraints of acoustic analysis and also by the quality and length of the original recordings. As with the auditory quantitative analysis described below, some speakers did not produce enough material to permit a valid acoustic analysis. In other cases there was so much background noise that it was impossible to obtain a sufficiently clear signal to analyse. In still other cases, because the speakers were elderly when they were recorded, their voices were very soft, or it proved impossible to obtain reliable formant readings from the spectrograms.

Because the tokens were extracted from continuous speech, at least 20 tokens were analysed for each vowel or diphthong, and 50–70 tokens for the front vowels and closing diphthongs, which are particularly characteristic of New Zealand English. Only words that received sentence stress were chosen for analysis. Close to 4,000 tokens were analysed across the ten speakers. Because of the limits of the original recordings, there was no acoustic information above 5 kHz. Tokens were digitised at 22.05 kHz using SndSampler and analysed on Soundscope 16, both programs for the Macintosh. Three formants were measured at the vowel target for monophthongs and at each of the targets for diphthongs. The formants were measured using the LPC analysis window and the default settings (14 coefficients, and 20 ms frame advance).

Normalisation was carried out using Lobanov's (1971) formula, which is based on a speaker's formant mean ($F_{n.mean}$) and standard deviation ($F_{n.sd}$):

$$F_{n.mean} = (F_n - F_{n.mean})/F_{n.sd}$$

(See also Harrington and Cassidy 1999.) Unless otherwise indicated, vowel plots are based on normalised data.

T-tests (with Bonferroni corrections because of multiple analysis of the data pool (see Portney and Watkins 2000)) were used to test for significance in the acoustic analysis. An individual normalised vowel plot for each speaker is presented in Appendix 5. Mean results are presented with the other data in Chapter 6.

3.2.1 Problems associated with acoustic analysis. Because the Mobile Unit archive consists of interviews, the words to be analysed acoustically were isolated from continuous speech. Deterding (1997) indicates that, although the vowel quadrilateral shrinks when vowels from connected speech are analysed, the relative positions of the vowels remain constant. The acoustic analysis should therefore provide a valid indication of the relative positions of the vowels for the speakers analysed. We also faced the problem that many of the Mobile Unit speakers were relatively elderly when they were interviewed. Mrs Cross, for example, born in 1851, was recorded in 1948 in her late nineties. We needed to be sure that people's vowel spaces did not change radically over their lifetimes. Rastatter and Jacques (1990) and Rastatter et al. (1997) demonstrated that older speakers produce more centralised vowels, but that their vowel patterns do not change markedly. We can therefore expect that the vowel diagrams obtained for the ten speakers who were analysed acoustically may be collapsed more towards the centre than would have been the case had we been able to analyse vowels in isolated words (citation forms) when the speakers were younger. Nevertheless, we consider that the vowel charts we obtained still give a valid representation of the vowel contrasts in their speech.

Normalisation can introduce unintended biases into the analysis (see Disner 1980). Because the five women whose speech was analysed acoustically had raised DRESS, TRAP, THOUGHT and LOT, and fronted GOOSE and START more than the men, the overall mean formant values for the men and women, on which the normalisation was based, were very different. The effect of this was to lessen the apparent extent of the raising and fronting of these vowels for the women. This effect is taken into account when the statistical analyses are interpreted in Chapter 6.

3.3 Auditory quantitative analysis

Auditory quantitative analysis was used to provide a more detailed analysis of specific variables. The auditory perceptual analysis had indicated the overall pattern of pronunciation. The auditory quantitative analysis was then designed to provide precise figures for variables selected from the perceptual analysis. Fifty-nine of the 115 speakers were analysed quantitatively. Men and women from different parts of the country were chosen from the middle of the decades represented in the database to provide as balanced a sample as possible (see Table 5.1 above).

The following variables were chosen for auditory quantitative analysis:

- presence of post-vocalic /r/
- presence of word initial /h/
- /h/~/hw/ contrast
- the pronunciation of KIT, DRESS, TRAP and START and the unstressed vowel

These variables were selected, on the basis of the perceptual analysis, as being likely to benefit from quantification. With the exception of KIT, all showed a reasonably large degree of variability. KIT was included to complete the picture of the short front vowel system.

The aim was to analyse a large number of tokens per speaker wherever possible (300 for post-vocalic /r/, 100 each for /h/ and /hw/, and 150–200 for each of the vowels), though in some cases speakers did not provide sufficient tokens. Only vowel tokens carrying sentence stress were included in the analysis, and no more than ten tokens of any single lexical item per speaker. All tokens were analysed twice by the same analyst (Andrea Sudbury) and the second analysis was blind, done several months after the initial one. Any tokens on which there was not consensus were discarded.

Following the analysis, each token was coded for relevant features, including: preceding and following environment, social factors such as the year of birth and gender of the speaker, the type of town in which they lived, and the parents' origins. The consonantal variables were also analysed for more detailed linguistic factors. Choice of appropriate linguistic factors was made on a variable-by-variable basis.

3.3.1 Statistical analysis. All statistical analysis of the quantified auditory analysis was conducted using R (The R Project for Statistical Computing: http://cran.r-project.org).

3.3.1.1 Linear regression modelling (modelling speakers). An index was calculated for each speaker for each variable quantified. In some cases, this index took the form of a percentage (for example, the percentage of /r/ tokens that were realised rhotically). In the case of the vocalic variables, the index was an average, indicating the degree of advancement of the vowel. (These indices are described under the specific variables in Chapter 6, and presented in Appendix 6.) Stepwise linear regression modelling was used to examine social factors that might predict an individual speaker's usage of each variable (following Venables and Ripley 1994). Social factors that are retained as significant in linear regression modelling should be considered relatively robust. If a result is reported as significant in a regression model, then it plays a role, even when all other factors are taken into consideration. Each speaker is represented just once in the data set, so there is little scope for outlier speakers to unduly influence the results. Throughout most of the discussion of the data, graphs present raw data, rather than correlation coefficients.[3] This is for ease of interpretation by readers who may be unfamiliar with regression techniques. However, in all cases where results are reported as significant, coefficients have been checked to ensure they line up with the directionality and (approximate) magnitude of effects displayed on the graphs.

3.3.1.2 Logistic regression modelling (modelling tokens). Logistic regression modelling is used to model which of two alternative variants a variable is realised as, and is akin to VARBRUL. We chose to implement logistic regression in R rather than in VARBRUL because VARBRUL is not well equipped to easily explore possible interactions, nor is it suited to deal with continuous dependent or independent variables. (See Bayley 2001 and Mendoza-Denton et al. in press, for discussion. A good practical guide to the implementation of logistic regression in R/S-Plus is given in Venables and Ripley 1994.) For such analysis, the multiple variants coded for each variable are collapsed into two discrete groups. As with linear regression, a stepwise procedure steps through the various independent variables, establishing the degree to which each variable (taking all the others into consideration) can predict the patterns in the data. This technique is valuable for investigating possible linguistic conditioners, and for assessing the relative weights of social and linguistic factors. However, it is important to note that multiple tokens from an unusual individual-speaker may unduly skew the social results in this type of analysis.

3.3.1.3 Classification and regression trees (CART). Classification and regression trees are used for additional data exploration. This technique is particularly suited to data exploration, because it handles interactions automatically and makes no assumptions about the underlying distribution of the data. This makes it less powerful for detecting patterns in data than the other techniques employed, but extremely reliable in terms of the patterns found.

A CART tree begins with the data to be analysed, and then attempts to split it into two groups (for example, one that maximises rhoticity, and one that minimises it). Splits are designed to minimise variation within categories and maximise variation across categories. The algorithm then attempts to split each resultant category into a further two groups. This technique is particularly useful, then, for revealing salient divisions in data sets, without imposing group membership from the outside. For example, as will be seen in Chapter 6, CART trees split many of our variables based on the date of birth of the speaker. Invariably, the place chosen to split by date of birth is somewhere in the mid-1870s.

[3] Correlation coefficients are similar to VARBRUL weights.

Thus, this technique enables us to identify a period in the history of New Zealand English in which there was clearly significant change underway.

As a technique for analysis, CART trees were fit both for speakers and for tokens for all of the quantified variables. Foundational literature on classification and regression trees includes Morgan and Sonquist 1963, Morgan and Messenger 1973, and Breiman et al. 1984. A good practical guide for their implementation in R/S-Plus can be found in Venables and Ripley 1994. For discussion of their use in sociolinguistics see Mendoza-Denton et al. in press.

3.3.2 Coding background information for Mobile Unit speakers.

3.3.2.1 Origin of parents. Several types of statistics we intended to conduct (logistic and linear regression models) require that the predictive variables are largely independent of one another. This means that we could only test the role of the mother's origin and the role of the father's origin if these two factors bore no relationship to one another. As it turns out, there is a strong statistical relationship between the mother and father's origin, and so we could not routinely test both factors simultaneously. Because the relationship was so strong (the mother's origin and the father's origin were often the same), we chose to collapse these codes into a combined 'parents' origin' code. If both parents were Scottish, then the parents' origin would be 'Scottish'. However, if one parent came from Scotland, and one from Australia, then this would be coded as 'mixed'. Because there were enough speakers for whom the parents shared place of origin, it seemed likely that this simpler coding scheme would probably capture any role of parental origin, while not violating the expectations of the statistics used.

Luckily, there was not an undue degree of collinearity between settlement type and parents' origins in the data set, and so we were able to include both in our statistical tests.

3.3.2.2 Settlement type. After some preliminary analysis of the data, it became apparent that some variables were behaving differently in different towns, and that certain towns appeared to cluster together in terms of their behaviour. In particular, it was felt that towns that contained settlers of quite mixed origins were undergoing linguistic change at a faster rate than the towns where the settlement was more homogenous. We therefore classified towns according to the majority of the settlers (i.e. the non-New Zealand born), or as 'mixed' if there was no dominant single origin for settlers. This was done using available census information (see Chapter 3). If, for every year that census data was available, the majority of migrants in a town were of Scottish birth, the settlement type was coded as 'Scottish'. Milton is an example of such a town; the relevant census information is shown in Table 5.2. Table 5.3 shows the census figures for Hamilton, a town coded as 'English'. Some towns showed a fairly even spread and no consistent majority across different census years. Lawrence is an example of a 'mixed' town, as shown in Table 5.4. There was no town that showed a clear majority of settlers from any area apart from England or Scotland. Census

Table 5.2 *Census information for Milton: example of a* ***Scottish*** *town*

Milton	1878	1881	1886
New Zealand	544	676	716
England	178	179	127
Scotland	**293**	**251**	**215**
Ireland	77	116	85

Table 5.3 *Census information for Hamilton: example of an* ***English*** *town*

Hamilton	1878	1881	1886	1891
New Zealand	485	637	660	722
Australian Colonies	108	86	55	57
England	**390**	**350**	**268**	**243**
Wales	1	4	6	5
Scotland	52	56	36	37
Ireland	171	192	144	120

Table 5.4 *Census information for Lawrence: example of a* ***mixed*** *town*

Lawrence	1874	1878	1881	1886
New Zealand	252	393	449	593
Australian Colonies	92	92	91	63
England	**126**	**144**	**184**	**143**
Wales	3	1	3	2
Scotland	**125**	**138**	**170**	**162**
Ireland	79	67	86	94

information was not available for all towns. In particular, more rural settlements, with a low population, were not included in the census. Such towns are classified as 'unknown'.

3.3.2.3 Year of birth. The year of the speakers' birth was tested for all quantified variables. This was treated as a continuous factor – that is, we did not collapse the speakers into discrete categories for the purposes of the statistics. However, we did do this when producing the graphics, to facilitate the display of information. For this purpose, we usually divide speakers into those born before 1875, and those born in 1875 or later. The year 1875 was chosen both because it marks the approximate midpoint of the period studied and because CART modelling of our data consistently identified the mid-1870s as an important time for many of our variables.

4 Terminology and phonetic symbols

There are numerous terms used in the literature for discussing varieties of languages and of English in particular; for example, *accent*, *dialect*, *traditional dialect*, *variety*, and *lect*, among others. Their meanings, while overlapping in part, are not the same. While their meanings are usually clear in specific publications, they can be confusing when used together or taken out of context. Therefore, in this book, we attempt to avoid any potential confusion by relying primarily on the term *variety*, alternating it at times with *dialect*; by these, we intend any clearly identifiable variety of a language, be it defined regionally, socially, or however.

Phonetic symbols are listed at the front of the book. We have used standard IPA symbols (1996 version) with the addition of [A] to indicate a central open vowel, a sound for which the IPA charts do not provide a symbol.

5 Methodological assumptions

This project faces the same methodological problem as all sociolinguistic work that employs some form of the apparent-time hypothesis. The informants, although in a few cases born as early as the 1850s, were recorded in the 1940s. Most of them do not sound like modern New Zealanders, but it is probable that a number of changes may have occurred in their speech between the second half of the nineteenth century when they reached late adolescence and their basic language system was formed (see, for example, Chambers and Trudgill 1998: 151; Ritchie and Bhatia 1999: 579ff.) and the 1940s when they were recorded. We regard the presence of conservative features and the absence of advanced features[4] in the informants' speech as unproblematic. Absence of conservative features, on the other hand, could be due to their loss during a speaker's lifetime. Our main safeguard here is in numbers: if none of the 108 New Zealand-born speakers analysed demonstrates a particular conservative feature, we regard that as not a coincidence. It is unlikely that they all once had the feature but have subsequently lost it; it was probably not present in their language. None of the New Zealand-born, for example, display the /w~v/ merger that results in *village* being pronounced as *willage*.

The presence of innovative features constitutes a potential problem of greater importance: such features could be the result of accommodation by the informants to younger speakers during the course of their lifetimes (cf. Giles 1973,

[4] As explained in Chapter 2, Section 2.2, we used the terms 'advanced' or 'innovative' to refer to those tokens or speakers that are further ahead in terms of a sound change that is underway.

1977). When small numbers of randomly occurring advanced tokens of a variable are combined with large numbers of conservative tokens in the one speaker, we assume that the conservative forms were the ones acquired in childhood. Less weight should be placed on innovative tokens that occur infrequently in the Mobile Unit interviews because they may represent accommodation by the interviewees to the speech of younger persons in the community. The small numbers of innovative tokens are not completely ignored, however, because they may represent embryonic variants of changes that are just starting (Gordon and Trudgill 1999).

There is recent converging evidence that, rather than language being relatively fixed after adolescence, speakers change their pronunciation over their lifetime (see, for example, Harrington et al. 2000; Sankoff et al. 2001; Yoneda 1993). Because speakers usually change in the direction in which the surrounding language is changing, this suggests that the Mobile Unit speakers will have changed towards modern New Zealand speech over their lives. An analysis of the speakers in the Mobile Unit archive will therefore somewhat underestimate the differences between early and modern New Zealand speech. Labov (1994: 111) says of this problem, 'From present indications, apparent-time studies may understate the actual rate of sound change, since older speakers show a limited tendency towards communal change, participating to a small extent in the changes taking place around them'. Recent evidence suggests this extent may not even be particularly small (see, for example, Harrington et al. 2000 on changes in the Queen's pronunciation over an extended period of time). Our own work on the speech of Sonja Davies (a well-known New Zealand union leader), interviewed seven times in the twenty-four years from 1976 to 2000, shows that her vowel space shifted significantly during this time (see Chapter 8 for further discussion of this).

Such results demonstrate that we cannot regard the Mobile Unit speakers simply as examples of the way in which people spoke in the nineteenth century. However, it also reassures us that the changes in their speech are likely to be towards the positions of modern New Zealand English. Therefore, when we make claims about how New Zealand English has changed over time, the results of our analyses are likely to be conservative and underestimate the extent of those changes.

In order to further assess the extent of this problem, seven speakers in the Mobile Unit archive were analysed who were born in Australia and Great Britain and came to New Zealand later in life. If these non-New Zealand-born speakers sound relatively like their dialects of origin (to the extent that we know what these dialects would have sounded like in the nineteenth century), and if they differ from the New Zealand-born Mobile Unit speakers, this provides one marker of the extent to which the Mobile Unit speakers represent a valid indication of early New Zealand speech.

Details of the seven non-New Zealand speakers, including a description of their speech, are in Appendix 4. The Australian-born speaker does not sound different from New Zealand-born Mobile Unit speakers of comparable age. We discuss this further in Chapters 4 and 7 when we consider the possibility of an Australian connection in the development of the New Zealand accent. All of the six speakers from Great Britain sound different from their New Zealand-born age peers in various ways, presumably as a result of not accommodating to the speech of the surrounding community. They provide an indication of the extent to which the speech of the New Zealand-born subjects in the Mobile Unit corpus really is different from that of speakers born elsewhere, and reassure us that the Mobile Unit speakers do give an appropriate representation of the development of the New Zealand accent during the nineteenth century.

6 Summary

The results described in the following chapter are based on a variety of analysis techniques. For some variables we are able to provide detailed quantitative analysis of linguistic and social factors, and for others we can simply comment on the degree to which that variable appeared to be present or absent on the recordings. By using a combination of very detailed, time-consuming techniques (i.e. acoustic and quantified auditory), and a rather more time-efficient, broad-brush, auditory perceptual analysis, our aim is to provide a reasonable balance of both breadth and depth of coverage. We hope that with this approach we are able to provide the reader with a reasonable overall impression of the nature of the recordings, together with detailed insight into the behaviour of a smaller number of variables.

6 The variables of early New Zealand English

By and large there are no fundamentally unhealthy sounds in New Zealand speech . . . However as a race, you are not very good at short vowels. You would, for instance, rather say 'yeees' than 'yes'; 'mulk' rather than 'milk'; and 'bull' rather than 'bill'. Your diphthongs frequently expire in a drawl or resolve themselves into triphthongs . . . Your long vowels tend to be placed in the wrong part of the mouth – 'harm', 'there' for example. And the things done to the final 'y' sound – 'Anthonee, gloree!' . . . Casting a quick (and tactful) glance at your consonants, may I observe that, as a whole, New Zealand tongues are idle. The 'l' sound is treacherous. Your plosives, too, tend to disappear without trace. And just a word about the way you 'manhandle' the name of your country . . . [I]s it to be 'New Zealand' or 'Nu Zilland?'

(Trinity College Examiner, Andrew Morrison, 'The New Zealand Voice', *NZ Listener* 19 (491) November 1948, p. 7)

1 Introduction

In this chapter, we present the main phonological variables important in the development of New Zealand English. We discuss each variable in turn. Firstly, we present what is known (or can be inferred) of the variable's antecedents in relevant parts of the British Isles.[1] Secondly, we consider what has been said in the written records about the variable in New Zealand. Mostly these written comments are complaints about 'improper' language, but are revealing about the history of New Zealand English. Thirdly, we give the results of the ONZE project's analysis for each of these variables. Some of the variables were investigated more intensely, subjected to in-depth auditory and acoustic analyses; other less central variables received less attention, though always sufficient to determine their nature both in the Mobile Unit speakers' speech and to relate this to the same variables in modern New Zealand English.

[1] We in no way attempt an exhaustive survey of British varieties for each feature discussed; rather, we concentrate on areas from which immigrants are known to have come to New Zealand or which have linguistic traits comparable to those found in New Zealand.

Table 6.1 *Order of treatment of variables*

Type of analysis		Auditory Perceptual	Auditory Quantitative	Acoustic
Number of speakers		95	59	10
Section 2	TRAP	√	√	√
3	DRESS	√	√	√
4	KIT	√	√	√
5	START	√	√	√
6	STRUT	√		√
7	FOOT	√		√
8	FLEECE	√		√
9	GOOSE	√		√
10	LOT (CLOTH)	√		√
11	THOUGHT	√		√
12				
12.2	MOUTH	√		√
12.3	PRICE	√		√
12.4	FACE	√		√
12.5	GOAT	√		√
12.6	CHOICE	√		√
13	Centring diphthongs	(√)		√
14	NURSE	√		√
15	Unstressed vowels		√	√
16	/r/	√	√	
17	/h/	√	√	
18	/hw/	√	√	
19	/l/	√		

As the results of the ONZE project show, the crucial formative period for the development of New Zealand English was the decades following 1840, especially 1860 to 1890. As seen in Chapter 3, English arrived in New Zealand mainly from the British Isles; therefore, if we are to gain an understanding of the processes involved in the development of New Zealand English, we must begin with the forms of mid-nineteenth-century British English that provided the main input to what became modern New Zealand English. The discussion begins with the first half of the nineteenth century, when people in the British Isles who were the parents of the first New Zealand-born anglophones (including some of the ONZE subjects) would have been born and acquired the varieties of English they brought with them to New Zealand.

The variables are considered in the order given in Table 6.1. The analyses performed on each variable are indicated, together with the number of speakers included in the analysis. The final sections of the chapter consider the relationships between the various variables analysed.

2 The vowel of the TRAP lexical set

Modern New Zealand English words of the TRAP vowel class have as their dominant variant [ɛ̝]; however, this vowel was already significantly raised (as [ɛ]) in major varieties of English that arrived in New Zealand from Britain.

2.1 British historical antecedents of the TRAP vowel

For the mid nineteenth century there is interesting and abundant evidence for the raised quality of the TRAP vowel in the south-east of England, which is particularly relevant to our study, since south-east features dominate in New Zealand English (see Chapter 4). For example, Sweet (1888: 275) noted tersely that in words of the TRAP lexical set the vowel 'tends to [[ɛ]] in Vg.' (see Bauer 1992: 266). Ellis (1889: 226) quoted from a Mr D'Orsey who writes of London English that '*cab* is *keb*, *bank* is *benk*, *strand* is *strend*', which Ellis interpreted as (E) [[ɛ]] (see Eustace 1969). Ellis also quoted from Field and Tuer's (1883) *The Kaukneigh Awlmineck*, which, in addition to having *almanac* with <e> in the title, also has many other words such as *bad*, *man*, *cat*, *rats* with <e>. Again, Ellis interpreted this as indicating [ɛ]. A German, Mr Baumann, is also quoted by Ellis (1889: 231) as representing London English words such as *cab*, *catch*, *standard* with <e>. Note that Ellis began his fieldwork in 1868. Significantly, Ellis reported that the vowel is raised in his own speech (all cited in Eustace 1969: 47):

> My own pronunciation of (æ) has been constantly misunderstood, and considered as (e) [[e̝]] or (E) [[ɛ]]. (Ellis 1869: 71)
>
> [Bell] supposes the true sounds of English *men*, *man* to be (mEn, mæn) [[mɛn, mæn]]. My own pronunciation of *man* he finds frequently the same as his pronunciation of *men*, so that to him I pronounce *men*, *man* as (men, mEn) [[me̝n, mɛn]]. (Ellis 1869: 106)[2]

Similarly, Wright (1905: 9, 22–4, 26–7, 29, 63, 112) shows much of Kent, Middlesex, south-east Buckinghamshire, southern Hertfordshire, southwestern Essex, and so on[3] – the areas immediately adjacent to London – as having the

[2] Ellis 1869: 1147 (reported in Eustace (1969: 47) says: 'My own /æ/ is sometimes mistaken for /ɛ/ on the telephone; and in casual speech, between velars, I have heard myself saying [igzɛkli] *exactly*. (At other times however I drop towards the modern [a].) When I hear my /æ/ recorded the effect is a little old-fashioned, but something yet closer sounds yet more so. Miss Russell as I say often had [ɛ] unmistakably.'

[3] Those readers less familiar with the locations of the counties of England may find it useful, from time to time, to refer to Map 11, at the end of Appendix 3.

pronunciation that he represents as <e>, which, from his description (pp. 13–15, 22) appears to represent [ɛ], or a vowel intermediate between [ɛ] and [æ].

This supposition that the TRAP vowel was already relatively close in the English dialects transported to New Zealand is further supported by evidence from the Survey of English Dialects (SED), 1962–71. The SED does not provide information about mid-nineteenth-century English, but is based on data obtained in the 1950s and 1960s from elderly speakers who were in some cases born as early as 1870. In a large area of south-eastern England the SED fieldworkers nearly always used [ɛ] as the transcription for the vowel in items such as *stack*, *hammer*, *apple*, *saddle*, *handle*, *rack*, *sack*, *mallet*, *paddock*, and so on. Map 2 (in Appendix 3), with data based on Orton and Wakelin 1967 and Orton and Tilling 1969, shows that this area straddles the Thames and includes all of Sussex, all of Kent and Surrey except for the areas closest to London, and south-eastern Essex. The geographical patterning indicates that the area used to be larger – as Wright (1905) indicated – and almost certainly used to include London itself, as shown by Ellis (1889).

There is also more recent evidence. Gimson (1962: 101) writes of refined RP and popular London as raising /æ/ to 'approximately *C* [ɛ]' (where *C* stands for 'cardinal'). It is known that RP and other south-eastern English English dialects generally used to have higher realisations of /æ/ than is currently the case. Wells (1982: 129) writes of /æ/ that 'it is a striking fact that the current trend in pronunciation of this vowel is . . . towards an opener [a]-like' quality, which 'is possibly to be seen as a reaction against the closer, [ɛ – ɛˈ] type of realisation associated with Cockney'. This vowel in RP is continuing to lower. A diagram in Gimson (1962: 101) shows RP /æ/ as being about a quarter of the way from [ɛ] towards [a]; twenty years later, Roach's (1983: 15) diagram shows RP /æ/ as being three-quarters of the way towards [a]. Indeed, Gimson (ibid.) specifically says, 'the quality is nearer to *C* [ɛ] than to *C* [a]', while Roach (ibid.) says that it is 'not quite as open as cardinal vowel no. 4 [a]'. (See also Bauer 1992: 256.)

Though the dates are less clear, a similar picture seems to hold for Devon in the south-west; Wright (1905: 22–3) lists the same raised feature in various words for speakers from north and north-west Devon. Downes (1998: 12) reports of educated dialectal pronunciations:

> One must also consider and wonder at the arrival of the long A which is affected by many young persons. Simple words like *black*, *that*, *cat* and *rat* appear to have developed an extra long vowel sound, perhaps by a swing of the linguistic pendulum **from the old fashioned prissy speech which caused these words to become *bleck*, *thet*, *ket* and *ret*** [our emphasis].

(See also Anderson [1987: 12], who discusses raising of ME /a/ beyond [æ] to [ɛ] in parts of Essex, Kent, Surrey, and Sussex, and sporadically in other dialects.)

It is clear, then, that in the middle of the nineteenth century regional accents in the whole area around London and the south-east had a TRAP vowel that was higher than [æ] and in some cases, according to Wright, even higher than [ɛ].

Map 2 shows the area of England where the [æ] pronunciation – as opposed to the more widespread [a] – was extant in local dialects as portrayed by the SED, as well as areas where the evidence indicates that variants around [ɛ] were found in 1850. As we have seen, RP, or its precursor, is also very likely to have had such qualities at that time.

On the subject of the raised TRAP vowel, Lass summarises as follows:

> By the 19th century this raising had begun to move from the Eastern Counties into London; it is remarked on as early as the 1780s . . . and condemned by Batchelor (1809). It is not however entrenched as prototypically London until quite late in the century . . . It was not typically metropolitan as late as the 1880s; but it was widespread in the rural SE . . . So while [æ] is generally southern, [ɛ] is pretty strictly SE; and its widespread occurrence in the southern ETEs [Extraterritorial Englishes] (where it is virtually a defining feature of local dialect-type) seems likely to reflect primarily an input from the SE hinterland rather than London itself. (Lass 1990: 256–7)

In most of Ireland and Wales, the TRAP vowel would have had 'fully open qualities' ([a] or [a̟]) during the period in question. In Scotland and Northern Ireland today, 'the possibility of a TRAP-PALM Merger' gives mostly central and even back qualities in TRAP words, though there is some phonetic variation in Scotland (Wells 1982: 129–30).

2.2 *Early New Zealand commentaries on the* TRAP *vowel*

In 1887 McBurney (reported in Ellis 1889) noted variable 'e' pronunciations for 'hand' words of the TRAP lexical set. He listed <hEEnd> [hɛːnd] and <hEnd> [hɛnd] as about equally common pronunciations in Nelson and Christchurch, with some instances of <hænd> [hænd]; for Auckland <hEnd> [hɛnd] was general for the girls, <hænd> [hænd] general for the boys; for Wellington and Napier <hEnd> [hɛnd] and <hænd> [hænd] were equally common; Dunedin had some <hEnd> [hɛnd], many <hænd> [hænd], and a few <hand> [hand] (in Ellis 1889: 1675; cf. Woods 2000a: 114).

One of the earliest comments is from *The Triad* (10 August 1910: 40), quoting Mr E. W. Andrews of Napier Boys' High School, who said:

> The broad 'a' of father and the narrow 'a' of fat appear to cause great difficulty, and are advanced in the mouth almost to the sound of 'e' in pen, so that 'last' becomes 'least', 'remark' 'reme-rk', 'camp' 'kemp' and 'standard' 'standerd'.

Arnold Wall (1939: 16) gave a somewhat contradictory report, confirming the existence of the close TRAP variant ([ɛ]), but suggesting (perhaps mistakenly, judging from the Mobile Unit results we report below) that it was uncommon: 'The Cockney "e" for the short "a" in "hat" [æ], while not entirely absent, is uncommon and is not one of our besetting sins'.

Table 6.2 *Distribution of TRAP variants*

	0 [æ]	1 [æ̝]	2 [ɛ̞]
Number of Tokens	2,334	1,294	2,078

2.3 *Results from the Mobile Unit speakers for the TRAP vowel*

2.3.1 Auditory analysis. Quantified auditory analysis of TRAP was conducted on 5,706 tokens from 59 speakers. Three variants were coded: 0 for [æ], 1 for raised [æ] (that is, [æ̝]), and 2 for lowered [ɛ] (that is, [ɛ̞]). The total number of each variant is shown in Table 6.2. This distribution provides clear evidence that a raised variant of the TRAP vowel was present in New Zealand from the very beginning.

The data were organised into two data sets. The first was designed to reveal the average degree of TRAP raising present in individual speakers. The second investigated factors influencing the likelihood that any individual token of TRAP will be raised. It should be noted that by 'TRAP raising' we mean the incidence of relatively close tokens of the TRAP vowel. We do not necessarily mean that the vowel was involved in a raising movement at the time the data were collected. We use similar terminology in discussing other variables in this chapter. See Section 20.2 for a discussion of the relationships between the vowels.

2.3.1.1 Speaker analysis. Each speaker was assigned an index score, which represents his or her average degree of raising of the TRAP vowel. This was formulated by interpreting the variant codes 0, 1 and 2 as numerical values related to degree of raising, and by calculating an average score for each speaker. The scores for each speaker for each variable analysed quantitatively are shown in Appendix 6. Their scores ranged from 0.09 (for little raising) to 1.83 (for considerable raising). A stepwise linear model was then fitted, considering gender, region, birthdate, and interactions between these factors, as possible predictors of an individual's index score. The model retained (i.e. revealed) gender as a highly significant predictor of a speakers' index score. Age, settlement type and parents' origins were not retained as significant predictors of the linear model. The averaged indexes for men and women are shown in Table 6.3.

A classification and regression tree (CART) was also fitted to the data. The resulting tree is shown in Figure 6.1. This, again, shows a strong gender effect, with a higher level of TRAP raising for females. The CART analysis also reveals a significant effect of age, with women who are born later showing a higher degree of raising. Higher numbers indicate higher degrees of raising. In each CART regression tree, the factors that are retained most strongly are on the higher branches and on the right-hand branch at each level.

The effects of gender and age are shown in Figure 6.2, with date of birth broken down into two categories. This figure clearly shows the females with

Table 6.3 *Averaged Index scores for* TRAP, *by gender*

Averaged Index Scores for TRAP raising (Higher scores = more raising)	
Male	0.81
Female	1.14

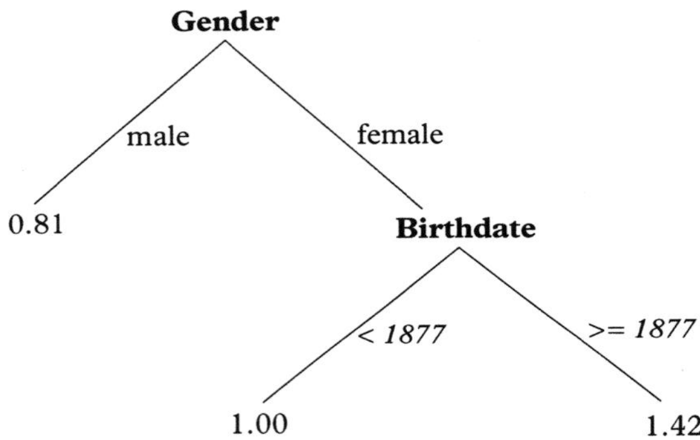

Figure 6.1 CART regression tree predicting individuals' index scores for raising of TRAP

more raised variants than males, and an increase in degree of raising over time. Figure 6.3 shows the distribution of raised variants by settlement type and age. Note that settlement type is not a significant predictor of the variation in TRAP, but nonetheless, some trends are revealed. The mixed settlements have the most raising, and TRAP is raising over time in all settlement types.

2.3.1.2 Token analysis. A second analysis was conducted on the entire data set of TRAP vowel tokens to investigate how social effects combine with possible linguistic conditioners (for example, preceding and following environment). For this analysis, the variants 0, 1 and 2 (described earlier, in 2.3.1) were collapsed into two categories – not raised (0) and raised (1, 2) – and a stepwise logistic regression model was fitted (see Chapter 5). Region, gender, and preceding and following environments (both manner and place of articulation) all have a significant effect on the likelihood of raising. Seventy-four percent of tokens produced by women are raised, and 53% of tokens produced by men are raised. Mixed settlements produced the most raising, and tokens produced by speakers with New Zealand, Scottish, and English parents were more likely to be raised than those produced by speakers with Irish parents, or parents of different origins. Age is also retained as a significant factor, with tokens produced by later-born speakers more likely

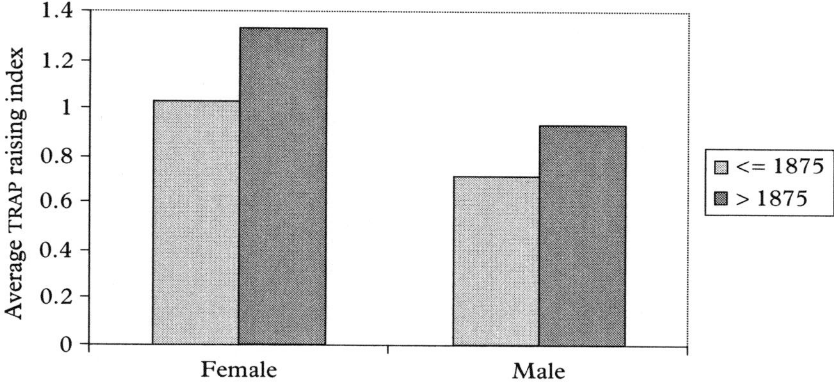

Figure 6.2 TRAP raising, by gender and birthdate

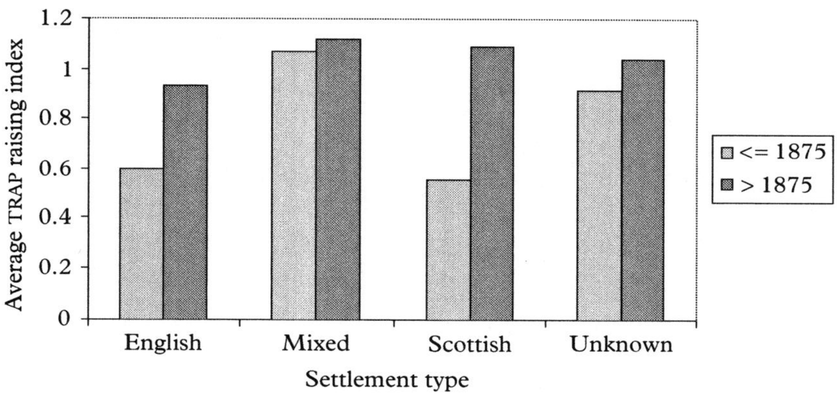

Figure 6.3 TRAP raising, by settlement type and birthdate

to be raised. If we split the time period in two parts, we can see the directionality of this effect: 54% of tokens produced by speakers born 1850–75 are raised, and 65% of tokens produced by speakers born after 1875 are raised.

The ranking of the environments is shown in Table 6.4. The TRAP vowel is maximally raised in words such as *gang* (followed by a nasal which is back, and preceded by a plosive which is back), and least raised in words such as *arid* (followed by a sonorant that is a coronal, preceded by a pause which obviously has no manner of articulation).

A CART analysis of the TRAP tokens again reveals gender as the most predictive variable. For tokens from male speakers, further divisions according to the manner and place of articulation of the following environment were also found to be predictive. The result is shown in Figure 6.4.

Table 6.4 *Linguistic constraints for* TRAP *raising (Ordering of environmental factors for following and preceding environment, as returned by a stepwise logistic regression)*

	Facilitation of raising	
Following environment	Manner	nasals > fricatives > plosives > approximants
	Place	back > labial > coronal
Preceding environment	Manner	plosives > approximants > nasals > fricatives > pauses > vowels
	Place	back > labial > coronal

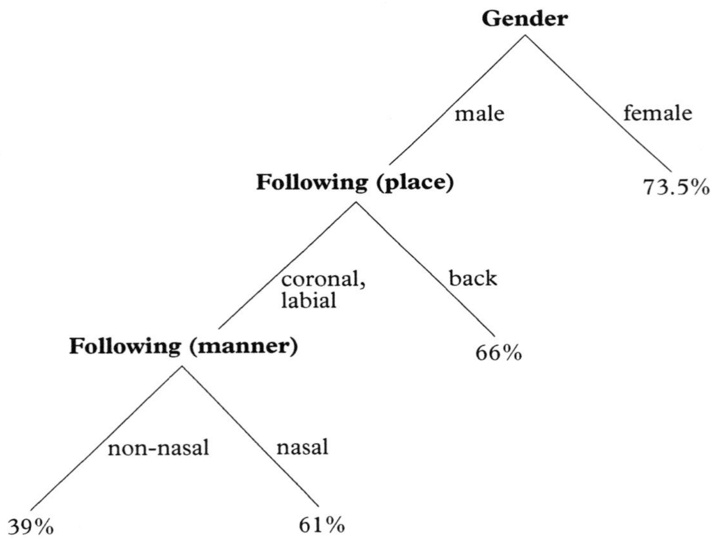

Figure 6.4 CART regression tree predicting percentage of raised TRAP tokens over the entire data set

2.3.2 Acoustic analysis. The acoustic analysis of speakers shown in Figure 6.5 agrees with the auditory quantitative analysis in showing that the five women analysed have closer TRAP vowels than the five men. The difference is not statistically significant for the acoustic analysis, but this is largely an artifact of the normalisation method used (see Chapter 5).

2.3.3 Summary. Overall, the analysis demonstrates an extremely strong gender effect. However we analyse the data, gender emerges as the strongest and most predictive factor affecting the raising of TRAP. Females show much higher

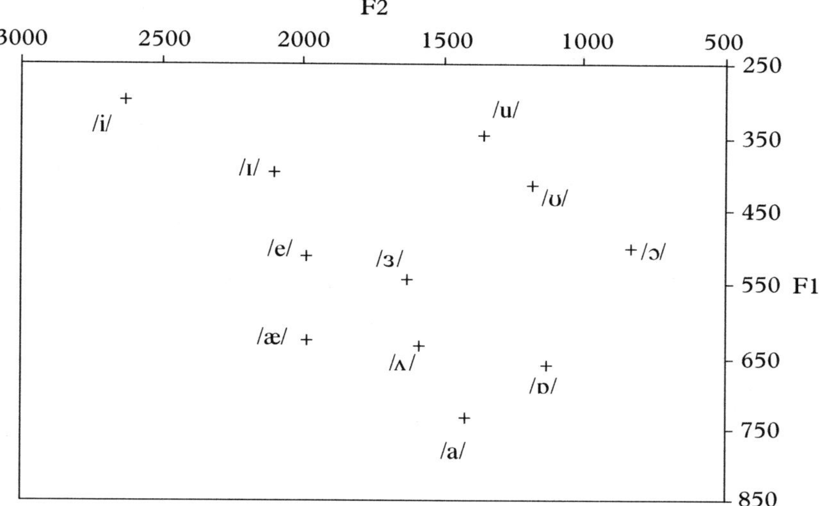

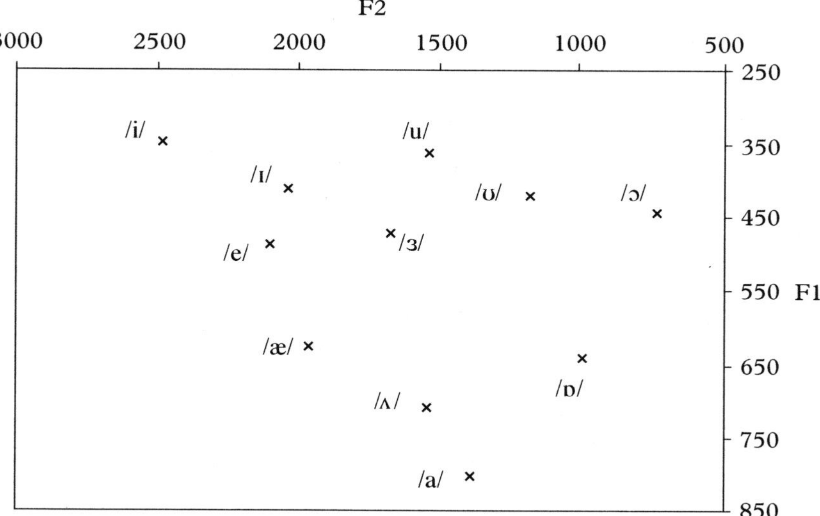

Figure 6.5 Normalised vowel spaces for the five men and the five women analysed acoustically (Note: The vowel charts for each of the ten speakers are presented in Appendix 5.)

degrees of raising than males. There also appears to be an effect of age, with later-born speakers showing more raising. However, we should perhaps interpret this result with some caution, since age did not emerge as a significant factor in the linear model of speakers. This suggests that the significant effect here may be unduly carried by a small number of speakers. While there is a clear tendency towards raising over the period of our corpus, the statistical reliability of this tendency is certainly not as robust as the observed gender effect. Similarly, while there is an indication that parents' origin and settlement type significantly affect the raising of TRAP, these patterns emerge only in the token analysis, which makes it possible that they may be unduly influenced by the extreme behaviour of individual speakers.

3 The vowel of the DRESS lexical set

The variants of the DRESS vowel in modern New Zealand English are generally perceived as distinctly higher, [e̝, ɪ̞], than in most British and American varieties. However, how it came to be so close is a significant story, in which we find it is not only the result of a New Zealand vowel shift.

3.1 British historical antecedents of the DRESS vowel

It is quite possible that higher variants of /æ/ (TRAP vowel) imply higher variants of /ɛ/ (DRESS vowel) too. There is evidence of higher realisations of the DRESS vowel in south-eastern England from the period of time when emigrants from there first came to New Zealand. Gimson (1962: 101) describes modern RP as having a vowel for the DRESS set of words half-way between [e] and [ɛ]. However, he also writes of 'that type of refined RP (and popular London) which realises /ɛ/ in the *C* [e] region [*C* = cardinal]'. The evidence shows that RP and other south-eastern English English dialects more generally *used to* have much higher realisations of the vowels of the DRESS lexical set than is currently the case. Wells (1982: 128), for example, writes, 'old-fashioned types of both Cockney and RP tend to closer [higher] varieties [of this vowel] than are now general'. Wright (1905: 51–2, 54, 161–2) also confirms the existence of the higher variants of the DRESS vowel in these regions.

There is also indirect evidence for how DRESS was pronounced in nineteenth-century Cockney – the SED tells us how these vowels were pronounced in the south-east and adjacent areas in the speech of people born around 1870. It is likely that many features of the accent current in London in 1800, although they may subsequently have been lost from London English itself, were still current in, for example, rural East Anglia in 1870. For the last several centuries, it has been usual for features of London English to spread outwards geographically from the metropolitan area until they eventually took root in neighbouring regions (as seen in Maps 3a–3d in Appendix 3). This takes time, and because of this time lag, we gain some idea of what earlier forms of London English were like by

Table 6.5 *Distribution of* DRESS *variants*

Variant	0 [ɛ]	1 [ɛ̝]	2 [e̞]	3 [e or e̝]
Tokens	3,357 (58.8%)	1,331 (23.3%)	1,010 (17.7%)	11 (1.9%)

examining chronologically more recent dialects in neighbouring areas. The SED transcriptions always write [ɛ]; however, their tape-recordings (supplemented by Trudgill's field research in this area) show that East Anglian informants employ pronunciations such as [bed] *bed*, with close realisations. Dialect 'spellings' of the following sort also suggest the same raising of /ɛ/ to /e/ for the traditional dialect of Devon: *laig* 'leg', *daid* 'dead', *mane* 'men', *raid* 'red' (Downes 1998; Marten 1992).

The DRESS vowel in Scotland is not raised, though in some contexts a centralised variant occurs (cf. Wells 1982: 404).

The quality of the DRESS vowel in early New Zealand attracted no significant written commentary.

3.2 Results from the Mobile Unit speakers for the DRESS *vowel*

Up to 100 tokens of DRESS per each of the 59 speakers were coded; the total number of tokens analysed was 5,709. Four codes were used for variants of DRESS, as shown in Table 6.5.

3.2.1 Speaker analysis. For each speaker an index score for the raising of DRESS vowel was calculated which averaged over all the tokens coded for that speaker. The index score could (theoretically) range from 0 (consistently [ɛ]) to 3 (consistently [e]). The actual index scores ranged from 0.2 to 1.29.

A stepwise linear model was fitted to the index scores, and this revealed the parents' origins, the settlement type, and the sex and birthdate of the speaker to be relevant factors. Also significant were two interactions, one between speaker gender and birthdate, and the other between settlement type and birthdate.

Figure 6.6 shows the effect of the origins of the parents. The significance of this factor is carried by the increased rates of DRESS-raising displayed by speakers who are children of Scottish parents. There is no significant variation among speakers with non-Scottish parents.

Figure 6.7 shows the interaction between gender and birthdate. Females show more advanced variants than males, and DRESS is raising over time, with later born speakers showing more raising. Gender and birthdate interact, in that the effect of time is more dramatic for the female speakers than the male speakers – the female speakers are raising more, and more quickly.

The interaction between settlement type and birthdate is shown in Figure 6.8. This reveals that, while mixed settlements show the overall highest rates of

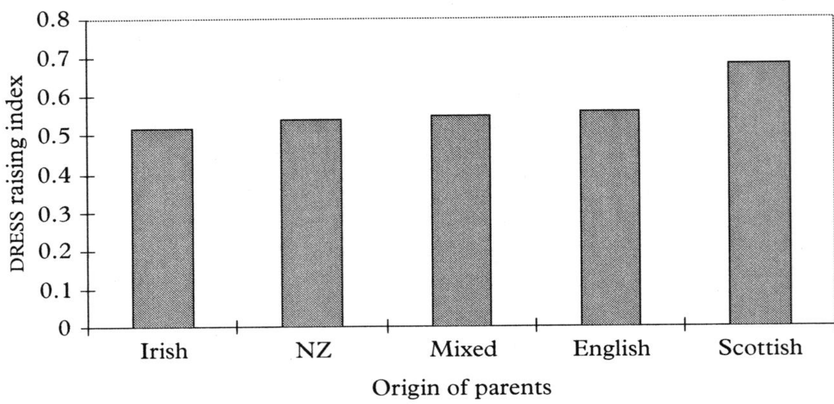

Figure 6.6 DRESS raising, by origin of parents

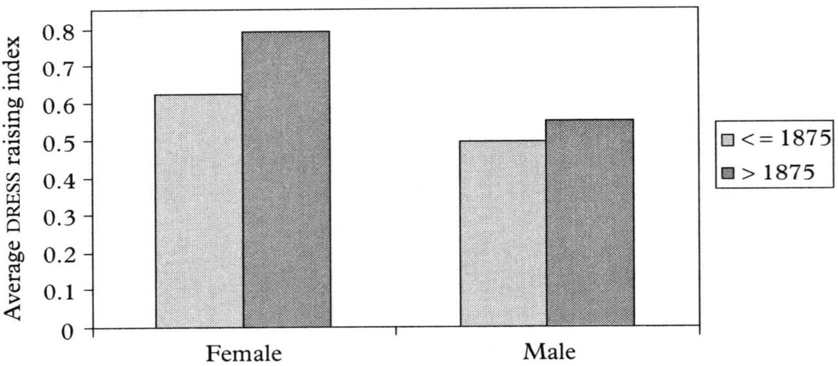

Figure 6.7 DRESS raising, by gender and birthdate

DRESS-raising, raised variants actually decrease over time in these settlements, while they are increasing everywhere else.

A classification and regression tree (CART) reveals gender to be the strongest predictor of raising, with the females having closer DRESS vowels than the males. Both mother and father's origin are identified as important – the mother for the female speakers, and the father for the male speakers. Finally, settlement type plays a role. The resultant CART regression tree is shown as Figure 6.9.

3.2.2 Token analysis. Two analyses were conducted – one that contrasted tokens coded as [ɛ] or [ɛ̝], with those coded as [e̞] or [e], and a second that contrasted tokens coded as [ɛ] with all other tokens. The same factors were retained as significant in both analyses. The results of the latter analysis, where the most open variant [ɛ] was contrasted with all other variants, are presented here.

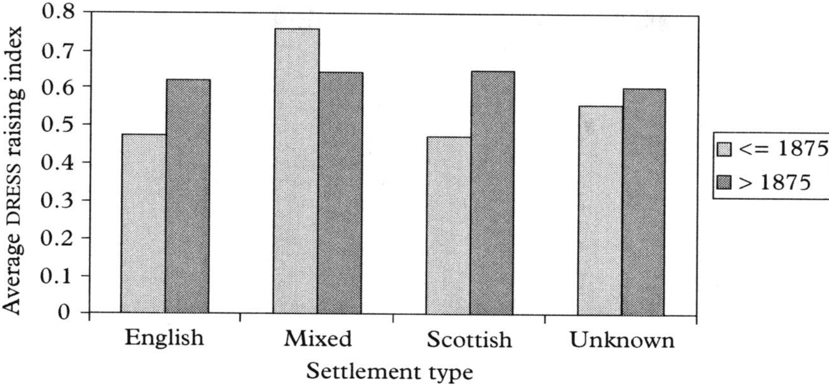

Figure 6.8 DRESS raising, by settlement type and birthdate

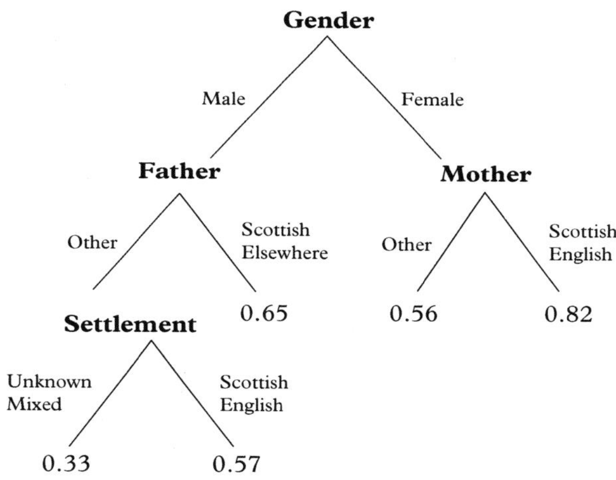

Figure 6.9 CART regression tree predicting individuals' index scores for raising of DRESS

The stepwise logistic regression retained age, gender, parents' origin, settlement type, preceding and following environments, and an interaction between age and gender. The token analysis thus largely confirms the results of the speaker analysis above. The ordering of the conditioning environments are shown in Table 6.6.

Finally, a CART regression tree on all DRESS tokens reveals gender, parents' origins and birthdate as significant predictors, as shown in Figure 6.10. The overall structure of this tree is very similar to that returned from the speaker analysis reported in 3.2.1.

Table 6.6 *Linguistic constraints on DRESS raising*

		Facilitation of raising
Following environment	Manner	nasal > fricative > approximant > plosives > vowel
	Place	back > coronal > labial
Preceding environment	Manner	vowel > fricative > pause > plosive > approximant > nasal
	Place	back > coronal > labial

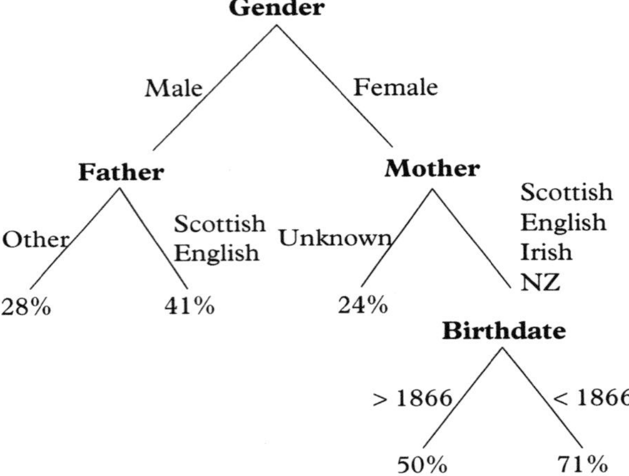

Figure 6.10 CART regression tree predicting percentage of raised DRESS tokens over the entire data set

The acoustic analysis of speakers confirms that the DRESS vowel for the five women studied is raised and fronted significantly more than for the five men (see Figure 6.5 in Section 2.3.2).

3.2.3 Summary. Almost 43% of DRESS tokens analysed showed some degree of raising. Female speakers showed more extreme raising than male speakers, and were increasing their degree of raising over time at a faster rate. Individuals with Scottish parents were more likely to use raised variants than other speakers, and the overall degree of raising was highest in the mixed settlement types.

4 The vowel of the KIT lexical set

The KIT vowel in modern New Zealand English has a special character. One of its most salient variants is centralised, realised towards [ə]. It has become a marker of New Zealand speech abroad, 'the sound which "stamps" speakers of NZE [New Zealand English]' (Woods 2000a: 115), as in the 'fush and chups' (fish and chips) stereotype of New Zealand speech in many Australian jokes, and an Australian airline's recent advertising campaign, announcing many 'trups' each week to Auckland. Therefore, we were especially eager to know what this vowel's character was in the British dialects brought to New Zealand. KIT centralisation has typically been thought to be recent; it is cited as an 'embryonic variant' by Gordon and Trudgill (1999), meaning a few early tokens – but only a few – have been found in our data.

4.1 British historical antecedents of the KIT vowel

There is some evidence to suggest that the /ɪ/ vowel of the KIT lexical set, which has shown 'considerable stability since Old English' (Gimson 1962: 98), may nevertheless have had a closer (higher) quality in some forms of nineteenth-century British English than is most current today. Gimson (1962: 97), for example, says, 'a conservative form of RP may be much closer than the general RP /ɪ/ . . . coming nearer to the quality associated with /iː/'. This is true also of many varieties of Cockney. Modern West Midlands dialects also have [i] rather than [ɪ] (Trudgill 1986b: 134). Older speakers in Milton Keynes have the closer variant (Williams and Kerswill 1999: 142). Wells (1982: 363) writes of Birmingham speech that 'phonetically, /ɪ/ is very close, [ɪ̝]'. Wright (1905: 70) notes that in monosyllabic forms, west Somerset and east Devon have [ɪ̝], as in *bid*, *bin*, *bit*, *bitch*, *chin*, *fin*, *skin*, *spin*, *stitch*. This is confirmed in dialect 'spellings' of traditional Devon speech such as 'een' *in*, 'een tu' *into*, 'weel' *will*, 'weend' *wind*, 'eel' *hill*, 'jean' *gin*, 'veesh' *fish* (Downes 1998; Marten 1992). (See also Wright 1905: 71, for dialects with *fish* and *dish* as /fiʃ/ and /diʃ/.) D'Orsey is cited by Ellis (1889: 226) with 'Myder-eel' for *Maida-hill*, confirming the closeness of the KIT vowel in some speech varieties in London in the nineteenth century.[4] As we will show, these close variants of /ɪ/ play a significant role in the history of both Australian and early New Zealand English.[5]

The KIT vowel in Scottish English in particular is significant to our discussion, since a number of scholars have thought that the New Zealand English vowel may owe something to Scottish input (for examples and discussion, see Bauer 1979; Trudgill 1986b: 142). McClure (1994: 65) describes this vowel in the Scottish dialects as being 'somewhat lower than the corresponding vowel in English'. Wells (1982: 128) reports 'very open, [ʌ]-like qualities . . . in some kinds of Scottish speech'. He also says (p. 404) that 'in more popular accents it may be considerably opener and/or more retracted [than in RP] . . . In Glasgow it ranges from [ɪ] to

[4] Ellis (1889: 226) mentions *edeeshon* 'edition' in this context, but believes that it 'seems to be confined to newsboys, and is merely emphasism'.

[5] It could be argued that modern New Zealand English has preserved remnants of the raised KIT vowel, since this is the most frequent allophone before velar nasals (as in 'king').

[ʌ̝], including various intermediate possible qualities'. Indeed, McClure (1994: 65) reports that, after /w/ and /hw/, KIT has merged with /ʊ/, as in /wʊt/ 'wit', and according to Wells (1982: 404) there may even be a total merger of the KIT and STRUT vowels in some Scots varieties.

Wright (1905: 70, 86) reported centralised versions of KIT words not only in various Scottish dialects, but also in some southern dialects (Somerset, Dorset, Devon, Buckinghamshire) in words such as *milk*, *silk*, *brim*, and so on (cf. Ellis 1889: 146–7). Branford (1994: 478) notes that Jane Austen has a cook saying 'I wull, I wull' in one of her works, and he cites seventeenth-century spellings of 'bushup' *bishop*, 'dud' *did*, and 'wuth' *with*. Finally, Lass and Wright (1986: 210–11) cite a number of dialects in England with centralised vowels as manifestations of Middle English /i/ (the KIT vowel).

Since in modern South African English the KIT vowel 'for most respectable speakers . . . is centralized' (Lass 1987: 304, see also Branford 1994: 475), we might wonder if some shared British dialect input has played a role in both New Zealand English and South African English. In contrast, the KIT vowel in modern Australian English tends to be close. Bernard (1970) showed it to be relatively raised, acoustically close to KIT in RP. More recently, Cox (1996) shows that in the thirty years since Bernard made his recordings, KIT was raised further, while DRESS did not change and TRAP fell. Both Bernard and Cox analysed speakers in Sydney.

We can thus expect that the immigrants who came to New Zealand in the nineteenth century may have brought some closer variants of the KIT vowel with them, as well as some more centralised ones.

4.2 Early New Zealand commentaries on the KIT vowel

The centralisation of the KIT vowel in New Zealand is so recent that few comments are found in the written records, and all are rather recent ones.[6] In 1939, Arnold Wall made the following observation about the vowels in unstressed syllables, which appears to reveal some awareness of centralisation at that time:

> One very serious and widespread mispronunciation gives an unstressed short 'i' whether as a syllable or in an independent word, the value of the obscure vowel [ə]. Thus 'Alice', 'Philip', 'Malice' become 'Allus' [æləs] Phillup or Phullup or even Phulp [fɪləp, fʊləp, fʊlp] 'mallus' [mæləs]. 'It' appears as 'ut' [ət] in 'is it' [ɪz ət]. (Wall 1939: 16)

[6] We find considerable commentary on unstressed vowels (see later in this chapter), and some of them could be taken to implicate also some KIT vowel forms, for example: 'Failure to appreciate the value of common vowel sounds . . . (and more recent developments) *ut* for "it", *plasuz* for "places"' (Wellington School Inspectors (*AJHR* E-1B, 1908: 16), and 'This carelessness or indifference on the part of the teacher is mainly responsible for such improprieties as . . . "plasuz" (places) "dishers" (dishes) "ut" for "it," "paintud" for "painted" . . .' (Wellington School Inspectors: *AJHR* E-2, 1914, Appendix C: xii–xiv). We take the 'ut' for *it*, nevertheless, to represent, not the centralisation of a stressed KIT vowel, but rather a reference to *it* in unstressed positions, as in *she saw it many times*.

Table 6.7 *Distribution of* KIT *variants*

	0 [ɪ]	1 [ɪ̟]	2 [ɨ]	3 [ɪ̝]
Token count	5,595	287	27	81

His spelling of 'Phullup' for *Phillip* seems to show that the characteristically centralised New Zealand English KIT vowel was being observed in stressed syllables, as well as in unstressed ones.[7]

Buzo (1994: 9) writes that the New Zealand cricketer Clarrie Grimmett, who played test cricket for Australia from 1925 to 1936, was called 'Grum' by his team-mates 'as an affectionate tribute to his New Zealand birth and accent'. This indicates that the centralization of the KIT vowel was sufficiently advanced by the 1930s to be observed by non-New Zealanders at least.

As noted above, the centralisation of KIT has become stereotypic in Australia as an indicator of New Zealand English (Turner 1994: 295), with Australian English being more associated with raising (e.g. 'Seedney' [siːdni] for *Sydney*; 'keeds' [kiːdz] for *kids*).

4.3 *Results from the Mobile Unit speakers for the* KIT *vowel*

4.3.1 Auditory analysis. Up to 100 KIT tokens per each of the 59 speakers were coded in the quantified auditory analysis, totalling 5,990 tokens. Only vowels carrying lexical stress were considered. Four variants were coded. Their distribution is shown in Table 6.7.

As can be seen in Table 6.7, the overall number of both centralised and raised tokens was extremely low – only around 5% of all tokens displayed centralisation, and less than 2% were raised variants. In addition, the degree of centralisation encountered was considerably less than in modern New Zealand English. Schwa was also included in the original coding scheme, but no schwa tokens were in fact encountered. Nor were any tokens of the Scottish centralized [ɜ] found. We conducted two separate analyses on this data set, one that investigated degree of centralisation (i.e. omitting raised [ɪ̝] tokens from the analysis), and one that investigated raising (comparing [ɪ̝] tokens with all other tokens).

We discuss each in turn, beginning with centralisation. The auditory perceptual analysis (which is carried out on 95 speakers rather than 59) agrees with

[7] Some have related comments about the unstressed vowels in New Zealand English to the centralisation of the KIT vowel (see, for example, Woods 2000b); however, it is not clear that the same phenomenon is involved. In the case of Wall's 'Phillip', it is possible that the environment before /l/ was influential, and it is unfortunate that he offers no observations about possible centralisation of the KIT vowel in other environments. We might suspect Wall's *ut* for *it* reflects another environment, but because in his phrase 'is it' [iz ət], 'is' is not centralised, it is probable that the 'it' here was unstressed. (See the discussion of unstressed vowels later in this chapter.)

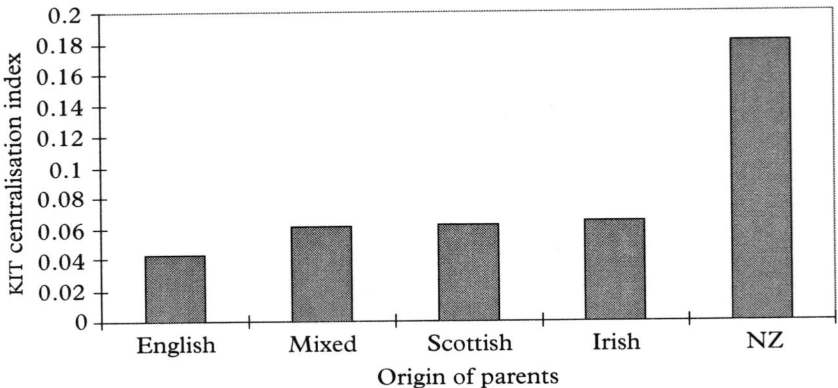

Figure 6.11 KIT centralisation, by origin of parents

the auditory quantitative analysis with respect to the low numbers of centralised tokens. The auditory perceptual analysis found that only 7% of the speakers used any centralised tokens in their speech. We emphasise that, because the numbers of tokens involved is very small, care must be taken in interpreting the results of the statistical analyses.

4.3.2 Centralisation of the KIT *vowel*

4.3.2.1 Speaker analysis. For the analysis of the data set for centralisation, an index score for each speaker was calculated by treating the variant coding for each of their tokens as a numerical value, as with the other variables discussed so far, and finding the speaker's average across all their tokens. An index score of 0 would therefore indicate no centralisation at all (consistent [ɪ]), whereas an index score of 2 would indicate highly consistent centralisation (consistent [ɨ]). Index scores in fact ranged from 0 to 0.45. The speaker with the highest index score was Miss Ada Aitcheson, born in 1878 to New Zealand-born parents, in a predominantly Scottish settlement.

A stepwise linear model returns speaker sex, settlement type, and parents' origin as significant predictors of centralisation – females, speakers with New Zealand-born parents and speakers from Scottish-settled towns show more centralisation. The directionality of these effects can be seen in Figures 6.11–6.13. Note that although the figures show that centralisation in general is increasing over time (Figure 6.12), this in fact is only true in the Scottish settlements (Figure 6.13).

A CART regression tree, which is not presented because of the small number of tokens analysed, splits the data first by settlement type (Scottish, versus other settlements) and then by gender (for non-Scottish settlements, women show more centralisation than men).

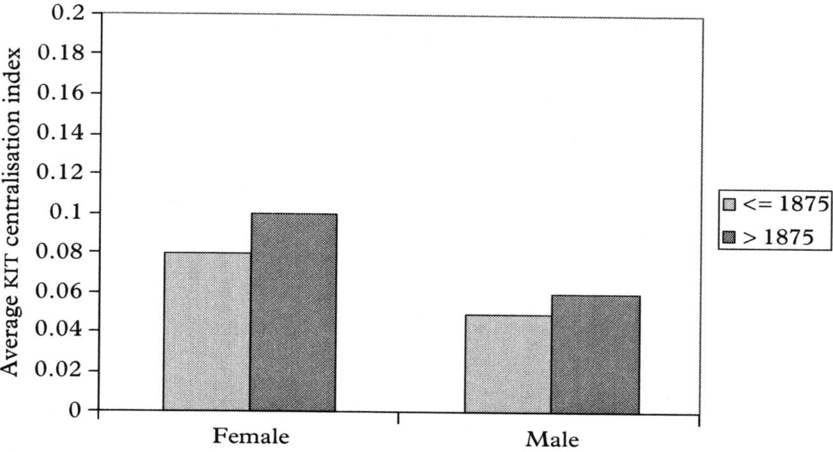

Figure 6.12 KIT centralisation, by gender and birthdate

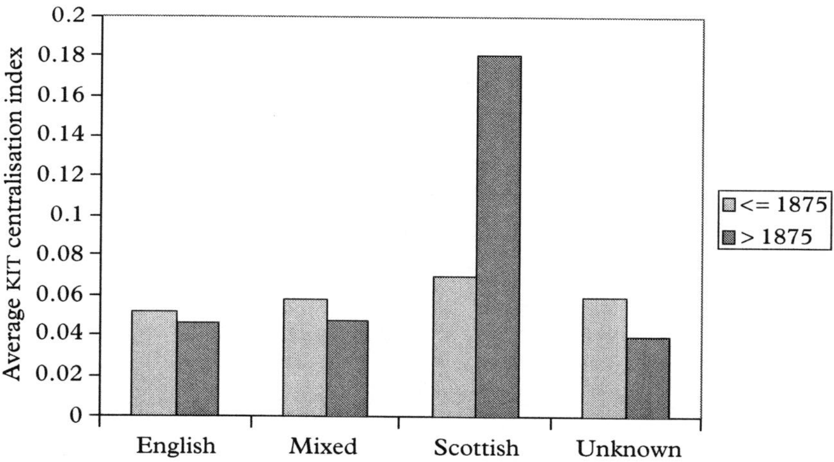

Figure 6.13 KIT centralisation, by settlement type and birthdate

4.3.2.2 Token analysis. The token analysis for centralisation of KIT returns birthdate, gender of speaker, the origins of the parents, settlement type, and the preceding and following environment as significant predictors of variation in the data set. For each of the social factors revealed in the token analysis, the direction of the effects mirror those revealed in the speaker analysis. This confirms that the results shown in 4.3.2.1 are not due to the uneven distribution of specific, favouring environments across different social groups. In addition, age is retained

Table 6.8 *Linguistic constraints on* KIT *centralisation*

	Facilitation of KIT centralisation	
Following environment	Manner	nasals > fricatives > sonorants > plosives > vowels
	Place	labial > coronal > back
Preceding environment	Manner	sonorants > plosives > fricatives > nasals
	Place	labial > coronal > back

as a significant factor in the token analysis, suggesting that we may be seeing a move towards centralisation over time.

The effect of linguistic environment is shown in Table 6.8.

4.3.2.3 Centralisation of KIT: Summary. Both speaker and token analyses reveal significant effects of gender, settlement type, and parents' origin. While there may also be an increase in centralisation with time, this result is less robust than the other social results reported. The statistical analyses indicate that interpretation of KIT centralisation in the data is not straightforward. Although there is more KIT centralisation in Scottish settlements, it is speakers with New Zealand-born rather than Scottish parents who display increased rates of centralisation, indicating that any suggestion of a Scottish origin for the modern New Zealand English centralised KIT must be treated with great caution.

4.3.3 Raising of the KIT *vowel.* As shown earlier in Section 4.1, there is some evidence that KIT used to be more raised in relevant British English varieties than it is now. We therefore expected that some raised tokens would have been brought with the earliest immigrants. The quantified auditory analysis showed only 2% of the tokens to be raised. In the auditory perceptual analysis (which was carried out on 95 rather than 59 speakers) almost one third of the speakers used some raised tokens in their speech, which suggests that the tokens of raised variants are quite widely distributed. This is confirmed in the quantified speaker analysis below.

4.3.3.1 Speaker analysis. As explained in 4.3.1, in the quantified analysis for KIT raising, we compared [ɪ̝] tokens with all other tokens. For the speaker analysis, we assigned raised tokens a value of 1, and other tokens a value of 0, and calculated an index score for each speaker. A score of 0 would indicate no raising, and 1 would indicate consistent raising. Speakers' index scores for KIT raising ranged from 0 to 0.05, that is, the overall degree of raising was very low. No speaker used raised variants for more than 5% of their KIT tokens, and less than 2% of the overall tokens were coded as raised.

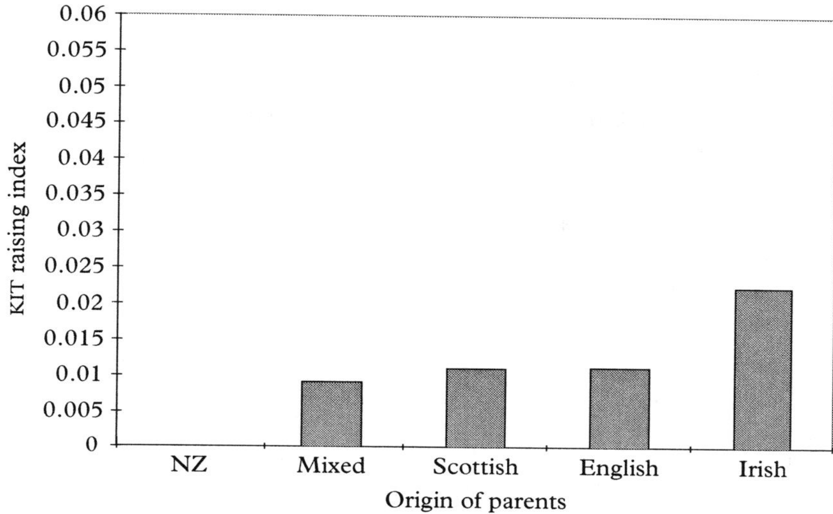

Figure 6.14 KIT raising, by origin of parents

A stepwise linear model retains birthdate, gender, parents' origins, settlement type, and an interaction between gender and settlement type. These results can be seen in Figures 6.14–6.16. The women display more raising than the men, and there are higher degrees of raising in predominantly English settlements. If both parents are Irish, this appears to facilitate raising. Finally, raised variants decrease significantly but slightly over the time period under investigation.

Recall that the reason that we collapse the origins of both parents into a single category (Scottish, Irish, New Zealand, English, or Mixed) relates to statistical convenience. Because mother and father's origin are highly correlated with one another, we cannot include both in the same statistical model. However, using the conjoined 'parents' origin' conceals some variation in the origins of the parents which may in some cases be important. We suspected this was the case with KIT raising, where it seemed possible that an Australian influence on a speaker may facilitate the use of raised tokens. However, because no speakers in our sample have *both parents* from Australia, the conjoined 'parents' origin' categories hide speakers with an Australian parent in the 'mixed' category. We therefore thought it worth checking the individual parents' origins for this particular variable. Two separate logistic models were run, identical to the model described above, except for one, the mother's origin was substituted for the parents' origin, and for the other, the father's origin was substituted.

The model containing the father's origin did not retain father's origin as a significant predictor of variation. However, the model containing the mother's origin did retain it as strongly significant of the patterns of the data, with speakers with Australian mothers using the most raising. The KIT raising index, broken down by origin of mother, is shown in Figure 6.17.

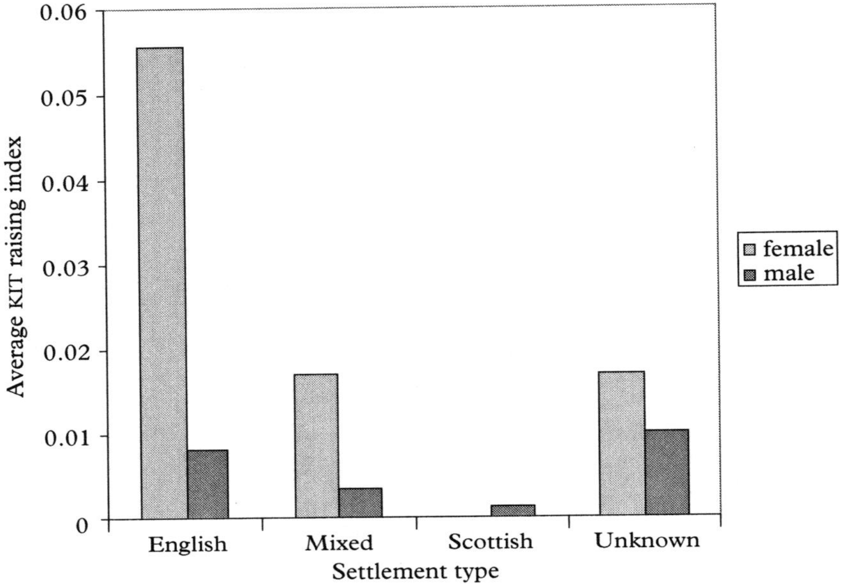

Figure 6.15 KIT raising, by settlement type and gender

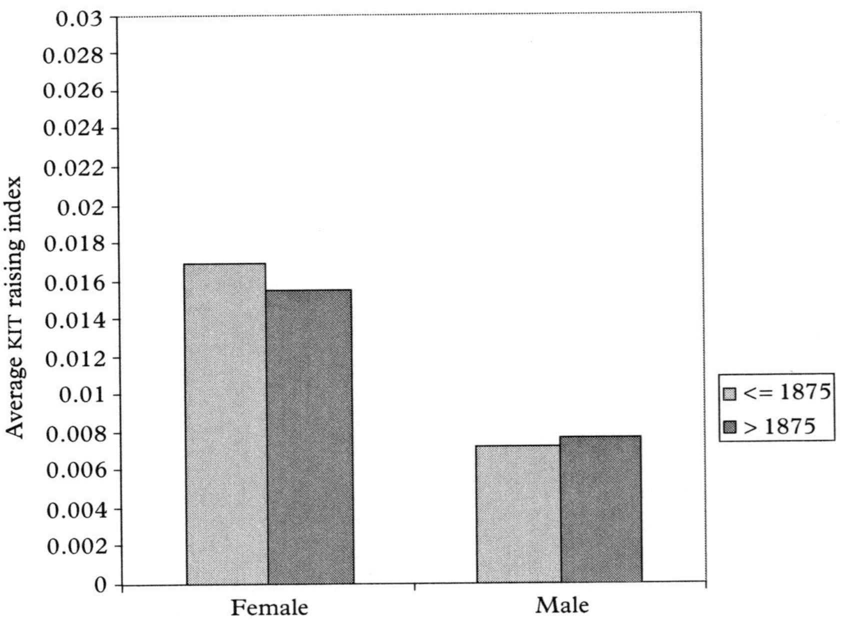

Figure 6.16 KIT raising, by gender and birthdate

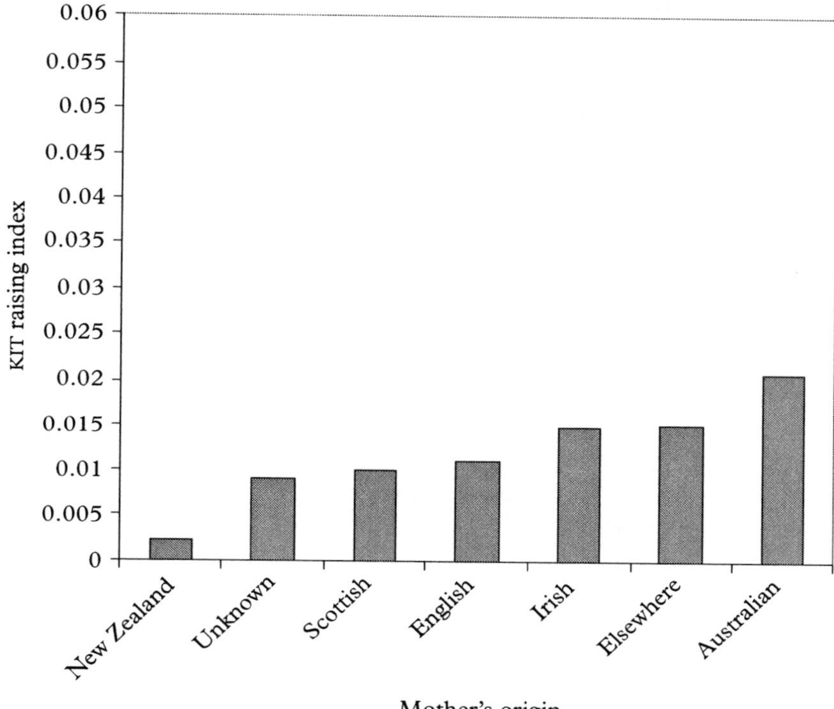

Figure 6.17 KIT raising, by origin of mother

Because CART analysis allows for inclusion of factors that are correlated with one another, both mother and father's origins were included in the CART model. This analysis retained speaker gender as the most predictive factor for KIT raising, and then, for both men and women, identified mother's birthplace as a predictive factor, with Australian mothers being in the most raised set in each case. The resulting tree is shown in Figure 6.18.

4.3.3.2 Token analysis. The token analysis for raising of KIT retains settlement type, parents' origin, birthdate, and the following and preceding environments as significant predictors in the data set. The lack of a gender effect here indicates that the significant gender effect in the speaker analysis may not be so robust as the other social effects reported. The linguistic effects are shown in Table 6.9.

4.3.3.3 Raising of KIT: summary. There are robust effects of settlement type, parents' origin, and birthdate upon KIT-raising. Raised variants are decreasing over time; they are most prevalent in English settlements, among speakers with Australian and/or Irish parents. The speaker analysis also revealed an effect

Table 6.9 *Linguistic constraints on* KIT *raising*

	Facilitation of KIT raising	
Following environment	Manner	fricatives > plosives > sonorants > nasals
	Place	back > coronal > labial
Preceding environment	Manner	plosives > nasals > fricatives > vowels > sonorants
	Place	back > coronal > labial

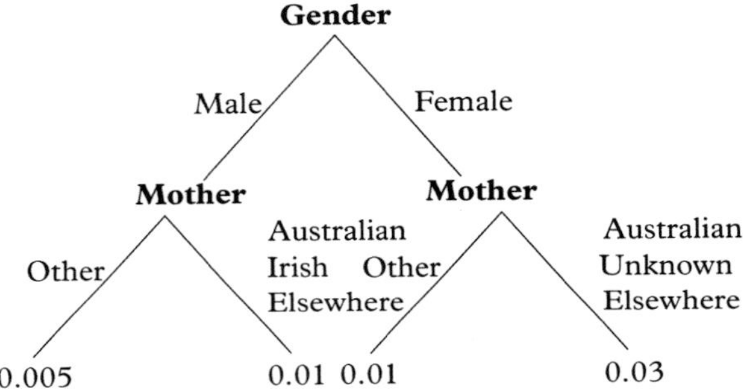

Figure 6.18 CART regression tree predicting individual's index scores for raising of KIT

of gender, with females displaying a greater proportion of raised variants than males.

4.3.4 Overall summary for KIT. The number of raised and centralised tokens for KIT is small. In spite of the small number, there are trends that are statistically significant, and they give indications of what was happening for the early New Zealand English speakers. KIT is more likely to be centralised by women, by those who live in Scottish-type settlements, and by those whose parents are New Zealanders. Although Scottish settlements facilitated centralisation, Scottish parents did not necessarily facilitate it. On the other hand, KIT is more likely to be raised by women, by those in English settlements, and by those with Australian and/or Irish parents. It seems likely that Australian and New Zealand English were formerly more similar in their realisations of KIT. Over the twentieth century, especially the second half, Australia raised KIT further (see Cox 1996) and New Zealand centralised it (see Bell 1997a; Maclagan et al. 1999) so that the two varieties are now clearly different for this vowel.

The acoustic analysis (see Figure 6.5 in 2.3.2) does not show KIT with a markedly raised quality. For the men, KIT is still slightly more fronted than

DRESS, but for the women KIT is already slightly more central than DRESS. The acoustic analysis thus supports the auditory analyses in indicating that any centralisation of KIT is small, and that the women show more centralisation than do the men.

5 The vowel of the START (or START/BATH/PALM) lexical set

Modern New Zealand English, especially in its broader varieties, is characterised by very front realisations of the START vowel (generally in the area of [a] to [ɐ̟̝]). In New Zealand, as in south-eastern England, this vowel occurs in the lexical sets of START (in words such as *star*, *sharp*, *farm*, *party*, *market*, etc.), BATH (in such words as *path*, *brass*, *shaft*, *fast*, *basket*, *laugh*, *calf*, etc.), including the *dance* subset (see below, in words such as *chance*, *grant*, *aunt*, *branch*, etc.), and PALM (in words such as *calm*, *ma*, *pa*, *father*, *spa*, *raj*, *Brahms*, etc.).

5.1 British historical antecedents of the START/BATH/PALM vowel

This vowel /a/ is a relatively new addition to the phoneme inventory of the English dialects involved, and many other varieties do not have it. These include many of the varieties of Scotland and the south-west of England where, for example, *lager* and *lagger* are homophonous (see Hughes and Trudgill 1995).

5.1.1 The TRAP-BATH split. This new /a/ vowel came into existence phonemically as a result of the two lengthenings of the TRAP vowel, which Wells (1982: 201) calls *Pre-R Lengthening* (which also affected words of the PALM class, p. 206) and *Pre-Fricative Lengthening* (p. 203). These changes led ultimately to the *TRAP-BATH Split* (p. 232). Also involved in this phonologisation was *R-Dropping* (p. 218, see below). Pre-R Lengthening was the earlier of the two lengthenings, and produced a lengthened version of the seventeenth-century TRAP vowel, namely [aː], while Pre-Fricative Lengthening produced a lengthened version of the eighteenth-century TRAP vowel, namely [æː], giving START and PALM with [aː] and BATH with [æː]. At some time subsequent to 1750, the BATH set merged with START and PALM to [aː], but not in all dialects. Accents in the north of England did not undergo Pre-Fricative Lengthening and thus have /aː/ only in the sets of START and PALM.

The back quality [ɑː] of RP and certain regional dialects is a more recent development resulting from *START-Backing*, which Wells (1982: 234) dates to the early 1800s. MacMahon (1998: 456) argues that this backing started amongst 'the lower sections of society' and a fully back vowel had become socially acceptable by the late 1860s. As Wells (1982: 234) says, 'many English provincial accents retain a front [aː]'. As seen in Map 4 (in Appendix 3), Wells could perhaps have said 'most'. The map shows that the areas of England where back [ɑː] occurs in the regional dialects, as seen in the SED materials, are located around London and Birmingham.

5.1.2 The BATH *vowel.* The BATH lexical set (see Wells 1982: 133–7) has a number of different subsets and complications. The bulk of the words in this set result from the later Pre-Fricative Lengthening of the TRAP vowel just mentioned, resulting in /aː/ before the front voiceless fricatives /f, θ, s/, as in *laugh*, *path*, *grass*. This change did not take place in the north of England, in the south-west of England, nor in Scottish varieties (which lack the /aː/ vowel altogether) (see Anderson 1987: 12, 16–17 for a slightly different distribution). Moreover, a number of words, particularly polysyllabic ones such as *classic*, *passage*, did not undergo this change even in the south. On the other hand, the word *master* often has /aː/ in the north, particularly in the north-east; Wells (1982: 354) explains this in terms of the association of this word with formal education, as in *schoolmaster*. South Wales varieties have /aː/ in *laugh* but /æ/ in *path*, *grass*, *nasty* (Thomas 1994: 116). The SED materials also show a corridor-like area of variability in central England in which isoglosses for individual BATH words do not coincide.

A subset of the BATH class of words, which we can call the *dance*-class (Wells 1982: 135), results from the lengthening of TRAP before certain clusters of nasals followed by obstruents, as in *sample*, *demand*, *plant*, *dance*, *branch*. There are, however, many exceptions, such as *ample*, *grand*, *ant*, *romance*. We suggest that this resulted from a change that took place later than Pre-Fricative Lengthening, suggested by the fact that a number of varieties around the world have Pre-Fricative-Lengthening but not *dance*-Lengthening. Many Australians (see Bradley 1991), for example, and speakers of certain Welsh varieties (see Trudgill and Hannah 2002; Hughes and Trudgill 1995) have a split system in which /æ/ occurs in words of the *dance* class, such as *sample*, which involve a nasal, but /aː/ occurs in words such as *laugh*, which involve voiceless fricatives. Wells (1982: 233) points out that Leeward Islanders in the Caribbean also have this split system, while other West Indians do not. Wells speculates that the split system that we find in Wales, Australia, and the Leeward Islands – all, in a sense, colonial varieties – but not elsewhere, 'may well be because in eighteenth-century south-east England these *dance*-type words were still fluctuating between a short and long vowel; or indeed they may still generally have had a short vowel, and have gone over to the long vowel only later'. This is true of New Zealand English, as we see below. The *dance* set had /æ/ in the speech of many Mobile Unit speakers, but this has now gone almost completely to /a/.

There is support for this from MacMahon (1998: 436–8), who dates Pre-Fricative Lengthening to 'a period of about fifty years' in which a gradual shift in favour of /aː/ took place. He cites Ward (1952: 95–7) as concluding that the lengthened vowels had become the norm by 1784. In the pre-nasal environments, however, words with <ant> 'retain /æ/ beyond the turn of the eighteenth century', although lengthening in words such as *command* was earlier. Ellis (1889) shows /æ/ in *chance* in three East Anglian localities, Ely, North Walsham and Great Yarmouth, which today have /aː/.[8]

Though most of modern New Zealand has the [aː] pronunciation of these *dance* words, it is still somewhat variable for some older speakers, and certainly [æ] was much more common earlier, as confirmed in the commentaries from written records.

5.2 *Early New Zealand commentaries on the* START, BATH, *and* dance *vowels*

Some of the written comments clearly refer to the BATH and *dance* vowels and others to START words in general. The earliest comments we have refer to the vowels of the BATH and *dance* words and these are considered first.

5.2.1 Comments on the BATH *and* dance *vowels.* McBurney in 1887 gave several variant pronunciations of *dance*: 'dens' (for few girls in Auckland, some people in Dunedin), 'dans' (general for girls in Auckland, for few people in Wellington, for many in Napier, and general in Nelson and Christchurch), and 'dæns' (general for boys in Auckland, some people in Wellington and Napier, and many in Dunedin) (Ellis 1889: 243). In a letter printed in *The Triad* (1 December 1909: 7) we read of reactions to the vowels of the BATH lexical set:

> Sir,–many people, especially those who boast a college education, give such words as grass, brass, castings, class, master, aspect, the absurd pronunciation of grarse, brarse, carstings, clarse, marster, arspect. Why is this thus? Can some of our educators, including Mr Hogben, explain? What is the use of sending our boys to college if they are not taught to pronounce their own language correctly? Pitman's Phonographic Dictionary shows that all the above-mentioned words are written in shorthand with the 'short a' not with the 'ah' sign.

Here we see the stigma attached to the long vowel in the BATH set (represented by the <ar> spellings) in early 1900, and such comments confirm that the vowel of BATH became lengthened before that of *dance*.

At a later time, Wall (1936: 29) wrote his impressions of the *dance* vowel (though without comment on his impressions of pronunciations of the BATH set):

> 'Chance', 'dance' etc. the two pronunciations of these words, one with the long a as in 'father', the other short as in 'hat' are equally good. The short is the traditional sound. The long sound was not known as a standard sound,

[8] In Irish English, the eastern dialects (the most conservative, stemming from before 1600) have a short /æ/, for example, *bath* is [bæt]. Other varieties of Irish English have a long [æː] in such words, but the lengthening is not adopted from English English, but is rather a general lengthening of low vowels that is also found in Irish (Gaelic) (Ray Hickey, personal communication 2000).

> in the eighteenth century . . . I personally prefer the long sound, because I am more accustomed to it; indeed I have rarely heard the short sound in England, though in this country it is, I think, more usual than the long.

J. A. W. Bennett (1943: 82) reported of both the BATH and *dance* vowels:

> In many other cases in which Standard (Southern) British English has [ɑː], New Zealand often has the short [æ], as in *dance*, *path* etc.; and this value is common in final syllables of such words as *telegraph*, *contrast*. Fluctuations in the pronunciation of this vowel seem to follow no precise pattern.

From the *Truth* newspaper (10 October 1909) we have the very telling early commentary:

> The proper authorities upon the pronunciation of a language are those who in the chief centre of population in its country of origin speak that language: and therefore, the people of New Zealand would do well to continue to pronounce grass, brass, castings, class, master as if they were written grahss, brahss, cahstings, clahss and mahster. The fault to be avoided is a prolongation and accentuation of the 'ah' sound. If this fault be avoided there is nothing objectionable in the 'ah' sound of 'a' and dance pronounced 'dahnce' is as good English as dance pronounced with the so-called 'short a'. May the Lord preserve the English language from prigs and pedants, and from the pushing, profit pouching publishers of pamphlets pertaining to alleged 'phonography'.

These comments show that both /æ/ and /a/ were common in New Zealand for BATH and *dance* class words during the first half of the twentieth century. The complaint about the 'prolongation and accentuation of the "ah" sound' may refer to the fronting of the START vowel.

5.2.2 Comments on the START vowel. There are fewer written comments about the front quality of the START vowel in New Zealand English, although this is mentioned as a 'fault' in guides to speech training and pronunciation in the early twentieth century (Stewart 1925; McLeod 1940) and in some discussions is compared to the bleating of a sheep.

> In a recent broadcast lesson by Miss D. Baster of the Christchurch Normal School, it was illuminating to hear the young voices attempting such exercises as 'Arthur has parked his large car in Armagh St.' In the course of correcting the vowel the gentle criticism was made that it sounded too much like the sound of the lamb . . . In looking around for someone to blame, one is almost tempted to the theory that the twenty-eight and a half million sheep up and down the land are responsible for an onomatopoeic quota. (A. N. Fitzgerald, *Education Gazette* 1 August 1934: 123 (quoted in Gordon and Deverson 1998: 36))

The fronted sound is explicitly criticised in the following quotation from a Department of Education Special Report on speech training:

> **a (path)** This is the long vowel sound in palm, far, path, clerk, heart, half. **Fault.**– Instead of this full vowel sound, there is sometimes substituted a kind of lengthened or double short ă as in (*tap*), resembling the 'baa' of a sheep. This sound corruption gives us *caar* for *car*, *haaf* for *half*. The remedy is to open the mouth vertically, not laterally, dropping the lower jaw sufficiently (New Zealand Department of Education 1925: 12)

A similar comment can be seen in *The Triad* (10 August 1910: 40) quoting Mr. E. W. Andrews of Napier Boys' High School: 'The broad "a" of father and the narrow "a" of fat appear to cause great difficulty, and are advanced in the mouth almost to the sound of "e" in pen, so that "last" becomes "least", "remark" "reme-rk", "camp" "kemp" and "standard" "standerd"'. The written representation of 'remark' as *reme-rk* suggests the more fronted [aː] of modern New Zealand English. Wall (1939: 17) wrote:

> *Long a*: 'Car,' 'farm' 'rather.' This is pronounced as [ǣ] approximating to long open 'e' [ɛ]. It is not a standard sound and there is no convenient way to represent it in ordinary spelling. It approximates to the [ɛ] in 'there' and 'fair' [ɛə(r)]. McBurney noticed it particularly in Auckland in 1887. 'A strange "a" was to be heard in Auckland. The boys calling the *Evening Star* shouted out sta. . . . . , perhaps [stææææ]. It had a strange effect.' The sound is now almost universal.

Finally, J. A. W. Bennett (1943: 82) reported:

> The treatment of Standard English [ɑː], as *in art*, *hard*, *large*, *master*, *task*, *Varsity*. In all such words, the vowel is given a much flatter sound than in Standard British English; it closely resembles the vowel found in the same positions in some New England speech, and can best be transcribed as [aː]. What Gradgent says of New England applies to New Zealand: '. . . Our grass really lies between the *grahs* of a British lawn and the *grass* of the boundless prairies.' Words in which the vowel is followed in the spelling by *r* and a consonant are particularly liable to receive this pronunciation (*r* in such words is generally silent, as in Southern England, except where the Scottish influence is felt).

5.3 Results from the Mobile Unit speakers for the START *vowel*

The acoustic analysis (see Figure 6.5 in Section 2.3.2) does not show any difference for START between men and women. The start vowel for the five women analysed is not significantly more front than that of the five men. The auditory analysis presents a different picture. A total of 2,273 tokens of START were coded for the quantified auditory analysis of 59 speakers. In the distribution of variants,

Table 6.10 *Distribution of* START *variants*

Variant	0 [ɑː]	1 [ʌː]	2 [a̟ː]
Token count	13 (1%)	1,185 (52%)	1,075 (47%)

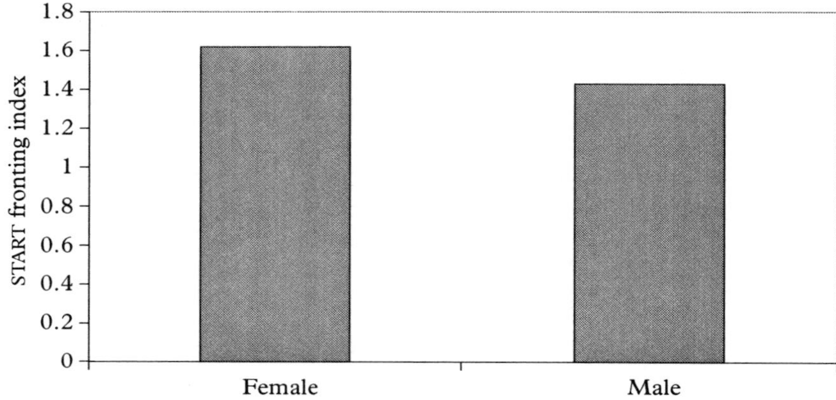

Figure 6.19 START fronting, by gender

as shown in Table 6.10, it is noticeable that there were very few examples of the back vowel [ɑː], which confirms that the earliest immigrants to New Zealand brought a relatively front START vowel with them from Britain.

5.3.1 Speaker analysis. Using the variant codes in Table 6.10 as numeric values, each speaker was assigned an index score, indicating an individual's average degree of fronting, where 0 indicates no fronting and 2 indicates consistent use of [ɑː]. The speakers' scores ranged from 1.01 to 2.

A stepwise linear model retains gender, settlement type, and birthdate as significant predictors of the data. The female speakers display higher fronting indices than male speakers (Figure 6.19); speakers born later produce more front variants (Figure 6.21); and the Unknown settlements display most fronting, with Scottish settlements displaying least fronting (Figure 6.20).

Figure 6.20 shows the averaged indices by settlement type. Note that the ordering of the coefficients returned by the linear model actually shows a slightly different ordering than Figure 6.20: Unknown > English > Mixed > Scottish. That is, once unevenness in the distribution of gender and birthdate across settlement types is taken into account, English settlements show a greater likelihood of fronting than Mixed settlements.

The effect of age can be seen in Figure 6.21, which shows speakers divided into two discrete age categories. As shown in Figure 6.22, the origin of the parents

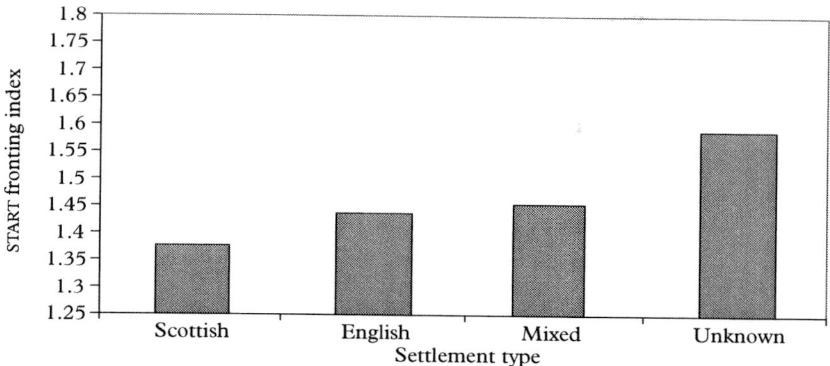

Figure 6.20 START fronting, by settlement type

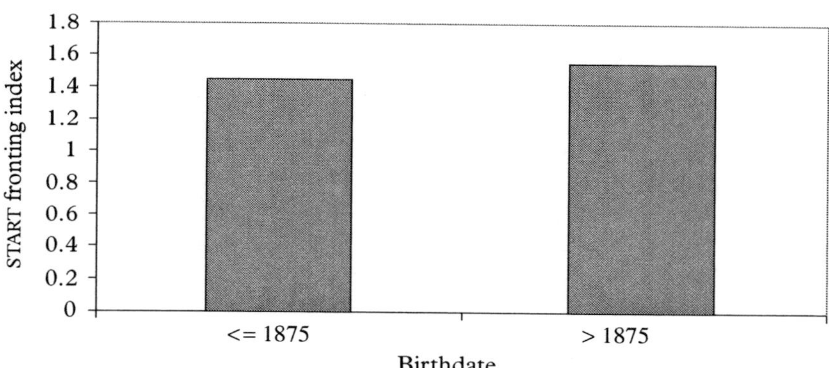

Figure 6.21 START fronting, by birthdate

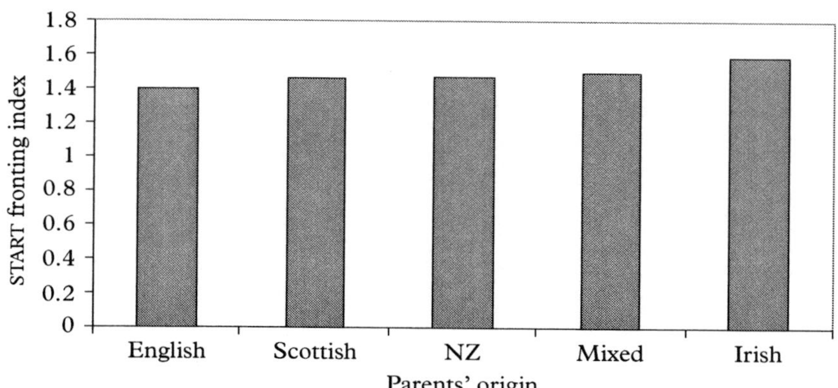

Figure 6.22 START fronting, by origin of parents

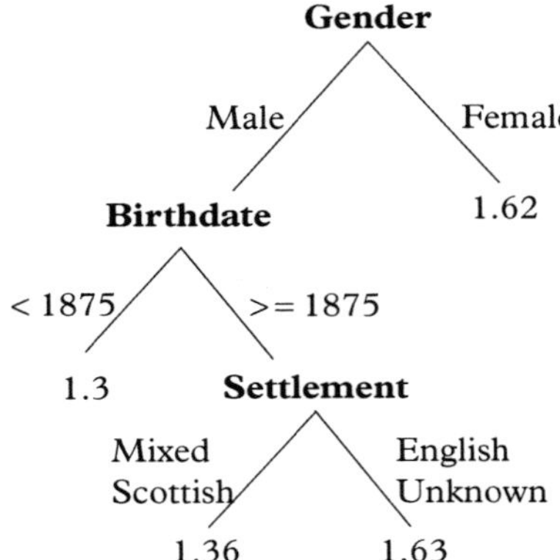

Figure 6.23 CART regression tree predicting individuals' index scores for START fronting

has no effect whatsoever on START fronting in the speaker analysis (but see the token analysis below). Put differently, Mobile Unit subjects in general reveal a fair degree of START fronting across the board, regardless of the locations from which their parents came.

The results of the linear model are also returned by CART analysis, which also selects gender, birthdate and settlement types as the predictive variables, but orders the settlement types slightly differently from the linear model. The resulting tree is shown as Figure 6.23.

5.3.2 Token analysis. The token analysis contrasts START tokens coded as [ɑː] and [ʌː] with the front variant [a̟ː]. A logistic regression analysis was fit, which retained settlement type, gender, birthdate, parents' origins, and the manner of articulation of a following consonant. Settlement type, gender, and birthdate all follow the patterns seen in the speaker analysis. In terms of parents' origins, the logistic model contrasts with the speaker analysis and returns a significant effect, with speakers of English descent less likely to show fronting of START.

The manner of articulation of a following phoneme has a very strong effect. Ordered in terms of decreasing facilitation of fronting, the environments are as follows:

pause > plosive > fricative > approximant > nasal > vowel

In general, the less sonorant the following environment is, the more likely START is to be fronted. Note that this is the only vocalic variable studied where the preceding environment has no effect, and the full conditioning effect is carried by a single phonological variable – manner of articulation of the following segment.

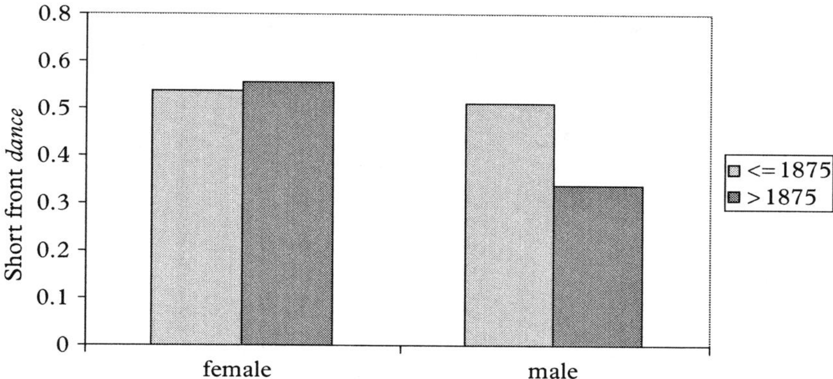

Figure 6.24 Proportion of short front *dance* variants, by age and gender

5.3.3 Summary. The quantitative analysis thus shows that the parents of the Mobile Unit speakers came to New Zealand with relatively front variants of START, and that productions of START fronted still more in New Zealand English over the time period analysed.

5.4 Results from the Mobile Unit speakers for dance

In this section we consider words involved in the *dance* class, which is a subset of the BATH lexical set. We consider whether they are produced with a long open START vowel, or with the short front TRAP vowel.

In our data set there are just 261 tokens of words belonging to the *dance* set, and of these 49% are realised with a short front vowel. Because there are so few tokens, it was not possible to conduct a speaker analysis of the data (as we only have a few tokens from each speaker); therefore we are limited to an analysis of the tokens. The multiple regression model returns preceding and following place of articulation, gender, birthdate, and parents' origins as significant predictors of the patterns in the data set.[9]

The effects of age and gender can be seen in Figure 6.24. The females use a higher proportion of short front *dance* variants than the males. And, while this variable remains fairly constant for the female speakers, the number of tokens with short front variants produced by male speakers decreases significantly over time. As can be seen in Figure 6.25, the proportion of short front variants varies considerably with the origin of the parents. Individuals with New Zealand parents or parents of mixed descent are less likely to produce short front variants in *dance*

[9] While considering the social results here, it is important to keep in mind that social results returned by a token-based analysis are susceptible to the undue influence of a small number of extreme speakers. These results should therefore be interpreted with appropriate caution.

Table 6.11 *Linguistic constraints on short front* dance *variants*

Preceding place of articulation	coronal > front > back
Place of articulation of following nasal	coronal > front

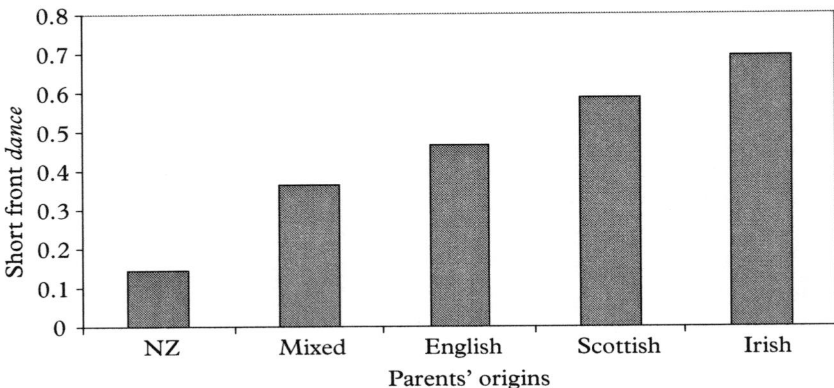

Figure 6.25 Proportion of short front *dance* variants, by origin of parents

words. Finally, Table 6.11 displays the effects of environment on *dance* words, with both preceding and following coronal consonants facilitating the production of short front vowels.

5.5 *Results from the Mobile Unit speakers for the* BATH *vowel*

Here we consider the production of words in the BATH lexical set apart from the *dance* class, considering whether they are produced with a short front TRAP vowel, or a long open START vowel. We analysed 975 tokens of BATH words, of which just 6.6% were produced with a short front vowel. The short front variant of BATH was therefore clearly ahead of that of *dance* in terms of its disappearance from New Zealand English. As with *dance*, we limited ourselves to a token analysis, due to the low number of tokens per speaker. A multiple regression shows that parents' origins, settlement type, gender, and the manner of the preceding consonant are significant predictors of the patterns in the data.

Figure 6.26 shows the distribution by gender, with males using a higher proportion of short front variants than females.

The effect of settlement type is shown in Figure 6.27. It is the Scottish settlements and the Unknown settlements (for which we have no census data but

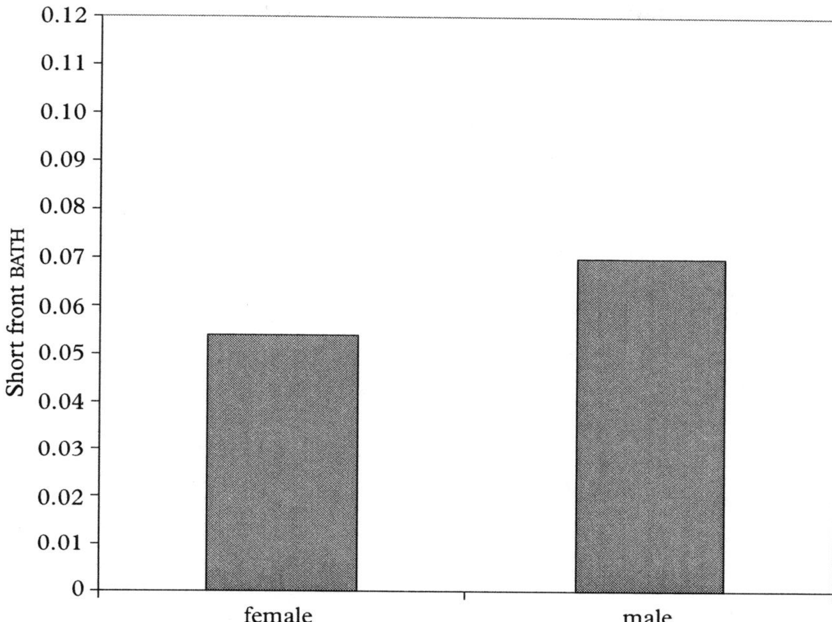

Figure 6.26 Proportion of short front BATH variants, by gender

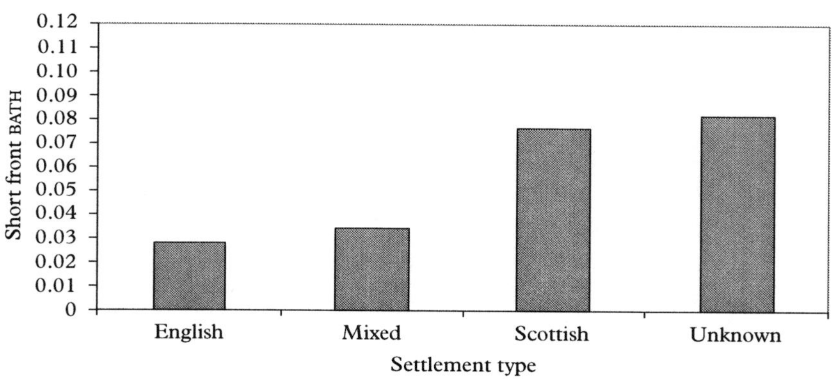

Figure 6.27 Proportion of short front BATH variants, by settlement type

which are likely to be small and rural) in which short front variants most often appear. The use of short front BATH variants in mixed settlements and predominantly English settlements is extremely small. Similarly, in Figure 6.28, we see the importance of the origins of the parents, where individuals with Scottish parents show the greatest incidence of short front variants.

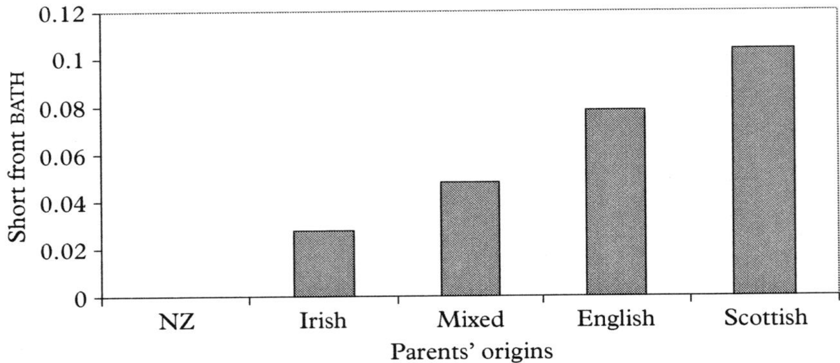

Figure 6.28 Proportion of short front BATH variants by origin of parents

The linguistic effects show that the manner of a preceding phoneme has a significant effect, as shown in decreasing order:

pause > nasal > vowel > plosive > approximant > fricative

The greatest number of short front variants occur after pauses and nasals, the fewest occur after approximants and fricatives.

Finally, we note that there is no effect of age on the realisation of BATH vowels. While the overall incidence of short front variants is low, it remains stable over the time period we have analysed.

6 The vowel of the STRUT lexical set

Modern New Zealand English typically has more open and relatively front realisations of the STRUT vowel than most British and American varieties do. Its range of variants is, approximately, [ɐ, ɐ̝, a̠], and it is differentiated from START chiefly by length.

6.1 British historical antecedents of the STRUT vowel

The STRUT vowel is relatively recent in origin in those dialects of English that have it, having split from the former /ʊ/ of the FOOT lexical set. What is known as the *FOOT–STRUT Split* (Wells 1982: 196) probably started in the south-east of England (Ihalainen 1994: 261), about the end of the sixteenth century (Brook 1958: 90; Strang 1970: 112). According to Strang (ibid.), this is 'one of the most unaccountable things that has happened in the history of English'. In her account, in around 1570 the vowel /ʊ/ began to lose its lip-rounding so that a quality more like back unrounded [ɤ] began to be more usual. This did not happen in certain labial environments, so that words like *put*, *butcher*, *pull* retained their original

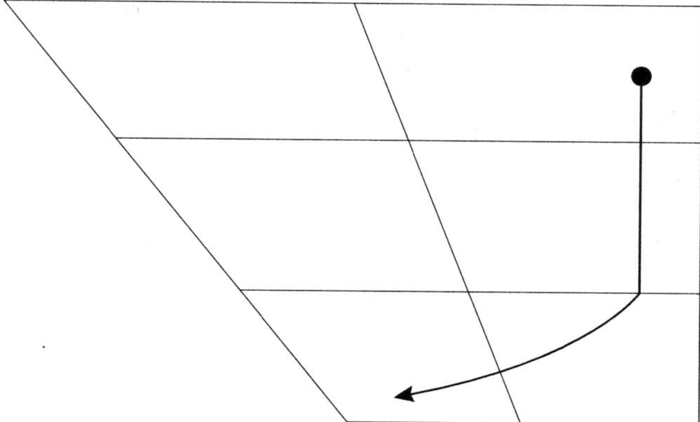

Figure 6.29 Historical movement of STRUT

/ʊ/ pronunciation. This eventually led to a phonemic split, reinforced by the shortening of /uː/ to /ʊ/ in a number of words such as *look*, giving rise to minimal pairs such as *look* and *luck*. According to Ihalainen (1994: 261) 'unrounded *u* was regarded as vulgar until the mid 17th century, when Simon Daines [(1640)], a Suffolk schoolmaster, described it as the accepted pronunciation'.

The relatively recent STRUT vowel innovation did not take place in local varieties in northern England. After the change of /ʊ/ to [ɤ] in south-east England in the late 1500s, it subsequently lowered to [ʌ]. Gimson (1962: 103) postulates that this took place in the eighteenth century. A vowel a little front of [ʌ] seems to have been the RP norm at the beginning of the twentieth century, and during the course of the century, it was then fronted to [ɐ], a somewhat lowered open-mid central vowel that is its pronunciation in RP today (see Roach 1983: 16), although in practice scholars continue to write /ʌ/ to symbolise this vowel phonemically. In the English of London and other parts of the south-east, however, the fronting progressed further, giving 'an open front vowel very close to *C* [a] = [ä]' (Gimson 1962: 103). The trajectory followed by this vowel over the last 400 years is shown in Figure 6.29. This diachronic pattern is reflected in a synchronic geographical distribution: the further from the south-east of England, the further back the vowel quality that is encountered. (Cf. Anderson 1987: 23, 31, 34–5, 37; cf. Lass 1990: 252.)

Though FOOT and STRUT have distinct vowels both in the south of England and in Scotland, the situation is rather different in the two cases. In Scots, the mediaeval /ʊ/ vowel was unrounded and lowered to /ʌ/. (This is also true of the very far north of Northumberland in England; see Map 5 in Appendix 3.) However, there are two major ways in which this process differed from the corresponding sound change in southern England. Firstly, the change in Scotland was much later than in England; according to McClure (1994: 65) it did not happen until the Modern Scots period, which he dates from 1700. Secondly, it involved *all* the words in the relevant lexical set, that is, there was no blocking effect in 'certain labial environments'. Thus, words such as *put*, *butcher*, *pull* have /ʌ/. Words such as *wood*, *blood*, *book*, moreover, have not separated off from the GOOSE set through a process of shortening, so that no phonemic split occurred.[10] These facts lead us to suppose that the changes in England and Scotland were not connected – that is, there was no diffusion from one area to another, which would be unlikely anyway given that the north of England was unaffected.

Map 5 shows the areas of northern and midland England (plus Pembroke in south-west Wales) that have retained the original five short vowel system. The shaded parts on the map in Norfolk, Cambridgeshire, Northamptonshire, Oxfordshire, and Gloucestershire are areas of England for which the SED shows southern pronunciations but which Ellis, seventy years earlier, gave as having the northern system, at least variably. The shaded part on the Scottish borders is the area shown by Ellis as having the Scottish system with /ʌ/ but which later has the northern England five-vowel system in the SED. The larger area indicated in Northumberland and Durham is shown by Ellis as *variably* having /ʌ/, but is not shown as such in the SED. Therefore it can be assumed that in the century between Ellis and SED, the southern system moved slightly to the north in southern England, while the northern system moved to the north to match up more or less with the Scottish–English border (see Trudgill 1999d). (Ellis' map is best consulted in Ihalainen 1994: 236.)

There is no evidence in the British dialectological literature for STRUT-fronting such as we see in modern New Zealand English, but Map 5 also shows the area of the south-east of England for which Kurath and Lowman (1970: 17) show a 'fully unrounded and lowered' STRUT vowel, that is, the most advanced form in their data. Therefore, most immigrants to New Zealand in the nineteenth century, given the numbers from the south-east (see Chapter 3), would have had relatively back versions of the STRUT vowel that were not particularly open (near to [ʌ̝]). This is confirmed in the Mobile Unit speakers' pronunciations.

6.2 *Early New Zealand commentaries on the* STRUT *vowel*

We have found only one relevant historical comment on the STRUT vowel in New Zealand. McBurney (in *The Press*, 5 October 1887) noted its relatively open nature and its similarity to the START vowel: 'The only point that has struck me in New Zealand as peculiar is the short u in "but", "tub", etc. which has a much more open sound than I have been accustomed to, approaching the "a" in "father", but difficult to describe.'

[10] The modern Scottish English usage of /u/ corresponding to English English /ʊ/ in items such as *put*, *pull* – giving an *apparent* FOOT-STRUT split – is thus the result of the redistribution of Scottish English words over Scots vowels as a result of influence from English English. In fact, Scottish English vocalic phonology generally can be seen as basically the result of the vowel system of Scots having been transferred to the lexical sets of English.

6.3 *Results from the Mobile Unit speakers for the* STRUT *vowel*

An auditory quantitative analysis was not carried out for STRUT. We present here the results of the auditory perceptual analysis of 95 Mobile Unit speakers, which found that approximately 40% consistently use a conservative pronunciation for their STRUT vowels, that is, they habitually use back variants that are above open-mid (i.e. [ʌ̝]). A further 15% use some fronted tokens ([ə]) and another 7%, while variable in their pronunciations, use some back realisations. This gives a total of more than 60% of speakers who use back variants of STRUT some or all of the time. Following the progression in the dialectological account above, we find that 20% of Mobile Unit subjects habitually use somewhat fronted variants of STRUT ([ɤ̞ ~ ə]) and nearly 15% habitually use variants that approximate the fronted and lowered modern New Zealand English form ([ɐ]). If we add in the speakers whose usage is variable, we find that nearly 60% (again) of Mobile Unit speakers use some fronted variants of STRUT some or all of the time.

Fronted and lowered STRUT tokens become more common over time. Of the informants born between 1850 and 1869, 35% have some fronting and lowering, while the corresponding figure for those born between 1870 and 1889 is over 60%. Only one of the speakers who habitually use very fronted versions of STRUT similar to the modern New Zealand English form is among the older rural speakers in the corpus. All the other speakers who use the most fronted variants are younger and/or from non-rural backgrounds.

Very few immigrants to New Zealand came from the north of England – the area which did not have the FOOT-STRUT split – and consequently we would not expect many of the Mobile Unit speakers to have the northern vowel system. There is, in fact, only one speaker, Mr Sam Temple whose father came from Lancashire and mother came from Cheshire, who does not distinguish FOOT and STRUT.

The acoustic results for ten speakers (see Figure 6.5, in Section 2.3.2) show that the women's pronunciation of STRUT is not significantly fronter or more open than the men's. For both the men and women, STRUT is significantly closer and significantly more front than START. Thus both men and women have a similarly fronted STRUT vowel. However, even though the women's STRUT vowel is still significantly closer than their START vowel, it has nevertheless proceeded slightly farther than the men's along the lowering process that led to the open STRUT vowel of modern New Zealand English. The two oldest speakers analysed acoustically produce closer variants of STRUT whereas the younger speakers are variable.

7 The vowel of the FOOT lexical set

In modern New Zealand English, FOOT is produced close to [ʊ] by older, more conservative speakers, while there is a tendency for younger speakers to front and somewhat unround FOOT, so that it is close to [ɘ̞]. Before /l/, KIT and FOOT have almost merged, and in a few words (here as elsewhere), even when FOOT does not precede /l/, it is difficult to decide which phoneme is intended (e.g. *good*, *look*).[11]

7.1 British historical antecedents of the FOOT *vowel*

Two historical issues are relevant to the FOOT vowel: the FOOT-STRUT split (discussed in Section 6) and the merger of FOOT and GOOSE. Wells (1982: 132, 400) indicates that Scottish and Ulster English are distinguished from all other varieties because they lack a distinction between FOOT and GOOSE. Because many immigrants to New Zealand came from Scotland and Ulster (see Chapter 3), we would expect some of their descendants to have the FOOT/GOOSE merger. This merger, however, has not survived in modern New Zealand English. Apart from the merger, once the words of the STRUT vowel set are set aside, there is nothing of relevance to report here on the British dialect history of the FOOT vowel.

There are no comments in the New Zealand written records on the pronunciation of FOOT, and comments on GOOSE make no mention of a possible merger with FOOT.

7.2 Results from the Mobile Unit speakers for the FOOT *vowel*

As expected, the auditory perceptual analysis of 95 speakers finds that the great majority distinguish the FOOT and GOOSE vowels and thus have no FOOT/GOOSE merger. However, 17 speakers do have the merger and a few merge the two vowels variably.

Twelve of the seventeen speakers who have the merger had parents who were both born in Scotland, but three speakers had English parents, one had an English and an Australian parent, and one had an Irish father (more precise origin is not known, and we have no details for the speaker's mother, who died four days after the speaker's birth). All the speakers who variably merge the two vowels had parents born in Scotland. However, some Mobile Unit speakers with Scottish parents do not have the merger. If parents do not distinguish between FOOT and GOOSE, we might expect that their children may also merge these vowels, but it is possible that, through association with children from other dialects lacking the merger, children whose parents have the merger may nevertheless

[11] The pronunciation of 'women' as [wʊmən] is very common in modern New Zealand; this appears to be a relatively late innovation, due to the rounding influence of the two adjacent labial consonants on the typically centralised KIT vowel. Though similar pronunciations are found in north Devon, for example, we assume that a British antecedent does not account for this word's recent history in New Zealand.

learn the FOOT/GOOSE contrast. In summary, within the Mobile Unit corpus we find speakers with the FOOT/GOOSE merger whose parents were very unlikely to have this merger, and we have speakers without the FOOT/GOOSE merger, whose parents very likely did have it. No evidence of the merger survives into modern New Zealand English.

The results of the acoustic analysis (see Figure 6.5 in Section 2.3.2) show no significant difference between men and women for FOOT. For all the speakers, FOOT is significantly further back than both START and GOOSE. The difference in F2 frequency between FOOT and GOOSE is significant for both men and women, reflecting the fronting of GOOSE, and this fronting is more advanced in the women than in the men.

8 The vowel of the FLEECE lexical set

Modern New Zealand English FLEECE is often diphthongised. The on-glide is more pronounced in Broad New Zealand English of working-class speakers, where it is [ᵊɪ]. More conservative pronunciations are closer to [iː] or [ɪi], though many General New Zealand English speakers use [ᵊɪ], and even [ᵊɪ].

8.1 British historical antecedents of the FLEECE vowel

We have very little evidence at all for diphthongisation of FLEECE from early dialect studies in England. However, Map 3e (in Appendix 3) shows the area with a slightly diphthongal FLEECE as [ɪi] as opposed to [iː], from Lowman's work in the 1930s. We can assume that this area is where the process must have started. We therefore do not expect that most of the early immigrants to New Zealand would have produced diphthongised versions of FLEECE.

There are no early New Zealand commentaries on the pronunciation of FLEECE, probably because the on-glide developed relatively late, but possibly also because it may not have reached the level of awareness (and it is also difficult to represent with ordinary English spelling).

8.2 Results from the Mobile Unit speakers for the FLEECE vowel

The auditory perceptual analysis of 95 speakers reveals that the majority of the Mobile Unit speakers did not diphthongise FLEECE. Approximately 30% use a slight diphthong some of the time, and a further 10% sometimes used a more pronounced diphthong starting with [ə]. More men than women produce diphthongised versions of FLEECE in general, but an equal number of men and women (four each) produced the more marked diphthongs with [ə].

The acoustic analysis (see Figure 6.5 in 2.3.2) shows the FLEECE vowel in the extreme front close position for all ten Mobile Unit speakers analysed. A comparison of normalised formant values shows that the men appear to have significantly closer and fronter FLEECE vowels than the women, but this is an artifact of the normalisation (see Chapter 5). What this analysis actually reveals is that women have fronted and raised so many of their other vowels, that FLEECE is no longer as isolated from the rest of their vowel system as it is for the men. Although the F1 distances between FLEECE and KIT and between FLEECE and DRESS are not significantly different when men are compared with women, the Euclidean distance between FLEECE and KIT is significantly different for men and women, and the gender contrast for the Euclidean distance between FLEECE and DRESS just reaches significance also. This provides further evidence that the women of the Mobile Unit corpus raised both KIT and DRESS relative to FLEECE. Women also centralised KIT and fronted DRESS relative to FLEECE.

9 The vowel of the GOOSE lexical set

In modern New Zealand English, GOOSE is a close vowel, central [ʉ] or front of central [ʉ̟]. It may be diphthongised, with the diphthongisation ranging from [ᵊʉ] to [ᵌʉ]. A back variant appears before dark /l/.

9.1 British historical antecedents of the GOOSE vowel

The vowel of GOOSE, as part of Diphthong Shift (see discussion later in Section 12.1), 'shifts from [uː] to [əʊ], though usually with the competing possibility of [ʉː]' (Wells 1982: 257). We should probably consider these two possible types of GOOSE-shift as mentioned by Wells – diphthongisation and centralisation – as separate but not necessarily mutually exclusive processes.

Very many varieties of English have fronted allophones of GOOSE after /j/, as in *new*, and we do not consider these variants to represent Diphthong Shift. While conservative RP has a fully back [uː] in GOOSE (Wells 1982: 281), modern RP has 'a somewhat centralised' variant, 'to the extent that there is no perceptible difference between the allophone used in the environment /j___/ and the phonemic norm' (p. 294). However, this centralisation does not typically occur before /l/ (Hughes and Trudgill 1995). Modern London also has fronted variants, shown by Wells (p. 310) as [ʉː ~ əʉ ~ ʊʉ], but again not before /l/ (p. 315).[12]

Fronted vowels also occur in the modern varieties of southern Lancashire, Devon, Milton Keynes, Reading, and East Anglia (Wells 1982: 347; Trudgill 1986b: 114; Williams and Kerswill 1999: 144), and diphthongal variants occur in Birmingham and northern Yorkshire (Wells 1982: 359). Liverpool has [ɨʊ] (p. 372). In Scottish English and Ulster English, where GOOSE and FOOT are not distinct (see Section 7.1 above), the GOOSE/FOOT vowel also typically has central or front realisations (Wells 1982: 402, also p. 148; see also Hickey 1999: 44).

[12] Trudgill (1986b: 46–9) shows the ongoing progress northwards into East Anglia of this sort of before-/l/-versus-elsewhere allophony.

For Ireland, Wells (p. 425) writes that the phonetic quality of /uː/ is 'generally unremarkable' except that in popular Dublin speech there are 'some strikingly diphthongal variants' such as [ɛʊ], [ĕuː].

The dating of this fronting and/or diphthongisation in London and elsewhere is not entirely clear, but it had certainly started in some areas in the 1800s. Ellis (1889) discussed the fronted GOOSE vowel as being a very well-known feature of the mid-nineteenth-century Norfolk dialect, and likens it to French [y]. For the traditional dialects of the 1930s, Kurath and Lowman (1970: 13) show central vowel qualities for Norfolk, eastern Suffolk, Kent, and Surrey. Cambridgeshire and the rest of Suffolk have [ɪʉ]. For the traditional dialects of the 1950s and 1960s, the SED materials show extreme fronting to [ʏː] in Devon and neighbouring areas of Cornwall and Somerset, as well as in the south Lancashire/north Cheshire region; and there is centralisation to [ʉː] in Leicestershire, as well as in Norfolk. It is noticeable that in these four regions in the SED materials, unlike in London and modern RP, the front and central variants also occur before /l/. Suffolk and Cambridgeshire are given as having diphthongal [ɪʉ] or [iu], but not before /l/, where [uː] occurs. Wright (1905: 131–2) gave fronted variants (with and without diphthongisation) for a wide range of dialects, both north and south. For example, he listed [ü] for *school* in eastern Kent, for *do* in east Suffolk, east Kent, west Somerset, Devon, and others (pp. 133–4). (The traditional dialects of the far north of England have a totally different vowel in this lexical set, of the type [iə] (see Wells 1982: 359, 360).)

Based on these data, we could expect that at least some speakers with fronted and/or diphthongised pronunciations of the GOOSE vowel would have arrived in New Zealand among the first immigrants.

9.2 *Early New Zealand commentaries on the GOOSE vowel*

Written comments from New Zealand appear to mention centralisation first, as in the earliest we have found, one from Robert Lee, a Wellington school inspector, in 1889: '. . . a tendency to pronounce "oo" as "ew". Thus "spoon" is pronounced "spewn"' (*AJHR* E-1B, 1889: 14). The next written comment, also by a Wellington school inspector, appears to refer to both possibilities of diphthongisation and fronting: 'toe' or 'tew' for 'two' (*AJHR* E-1B, 1900: 14).

The following comments focus on diphthongisation. Though the spellings may seem to indicate a diphthong like [iʉ], some could also be attempts at indicating a central pronunciation for /u/:

> 'skee-ool' for 'school' (*The Triad*, 10 December 1912: 12)
>
> There is a strong tendency here, as in Cockney, to pronounce the long 'u' [ʊu], especially after labial consonants, as 'iu' [iʊu], 'bee-oots' [*boots*], 'mee-oon' [*moon*]. A visitor to Auckland in 1877 noticed this but observed it as less prevalent than in Australia. (Wall 1938: 17)

> My own pet aversion is the inability of announcers to pronounce the 'oo' sound in 'two' . . . Why must it always be 'ee-oo?' (*The Listener*, 4 August 1944: 5)

> I have heard my small son, when about five, pronounce *too* as [tou]. (Turner 1966: 100)

It is not readily possible to determine whether some of these comments refer to the type of [ɪʉ ~ iu] diphthong or to some other form of diphthong.

9.3 Results from the Mobile Unit speakers for the GOOSE *vowel*

Both the trend towards fronting and the trend towards diphthongisation are seen in the Mobile Unit speakers. The auditory perceptual analysis shows that approximately 40% of the 95 speakers consistently use back variants of GOOSE. About a quarter have variants just front of back, almost 10% use variants as central as modern New Zealand English, and almost 15% use variants that are both fronted and diphthongised. The remaining 10% of the speakers use the FOOT vowel for words from both the GOOSE and FOOT lexical sets, and therefore are not relevant in this analysis. Within the Mobile Unit corpus, therefore, nearly half the speakers have fronted realisations of GOOSE, although less than a quarter produce variants that approximate to the modern New Zealand English pronunciations. At the same time, significantly, almost half use the back variants that have essentially disappeared in modern New Zealand English. We did not make a systematic analysis of tokens of GOOSE before dark /l/, but many speakers who used a fronted variant of GOOSE used the same variant before dark /l/.

The acoustic results (see Figure 6.11 in Section 2.3.2) clearly show the centralisation of GOOSE. For both men and women, GOOSE is significantly farther forward than FOOT. For the women, GOOSE is also significantly farther forward than their START vowel. For the men, it is farther back than START, but not significantly so. The women's realisations of GOOSE are also significantly more fronted than the men's, indicating again that the women are closer to modern New Zealand English than the men are.

10 The vowel of the LOT lexical set

Modern New Zealand English has a raised LOT vowel /ɒ/ (for which the lexical set includes words such as *stop*, *pot*, *sock*, *rob*, *odd*, *cog*, *doll*, *box*, *romp*, *bother*, *honest*, *swan*, *watch*, *knowledge*, etc.) with realisations above [ɔ̈] to [ɔ̞̈]. Today it is always rounded, though this has not always been the case. We also consider here the CLOTH lexical set (*off*, *across*, *cloth*, etc.) which is defined as consisting of those words that use the THOUGHT vowel /ɔ/ in General American English but /ɒ/ in RP (Wells 1982: 136). These words are now usually realised by the LOT vowel in New Zealand English, but some older New Zealand English speakers still use THOUGHT in some CLOTH words.

10.1 British historical antecedents of the LOT *vowel*

Irish English and most varieties of North American English have an unrounded vowel in the lexical set of LOT, whereas English English usually has back and rounded variants [ɒ, ɔ] (Wells 1982: 130). However, we also find 'the recessive unrounded variant [ɑ] in parts of the south of England remote from London' (ibid.), and the vowel 'often appears to be unrounded in the west [of England]' (p. 347); and 'in Norfolk the LOT vowel has an unrounded variant' (p. 339). The SED materials are not very helpful on this point; however, Lowman's data (Kurath and Lowman 1970: 22) coincide with Wells' interpretation. They indicate unrounded vowels in most of the south of England, apart from Suffolk, Essex, Cambridgeshire, Hertfordshire, and Middlesex. This gives the geographical pattern in which the south-east and south-west of England form two areas with unrounded vowels, separated from one another by an intervening area of rounded variants that includes London. This strongly suggests that the [ɑ] area in England was much larger in the mid-nineteenth century than it is now. Many Modern Scottish speakers do not distinguish between LOT and THOUGHT (Wells 1982: 399, 402) and this would probably have been the case in the mid-nineteenth century also. Thus we expect that many of the early immigrants to New Zealand, a great number of whom came from the south-east or south-west of England, would have had unrounded variants for the LOT vowel, and some immigrants from Scotland would not have had a LOT vowel distinct from THOUGHT. This is confirmed in the analysis of the Mobile Unit speakers' pronunciation of this vowel.

There are no commentaries on the pronunciation of LOT in the New Zealand written records.

10.2 Results from the Mobile Unit speakers for the LOT *vowel*

The auditory perceptual analysis shows that 8 of the 95 Mobile Unit speakers analysed do not have a separate LOT phoneme, but have LOT words with the THOUGHT vowel. As would be expected (see Wells 1982: 399), the parents of all but one of these speakers were born in Scotland and none of them makes a distinction between FOOT and GOOSE either. Of the 87 speakers who do have a separate LOT phoneme, approximately 40% consistently use an unrounded variant, [ɑ] or closer (higher), while approximately 30% have a rounded variant, [ɒ] or closer (higher). A further 30% variably use some unrounded variants. Therefore, from the Mobile Unit sample of speakers it looks as though slightly more early New Zealanders used unrounded variants than rounded variants during the nineteenth century.

Acoustic analysis of Mobile Unit speakers (see Figure 6.11 in Section 2.3.2) indicates that the LOT vowel is raised towards the modern New Zealand English position in the women's speech, but not in the men's. There is no significant difference between men and women for F1 height but there is for the Euclidean distance between LOT and START, indicating that both LOT has raised and START fronted for the women. For all speakers, the position of LOT is roughly parallel to TRAP: as TRAP raises ([æ] to [ɛ]), so does LOT ([ɒ] to [ɔ]). Individual speakers may have closer realisations of either LOT or TRAP, but the difference between the height of the two vowels is not significant.

10.3 The CLOTH lexical set

As mentioned above, the vowel in the CLOTH lexical set is realised as LOT in modern New Zealand English (/ɒ/). However in the eighteenth century, Pre-Fricative Lengthening (see discussion of this earlier in Section 5.1.1) in the set of CLOTH led to /ɒ/ becoming /ɒː/ before /f, s, θ/, as in *off*, *cross*, *cloth*, and being pronounced as THOUGHT (/ɔ/) rather than LOT (/ɒ/) (Wells 1982: 203, 204). A complaint in *The Triad* (quoted in Section 11.2, under THOUGHT) about the pronunciation 'rorth' for *wrath* probably represents this THOUGHT pronunciation.

The auditory perceptual analysis shows that nearly half of the Mobile Unit speakers use the THOUGHT vowel in words in the CLOTH set and just over a quarter use LOT. The remaining speakers have no examples of the relevant words or do not make a contrast between LOT and THOUGHT.

11 The Vowel of the THOUGHT Lexical Set

Like modern RP, and many other English English varieties, modern New Zealand English has a single vowel, /ɔː/, in the lexical sets of THOUGHT, NORTH and FORCE, and we will use the key word THOUGHT to refer to this set. This THOUGHT vowel also occurs in some words from the lexical set of CURE in items such as *poor*, *moor*, and for some speakers in items such as *sure*, *tour*, *cure*. A very few older New Zealanders today still use THOUGHT in the lexical set of CLOTH. Modern New Zealand English has a raised THOUGHT vowel, above close-mid and back, [ö̝ə] or even [ö̝ɐ]. It is produced with lip rounding. A marked characteristic of modern New Zealand English is the off-glide, which can be present in closed syllables as well as in open ones.

11.1 British historical antecedents of the THOUGHT vowel

The /ɔː/ vowel is a relative newcomer to English phonology, and its occurrence and distribution vary widely from variety to variety. In RP and similar varieties, as well as in New Zealand English, it has a number of different sources. Firstly, it occurs in the lexical set of THOUGHT as a result of what Wells (1982: 191) calls *THOUGHT Monophthonging*. This was a development that took place around 1600 in which late Middle English /au/ became monophthongised to [ɒː]. Secondly, it developed in the set of NORTH, originally [nɒrθ], as a result of Pre-R Lengthening (see earlier, in Section 5.1.1) to [nɒːrθ], followed by R-dropping, which gave [nɒːθ]. By the eighteenth century, therefore, the sets of THOUGHT and NORTH had merged in the dialect that can be considered the precursor to RP. Thirdly, also in the eighteenth century, *Pre-Fricative Lengthening* (see earlier, Section 5.1.1) in the set of CLOTH led to [ɒ] becoming [ɒː] before /f, s, θ/, as in *off*, *cross*, *cloth*. However, this change has subsequently been reversed ([ɒː] > [ɒ]) in a number of varieties (Wells 1982: 204). From the chronology, each of these three innovations must be considered as constituting part of the mid-nineteenth-century input to New Zealand English.

Fourthly, in the lexical set of FORCE, originally [fo:rs], Pre-R Breaking (Wells 1982: 213), giving [foːərs], was followed by Pre-R Laxing (ibid.), resulting in [fɔərs]. Then eighteenth-century R-Dropping produced [fɔəs], and thus a new vocalic nucleus [ɔə]. During the nineteenth century, [ɒː] in THOUGHT and NORTH and CLOTH raised to [ɔː]. This led to a situation in which the difference between the [ɔə] in FORCE and the [ɔː] in THOUGHT and NORTH and CLOTH was very small and, not surprisingly, in many varieties the *First FORCE Merger* (Wells 1982: 235) occurred, whereby [ɔə] monophthongised to [ɔː], and *horse* and *hoarse* became homophonous. The timing of the beginnings of this change means that its result has to be considered as part of the input to New Zealand English. Many English dialects, however, have not undergone this merger, and indeed in conservative RP the distinction between THOUGHT/NORTH and FORCE survived well into the twentieth century. Interestingly, although the phonological merger is complete in London, both vowel qualities have survived there as allophonic variants, with the diphthong occurring word-finally – as in New Zealand – as in *floor*, *flaw*, and the monophthong pre-consonantally, as in *court*, *caught*.

Fifthly, the *Second FORCE Merger*, which is 'now under way' (Wells 1982: 237, 287), is leading to the lowering and monophthongisation of the /ʊə/ of *cure* [ʊə] > [oə] > [ɔə] > [ɔː], with the result that *poor*, *pour*, *pore* and *paw* now can all be homophonous. The current ongoing status of this change in the UK might suggest that it was not part of the mid-nineteenth-century British input to New Zealand English, though its results are also variably present in modern New Zealand English.

11.2 Early New Zealand commentaries on the THOUGHT vowel

There are very few comments specifically on vowels of the THOUGHT lexical set, but we can glean some information about THOUGHT from commentaries on other vowels. In 1895 *The Triad* reported: 'The usual mispronunciation of words, for which one learns to look in New Zealand, were pronounced as usual. What are *rorth*, *cuvernunt*, *heavun*, *trinurty*, *glowry*?' (*The Triad*, September 1895, cited in *Music in New Zealand*, Autumn 1993: 54). This can be interpreted mostly as a complaint about the schwa ([ə]) pronunciation of the unstressed vowels ('cuvernunt', 'heavun', 'trinurty'). However 'rorth' for *wrath* appears to indicate the Pre-Fricative Lengthening of the CLOTH vowel (see Section 10.3) and 'glowry' seems to be an attempt to indicate the raising of the THOUGHT vowel, which is characteristic of modern New Zealand English.

In 1903, R. N. Adams wrote a booklet entitled 'How to Pronounce Accurately on Scientific Principles', to guide those who wished to avoid the 'colonial twang'. In it he commented on THOUGHT and GOAT together, indicating that they should both be pronounced with monophthongs. He describes a pronunciation '"aw" or "awh" instead of oar'. His spelling <aw> again seems to indicate the raising of THOUGHT, and <awh> seems to indicate the final [ə] off-glide as well. (The full quotation is reproduced under GOAT in Section 12.5.2.)

11.3 Results from the Mobile Unit speakers for the THOUGHT vowel

The acoustic analysis of the Mobile Unit speakers (see Figure 6.5 in Section 2.3.2) shows that the THOUGHT vowel is raised towards the modern New Zealand English relatively close position, as reported with LOT. The women have raised THOUGHT significantly more than the men. Women do not show a greater difference than men between the F1 heights of LOT and THOUGHT, indicating that the two vowels are being raised together, however THOUGHT, but not LOT, is significantly closer (higher) than START for the women, but not for the men. This could indicate that LOT was raised first and had stabilised during the period under study, while THOUGHT was still actively raising, parallel to the situation with TRAP and DRESS (see Sections 20.2 and 20.3).

12 Closing diphthongs

The closing diphthongs of the MOUTH, PRICE, FACE, and GOAT lexical sets have long been noted as having a different character in modern New Zealand English from RP and many other varieties (Bauer 1986; Gordon and Deverson 1998: 41; Maclagan et al. 1999). They were among the first sounds to be criticised as part of the new variety, and today they are among the most salient markers of social class (Maclagan et al. 1999). CHOICE, which is also included in this section, does not attract comments.

12.1 Diphthong shift and glide weakening

In our discussion of the closing diphthongs we make use of two terms introduced by Wells (1982): *diphthong shift* and *glide weakening. Diphthong shift* (Wells 1982: 256) refers to the ongoing developments that many associate with the Great Vowel Shift in which what are called the closing diphthongs, /ei, oi, ou, ai, au, iː, uː/, show continuing movement of their first elements, beyond those reached by RP. Thus, /ai/ (the PRICE vowel) is the result of the diphthongisation of Middle English /iː/ (e.g. *tide* [tiːd] > [taid]), in which the first element has gone from [i] through [ɪ] and [ə] and [ɜ] to [ɐ] and [ʌ].[13] Diphthong shift of /ai/ involves more recent and continuing movement of the type [ʌ > ɑ > ɒ > ɔ], for example [tɔɪd] for *tide*. Similarly, diphthong shift of /au/ (the MOUTH vowel) involves a first element fronter than [ʌ] or closer (higher) than [a], for example [kɛʊ] *cow*; diphthong shift of /ei/ (the FACE vowel) has a first element more open (lower) than [e], as in [plæɪs] *place* (cf. RP [pleɪs]); diphthong shift of /ou/ (the GOAT vowel) involves a first element fronter and/or more open (lower) than [o], for example [kɐʊt] *coat* (cf. RP [kɵʊt]). In diphthong shift, the first element of the diphthong moves farther away from the second element, so that the new versions are wider diphthongs involving a greater degree of tongue movement.

Glide weakening (Wells 1982: 614–15) reduces or 'weakens' the newly widened diphthong shifted diphthongs by reducing the distance between the two vocoids in the diphthong. This occurs when the second element moves towards the first element, as in, for example, glide-weakened FACE, where the second element moves from [fæɪs] > [fæes], and in MOUTH, where it moves from [mɛʊθ] > [mɛəθ].

The historical analysis below shows that diphthong shift began with MOUTH and PRICE, probably in that order, before spreading later to FACE and GOAT, in that order. Diphthong shift finally spread to GOOSE and FLEECE (if at all), in that order.[14] All of these developments involving the closing diphthongs, with the possible exception of the fronting and/or diphthongisation of GOOSE, appear from the configurations on our maps to have begun in the English south-east; and, with the exception of FLEECE, are considered to have been under way by the mid-nineteenth century and hence available to be brought to New Zealand by the parents of the Mobile Unit informants.[15]

In those regional dialects that did not have diphthong shift at the time when the Mobile Unit speakers' parents were growing up, the qualities of the closing diphthongs may simply have been those corresponding to RP and other unshifted dialects. For RP, we are able to date the modern qualities of these

[13] [ʌ] is not an IPA symbol, but is nevertheless found useful by numerous scholars writing on English pronunciations; it is used to represent a fully open central vowel, [ɐ̞] (see the chart at the front of this book).

[14] Wells (1982) considers the vowels of FLEECE and GOOSE, which undergo diphthongisation in many regional dialects, to be part of 'diphthong shift', when the /iː/ of FLEECE is more open than [ɪ], as in [fləɪs] and when the /uː/ of GOOSE is fronter and/or more open than [ʊ], as in [gəʉs]. We have very little evidence at all for Diphthong Shift in FLEECE from dialect studies. However, Map 3c (in Appendix 3) shows the area with slightly diphthongal [ɪi] as opposed to [iː] in FLEECE from Lowman's work in the 1930s. We can assume that this area is where the process must have started, and that it is a very late development in England. Although some Mobile Unit speakers do produce diphthongised versions of both FLEECE and GOOSE, we have treated these vowels separately in this chapter, rather than with the closing diphthongs.

[15] We note that another colonial variety, the English of Tristan da Cunha, which developed in the nineteenth century and had probably become fully focused by about 1860 (see Schreier 2003) has Diphthong Shift of PRICE and MOUTH, but not of FACE and GOAT – indeed, it does not even have Long Mid Diphthonging (see Schreier 2002a, 2003).

vowels reasonably precisely, for example the modern quality of the first element of MOUTH in RP – [ɑ] – is thought to have developed by the last quarter of the nineteenth century (MacMahon 1998: 464, 466). In the case of those dialects that are historically more conservative than RP (such as Scottish English), monophthongs were normal for /ei/ [eː ~ ɛː] and /ou/ [oː ~ ɔː], while /ai/ began with a vowel of the type [ə – ɜ – ɐ], and /au/ with a vowel of the type [ɞ – ɜ – ɐ]. In order to date the origins of diphthong shift beyond typical RP qualities, we clearly need to examine varieties other than RP. We now look at each of the closing diphthongs in greater detail.

12.2 The MOUTH vowel

In modern New Zealand English, MOUTH usually starts above START at [æ]. For older and/or more conservative speakers, it moves towards a second element of [ʊ], and for some younger and/or less conservative speakers it moves towards [ə]. In broader accents, MOUTH is realised as [ɛə] and in more conservative ones as [a̝ʊ].

12.2.1 British historical antecedents of the MOUTH vowel. As noted in Section 12.1, in those regional dialects that did not have diphthong shift, the qualities of the closing diphthongs may simply have been those corresponding to RP and other unshifted dialects. For traditional RP MOUTH, the development of the modern quality of the first element – [ɑ] – is dated by MacMahon (1998: 464, 466) to the last quarter of the nineteenth century. However, in those dialects that are historically more conservative than RP, /au/ began with a vowel of the type [ɞ – ɜ – ɐ].

For nineteenth-century regional dialects, Ellis (1889) cites diphthong-shifted variants of MOUTH as being typical of the eastern division, that is, Bedfordshire, Buckinghamshire, Cambridgeshire, Essex, Hertfordshire, Huntingdonshire, Middlesex, Northamptonshire, Rutland, and Suffolk, and parts of Norfolk (Trudgill 1974). Ellis (1889: 226) also cites D'Orsey on London, who says, '*mountain* is "meowntain"'. Lowman's fieldwork in England in the late 1930s (Kurath and Lowman 1970) shows a rather larger area for this, and even larger is the area that has predominantly shifted forms in the SED materials. Diphthong shift in words of the MOUTH set (i.e. with variants such as [ɛʊ ~ æʊ]) in regional dialects is portrayed for different chronological periods in Map 3a (see Appendix 3). (See Wright 1905: 146–7 for the various dialects he listed with /eu/ for this diphthong.)

Based on the information summarised on Map 3a, we would expect that the input to New Zealand English would have included a range of variants from the more conservative (starting with [ɞ – ɜ – ɐ]) to diphthong-shifted variants such as [ɛʊ ~ æʊ].

12.2.2 Early New Zealand commentaries on the MOUTH *vowel.* Written records show very clearly that the pronunciation of the /au/ vowel was a salient feature of early New Zealand English, with frequent mentions from the end of the nineteenth century. McBurney in 1887 listed diphthong-shifted pronunciations of *now* and *town* with <éeu> [e̝ʊ] and <ææ'u> [æʊ] in towns in various parts of the country (in Ellis 1889: 241). Bauer (1994: 392–3) interprets McBurney's 1887 comments on these diphthongs to mean that initially Australia was much ahead of New Zealand in diphthong shift and that New Zealand had little of it. However, judging from later negative commentaries in written records, he concludes, 'New Zealand appears to have caught up with Australia in the pronunciation of the diphthongs in a period of something like thirty years' (p. 393).

One of the earliest comments we have found on MOUTH is by one no less renowned than Rudyard Kipling, who commented on both PRICE and MOUTH: 'In 1892, when he was in New Zealand, Rudyard Kipling wrote a story exclusive to the *Auckland Herald* and the *Auckland Weekly News* . . . In it he refers to a New Zealand women, who talked about "ke-ows" and "bye-bies"'. (Cited in a letter to *The Listener*, 22 March 1957: 11.)

Comments from school inspectors started in 1902: 'Reading and recitation are usually well taught, though in some parts a twangy pronunciation, particularly of the "ou" and other vowel sounds, prevails' (Nelson school inspector W. Ladley, *AJHR* E-1B, 1902: 28). These comments continue to modern times:

1903: 'Cow is converted to "keow," brow into "breow" . . .' (Adams 1903: 20–21).
1904: Wanganui school inspector: '. . . words which might profitably be given every day in school – *house*, *pound*, *ground*, *round*, *bounce*, *how*, *cow*, *now*, *brown*, *gown* etc.' (*AJHR* E-1B: 10).
1908: Wellington school inspector: 'teown' (*AJHR* E-1B: 16).
1910: *The Triad* (10 August: 39): '. . . the broad "a" diphthong diverges "ah-oo" into "e-oo" – noun (nah-oon) becomes "ne-oon".'
1912: *The Triad* (10 December: 13): '"nee-ow" for "now".'
1912: *The Cohen Commission on Education*: 'the word is "house" not "heouse"' (*AJHR* E-12: 623).
1919: Otago inspectors: '"How" is "heow"' (*AJHR* E-2, Appendix B: xviii).
1924: *Education Gazette* (1 August: 130): 'the pronunciation of "ou" or "ow" as "eow".'
1947: *The Listener* (4 July: 13): '"bree-a-oon" (brown).'
1948: *The Listener* (16 January: 8): 'heow, neow, eout', and also (12 November: 7): 'Heyow neyow breyown ceyow.'
1966: *The Listener* (28 October: 13): '"AOU" for "ow".'

We can assume that these spellings are intended to represent [ɛʊ], a major variant of this diphthong in modern New Zealand English (see above and Chapter 2).

12.2.3 Results from the Mobile Unit speakers for MOUTH. The auditory perceptual analysis shows that approximately 20% of the speakers produced non-shifted dialect forms of MOUTH such as [ɜu, œʉ, ɐʉ], nearly 10% showed no diphthong shift or glide weakening, producing forms such as [ɑu, ɑʊ], and nearly 70% showed some degree of diphthong shift or of diphthong shift plus glide weakening. Speakers produced a wide range of variants [ʌu, æ̞ʉ, æʉ, ɛʊ, æᵊ, ɛɤ]. Most of the individuals who use diphthong-shifted variants of the closing diphthongs (with or without glide weakening) are among the younger speakers in the Mobile Unit archive or grew up in non-rural areas. Only four speakers born after 1870 who are from non-rural areas do not produce diphthong-shifted or diphthong-shifted and glide-weakened variants for MOUTH.

The acoustic analysis shows that the five women, as a group, are again more advanced than the five men (see Figure 6.30). For the women, MOUTH starts just above their TRAP vowel, whereas for the men it starts just below their TRAP vowel, with the women's MOUTH diphthong starting significantly closer (higher) than the men's. For the women the glide is horizontal, towards the centre of the vowel space. There is no remnant of raising towards [ʊ]. For the men, the glide moves towards a close position, with the difference between men and women being significant.

12.3 The PRICE *vowel*

In modern New Zealand English, PRICE starts relatively back, around [ɑ] or [ɒ], and moves towards [e]. More conservative variants are [ɑe] and broader variants are [ɔ̞ë].

12.3.1 British historical antecedents of the PRICE *vowel.* As with MOUTH, in those regional dialects that did not have diphthong shift in the mid-nineteenth century, PRICE may simply have corresponded to qualities in RP and other unshifted dialects, beginning with a vowel of the type [ə – ɜ – ɐ]. For traditional RP, the origins of the modern quality of PRICE with a first element of [a] can be dated to the last quarter of the nineteenth century (MacMahon 1998: 464, 466). Ellis (1889) reports that at the period when he was writing, diphthong-shifted forms of PRICE were typical only of London. For example, he quotes D'Orsey that '*light* is almost *loyt*' and others that *isle* is [oil] in London (Ellis 1889: 226, 228). Nevertheless Ellis also gives cases, for example, *I* and *fire* as '(ɔ́*i*) . . . (ói)' and '(fó*i*ɐr)' for Wingham in east Kent (pp. 142, 228), and only a few years later Wright (1905: 59, 125, 127, 153, 171) listed words such as *die*, *tie*, *height*, *fight*, *light*, *bright*, and so on with /oi/ in various locations, including the areas around London and the south-east. Map 3b (in Appendix 3) shows areas from the SED materials that have predominantly diphthong-shifted forms, with first elements indicated by [ɑ] or [ɔ]. The area may have been larger than Ellis reported, or, if it was not, then the spread outwards from London was rather rapid, and there

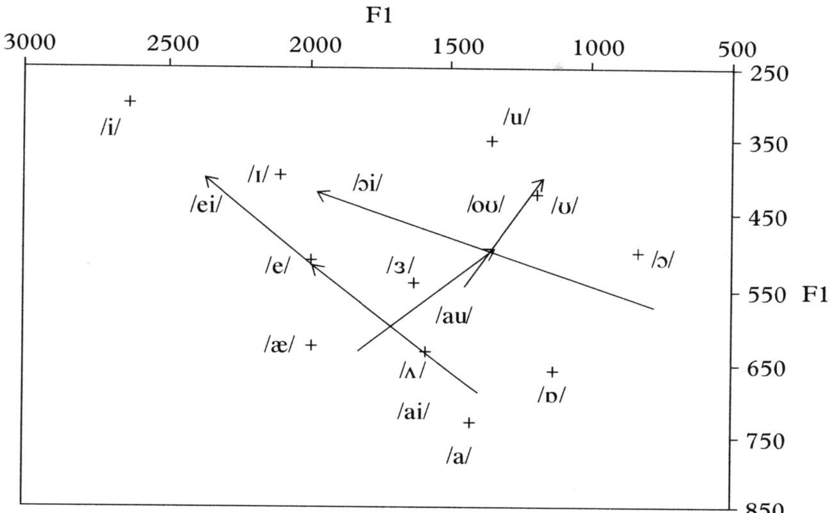

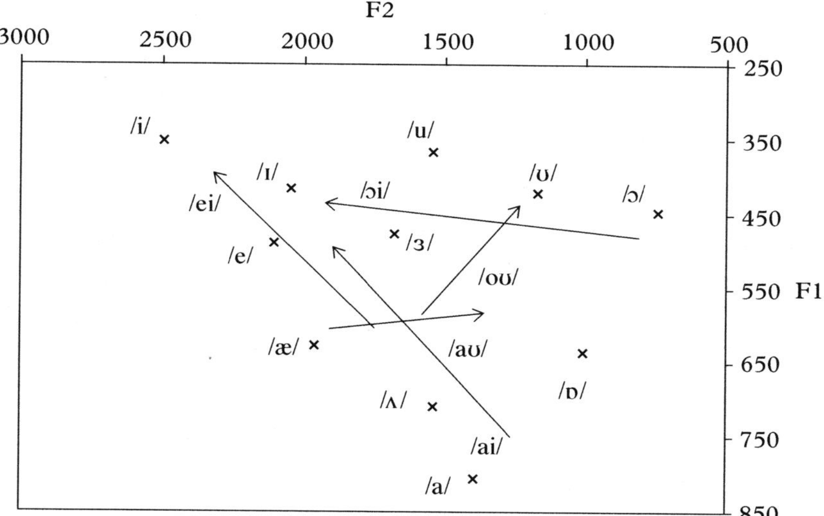

Figure 6.30 Acoustic vowel charts including closing diphthongs for men and women

were a few peripheral areas that shifted MOUTH without shifting PRICE, and vice versa.

As indicated above, Scottish English does not have diphthong shift. Nevertheless, two present-day phonetic versions of PRICE that are similar to diphthong-shifted variants are typical of many speakers: [a > e] in Aitken's Law environments (before voiced fricatives, /r/, and morpheme-finally) and [ʌi] in other environments (with [ɛ̈ɪ] in working-class speech) (Wells 1982: 405).

We could therefore expect that fewer diphthong-shifted variants of PRICE than of MOUTH would have been brought to New Zealand with the earliest immigrants.

12.3.2 Early New Zealand commentaries on the PRICE vowel. The earliest written references found concerning PRICE are from the late 1880s. Samuel McBurney in 1887 spoke of the 'broadening *ii* in *die*', saying that in parts of New Zealand it approached *oi*, '*I die* sounding *oi doi*' (in Ellis 1889: 238). In 1889, Robert Lee, a Wellington school inspector, refers to 'a tendency to pronounce "i" as "oi" . . . thus "fine" is "foine"' (*AJHR* E-1B, 1889: 14). He commented again in 1900 on 'foive' for *five* (*AJHR* E-1B, 1900: 14).

Diphthong shift in PRICE was also well established in New Zealand English early on, as revealed in these comments from the early twentieth century:

> I believe it would engage the children's attention if each class-room has a few placards on the wall, printed in big heavy type, such as '**c o w**' spells 'k-ah-oo' not 'ke-oo' or '**f l y**' spells 'fl-ah-i' not 'flaw-i' (*The Triad*, 10 August 1910)

> Among defects in pronunciation still prevalent in certain quarters, but by no means common . . . the broadening of the vowel 'i' until it resembles 'oi'. (Nelson Inspectors, *AJHR* E-1B, 1900: 30)

> Failure to appreciate the value of the common vowel sounds – e.g. moine. (Wellington Inspectors, *AJHR* E-1B, 1908: 16)

Comments continued up to modern times, so that in 1978 a contributor to *The Listener* (25 November: 10) wrote, 'I watched at a local competition, a perfect delivery of a piece of prose by a prize-winner – to be astounded to hear, when he returned to his seat beside me, his request to his mother – "Can oi boi an oice cream, Mum?"'

12.3.3 Results from the Mobile Unit speakers for the PRICE vowel. The auditory perceptual analysis shows that fewer speakers produced diphthong-shifted or diphthong-shifted and glide-weakened versions of PRICE than of MOUTH. One sixth of the Mobile Unit speakers used traditional versions of PRICE typical of regional varieties, such as [ɜɪ, ɐɪ, ɛɪ], and a further 30% showed no diphthong shift or glide weakening, producing versions like [aɪ]. Approximately half of the speakers showed evidence of diphthong shift of PRICE (with or without glide weakening) such as [a̟ᶦ, ᴀᶦ, ᴀᵋ, ɑ̠ᶦ, aᵉ]. Mr Malcolm Ritchie (born 1866) is the only speaker to produce some diphthong-shifted variants of PRICE (with or without glide weakening) without also producing diphthong-shifted versions of MOUTH (with or without glide weakening).

The acoustic analysis (see Figure 6.30 in Section 12.2.3) shows that PRICE starts slightly farther back than START for both the men and the women, with the women showing significantly greater retraction than the men. Neither diphthong shift nor glide weakening is as marked acoustically for PRICE as it is for MOUTH. For the men, the second element of the PRICE diphthong reaches DRESS, whereas for the women it is as close as DRESS, but more centralised. This difference is not significant.

12.4 The FACE vowel

Modern New Zealand English has relatively wide diphthongs for FACE. The most common pronunciation is [ɐe], with more conservative pronunciations being [æ̟e] and broader ones [ɐ̟e].

12.4.1 British historical antecedents of the FACE vowel. Long Mid Diphthonging, which created diphthongs from earlier long mid vowels, for example [eː] to [ei] in the FACE class (Wells 1982: 210), preceded chronologically the diphthong-shifted pronunciations of FACE words, and places which did not have Long Mid Diphthonging in the mid nineteenth century obviously did not have diphthong shift of these vowels. Wells (1982: 210) dates Long Mid Diphthonging for FACE to around 1800 in the precursor of RP, although MacMahon (1998: 450) finds references to it in 1711.[16]

In nineteenth-century regional dialects as shown in Ellis, Long Mid Diphthonging as a process had barely begun. (Indeed, many dialects in all parts of England are shown in Ellis as still having falling diphthongs, such as [fɪəs], for FACE words, rather than monophthongs or rising diphthongs.) There would probably have been more diphthongisation in urban speech, and at higher social class levels, and Ellis (1889: 226) refers to the rising diphthongs as typically a London feature, though also present in the regional speech of Hertfordshire and Essex. He quotes D'Orsey's comments on London: 'such words as *paper*, *shape*, *train*, are pronounced *piper*, *shipe*, *trine*' (p. 226), but believes these probably are represented by '(ᴇ'*i*) [ɛɪ] or (æ'*i*) [æɪ], and only rarely (á'i) [ai]' (p. 226); Ellis said of this, 'to my ears it seldom reaches this [ai] in London', though he had heard '(læ'id*i*z)' [læidɪz] in Hyde Park (p. 226). (Ellis also cites others with

[16] Note that, as is still true of some twenty-first-century varieties, the vowels of the sets of *made* and *maid*, and of *moan* and *mown*, were distinct in many nineteenth-century dialects, the first member of each pair coming from the Middle English monophthongs *a*< and *o*< respectively, the second from the Middle English diphthongs *ai* and *ou*. Long Mid Diphthonging is relevant, of course, only to the former.

observations about diphthong-shifted FACE forms in London (p. 229).) Wright (1905: 39, 46, 65) gave [ai] as the realisation of FACE in Hertfordshire, London, Essex, Kent, western Worcestershire, Dorset, Northampton, Gloucestershire, Berkshire, Wiltshire, Suffolk, Somerset, Devon, and so on. Map 3c (in Appendix 3) shows Long Mid Diphthonging of FACE in the 1990s (from Trudgill 1999d), in the 1950s/60s (from the SED), in the 1930s (from Lowman's data), and in Ellis 1889. Map 3d shows areas in which diphthong shift of FACE to [ɛɪ] or [æɪ] predominates in the SED materials.

The FACE vowels are generally monophthongal in Scotland (Wells 1982: 407). As for the other closing diphthongs, the first immigrants to New Zealand probably brought with them a range of variants for FACE, including diphthong-shifted variants, though the latter would probably not have been in the majority.

12.4.2 Early New Zealand commentaries on the FACE *vowel.* In 1887 McBurney listed diphthong-shifted pronunciations of some FACE words for various New Zealand towns; of the pronunciation <dææ′*i*> [dæɪ] for *day*, he said there were a 'few' in Wellington and Napier (in Ellis 1889: 241). An early written comment on FACE came from Adams (1903: 15):

> age, babe, date, fade . . . name etc.
> This is the natural sound that 'colonial twang', as we call it, has painfully corrupted into ige, bybe, dyte, fyde, nyme, and so on. There is some consolation, however in being able to believe that this sound is much less common amongst us than it was about five years ago [!]. Mr J. M. Clarke mentioned that scarcely had he observed it in any of the recent competitions, somewhat to his surprise. But we are by no means free from this vulgarism. The other Sunday the whole of the trebles in a city choir broke out with the words:
> Awyke, ye syents, awyke
> And hile this soicred dye.

School inspectors did not start to complain about FACE until 1909, considerably later than for either MOUTH or PRICE: 'the substitution of "a-ee" or "i" for "a"' (Westland inspectors, *AJHR* E-2, 1909: 124); and 'Mail is mile, tail is tile' (Marlborough inspectors, *AJHR* E-2, 1911, App. C: xxvi). In 1939, Arnold Wall wrote:

> ei as in London, 'ei' is pronounced as, approximately, 'ai' represented in ordinary spelling by long 'i' or 'y': 'syme' 'dy', 'die' for *same* and *day* . . . it is certain that this sound is not abused to the same extent in New Zealand as in Australia. The Australian 'nyme' or 'nime' for 'name' [naim for neim] has become almost proverbial, but in New Zealand this fault, though not altogether absent, is far less common. (Wall 1939: 18)

12.4.3 Results from the Mobile Unit speakers for the FACE *vowel.* The auditory perceptual analysis of 95 Mobile Unit speakers shows that nearly 20% produce monophthongal [e] variants of FACE or variants with very short glides [eᴵ]. Approximately 40% produce variants with no diphthong shift or glide weakening, such as [eɪ], and just over 40% show some degree of diphthong shift, producing variants like [ɛɪ, æ̞ɪ, æɪ, æ̞ɪ]. None of the Mobile Unit speakers produces glide-weakened versions of FACE. Thus, considerably fewer speakers produce diphthong-shifted variants of FACE than of MOUTH or PRICE. There are only six speakers who produce diphthong-shifted variants for this vowel without also producing diphthong-shifted variants (with or without glide weakening) for MOUTH.

The acoustic analysis shows that the women produced considerably longer glides for FACE than the men (see Figure 6.30 in Section 12.2.3). On average, the women's FACE starts near to TRAP whereas the men's starts just below DRESS. The difference just reaches statistical significance. Both men and women showed no noticeable glide weakening, with the average second element for FACE being as close (high) as KIT and as front as FLEECE (considerably fronter than KIT).

12.5 The GOAT vowel

In modern New Zealand English, GOAT is a relatively wide diphthong, starting from approximately [ɐ] and rising up towards [ʊ], [ɵ] or [ʉ] or even [ʏ]. More conservative versions start somewhat above [ɐ] and move towards [ʊ], while broader versions lengthen the first element.

12.5.1 British historical antecedents of the GOAT vowel. As with FACE, diphthong-shifted pronunciations of words in the lexical set of GOAT were preceded chronologically by Long Mid Diphthonging ([oː] to [oʊ]) (Wells 1982: 210). Places that did not have Long Mid Diphthonging in the mid nineteenth century clearly could not have diphthong shift, and monophthongs such as [oː ~ ɔː] for GOAT words were in fact normal in many dialects. Wells (1982: 210) dates Long Mid Diphthonging for GOAT to around 1800 in the precursor of RP, and MacMahon (1998: 450, 459) finds references to it in 1795. However, Gimson (1962: 130) states '[oː] was diphthongised to [oʊ] in the eighteenth and nineteenth centuries', indicating that the long monophthongal pronunciation could have survived longer. As with FACE, many regional dialects in all parts of England are shown in Ellis as having falling diphthongs, such as [gʊət]. There would probably have been more rising diphthongisation in urban speech, and at higher social class levels, and within London. Ellis (1889: 196) cites diphthongal GOAT as being typical (though recent) in the regional speech of his 'Mid Eastern' area, that is, Essex, Hertfordshire, Huntingdonshire, Bedfordshire, and central Northamptonshire. It is also clear from Ellis that diphthongisation was more advanced for FACE than for GOAT (as also suggested by MacMahon 1998: 450, 459). The GOAT vowels are generally monophthongal in Scotland (Wells 1982: 407).

We would expect, then, that many of the earliest immigrants to New Zealand would have had monophthongal pronunciations of GOAT, though some would have used diphthongal variants, and even diphthong-shifted variants.

12.5.2 Early New Zealand commentaries on the GOAT *vowel.* Once again, the first comments we have are from McBurney (1887) (in Ellis 1889: 241). He cites the pronunciation of the words *no* and *toe* in the various towns. For *no* as <náˈi*u*> [naʊ] he listed 'few' in Wellington and Napier, and 'some' for girls in Nelson and Christchurch; however, for *toe* as <táˈi*u*> [taʊ], diphthongisation appears to have been more widespread: 'many' in Auckland, 'general' in Wellington and Napier, and 'many' for girls in Nelson and Christchurch, with 'some' in Dunedin. The alternate pronunciation of <n*oo*> [no̝ː] for *no* was 'general' in all New Zealand towns, while <t*oo*> [to̝ː] for *toe* was only given as 'some' in Auckland, 'few' in Wellington and Napier, about half-and-half in Christchurch, 'general' in Nelson, and 'many' in Dunedin (Ellis 1889: 241). The earliest comment after McBurney is by Adams in 1903:

> The diphthong 'oa' has but one uniform sound, a full round 'o' as in oar, boat, coat, foam, roam, load. Like the one sound of 'a', this sound of 'o' is frequently blunted into a gross distortion, in which we have something like 'aw' or 'awh' instead of oar, 'bout' instead of boat, 'caut' instead of coat, 'vaut' for vote, 'naut' for note, and if you listen carefully we may hear some who have passed through a high school speak of such sentences as: 'We shall "tyke" a "baut" and have a "raow" on the "bie"' or 'while aout in the baut my auvaceaut blew auvabaud and we lost an awh in trying to ketch it.' . . . Why should not the ear be disgusted with the vulgarity of uncouth sounds? (Adams 1903: 20)

Adams refers at the start to an older pronunciation where GOAT was realised as a long monophthong (see Gimson 1962). His spellings *baut* and *raow* appear to indicate diphthong-shifted pronunciations of GOAT. The Cohen Commission on Education (1912) noted: 'A great many, instead of saying "oh no" say "ow, neow"'. School inspectors' comments on diphthongisation of GOAT begin in 1916: '"o" changes to "ah+o"' (Wanganui inspectors, *AJHR* E-2, 1916, App. B: ix); and again: '"home" is "haome"' (Otago inspectors, *AJHR* E-2, 1919, App. B: xviii).

In 1939 Arnold Wall noted:

> *ou*, 'home', 'note'. The diphthong 'ou' is mispronounced, as in London, with the sound 'ow' [au]. 'Cold' becomes 'cowld' [kauld or even kæuld]. This like the last [ei] is a sound far less commonly and less cruelly abused in New Zealand than in Australia. (Wall 1939: 8)

12.5.3 Results from the Mobile Unit speakers for the GOAT *vowel.* The auditory perceptual analysis shows that approximately one sixth of the Mobile Unit speakers produce monophthongs [o] or [ɔ] or dialect versions of GOAT such as [ɵʉ, o̞, ou], with these versions being particularly common amongst the oldest speakers. Some of the older speakers in the Mobile Unit habitually use a monophthongal variant that sounds extremely similar to THOUGHT (which is in agreement with the comments from Adams given in Section 12.5.2). Approximately 35% of the speakers produce versions with [ou, oʊ], that is, diphthongs with neither diphthong shift nor glide weakening, and over 40% of the speakers produce versions with diphthong shift, [ɔu, ʌu, ɞʊ, ɵʊ, ɐʊ, a̠ʊ]. As with FACE, no speakers produce glide-weakened tokens for GOAT. Slightly more speakers produce diphthong-shifted variants of GOAT than of FACE.

The acoustic analysis shows no glide weakening for GOAT (see Figure 6.30 in Section 12.2.3), with the diphthong ending on FOOT for both men and women. The women's GOAT diphthongs start significantly more front but not significantly more open than do the men's.

The auditory perceptual and acoustic analyses thus confirm the historical order of diphthong shift given earlier in Section 12.1: MOUTH followed by PRICE then FACE and GOAT.

12.6 The CHOICE vowel

In modern New Zealand English, CHOICE starts from a relatively close back position and moves towards a close front position, [o̝i̞̠]. There is little variation in its pronunciation.

12.6.1 British historical antecedents of the CHOICE vowel. The CHOICE vowel mostly derives from Middle English /ɔi/ or /ui/. All CHOICE words are ultimately loanwords, mainly from Old French (Wells 1982: 150). Wells (p. 209) indicates that the relationship between CHOICE and PRICE is complicated. Before the eighteenth century, CHOICE words such as *coin*, *join* and *oil* (derived from Middle English /ui/) developed a pronunciation of [əɪ] or [ʌɪ] and so rhymed with PRICE (Strang 1970: 112). Later, in popular speech in some parts of the south of England CHOICE apparently merged with PRICE as [ɒɪ], so that *boil* (v.) could be a homophone of *bile*, or *joined* rhyme with *find* (Wells 1982: 209). The same merger can be found in Ireland as well as the colonies of Newfoundland and the West Indies (Wells 1982: 210), which predate the British settlement of southern hemisphere countries like New Zealand. The [ɔi] pronunciation was apparently 'artificially' restored during the eighteenth century because of the spelling (Wyld 1936: 250), though the process of restoration did not initially affect all CHOICE words. On this basis, therefore, not many English emigrants to New Zealand would have brought a merged PRICE/CHOICE vowel with them, but some from Ireland might have.

12.6.2 Early New Zealand commentaries on the CHOICE vowel. There are no significant written comments on the CHOICE vowel. McBurney (in Ellis 1889:

247–8) says of 'boy' and 'voice', '*oy* most unfortunately escaped my notice . . . but I have not heard anything peculiar except in rare cases'. (He notes slightly higher and longer 'o' in the speech of 'Scotch' teachers in Napier.)

12.6.3 Results from the Mobile Unit speakers for the CHOICE *vowel.* There is so little variation in contemporary Englishes in the pronunciation of CHOICE, that we did not do a detailed auditory perceptual analysis of it. Nevertheless, no examples of a merger between CHOICE and PRICE were noted in the Mobile Unit speakers; most produced very few tokens of CHOICE, so all available tokens were analysed acoustically. The acoustic analysis (see Figure 6.30 in Section 12.2.3) showed that the first element of CHOICE was closely associated with THOUGHT for all speakers and is relatively close (high). As THOUGHT rose over the period we are considering, so the first element of CHOICE followed with the result that there is no significant difference between the positions of THOUGHT and the first element of CHOICE.

13 Centring diphthongs

As the centring diphthongs are relatively rare in contextual speech, we did not attempt a full analysis of them, nor do we provide a detailed account of their historical origins. However, because of the ongoing merger of NEAR and SQUARE in modern New Zealand English (see Chapter 2, Section 2.3.3), we performed an auditory perceptual analysis for those speakers who produced stressed tokens of NEAR and SQUARE. A total of 65 of the 95 speakers analysed produced stressed tokens of NEAR and SQUARE that we could analyse. None of these speakers completely merged the two diphthongs, but 12 of them produced variants of NEAR and SQUARE that were extremely similar. Four of these speakers were born before 1875 and eight of them after 1875.[17] A separate acoustic analysis has been carried out on four of the younger speakers in the Mobile Unit database, born around 1900 (see Watson, Maclagan, and Harrington 2000). Compared with young speakers of modern New Zealand English (see Maclagan and Gordon 2000), who exhibit an almost complete merger of NEAR and SQUARE, all four of the Mobile Unit speakers in Watson et al.'s study kept the starting points of these diphthongs distinct. NEAR started close to the position of FLEECE and SQUARE started close to the position of DRESS, with FLEECE and DRESS still being well separated (as in Figure 6.30 in Section 12.2.3). From this analysis, we would conclude that the merging of NEAR and SQUARE, which is a distinguishing characteristic of modern New Zealand English, did not begin until well into the twentieth century. The onset of the merger was sufficiently late so that the Mobile Unit speakers do not seem to have accommodated to it later

[17] See Gordon and Trudgill 1999: 113 for comments at an earlier stage of this analysis, where the Mobile Unit speakers are described as producing 'embryonic variants' of the current NEAR/SQUARE merger.

in life (see Chapters 5 and 8 on individuals' linguistic accommodation in later life).

14 The vowel of the NURSE lexical set

The modern New Zealand English variant is typically fronted and raised, and is also lip-rounded, [œ̞̈ ~ ø̞]. As Bauer (1979: 65) has pointed out, 'it is generally assumed to be unnatural for a language with only one front rounded vowel to have [œ] rather than [y]', though he suggests a link with the fronting of /u/ to [ʉ] (see the discussion of the GOOSE vowel) and suggests that Australasian English may be 'in the process of developing a set of front rounded vowels'.

14.1 British historical antecedents for the NURSE vowel

The NURSE vowel is relatively new in the history of English. It comes from Middle English /ɪr/, /ɛr/ and /ʊr/, where the /r/ was non-prevocalic, as in *bird*, *earth*, *hurt*, *fir*, *fur*. In Early Modern English these vowels underwent the *First NURSE Merger* (Wells 1982: 200), all three resulting in /ər/. Wells dates this to the sixteenth century, while MacMahon (1998: 415–18) suggests that it might have been later than this, certainly so in some geographical areas of England. (The merger did not occur in Scotland, where the pronunciations are still distinct, /ɪr/, /ɛr/ and /ʌr /. In some varieties of Irish English, the merger has affected /ɪr/ and /ʌr/, while /ɛr/ remains distinct.) Subsequently, Pre-R Lengthening took place in the seventeenth century (Wells 1982: 201), in which /ər/ became /əːr/. Then the quality of the vowel became more open, so that /əːr/ became /ɜːr/. Finally R-Dropping took place (p. 218), resulting in /ɜː/ in RP and similar varieties.

This vowel /ɜː/, of course, occurs only in non-rhotic varieties, rhotic ones having instead [əːɹ], [ɹ̩], [ɜːr], [ɚ] etc. Even in non-rhotic varieties, however, the RP-type vowel [ɜː] in *nurse*, *girl*, *bird*, and so on is not an especially common vowel in varieties of English either in England or around the world. The *Linguistic Atlas of England* shows very few areas that consistently have [ɜː] (written [əː]) in the relevant lexical set for traditional dialects in the 1950s–1960s: Cheshire, Staffordshire, Warwickshire, Northamptonshire, Huntingdonshire, Hertfordshire, and Essex. We can assume that this area was smaller a hundred years earlier.[18] Of London, Wells (1982: 305) writes that the NURSE vowel is 'often much the same in London speech as in RP' but that it is 'on occasions somewhat fronted and/or lightly rounded'. He mentions the 'Cockney variant' [œː] (ibid.) Relevant to New

[18] East Anglian English used to have [ɐ] in closed syllables and [aː] in open syllables in NURSE until the mid-twentieth century (Trudgill 1997a), and Tristan da Cunha still has this system today (Schreier 2003). The English English of Newcastle has [ɒ]; Liverpool, Middlesborough, Hull, Coventry, and a number of other places have [ɛː], identical with the vowel of THERE; Birmingham has a raised [ɨː] (Wells 1982).

Zealand is the implication that this lip-rounding could be a recent development, since it is not mentioned in other sources, including Sivertsen (1960). A number of Lancashire (Shorrocks 1998) and south-east Welsh dialects (Wells 1982: 381) also have a rounded vowel of the type [œː] – also seen for Monmouthshire in the SED materials. Wells (1982: 139) mentions as a sub-type 'lip-rounded variants, common in south Wales and in New Zealand'. Branford (1994: 481) (quoting personal communication from Lass) says of England that the NURSE vowel is the 'relatively long unrounded mid-central vocoid' of Wells (1982: 137) only in 'the most RP-focussed conservative communities' but is otherwise characteristically rounded to [ø].

Outside of the British Isles, some forms of Caribbean English have [ɔ]; and some non-rhotic American accents such as New York City and New Orleans have a diphthong [ɜɪ] in NURSE (stigmatised and not infrequently hypercorrected, hence the 'Toidy toid street' stereotype of so-called 'Brooklynese', and Archie Bunker's 'turlet' for *toilet*). Other comparable colonial varieties, however, also have the rounded vowel. Given this range of variation, we assume that the nineteenth-century immigrants to New Zealand came with a variety of NURSE realisations, possibly including a rounded vowel (see later). Both Australia and South Africa, like New Zealand, have rounded variants of this vowel.

14.2 Early New Zealand commentaries on the NURSE vowel

The earliest reference, of which there are very few, to the rounded NURSE vowel typical of New Zealand English comes from McBurney in 1887. He reported the pronunciations of *ferns* as: 'fœœnz' (general in Auckland, Wellington, Napier, Nelson, Christchurch, and Dunedin; attested also well in Australia); he gave *pearls* as: 'pœœlz' (several in Wellington and Napier; more in Australia: few in Tasmania and Sydney, half-and-half in Brisbane), also 'pəɾlz' (half-and-half in Nelson and Christchurch, many in Dunedin) (cited in Ellis 1889: 245).

In 1947, A. R. D. Fairburn, in the column 'Spoken English', complained about New Zealanders attempting to speak a form of RP – a variety he named 'colonial-genteel' (*The Listener*, 13 June: 23–5); his list of dislikes includes the pronunciation of NURSE as follows: '"First" is turned into "fust" or even "fast" and "persons" become "pahsons"'. His spellings, <fust>, <fast> and <pahsons>, all appear to indicate relatively open (low) vowels. The complaint against such pronunciations therefore appears to imply that a closer (higher) version was the unmarked one in New Zealand English. It seems clear that these 'colonial-genteel' pronunciations were unrounded, but it is not certain that we may infer from this that the more common pronunciations of the NURSE vowel at this time were rounded.

14.3 Results from the Mobile Unit speakers for the NURSE vowel

The auditory perceptual analysis reveals that one sixth of the Mobile Unit speakers variably retain the Scottish vowel system, with a three-way contrast in the vowels that later became the NURSE vowel, and all but one of these speakers had Scottish parents. A further 40% of speakers variably produce forms of NURSE that are at least partially rhotic (see Section 16). A further one sixth of the speakers use non-rhotic NURSE vowels, and the final 20% use variants of NURSE that are lip-rounded, including three speakers with both lip-rounding and raising of this vowel. Half of the speakers with lip-rounded NURSE have parents who came from either Scotland or Ireland and who would not, therefore, have produced rounded variants of NURSE. One of the speakers who use rounded variants was born in 1865, and the rest in 1869 or later. Most of them come from urban areas in the North Island. The oldest South Island speaker to produce lip-rounded NURSE was born in Arrowtown (a 'mixed' town) in 1877. This would seem to indicate that lip-rounding increased throughout the time period represented in the Mobile Unit database, and that, like other changes, it showed most movement in the mixed settlements.

The acoustic analysis (see Figure 6.5 in Section 2.3.2) shows that the women have raised NURSE significantly more than the men have. There is no significant difference in the F2 values for the men and women, indicating that the women have not significantly fronted NURSE. NURSE has raised in parallel with DRESS for both men and women, but for the women it is slightly closer than DRESS while for the men it is not quite as close. Although these differences are not significant statistically, again they show that the women are moving further towards the modern New Zealand English form of NURSE than are the men.

15 Unstressed vowels

We have considered to this point the various vowels that can appear in stressed syllables in New Zealand English. We turn now to the vowels that can appear in unstressed syllables. Wells (1982) gives three key words for unstressed vowels in word final syllables in modern English, *comm*A, *lett*ER, and *happ*Y (in each case the vowel in question is in the final syllable of the key word). We will first treat *comm*A and *lett*ER together, followed by *happ*Y.

15.1 The vowels of commA *and* lettER

The *comm*A and *lett*ER vowels may be used in non-word-final environments, as well as word finally. Modern New Zealand English is non-rhotic, and there is now no contrast between the vowels in the *lett*ER and *comm*A sets – all are usually realised with /ə/, [ə ~ ɐ] in modern New Zealand English. Wells (1982: 167) states that in non-final environments, some varieties have the possibility of a distinction between [ɪ] and [ə], so that contrasts like *Lenin* /lenɪn/ vs *Lennon* /lenən/ or *roses* /roʊzɪz/ vs *Rosa's* /roʊzəz/ can occur. The contrasting pronunciations are referred to as the *rabbit* /ræbɪt/ and *abbot* /æbət/ classes of words. Such contrasts are not possible in modern New Zealand English, which has undergone what Wells (1982: 167) calls the *Weak Vowel Merger*.

15.2 British historical antecedents for unstressed vowels

The different spellings in unstressed syllables give an indication of their pronunciation at earlier stages of English. Originally, *about*, *undo*, *colour*, *sitter*, *company*, and *harmless* had different vowels in their unstressed syllables. Wyld (1920: 258–82) indicated that by the eighteenth century, well before the Mobile Unit speakers' parents departed for New Zealand, this range had narrowed to two realisations, [ɪ] and [ə] (p. 260). He indicates that a contrast was preserved in the 'Received Standard speech' (or 'best usage') with [ɪ] used regularly for words now written with <*e*>, such as *knowledge*, *blanket*, or *harmless*, and also for some words spelled <*-as*> such as *Thomas*, *purchase*. Other unstressed syllables spelled with <*a*> or <*o*>, such as *stomach*, *infant*, *bishop*, were pronounced with [ə]. Word-initial unstressed syllables all had [ə]. This distinction was broken down in lower-class speech ('vulgar speech') or in the 'regions'. Most of the examples Wyld gave for nonstandard pronunciations involve [ə] where the 'Received Standard' has [ɪ], such as '[ɪntrəst], which is provincial' (1920: 261), but there are examples of the reverse trend, such as *wagon*, with [ɪ] instead of the expected [ə] (p. 264). The lack of contrast in these unstressed vowels, which Wells (p. 167) calls the *Weak Vowel Merger*, was also apparently a feature of lower-class London English, since Smart (1836) cited among errors to be avoided in his *Hints to Cockney Speakers* 'perp*u*trate, affin*u*ty, provid*u*nce' (in Ellis 1889: 227). Map 9 (Appendix 3) shows the extent of the weak vowel merger in the SED materials. Here the merger is restricted to a band across the north of England, the south-west and a smaller area in the south-east.

In Scottish English, the analysis of unstressed syllables 'presents problems' according to Wells (1982: 405). He reports that a phonemic contrast in unstressed vowels is mostly unclear (except for those who make a contrast between 'except' and 'accept' in non-final syllables); the pronunciation tends to be [ʌ] word-finally, but elsewhere a 'very [ə]-like' /ɪ/, though in Edinburgh a phoneme /ə/, [ə] 'seems more realistic'.

Because many of the early New Zealand settlers came from the lower classes or 'the regions', it is likely that the clear distinction between [ɪ] and [ə] in unstressed syllables was not present in the speech of most of them. Wells says that in modern Irish English 'the merger of KIT and schwa is well advanced' in unstressed checked syllables (1982: 427). If this merger was already underway in the nineteenth century, Irish immigrants to New Zealand could have added to the number of speakers who did not make clear distinctions in unstressed syllables.

15.3 Early New Zealand commentaries on unstressed vowels

The earliest written comment we have found about the pronunciation of unstressed vowels in New Zealand English is in *The Triad* in 1895 (cited earlier in the discussion of other vowels): 'The usual mispronunciation of words, for which one learns to look in New Zealand, were pronounced as usual. What are *rorth*, *cuvernunt*, *heavun*, *trinurty*, *glowry?*' In this extract, *cuvernunt*, *heavun* and *trinurty* all appear to indicate the use of [ə] in the unstressed position, where speakers who have not undergone the weak vowel merger would use [ɪ]. By 1900, school inspectors were also commenting:

> Some teachers . . . speak so badly as to be quite disqualified . . . Those who say . . . 'systum' for system are manifestly unfit to teach reading. (Robert Lee, Wellington school inspector, *AJHR* E-1B, 1900: 14)
>
> Failure to appreciate the value of common vowel sounds . . . (and more recent developments) *ut* for 'it', *plasuz* for 'places'. (Wellington inspectors, *AJHR* E-1B, 1908: 16)
>
> This carelessness or indifference on the part of the teacher is mainly responsible for such improprieties as . . . 'plasuz' (places) 'dishers' (dishes) 'ut' for 'it', 'paintud' for 'painted' . . . (Wellington school inspectors *AJHR* E-2, 1914, Appendix C: xii–xiv)

Comments in *The Triad* continued to complain about the vowels used in unstressed syllables:

> Miss Plummer is a very clever little lady, who will do something one day. In this recitation there were many mispronunciations, such as: . . . 'sullun' 'lansuz' (lancers) 'evun' . . . (*The Triad*, 1 February 1909: 9)
>
> Included in a list of 'mispronunciations': 'voisuz' for 'voices', 'viol-uts' for 'violets', 'siluncе' for 'silence', 'darknuss' for 'darkness', 'evul' for 'evil'. (*The Triad*, 10 December 1912)

The lack of contrast in unstressed syllables in New Zealand has sometimes been linked with the centralisation of the KIT vowel (e.g. Bauer 1994: 390), though the weak vowel merger seems to have an older and cleaner pedigree of British historical antecedence, both in New Zealand and elsewhere, than the centralisation of KIT does. This suggests they may not be causally linked, at least not so much in the beginning.

15.4 Results from the Mobile Unit speakers for unstressed vowels

Because many of the Mobile Unit speakers were at least partially rhotic, the final syllables of *lett*ER and *comm*A words words may be distinguished in their speech. Most do not produce centralised versions of the KIT vowel, and some still make the [ɪ] ~ [ə] distinction described by Wells. One of the noticeable features of the Mobile Unit speakers' speech in comparison to modern New Zealand English is the extent to which tokens of unstressed syllables are pronounced with [ɪ] rather than [ə]. However, the auditory analyses show that half of the speakers actually

Table 6.12 *Distribution of variants for unstressed vowels*

Variant	0 [ɪ]	1 [ɨ]	2 [ə]
Token Count	1,221 (51%)	774 (32.4%)	397 (16.6%)

used centralised vowels in unstressed syllables. The impression that [ɪ] vowels are frequent comes from the third of the speakers who use [ɪ] consistently.

15.4.1 Unstressed vowel centralisation. In our analysis of the unstressed vowel we do not consider the degree to which individuals make the contrast between [ɪ] and [ə], but rather the degree to which unstressed vowels in the former set are produced with centralised variants. That is, our analysis concentrated on the *rabbit* class of words (where RP, for example, would have KIT), not the *abbot* class (where one might expect schwa), and did not contrast speakers' production of the two word classes. We expect, of course, that greater degree of centralisation of the vowel in the *rabbit* class is likely to be correlated with greater degree of weak vowel merger, but the former is much easier to see in the evidence than the latter is. 2,392 tokens were coded, with variants distributed as shown in Table 6.12.

15.4.1.1 Speaker analysis. For each speaker, the average degree of centralisation was calculated, by using the coding of tokens – 0, 1, 2 (see Table 6.12), as numeric values. Thus, an index score of 0 would indicate consistent lack of centralisation, and an index score of 2 would indicate consistent complete centralisation. Scores ranged from 0.18 (Mr Robert Ritchie, born 1864 of Scottish parents in a mixed settlement), to 1.24 (Mrs Annie Hamilton, born 1877 of Irish parents in a mixed settlement).

A stepwise linear model containing parents' origin, birthdate, gender, and settlement type retains none of the above as significant predictors of patterns in the data. There do appear to be some non-significant tendencies, though, as shown in Figures 6.31–6.34. Speakers of Scottish and English descent show reduced rates of centralisation in comparison with other speakers (Figure 6.31).

Centralisation in the unstressed vowel shows a tendency to increase over time (Figures 6.32–6.34), this trend being particularly marked in mixed settlements (Figure 6.32). Overall, women appear to display more centralisation of the unstressed vowel than men (Figures 6.33; 6.34), although this appears to be true only of mixed and rural settlements (Figure 6.35), and not of predominantly Scottish or English ones.

Figure 6.34 shows the gradual increase in centralisation of the unstressed vowels. Overall, females are more advanced than males. The dip in the solid line fit through the female speakers is most probably an artifact and reflects the smaller number of women who were available for analysis.

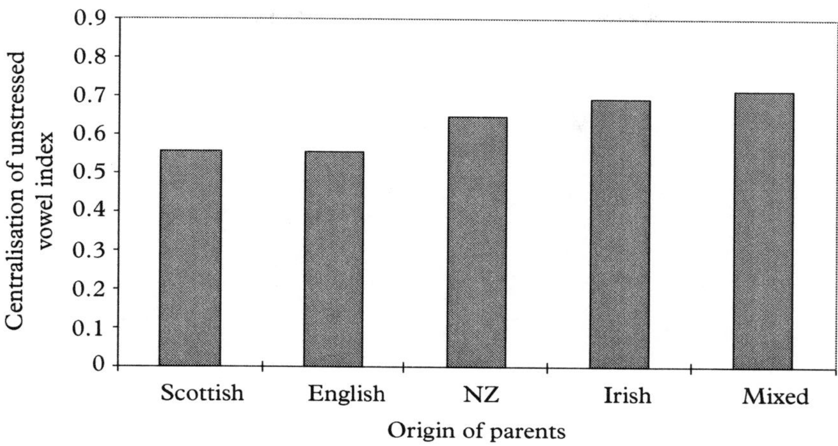

Figure 6.31 Unstressed vowel centralisation, by origin of parents

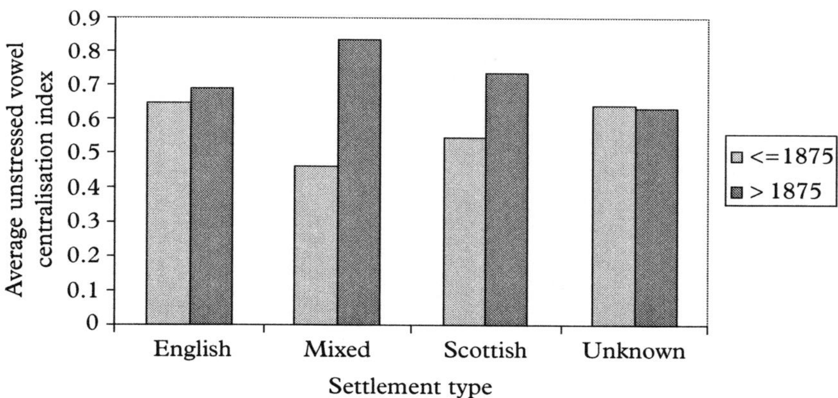

Figure 6.32 Unstressed vowel centralisation, by birthdate and settlement type

Despite the non-significance of these results in the linear model, CART analysis does provide some significant results, pinpointing the origin of the father and the speaker's birthdate as playing a pivotal role in the centralisation of the unstressed vowel. Australian and Irish fathers significantly facilitate the use of centralised variants, and later-born speakers show more centralisation than older speakers.

15.4.1.2 Token analysis. In the token analysis we compared uncentralised variants ([ɪ]) with variants with some centralisation ([ɨ] or [ə]). Despite the non-significance of the social variables in the speaker-based linear model, all social

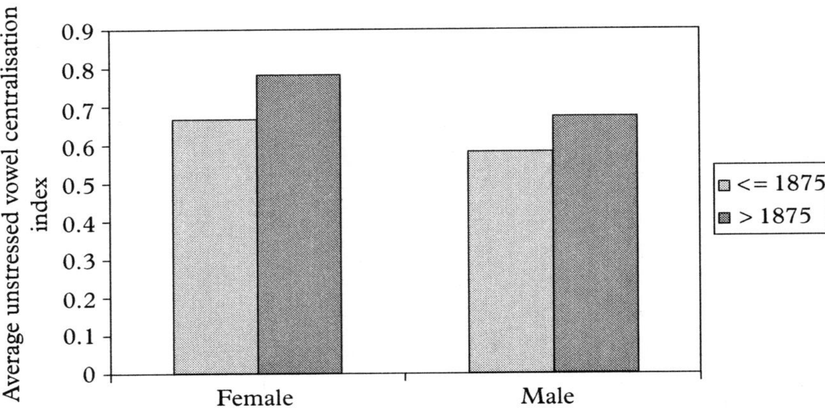

Figure 6.33 Unstressed vowel centralisation, by birthdate and gender

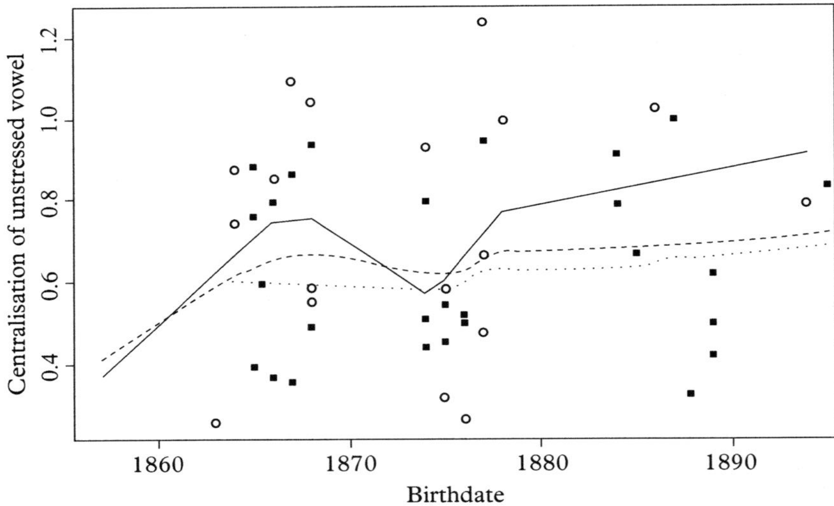

Figure 6.34 Unstressed vowel centralisation (Each point represents a speaker. Filled square points represent male speakers, unfilled round points represent female speakers. Each line represents a non-parametric scatterpoint smoother fit through the points. The solid line is fit through the female speakers, the dotted line is fit through the male speakers, and the dashed line indicates the line of best fit through all speakers in the sample. Higher values indicate greater centralisation of the unstressed vowel.)

Table 6.13 *Linguistic constraints on centralisation of unstressed vowels*

		Facilitation of centralisation
Following environment	Manner	nasals > plosives > approximants > fricatives
	Place	labial > coronal > back
Preceding environment	Manner	vowels > pauses > fricatives > approximants > nasals > plosives
	Place	labial > back > coronal

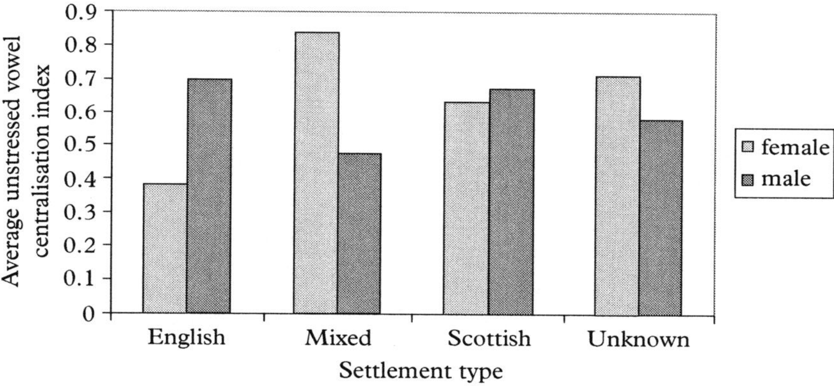

Figure 6.35 Unstressed vowel centralisation, by settlement type and gender

variables are retained in a stepwise logistic model of the data (gender, birthdate, parents' origins, settlement type). In addition, interactions between settlement type and sex, and settlement type and age are also retained. The linguistic factors retained are shown in Table 6.13.

One interpretation of the fact that so many social variables were non-significant in the speaker analysis but emerged as significant in the token analysis considers the presence of linguistic environmental effects. As the environmental effects are fairly strong it seems plausible that it was these effects that were responsible for the lack of significance of the social factors in the linear model used in the speaker analysis, which could not take the linguistic environment into account. Once environment is factored in, all social variables emerge as strongly significant. The direction of the patterns is consistent with the graphs in Figures 6.31–6.35. Females show significantly more centralisation than males, centralisation is increasing with time, and the biggest shift takes place in mixed communities. While women in general are leading the change, this is not true in the settlements that are settled by primarily English or Scottish immigrants. As the token-based graphs echo almost exactly the patterns shown in Figures 6.31–6.35, they are not repeated here. In this interpretation, then, the findings of the speaker analysis

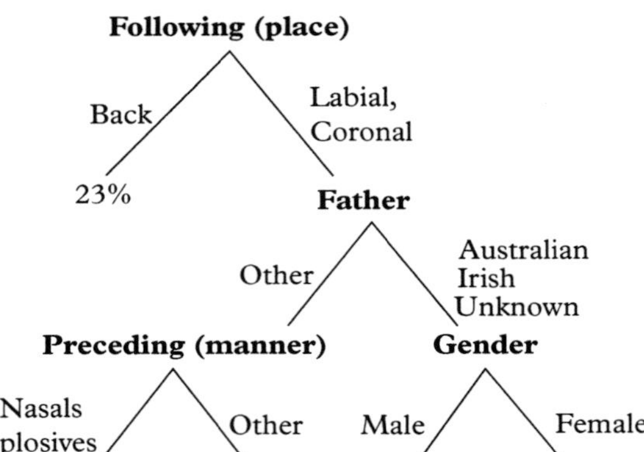

Figure 6.36 CART regression tree showing percentage of unstressed vowel centralisation of unstressed vowels across all tokens

are likely to reflect genuine differences, the significance of which was formerly masked by the presence of strong environmental conditioners.

A second interpretation is that the differences in significance between the speaker and the token analyses might arise if a relatively small number of speakers were carrying most of the variation. However, examination of the data suggests that the results reported here are fairly robust across speakers. Figure 6.34, for example, shows that the reported gender effect is not simply due to one or two outlier speakers.

Finally, a CART regression tree selects place of articulation of the following segment, father's origin, gender, and the manner of articulation of a preceding segment as significant predictors of the variation in the data, as shown in Figure 6.36. The fact that a linguistic factor is selected by the CART model as the primary predictor of the data lends weight to the interpretation that the speaker-based analysis failed to reach significance primarily because it was unable to take into account the effects of linguistic environment.

15.5 Happ*Y-tensing*

New Zealand English appears to have undergone the change Wells (1982: 257–8) calls *happY-tensing*, where the final syllable of words like *city* are now realised with the FLEECE vowel rather than the traditional KIT vowel.

15.5.1 British historical antecedents of happY*-tensing.* Wyld (1914, 1936) showed that reflexes of the diphthongs *-ei* and *-ai* had become [ɪ] well before the start of the nineteenth century. Names for days of the week were also usually pronounced with [ɪ]. As Wells (1982: 258) points out, this vowel was regularly seen by phoneticians as [ɪ] between the seventeenth century and 1950, though there is 'an increasing tendency throughout the English-speaking world to use a closer quality [i(ː)]' and this pronunciation 'has probably been in use in provincial and vulgar speech for centuries'. Scottish varieties have vowel qualities similar to [e] of FACE (Wells 1982: 166). Bauer (1999: 292) sees *happ*Y-tensing as restricted to the English traditional dialect of the south-west, which is the area shown from the SED materials in Map 10 (Appendix 3). Wells (1982: 166) reports, 'consistent final [i] in much of the south of England, as well as in the peripheral north' and that it is invading RP (pp. 106, 405). This is consistent with the much greater area found by Trudgill and also shown in Map 10. Because the [i] pronunciation is so common in the southern hemisphere, Wells assumes that it must have been 'prevalent in the local accents of south-east England by the early nineteenth century' (p. 258). The Mobile Unit speakers provide concrete evidence with which to evaluate this assumption.

15.5.2 Early New Zealand commentaries on happ*Y-tensing.* There are relatively few comments on *happ*Y-tensing. The first we found comes from McBurney in 1887, as reported by Ellis:

> *Symplicity* with final *y* as (-i, -ii) [i] and not (-*i*) [ɪ]. This was not tested by Mr. McB[urney] till he came to Br. [Brisbane], and there he found it very common in [Brisbane, Sydney, Auckland, Wellington, Napier, Nelson, Christchurch, Dunedin]. His attention had been drawn to it by two Englishmen as a colonial impurity. (Ellis 1889: 245, fn. 3)

McBurney also gave variant pronunciations of *city*, with final [ɪ] said to be general in most locations, but with final [i] given as 'few' in Wellington, Napier, and Dunedin (in Ellis 1889: 241) Twenty years later, an article in *The Triad* quoted Mr E. W. Andrews of Napier Boys' High School: 'I have been constantly annoyed, too, by the substitution of a long "e" for the short final "y," which produces such words as "beautee", "babee", "badlee" – a peculiarity that I have noticed before only in the Eurasians in Bombay.' (*The Triad*, 10 August 1910: 39.) Finally, in Arnold Wall (1936) we find the following:

> Y, final as –ee
> 'Dirtee' for 'dirty' etc. A correspondent asks why so many people in New Zealand pronounce final *y* in this way, since it is not standard English . . . The peculiar ee is almost universal, is indeed very distressing, and seems likely to resist all attempts to eradicate it. I do not think it 'comes from' anywhere, certainly not India, though it is very marked in 'chi chi' English. In most cases where a sound varies from the standard in New Zealand speech, it is simply Cockney, and those who think otherwise have probably not had my experience behind them, for I spent my whole life, from the age of 9 to 29, in and about London. But this final ee seems to have arisen here spontaneously. (Wall 1936: 136)

15.5.3 Results from the Mobile Unit speakers for the happY *vowel.* Approximately half of the Mobile Unit speakers realise the *happ*Y vowel with [ɪ]. Just over a quarter of the speakers use [i], and the rest vary in their pronunciations. It therefore does not seem that the majority of early New Zealanders used the [i] realisation (though nearly 40% did, if we combine those with consistent [i] and those with variable pronunciations). There is an increase in the usage of [i] over time. If we combine those who use [i] consistently with those who use it variably, approximately 35% of the speakers born before 1875 use [i] for *happ*Y at least some of the time. The percentage rises to nearly 50% for those born in 1875 or later. Wells' (1982: 258) observation of this form in vulgar and regional speech by the early nineteenth century would appear to be correct, since many of the ONZE speakers do have [i]. Thus, *happ*Y-tensing probably did not start its life independently in New Zealand, though its frequency of occurrence appears not to have been in the majority at the beginning.

Although we have not attempted a systematic analysis of the pronunciation of the days of the week, pronunciations of *-day* with [ɪ], [i] and [ei] can all be heard from speakers in the Mobile Unit, though [ei] pronunciations are more common from the younger speakers in the group.

Structural properties may have aided the increase of *happ*Y-tensing. That is, English has no other lax (open) counterparts of [ɪ] in final position, no final [ɛ], [ʊ], or [ɒ]. Also, the contrast in unstressed syllables of [ɪ] and [ə] was merging to [ə] in New Zealand (see *Weak Vowel Merger* in Section 15.4.1), leaving no counterpart of final [ɪ] in other unstressed syllables. These system-internal pressures could have contributed to the increase in final [i] for the *happ*Y vowel (see Hickey 2002: 14; Wells 1982: 76, 291).

16 The 'r' variable (/r/ in non-prevocalic position)

As we have seen, modern New Zealand English is non-rhotic, with the exception of Southland and parts of Otago, in the far south of the South Island (see Bartlett 1992, 2003). That is, /r/ occurs only in prevocalic position, as in *rat*, *trap*, *carry*, *car appliance*, but not in non-prevocalic position, as in *cart*, *car wash*, *car*. The history of this variable in New Zealand is a surprising one.

16.1 British historical antecedents of the 'r' variable

Some of the main rhotic varieties of English include Scottish and Irish varieties and dialects of south-west England, much of the English spoken in the United States, including General American (though excluding parts of the South – see Wolfram and Schilling-Estes 1998: 94–6), Canadian English and Barbados English (Wells 1982). The non-rhoticity of general New Zealand English is the result of the sound change that Wells (1982: 218) labels *R Dropping*, which is well known to have begun in some regions of England (cf. Anderson 1987: 14, 19). The chronology of this change is of considerable importance for our purposes. The general consensus on the development of the southern hemisphere Englishes and the loss of non-prevocalic /r/ in English suggests that the absence of rhoticity in Australia, (most of) New Zealand and (much of) South Africa can be explained by the timing of colonisation in the southern hemisphere, namely that it postdated the loss of non-prevocalic /r/ in the parts of Britain from which the immigrants to these countries largely originated (Trudgill 1986b; Lass 1987, 1990; but see another view in Trudgill 1999a).

Non-prevocalic /r/ began disappearing in English in the seventeenth century, at least in certain environments (Strang 1970: 112), though this process was not widespread in southern England until, at the earliest, the middle of the eighteenth century (Wolfram and Schilling-Estes 1998: 94). Wells (1982: 218) dates it to 'the eighteenth century, when /r/ disappeared before a consonant or in absolute final position'. Strang (1970: 112) writes that 'in post-vocalic position, finally or pre-consonantally, /r/ was weakened in articulation in the 17c and reduced to a vocalic segment early in the 18c'. Bailey (1996: 100) dates the shift even later: 'The shift from consonantal to vocalic /r/, though sporadic earlier, gathered force at the end of the eighteenth century'. The dates given by Strang and Bailey do indeed seem to be accurate for London. John Walker, in his *Critical Pronouncing Dictionary and Expositor of the English Language* (1791, quoted in Beal 1993: 7–8) says that non-prevocalic /r/ is 'sometimes entirely sunk'. However, according to Beal, Walker is referring here 'only to the most advanced dialect' of his day, colloquial London English, and Beal further argues that the loss of /r/ was still stigmatised in the first decades of the 1800s. Hallam, quoted in MacMahon (1983: 28), also shows that variable rhoticity continued to be a feature of some upper-class speech into the 1870s, citing the accents of Disraeli (b. 1804) and Prince Leopold (b. 1853), the fourth son of Queen Victoria. Ellis (1889: 131) confirms the retention of non-prevocalic /r/ in various southern dialects.

It is clear, too, that most regional dialects lagged behind London English and the prestige norm that was to become RP. Bailey's (1996: 102) statement that 'resistance to the spreading London fashion was, however, not long sustained' is a considerable exaggeration as far as regional dialects are concerned, many of which are still rhotic today. If we work backwards chronologically, the evidence from dialectology is rather clear on this point. Map 6 (in Appendix 3) shows areas of England that were rhotic in different ways at different periods in local dialects. We note the following numbered areas marked out on Map 6:

1. Areas that were fully rhotic in the SED (large parts of the south-west and the north-west, plus the north-east). Also included are parts of Wales that are indicated to be rhotic by Thomas (1994): these are 'the rural communities of the west and the north' where it is said to be a feature 'carried over' from Welsh (p. 128); and the long-term English-speaking areas of southern Pembroke (p. 131), and Gower, where, however, it is 'infrequent'; and the Marches, which are the counties of Wales bordering directly on Herefordshire, Shropshire and Gloucestershire (p. 130).

2. Areas of eastern Yorkshire which in the SED retained non-prevocalic /r/ only in unstressed final syllables, as in *butter*.

3. Areas of Essex which in the SED retained non-prevocalic /r/ only after /ɜː/, as in *worms*.

4. Additional areas that are shown to be fully rhotic in the 1930s in Kurath and Lowman (1970).

5. Areas of the south and east Midlands, and of Essex and Suffolk, which Lowman's research showed as having /r/ after /ɜː/ in the 1930s (from Kurath and Lowman 1970: 29).

6. Areas that are shown in Ellis (1889) as being rhotic. The details for Ellis are as follows for the areas not shown as rhotic at later dates:

In area 20, 'Border Midland', which is equivalent to Lincolnshire, Ellis explicitly states (p. 297) that /r/ is vocalised or omitted. This is confirmed by the transcriptions he cites.

In area 24, 'Eastern West Midland', which is essentially South Yorkshire, rhoticity is variable but present, including Sheffield and Rotherham.

In area 25, 'Western Mid Midland', which centres on Cheshire, the transcriptions all show rhoticity.

In area 26, 'Eastern Mid Midland', which centres on Derbyshire, transcriptions show total rhoticity except in the far east of the county.

In area 27, 'East Midland', which is equivalent to Nottinghamshire, transcriptions show lack of rhoticity, except in East Retford in the north bordering the Eastern West Midland.

In area 29 'Eastern South Midland', all the transcriptions show rhoticity except for those for Lichfield, Staffordshire, and Atherstone and Enderby, Leicestershire.

In area 30 'East Northern', transcriptions generally do not show rhoticity (except in the east where it shows up in items such as *butter*).

The whole of area 31 'West Northern' has transcriptions showing rhoticity.

7. Welsh-speaking areas in the mid-nineteenth century, where we can assume, following Thomas (1994), that there was rhoticity in the second-language English spoken.

Thus, the only areas of England and Wales for which we have *no* evidence of rhoticity in the mid-nineteenth century lie in two separate corridors. The first runs south from the North Riding of Yorkshire through the Vale of York into north and central Lincolnshire, nearly all of Nottinghamshire, and adjacent areas of Derbyshire, Leicestershire, and Staffordshire. The second includes all of Norfolk, western Suffolk and Essex, eastern Cambridgeshire and Hertfordshire, Middlesex, and northern Surrey and Kent.

In all the r-pronouncing areas, it is possible that many speakers would nevertheless have been non-rhotic, or variable, depending on their position on the social-class scale, and on the degree of conservatism of the area in question.

Thus, at the time of the spread of English into the English-speaking northern hemisphere colonies (USA, parts of the Caribbean, Canada, Ireland), from approximately the mid-seventeenth–mid-eighteenth century, non-prevocalic /r/ would have been a feature of most English dialects, and so rhoticity would have been transported with the settlers.[19] Although it is hypothesised that /r/-loss was probably not complete in southern Britain until at least the early nineteenth century (Lass 1987: 275; 1997: 289; Bailey 1996: 105), it has generally been assumed that it had spread sufficiently by this time, for the majority of settlers to the southern hemisphere (with the exception of those from Scotland, Ireland, or the south-west of England) to have already lost /r/ before they left Britain:

> Despite blusterings about the 'vulgar' and the Cockney early in the century, the weakening and loss of /r/ (and the consequent rise of linking and intrusive /r/) came to completion early and at all social levels influenced by London fashion, just in time for the English of Australia, New Zealand, and South Africa to be drawn within the sphere of change. (Bailey 1996: 105)

The fact that Australian English, New Zealand English, and South African English are (mostly) non-rhotic is generally cited as support for this claim.

The local variety spoken in Southland and parts of Otago in the South Island is often claimed, by both linguists and lay people, to be New Zealand's only regional dialect, because of the presence of rhoticity – the 'Southland /r/' (Bayard 1990b: 155). This is usually attributed to the high proportion of Scottish settlers in that area. It is important to note, however, that Southland speakers are not fully rhotic. Recent research (Bartlett 1992, 2003) suggests that non-prevocalic /r/ is maintained most fully in the NURSE lexical set and varies considerably in other environments. Moreover, Bartlett shows that rhoticity in Southland is disappearing in all contexts except the NURSE set (1992: 7). Interestingly, similar patterns have been reported in other dialects, such as Levine and Crockett's (1966) study of rhoticity in Hillsboro, North Carolina, which found that speakers consistently had r-colouring after NURSE lexical items (cited in Wells 1982: 542). A small region in Massachusetts and Maine, in the transition zone between the non-rhotic Atlantic seaboard and the rhotic inland area, also has /r/ in NURSE but not elsewhere (Jack Chambers, personal communication, 2001), and in England, Williams and Kerswill (1999: 147) report that younger speakers in Reading retain non-prevocalic /r/ in the case of the NURSE vowel only.

There is also some debate as to whether South African English can really be described as non-rhotic. Lanham (1978) notes that rhoticity may be heard in 'extreme' varieties of South African English. He attributes this to a direct result of contact with Afrikaans (p. 55); Lass and Wright (1986) argue that

[19] Note that Lass (1987) and others (Wolfram and Schilling-Estes 1998: 93ff.; Romaine 1994: 137, 144–8) argue that non-rhoticity would also have been taken to the colonies.

South African English is actually 'semi-rhotic', particularly in lower social varieties, not necessarily as a contact phenomenon from Afrikaans, but as a relic feature from the input dialects of the early English settlers (p. 204). Branford (1994: 346) suggests that in the early Xhosa borrowing *tichela* from English *teacher*, /l/ replaced post-vocalic /r/ (Xhosa did not have an /r/ phoneme). This has been explained as coming from Scottish missionaries; however, it could also be an indication that early South African English was variably rhotic.

We would expect numerous kinds of /r/ to be part of the original input into New Zealand English from the different dialects brought by immigrants, including Scottish [r], [ɾ], [ɻ] or [ɹ] (Grant 1913 cited in Wells 1982: 411), Irish [ɹ] or [ɻ] (Wells 1982: 432), and various regional varieties of English English.

16.2 Early New Zealand commentaries on 'r'

A number of comments concerning rhoticity in early New Zealand English, both its presence and absence, were found. For example, McBurney, in *The Press*, 5 October 1887 remarked:

> Where the young colonial finds himself understood by half the oral exertion necessary, he forthwith abbreviates . . . and the strong trilled final r is avoided as an unnecessary exertion, when it is noticed that the majority of arrivals habitually neglect it. It is therefore quite common for the children to call farther *fahthu* (u of *but*) when the parent says farrthurr with a very loud trill: world, *wu'ld*, instead of *wurruld* and so forth. The insertion of r where it is not wanted, as in idea-r-of, is also explicable, as it is easier than to make the necessary hiatus between two tongue positions of the several vowels.

McBurney in 1887 listed his impressions of the frequency of final 'r' in several words for several New Zealand locations. Unsurprisingly, all were preserved with 'r' in Dunedin; 'poor' had a few with final 'r' in Nelson but was about equal with and without in Christchurch; 'sure' had few in Auckland and some in Christchurch; final 'r' in 'more' was general in Nelson and Christchurch, as was the 'r' of 'morning'; and 'r' in 'pearls' was half and half in Nelson and Christchurch (in Ellis 1889: 241–5).

From G. Harkness, Nelson school inspector, in 1908, we have his complaint concerning 'in certain localities faulty pronunciation such as . . . the omission of the final "r" as well as its opposite, the addition of one to a final vowel' (*AJHR* E-1B, 1908: 16). Two years later, *The Triad* (8 August 1910: 39), quoting Mr E. W. Andrews of Napier Boys' High School, confirms the presence of rhoticity, but also its absence for some, plus the existence of intrusive 'r':

> the letter 'r' which in England is pronounced only before a quickly-following vowel, is here commonly sounded before a consonant (as in 'Turkey' and 'heard') and is even inserted to fill a hiatus (as in 'I sawr it,'

'the idear of it.' 'the lor of Nature.') On the other hand, many colonial children are unable to trill the 'r' at all.

School inspectors noted the presence of both intrusive and linking 'r':

> . . . on several occasions pupils pronounced 'saw' as 'sor', 'idea' as 'idear' . . . [these are] simply barbarisms. (D. A. Strachan, Marlborough school inspector, *AJHR* E-1B, 1907: 23)

> This carelessness or indifference on the part of the teacher is mainly responsible for such improprieties as . . . the joining of the final consonant of one word on to an initial vowel of another, as 'ourise,' 'yourears' for 'our eyes' 'your ears' etc . . . (Wellington school inspectors, *AJHR* E-2, 1914, Appendix C: xiii–xiv)

16.3 Results from the Mobile Unit speakers for 'r'

The auditory perceptual analysis confirmed that a variety of realisations of /r/ were brought to New Zealand. Almost three-quarters of the 95 speakers analysed used alveolar approximants as their most common variant of /r/, but more than half of these speakers also produced some tapped (flapped) and retroflex tokens, as well. The remaining quarter of the speakers consistently used tapped or retroflex variants of /r/. The majority of the parents of this last group came from Scotland or Ireland.

In the auditory quantitative analysis, up to 300 tokens were analysed for non-prevocalic /r/ for each of the 59 speakers. To avoid lexical bias in the results, a maximum of ten tokens of any single word was used per speaker. Two variants were treated: the absence of non-prevocalic /r/ and the presence of non-prevocalic /r/. (Different phonetic variants were not distinguished, though most tokens were approximants.) In total, 13,700 tokens of words where there was a potential for non-prevocalic /r/ to occur were analysed; /r/ was produced in 9.1% of these tokens.

The data were organised into two data sets. The first was designed to analyse the average degree of rhoticity of individual speakers. The second investigated factors influencing the likelihood that any individual token will contain an /r/.

16.3.1 Speaker analysis of 'r'. The average rhoticity of each speaker was calculated. This figure ranged from 0 to 56%. The most rhotic speaker was Mrs Ellen Dennison, born to Scottish parents in 1874 in Arrowtown in the South Island, orphaned at the age of eight and taken in by a rural family who were most likely Scottish. Twenty-nine speakers (almost half) were less than 5% rhotic. A stepwise linear model was then fitted, considering gender, settlement type, birthdate, mother's and father's origin, and interactions between these factors as possible predictors of an individual's rhoticity. The model retained settlement type, birthdate, and the origin of the parents as highly significant predictors of

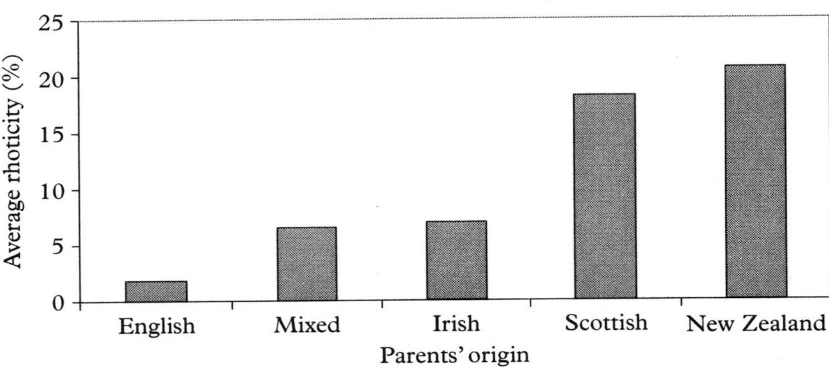

Figure 6.37 Average rhoticity by origin of parents

rhoticity, together with an interaction between settlement type and birthdate. Being in a Scottish settlement strongly influenced the degree of rhoticity; mixed settlements also showed a fairly high degree of rhoticity, but English settlements showed very little. Similarly, while individuals with Scottish parents showed the highest degree of rhoticity, individuals with English parents showed the lowest. Rhoticity decreased faster in mixed settlements than other types of settlements.

The effect of the parents' origin on rhoticity is shown in Figure 6.37, with individuals directly descended from English parents showing the lowest rates of rhoticity. Note that the facilitating influence of New Zealand parents upon rhoticity appears anomalously high in Figure 6.37. When we investigate the specific individuals involved, we find that most of the speakers in our database with New Zealand-born parents are living in Scottish settlements (see Appendix 6 for details).

Figure 6.38 shows the average rhoticity by settlement type and birthdate. The significant effect of settlement type can be seen in the higher rates of rhoticity in the mixed and Scottish settlements than in the English settlements, or the rural areas (settlements labeled 'unknown' were too small to have census data). The significant effect of birthdate can be seen by the decrease in rhoticity over time, which occurred in all settlements. The significant interaction between birthdate and settlement type arises because rhoticity decreases at a much faster rate in the mixed settlements than all other settlements.

While gender is not retained in the linear model as a predictor, the female speakers do appear to show quite a dramatic reduction in rhoticity, which is unparalleled by the male speakers. This pattern is shown in Figure 6.39.

A CART regression model identifies the same three factors – parents' origin, settlement type, and birthdate – as significant predictors of rhoticity, with Scottish towns and/or parents facilitating rhoticity, and with rhoticity declining fairly sharply with time. The regression tree is shown in Figure 6.40.

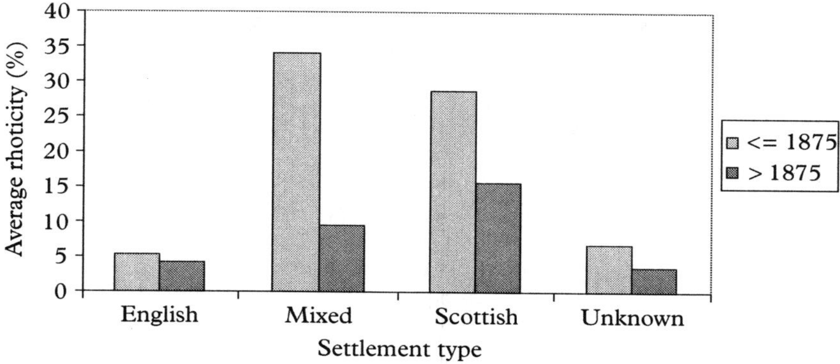

Figure 6.38 Average rhoticity by settlement type and birthdate

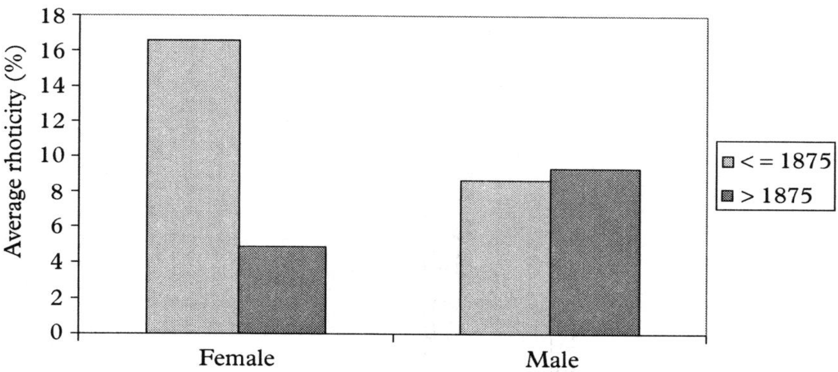

Figure 6.39 Average rhoticity by gender and birthdate

16.3.2 Token analysis of 'r'. A second analysis was conducted on the entire data set of tokens, to investigate how social effects combine with possible linguistic conditioners. Because a larger number of tokens were analysed for rhoticity than the other variables, we chose to analyse a larger number of linguistic conditioners than for the vocalic variables. These tokens were coded for linguistic and social factors, and analysed with a stepwise logistic regression. Nine factors were retained as highly significant predictors of rhoticity in this data set. These are outlined below.

16.3.2.1 Social factors as predictors of 'r'. The same social factors were retained in the token analysis as in the speaker analysis: parents' origin, birthdate of speaker, and settlement type. In addition, speaker gender was identified as a significant predictor of 'r'.

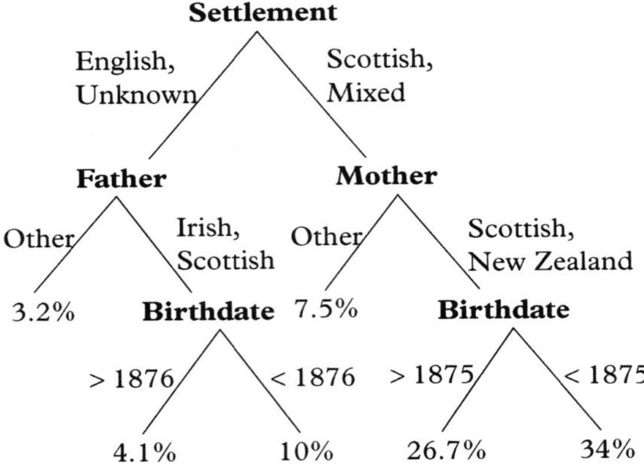

Figure 6.40 CART regression tree predicting speakers' average degree of rhoticity

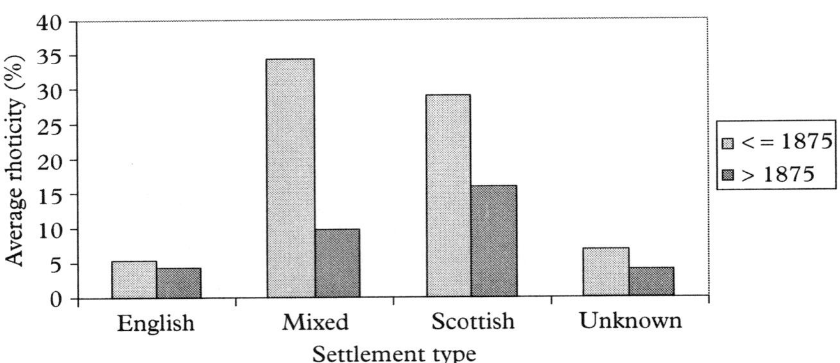

Figure 6.41 Average degree of rhoticity, by birthdate and settlement type

Later-born speakers were less rhotic. While this is modelled as a continuous factor in the statistics, Figure 6.41 shows the result using a binary division between speakers born before 1875, and those born in 1875 or later. The effect of age in the different settlement types is also shown. Note that, while in the early stages, the mixed towns show a high degree of rhoticity, the rhoticity decreases at a much faster rate than it does in the towns that have a clear majority of Scottish settlers.

16.3.2.2 Linguistic factors. 1. **Following segment.** Three factors relating to the following segment are significant: the voicing, the obstruency, and the coronality. For tokens with a following voiceless sound, 11.5% are produced with

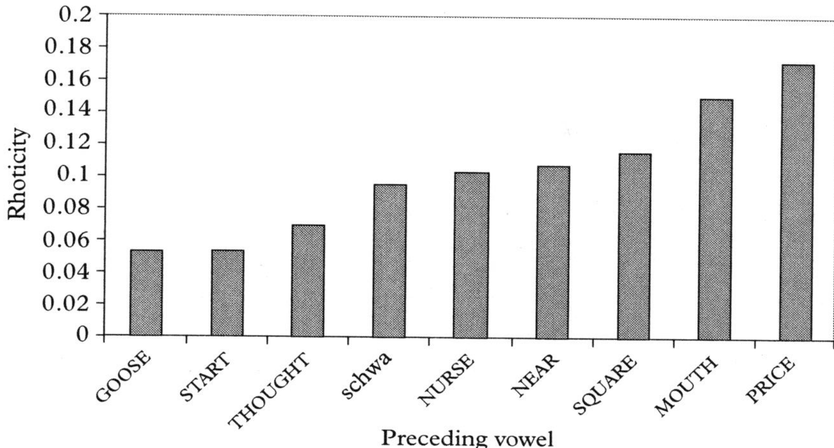

Figure 6.42 Average degree of rhoticity (across tokens), as conditioned by the preceding vowel

/r/, compared with 7% of tokens followed by voiced sounds. For tokens with a following non-coronal sound, 11.3% are produced with /r/, as opposed to 7.7% of the tokens followed by coronals. Finally, 9.4% of tokens followed by obstruents are rhotic, as opposed to 8% of tokens followed by sonorants.

2. **Preceding vowel.** As shown in Figure 6.42, preceding diphthongs clearly facilitate the production of /r/. For MOUTH and PRICE, the /r/ took longer to disappear and left a trace in the form of schwa, *fire* /aiə/ and *power* /aʊə/, in modern New Zealand English. The short vowels, KIT and DRESS also retained /r/ for a relatively long time, and also left a trace in modern New Zealand English as NEAR and SQUARE. The high back round FOOT vowel showed least rhoticity in this corpus. It retained a trace in the form of schwa as CURE, even though this phoneme is currently marginal, and so appears to form an exception to the apparent link between r-retention and its eventual replacement by schwa. We should note that we have very few tokens for CURE (38), PRICE (59) and MOUTH (66). All other vowels have more than 800 tokens. Of the long vowels, NURSE is the most likely vowel to facilitate /r/, consistent with patterns noted in other dialects (see Section 16.1 above).

3. **Lexical stress.** The logistic regression model shows stressed syllables are significantly more likely than unstressed ones to be produced with /r/, yet 9% of both stressed and unstressed syllable tokens contain /r/. This indicates that the distribution of other predictive variables (such as preceding and following environment) was not equal across stressed and unstressed syllables, and while the unstressed syllables were predicted to be less rhotic overall, due to these other

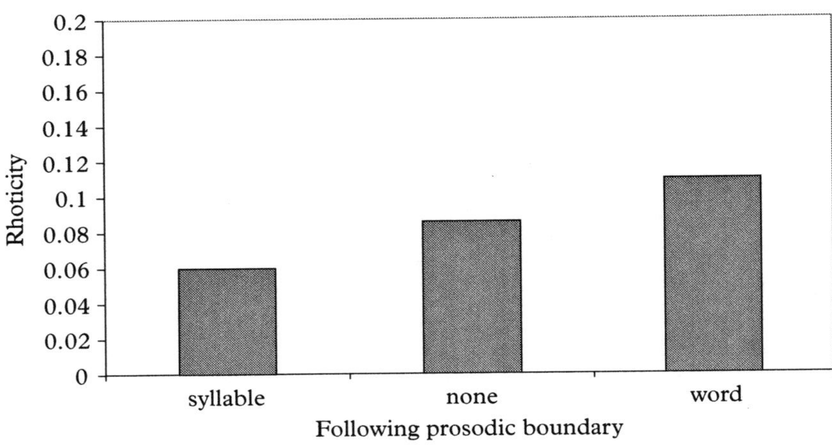

Figure 6.43 Effect of the following prosodic boundary on the realisation of /r/

factors they showed higher levels of rhoticity than expected. This is evidence that stress affects the production of /r/.

4. **The strength of a following prosodic boundary.** As shown in Figure 6.43, the strength of a following prosodic boundary affects the likelihood of /r/. Tokens with a following word boundary (e.g. *car door*), are most likely to be produced with /r/.[20] Tokens with a following syllable boundary are least likely (e.g. *carpet*). Tokens with no prosodic boundary following (e.g. *harp*) showed an intermediate degree of rhoticity.

5. **Semantic domains.** We classified words according to the semantic domains in which they occurred. We had gained the impression when listening to the recordings that words associated with old-time activities and activities strongly associated with the settler lifestyle were more likely to retain non-prevocalic /r/. We distinguished 6 sets of words:

Mining: e.g. quartz, miner, ore
Farming: e.g. turnip, tractor, rooster
Army: e.g. sword, spear, soldier
Proper Names: e.g. Parker, Martin, Sutherland
Home/School/Church: e.g. servant, teacher, church[21]
Other: (all other words)

[20] Note that tokens with a following vowel-initial word were not included in the analysis. In such an environment non-rhotic speakers will often produce an /r/ as part of a sandhi process.

[21] Although it would have been ideal to separate home from school/church, since in traditional dialectology these are generally seen as having different effects on the vocabulary, there was insufficient data to allow this.

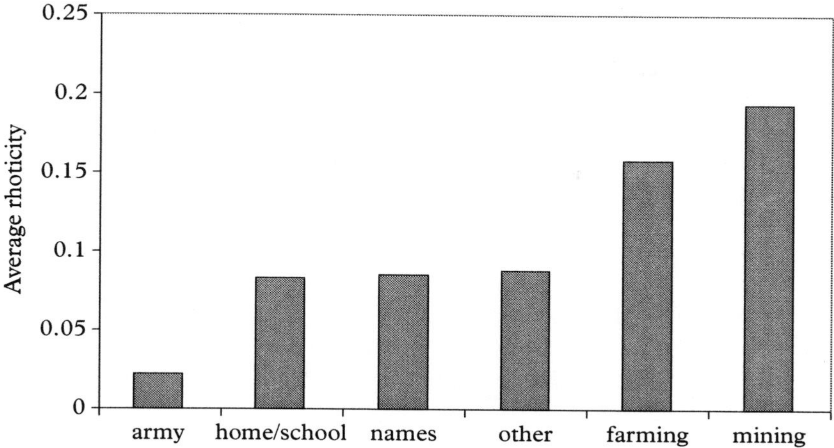

Figure 6.44 Semantic domain as a predictor of production of /r/

Words relating to mining and farming were strongly and significantly more likely to contain an /r/ than other types of words. This result is shown in Figure 6.44.

Finally, a CART analysis was conducted on the full data set, including all nine factors identified already as significant predictors of /r/. This analysis retained just two factors as overwhelmingly significant: the settlement type and, for Scottish and Mixed settlements, the birthplace of the mother.

The finding that frequency of use of a variable may be conditioned by semantic domain is generally quite unexpected from the perspective of traditional outlooks on sound change, and therefore this has very important implications. These are taken up in more detail in Chapter 7.

16.4 Summary of rhoticity

In sum, a large number of both social and linguistic factors affected rhoticity over the time period analysed. Of all these factors, there are two that are highly and strongly robust – standing out in all types of analysis on both the token-based and speaker-based data sets: the type of town in which the speaker lives and the birthplace of the speaker's parents. As rhoticity declined, so did linking /r/ (*the car is*), though to a much lesser extent. Intrusive /r/ (*the idea-r-of it*) appeared before post-vocalic /r/ had disappeared so that there are speakers in the Mobile Unit database who are partially rhotic and also produce examples of intrusive /r/. With the loss of rhoticity, intrusive /r/ increased and linking /r/ remained at relatively high levels, so there was never a period of /r/-lessness in New Zealand English (see Sudbury and Hay 2002).

17 H-dropping

Modern New Zealand English typically does not have h-dropping but the phenomenon was noted earlier in the history of the variety. H-dropping is the loss of word-initial /h/ in words such as *hill*, *house*, *hammer*, with the result that pairs such as *ill* and *hill* become homophonous. It is not to be confused with the absence of /h/ in unstressed grammatical words such as *him*, *his*, *he*, *her*, *have*, *has*, *had*, where all varieties of English can leave the /h/ out. Lack of this kind of /h/ is not considered h-dropping; neither is the absence of /h/ in words for which, although they have orthographic <h>, the /h/ is not pronounced in most varieties of English. This happens with some words borrowed from French or Latin, such as *heir*, *hour*, *honest*, *honour*; however, care has to be taken with older speakers because there are certain words in this category that used to lack /h/ but saw it restored as a result of spelling pronunciation, for example *hotel*, *hospital*, *humble*, *humour*, *herb*.[22] Other words in this class (see MacMahon 1998: 477–8, Wells 1982: 255) have had /h/ restored for so long that productions of them without /h/ can now safely be considered h-dropping: *habit*, *heritage*, *hospitable*, *host(ess)*, *human*.[23] Care also has to be taken with data from older speakers in the case of words such as *historic*, *hysteria*, which have unstressed first syllables and which in conservative RP lacked /h/ also (see Wells 1982: 286). A final group of words in which absence of /h/ cannot be considered h-dropping because English speakers generally do not employ /h/ in such words (Gimson 1962: 186) consists of certain words with non-initial <h> such as *exhaust*, *exhilarate*, *exhibit*, *shepherd* (plus, at least in Britain, place names such as *Durham*, *Birmingham*).[24]

17.1 British historical antecedents of h-dropping

H-dropping is seen by some scholars as representing the end-point of a very long historical process in which the original Old English phoneme /h ~ x/ was gradually subjected to more and more phonotactic restrictions. It was lost word-initially before /r/ as in *hring* = *ring*, before /l/ as in *hlāf* = *loaf*, and before /n/ as in *hnutu* = *nut* in late Old English or early Middle English; it was lost in

22 In regional varieties of American English, pronunciations of *herb* vary; many lack /h/ altogether; others pronounce /h/; still others have a lexical contrast, where *herbs* without /h/ are associated with more elite culture, for example commercial matters, spices, cooking ingredients, whereas *herbs* with /h/ designate things more in common, non-elevated culture, for example medicinal or locally grown plants.

23 *Homage* is given as a member of this class, though prematurely, since numerous Americans say it without /h/, reflected, for example, by the entry in *The American Heritage Dictionary of the English Language* which lists both pronunciations, with and without /h/, as acceptable, standard, and equal.

24 Again, some words may have been prematurely assigned to this class, since, for example, though *vehicle* and *vehement* are said not to be pronounced with /h/ by any English speaker, in fact the /h/-less pronunciation would be found odd by speakers of a number of American dialects.

other preconsonantal positions after back vowels during the 1300s as in *daughter*, *brought* (reflected by the orthographic <gh>), and during the1400s after other vowels, as in *night*, *sigh*, at least in the south of England (McLaughlin 1970: 110). The change of 'wh' to 'w', whereby *which* becomes homophonous with *witch*, is considered by some to be a loss of /h/ before /w/; it is much more recent, and many varieties remain unaffected (see Section 18.1). The loss of /h/ in absolute initial position, as in *hill*, is more recent still: Sweet (1888: 259) dates it to the late 1700s: 'initial *h* began to be dropt everywhere in colloquial speech towards the end of thMn [= third Modern period = 1700–1800]'. This would place it about 25–50 years before the beginning of the period in which we are interested. James Milroy (1983), however, has argued that it is a much older development than suggested by Sweet, and Jones (1989: 268) cites a number of examples from *The Diary of Henry Machin*, written in the 1550s and 1560s, and even some from *Lagamon's Brut*, written in the 1200s.

However, although h-dropping has been traced back at least as far as the thirteenth century (Jones 1989: 265), if not earlier (Lass 1987: 96; J. Milroy 1983: 39), it was probably not widespread in London (and perhaps the south-east) until at least the eighteenth century (Wells 1982: 255) and took until the end of the nineteenth century to become geographically widespread in England (Bailey 1996: 131). The geographical distribution of h-dropping in the history of colonial varieties of English supports these dates – h-dropping is virtually non-existent in the English varieties spoken in North America and parts of the Caribbean (colonisation sixteenth–seventeenth centuries), but was found, albeit variably, in the southern hemisphere Englishes (colonisation late eighteenth–nineteenth centuries) (Horvath 1985; Holmes et al. 1991).

H-dropping has been described as 'the single most powerful pronunciation shibboleth in England' (Wells 1982: 254), yet in spite of its early appearance in English, its social meaning only manifested towards the end of the eighteenth or early nineteenth centuries (Bailey 1996: 126; Ihalainen 1994: 216). With the spread of h-dropping in nineteenth-century England came a related phenomenon, h-insertion: the addition of a hypercorrect epenthetic /h/ in historically (and orthographically) /h/-less words (Bailey 1996: 127ff.), for example, *dozen [h]eggs* (Tollfree 1999: 173). As with h-dropping, h-insertion was regarded negatively and was used by mid-nineteenth-century authors such as Dickens to portray lower class and non-standard speech (Bailey 1996: 132).

If the chronological picture is not entirely clear, the geography of this change is similarly complex, although we can be sure that Sweet's 'everywhere' is a considerable exaggeration. Word-initial h-dropping is found in most working-class dialects of England and Wales, but not in Scotland or Ireland (Wells 1982: 253–4). The major exceptions to this in England are the varieties of the north-east and East Anglia, although in keeping with the gradual historical spread of this feature, modern East Anglia is currently acquiring h-dropping: the East Anglian h-pronouncing area is certainly smaller today than it was at the time of the SED fieldwork (Trudgill 1986a: 44–6). According to Wells (1982: 255), 'historical details of the spread of h-dropping through England are lacking'. However, there is much that we can deduce about the situation in the mid-nineteenth century, most obviously by noting modern trends and working backwards.

On Map 7 (Appendix 3), in the areas labelled (1), we see the extent of h-pronouncing ('h-retention') in current English dialects (from Trudgill 1999d). However, in the most conservative varieties for which we have current information, namely the traditional dialects investigated by the SED in the 1950s–60s, the areas involved are much bigger, as can also be seen from Map 7 in the areas labelled (2). Note, too, that at this stage, in addition to the north-eastern and East Anglian areas, there is another in the south-west and a small one in northern Kent that are also characterised by absence of h-dropping, as is the Isle of Wight. Kurath and Lowman (1970: 32), using data gathered by Lowman in the late 1930s, also say that, 'initial [h] is regular in a continuous area extending from Norfolk into Essex'. We can extrapolate backwards further from this pattern to a supposition that absence of h-dropping was even more widespread in the period 1825–65. In fact, Kurath and Lowman (1970: 32) say of the south-western area in the 1930s that 'initial [h] occurs with some frequency in Somerset-Wiltshire-Hampshire' (and see their map on p. 33); we take 'some frequency' to mean that lack of h-dropping was extensive here. Ellis (1889) provides some very helpful data for an even earlier period, showing that the East Anglian h-pronouncing area at the time of his work extended into parts of south-east Lincolnshire, northern Cambridgeshire, and northern Huntingdonshire (see transcriptions on pp. 211, 249–52, 298–9). He also shows absence of h-dropping in a rather larger area of Kent (p. 142). There is also evidence from the transcriptions that /h/ is retained in Devon (p. 167) and in Cornwall (see pp. 167, 169, 172–3). In Ellis too we find evidence that the north-eastern area lacking h-dropping was considerably larger: most of his West Northern area, which includes south Durham, Westmoreland, northern Lancashire, and western Cumberland, is described as a region in which 'the aspirate . . . is employed with much uniformity in the country part' (1889: 542, and see the transcriptions on pp. 563–94). Note that most of Ellis' data were obtained in the 1870s. These areas are labelled (3) on Map 7.[25]

By working backwards from our oldest information for any given region, we can produce the most extensive area shown on Map 7. It can be seen from this that most of Britain, including much of England, was h-pronouncing at the time

[25] H-dropping is found today in the English of south Wales (Wells 1982: 391), though this may not be of much significance, given the small numbers of Welsh who came to New Zealand. In the Welsh-speaking area of north and west Wales, however, h-dropping does not occur in English for the good reason that /h/ is found in the Welsh of this region (Thomas 1994: 128; labelled (2) on Map 7). The Welsh-speaking area was of course larger in 1850 than it is today; Ellis (1889: 13–14) has information on where the language frontier ran in the 1860s (see his Map of the English Dialect Districts) – these areas are also labelled (3).

in question, the mid-nineteenth century when the British settlement of New Zealand began in earnest.

In all of the areas where h-dropping is known today, it is (and presumably was in 1850 also) variable for many speakers. H-dropping is socially stigmatised and becomes considerably less frequent as speakers' social status increases, or as the formality of the context increases (see, for example, Bailey 1996: 127; MacMahon 1998: 477; Mees and Collins 1999; Strang 1970: 81; Trudgill 1974).

17.2 Early New Zealand commentaries on h-dropping

Written records confirm that at least some immigrants arrived with h-dropping and instances of hypercorrection. For example, Jane Oates, who emigrated with five children in 1856 to join her husband Samuel in the Wairarapa (in the North Island), uses spelling that reflects her Derbyshire dialect, with h-dropping and hypercorrect h-insertion:

> We have not got bullocks to plow yet but he [Samuel] **as** [has] a plow so we must trie to hire bullocks to plow till we have got of **hour howne** [our own] . . . When we can grow **howr** own crops we shall be rite a nuf. . . . We are go in **hour** new house but it is not quite finished yet . . . (quoted in Porter and Macdonald 1996: 165–6, our emphasis)

In perhaps the earliest recorded observations on New Zealand English, school inspector John Smith, in Westland, noted in 1880 that 'it is a common experience to find children repeating such lines as "o 'appy 'appy 'ummingbird"' (*AJHR* H-1I, 1880: 25, quoted in Gordon 1983a: 33). Samuel McBurney (in *The Press*, 5 October 1887) also observed that h-dropping and h-insertion could be heard in New Zealand, though he commented that h-dropping was notably less common here than in Australia. Other early commentaries were critical of the loss of /h/ in New Zealand speech, as Gordon (1983a, 1998) found to be the case with early New Zealand school inspectors. Thus, it is clear that h-dropping was exported to New Zealand, because in every year between 1880 (when the school inspectors' reports began) and 1913, at least one of the school inspectors refers to the 'aspirate' (Gordon 1998: 70–1). The following comments suggest much variability; they make it clear that h-dropping was not universal, but occurred only in certain schools or areas:

1883 Southland: '. . . the initial h too is cruelly neglected in many quarters' (John Gemmel, *AJHR* E-13, 1883: 24).

1884 South Canterbury: 'In a few schools . . . the pupils frequently drop the "h" . . .' (*AJHR* E-1B, 1884: 23)

1884 Westland: 'In one school the teacher of which habitually disregards the aspirate, both in speaking and reading the sound of the letter "h" is scarcely ever heard' (*AJHR* E-1B, 1884: 23).

1886 Taranaki: 'Dropping the final consonant and misplacing the aspirate are also very common in some parts of the district, the latter being very difficult to overcome' (W. E. Spencer, *AJHR* E-1B, 1896: 8).

1903 Nelson: 'The aspirate difficulty, particularly in connection with the Waimea schools . . .' (*AJHR* E-1B, 1903: 30).

1905 Nelson: 'The use of the aspirate still presents difficulty in some localities' (*AJHR* E-1B, 1905: 26).

1906 Marlborough: 'In one or two schools the difficulty with "h" was observable' (*AJHR* E-1B, 1906: 26).

After about 1905 some inspectors' comments seem to indicate that h-dropping was declining:

1907 Marlborough: 'The trouble with "h" was less pronounced this year . . .' (D. A. Strachan, *AJHR* E-1B, 1907: 23).

1909 Westland: 'This does not apply to the initial "h" the omission of which is now infrequent' (A. J. Morton, *AJHR* E-2, 1909: 124).

1913 Grey school district: 'The misplacing of the aspirate [was] hardly ever met with' (W. Austin, *AJHR* E2, 1912 Appendix C: xxxvii).

Nevertheless, in 1910 E. W. Andrews in *The Triad* makes an observation that suggests hypercorrection occurred as h-dropping declined:

> With regard to 'h', which is so commonly misplaced in England as a sin of both omission and commission, I have never come across a boy, born and educated in New Zealand, who had any great difficulty with this refractory letter. He rather overdoes the sound, if anything, triumphing over the obstacle so vigorously that victory then becomes defeat . . . It would almost make the hearers think that the ancestors of the New Zealander had been dropping h's for generations, and that now he is engaged in picking them up several at a time. (*The Triad*, 10 August 1910: 37)

In 1912, the *Cohen Commission on Education* was told: 'you very rarely find a boy dropping his h's' (*AJHR* E-12, 1912: 623). Finally, in 1939, Arnold Wall (p. 19) wrote: 'The dropping of the initial "h" and the final "g" of "ing", noted by McBurney as typically Cockney, but really occurring in most parts of England, is not at all usual in New Zealand and is confined to very careless and illiterate speakers'.

17.3 Results from the Mobile Unit speakers for h-dropping

The auditory quantitative analysis of /h/, as with other variables, is made up of two data sets: (1) a speaker analysis data set using individual speaker's scores for h-dropping, aimed at revealing the effect of social factors on individuals' rate of h-dropping, and (2) the token analysis data set, aimed at revealing possible

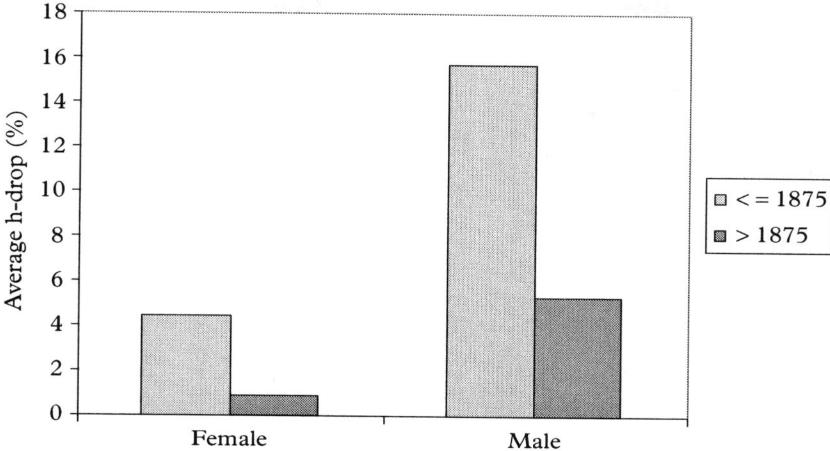

Figure 6.45 Average h-dropping by gender and birthdate

linguistic conditioning across all tokens. As with /r/, a maximum of ten tokens of any single word was used per speaker to avoid lexical bias in the results. The coding was limited to stressed content words only. Realisations of /h/ were coded either as presence [h] or absence Ø; the preceding environment and following environment and lexical frequency were also coded, in addition to the social variables. Where possible, 100 /h/ tokens were coded for each speaker. A total of 3,977 tokens was analysed, 9% of which showed h-dropping.

17.3.1 Speaker analysis. A stepwise generalised linear model of the speakers' percentage scores for h-dropping revealed gender, settlement type, and birthdate all to be significant predictors of rate of h-dropping. Figure 6.45 shows the clear gender pattern present in the results, together with the decline in rate of h-dropping over the period of the corpus. Female speakers in the Mobile Unit were much less likely to drop /h/ than male speakers, and both groups decreased their use of h-dropping over time.

Overall, the results showed a decline of h-dropping correlated with year of birth, from an average of 12% for speakers born before 1870, to only 4% for those born in the 1890s–1900s. However, the frequency of h-dropping was never particularly high. Although the most consistent h-dropper had a remarkable 72% of h-dropping and a further six speakers had at least 30% h-dropping, the majority of speakers (78%) used less than 10% of h-dropping overall, and 29% of speakers used no h-dropping at all.

The distribution across different settlement types is shown in Figure 6.46. The most h-dropping occurred in English settlements. This is consistent with

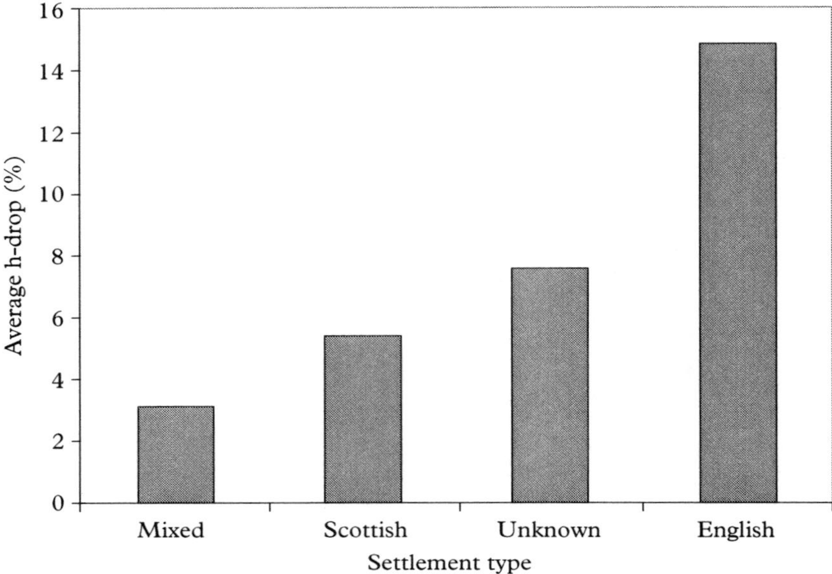

Figure 6.46 Average h-dropping by settlement type

the observation that, while England has a long history of h-dropping, this is not a feature of Scottish English (see Section 17.1).

The origins of the parents play no significant role in predicting the degree of h-dropping displayed by any individual speaker. A classification and regression tree analysis of this data set retains birthdate and gender as the most predictive factors. The resultant tree is shown in Figure 6.47.

17.3.2 Token analysis. A number of linguistic factors were coded in the h-dropping data set. The statistical analysis was limited to three linguistic factors: the preceding environment, following environment, and lexical frequency, and a stepwise binomial logistic regression returned all three factors as highly significant predictors. Table 6.14 shows the breakdown of model coefficients returned for different preceding and following environments. The lowest rates of h-dropping follow a vowel or a pause, and the highest rates of h-dropping (or lowest rates of production of /h/) occur following sonorant consonants. Treiman and Danis (1988) found that increasing sonority led to increased rates of ambisyllabicity. This may help explain why sonorant consonants facilitate h-dropping in the Mobile Unit corpus: in connected speech the preceding sonorant can easily step in to act as onset for the following h-less syllable. The highest rates of h-dropping occurred before the START vowel, and the lowest rates before the SQUARE vowel.

Table 6.14 *Linguistic constraints on h-dropping*

	Facilitation of h-dropping
Preceding environment	sonorant consonant > plosive > fricative > pause > vowel
Following environment (environments with less than 20 tokens not shown)	START > THOUGHT > yod + GOOSE > GOAT > NURSE > TRAP > KIT > STRUT > MOUTH > PRICE > LOT > DRESS > FACE > FLEECE > SQUARE

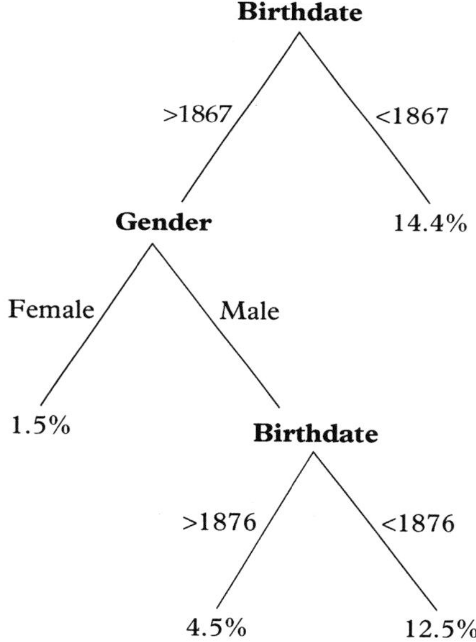

Figure 6.47 CART regression tree predicting individuals' percentage h-dropping

Finally, log lexical frequency, as calculated with CELEX (see Baayen et al. 1995) was a significant predictor of (h). The more frequent a word is, the more prone it is to h-dropping.

17.4 Discussion of the auditory quantitative analyses for h-dropping

Overwhelmingly men are the main h-droppers in the data. This agrees with other studies of h-dropping, both in modern New Zealand English (e.g. Holmes et al. 1991) and elsewhere (e.g. in Sydney: Horvath 1985; in Norwich: Trudgill 1974), where women drop /h/ less frequently than men do. As h-dropping was clearly regarded as non-standard in late nineteenth-century New Zealand (see the comments from the historical records in Section 17.2), this is consistent with the widespread observation that women are more likely to conform to overt linguistic norms than men (see Labov 2001).

The decrease in h-dropping over time is consistent with the comments by the early school inspectors (in Section 17.2). Moreover, it also coincides with the introduction of free and compulsory schooling in New Zealand. Just as the increase in /hw/ (explained in the next section) may have been influenced (in part) by spelling norms and higher levels of education (see Section 18.1), so too may the decrease in h-dropping have been influenced to some degree by these factors.

It seems curious that a preceding pause or vowel led to both the lowest rates of h-dropping and the lowest rates of /hw/-retention (see below). If an environment inhibited aspiration in one environment (i.e. limited /hw/ use), we might expect it to also inhibit aspiration in the other (i.e. facilitate h-dropping), but this is not the case. The reason that preceding pauses and vowels maximise /h/ but seem to minimise retension of /hw/ appears to relate to syllable structure. The loss of aspiration in /hw/ (hw > w) still leaves /w/ to serve as the onset of the syllable. In contrast, h-dropping leaves a syllable with no onset. The low rates of h-dropping after pauses and words that end in vowels can therefore be ascribed to the fact that h-dropping leaves a syllable with no onset, and is therefore likely to be most avoided in those contexts in which there is no segmental material that can step in and fill this position. Resyllabification is possible with preceding consonants, but not with vowels, or pauses.

Finally, there is a significant effect of lexical frequency upon h-dropping – frequent words are more likely to be produced without an /h/. This is consistent with a growing body of literature that indicates that, in more commonly produced words, the variant with greater articulatory reduction of phonological variables tends to occur with greater frequency than the less reduced variants (see, e.g., Wright 1997; Bybee 2001; Jurafsky in press). The finding that lexical frequency affects content words is also consistent with the observation that highly frequent function words are prone to h-dropping, even in non-h-dropping dialects. The more frequent and predictable a word is, the less articulatory effort is required for it to be accurately perceived (cf. Lindblom 1990).

18 The /hw/ ~ /w/ merger

The distinction between initial /hw/ and /w/, as in *which* versus *witch* (called the /hw/-variable[26]) is variably preserved in New Zealand English. In varieties that still have this distinction, /hw/ may be realised phonetically as [hw], [hʍ]

[26] Our use of /hw/ rather than /ʍ/ is a matter of orthographic convenience, and not a theoretical statement.

or [ʍ]. The unmerged /hw/ pronunciation is not a general characteristic of southern hemisphere varieties of English (Australian English, South African English, Falkland Islands English), although there are exceptions. Specifically in parts of Otago and Southland in the South Island, /hw/ is still retained by some speakers, though it does seem to be in decline (Bauer 1986: 229; Gordon and Sudbury 2002: 83), and /hw/ is still used by some broadcasters in New Zealand. Although a good number of other New Zealanders across the country in self-report say they maintain the contrast, this is a complicated matter; typically they make the contrast in reading contexts, but with some inconsistency, and it is mostly absent in unmonitored speech (see Gordon and Maclagan 2000).

18.1 British historical antecedents of the /hw/-variable

The merger of /hw/ with /w/ is referred to by Wells (1982: 228) as *Glide Cluster Reduction*. He suggests that the merger began in lower-class speech in the south of England in early Middle English, became current in educated speech in the 1700s, and was 'usual by 1800', but the history of this merger is treated differently by different scholars. Strang (1970: 45) goes as far as to claim that the /w/ ~ /hw/ contrast 'has been largely absent from Southern English since the Norman Conquest'. The merger of /hw/ with /w/ is part of, claims Chambers (2001: 356), a 'three millennium lenition, a weakening from stop to fricative to approximant, and from voiceless to voiced' (as claimed also for h-dropping, as mentioned earlier). The final stage of this lenition – the merger of /w/ and /hw/ – has carried low social prestige and was resisted in 'educated' speech. During the eighteenth century, [w] spread at the expense of /hw/ and became the norm in educated English accents of England by the beginning of the nineteenth century. In spite of the spread of [w], /hw/ retained prestige, and was retained (or reintroduced) in dialects such as RP, largely as a result of the spelling system (Strang 1970: 45). MacMahon (1998: 467) says that /hw/ was retained 'by most speakers of educated Southern English until at least the second half of the nineteenth century'. Map 8 (Appendix 3) shows the area that had /hw/ according to Ellis, and the rather smaller area in the SED.

The merger is generally held to be related to the loss of /h/, the h-dropping variable described in Section 17.1, and so speakers who retain /hw/ also retain /h/, while the reverse is not necessarily true, but speakers who lack /h/ also lack /hw/, with /w/ instead. The loss of /hw/ in this merger does not occasion the loss of much information, since /hw/ carries a low functional load. While it does differentiate homophones such as *whine/wine* and *whether/weather*, the contexts and grammatical functions are usually strong enough that serious ambiguity does not arise (Strang 1970: 45).[27]

[27] The fact that /hw/ is distributionally defective, occurring only morpheme-initially, may also contribute to its loss, as a marked feature of the language (cf. Chambers 2001).

The /hw/-variable has not been lost in Scottish and Irish English, some varieties spoken in the north-east of England (Wells 1982: 228), and many varieties of American English, but it has now disappeared from most of England except the far north. In RP the use of /hw/ is variable, being 'widely considered correct, careful, and beautiful' (ibid.), although Wells also notes that such /hw/ realisations in RP are not 'natural' but self-conscious decisions: 'Thus /hw/ is nowadays in England found principally among the speech-conscious and in adoptive RP' (p. 229). He also notes that women tend to use /hw/ more than men.

18.2 Early New Zealand commentaries on the /hw/-variable

The /hw/-variable is little mentioned in nineteenth-century reports of New Zealand English. However, Samuel McBurney (1887, cited in Turner 1967) did mention that the /hw/~/w/ distinction was in frequent use, and claimed that it was more often used by girls than by boys. As reported in Ellis (1889: 245), McBurney listed under 'wh-' his impressions of the /hw/-variable in New Zealand cities: In Auckland few <wh->, general <w->; in Wellington <wh-> general for girls, <w-> general for boys; in Napier about equal numbers of each; for Nelson, few <wh->, many <w->; in Christchurch many <wh-> and some <w->; and in Dunedin <wh-> general for girls and many for boys, with <w-> having some for boys.

J. A. W. Bennett (1943) commented that words spelled with *wh-* were usually pronounced as [hw]. He claimed this was the case throughout New Zealand, while noting that the strong Scottish links in Otago may have had some influence on the spread of /hw/. Bennett (1943: 83) also noted the possible reinforcing effect of spelling norms (and prestige) on the /hw/ pronunciation: 'All official radio announcers use it [hw] and are encouraged to do so. The habit is confirmed by the tendency, natural in a country where the tradition of Standard British English is not too strong, to pronounce words as they are spelt.'

Arnold Wall (1939: 5) observed a strong tendency to discard the 'wh' sound (i.e. to lose it through merger with /w/), but notes that its usage was nonetheless more widespread than in England, also mentioning the possibility of Scottish influence:

> The spelling wh-, as in *when*, *wheat*, *which*, *while*, usually represents breathed [ʍ]. This speech habit is equally strong in all parts of the country, for both stressed and unstressed positions, in anything that approaches 'careful' pronunciation. The presence of a large Scottish element in the original community, especially in the Otago district of the South Island, may have assisted in its growth. All the announcers in the main stations in this country maintain, very rightly, I think, the traditional 'wh'. And there is no doubt that in New Zealand generally it is better preserved than at home. Whether this fact is due to the large number of Scottish and Irish

settlers in our population it is hard to say, but if it is, it is curious that the influence of these speakers does not seem to have affected our speech in any other direction.

While most of the school inspectors' comments on 'the aspirate' referred to h-dropping, some referred to /hw/: 'A habit of dropping the aspirate in such words as "why", "when", "where" is also becoming disagreeably prevalent' (E. A. Scott, Grey School district inspector, *AJHR* E-1B, 1908: 16).

Bauer (1994: 395) is of the opinion that 'this feature [/hw/] is kept alive by overt teaching: /hw/ is perceived as being a prestige pronunciation'. (The question of whether prestige played a role comes up again in the following sections and in Chapter 7.)

18.3 Results from the Mobile Unit speakers for /hw/

Since <wh> words are relatively uncommon, all /hw/ tokens (where auditory consensus was reached) were used for analysis, regardless of the frequency of occurrence of specific words. The number of /hw/ tokens from any given speaker ranged from 5 to 100 tokens, 2,200 tokens in all. To avoid lexical bias in the results, a maximum of ten tokens of any single word was used per speaker (as was the case for /r/ and h-dropping). Two variants were coded: [w] and /hw/.[28] In addition to the social variables of birthdate, sex, parental origins, and settlement type, /hw/ tokens were also coded for preceding and following environment, lexical frequency (from the CELEX database, Baayen et al. 1995), and were categorised as to whether they were embedded within a word (e.g. *somewhere*) or unembedded (e.g. *where*) and whether they were function words (e.g. *where*, *when*) or content words (e.g. *wheel*, *wheat*). Overall, /hw/ occurred in 25% of the tokens analysed.

18.3.1 Speaker analysis. Each speaker was assigned a score representing their percentage of /hw/, and a stepwise generalised linear model was fitted. Testing was carried out for the influence of speaker sex, birthdate, settlement type, parents' origins, and for possible interactions among these factors. All four factors were proved to be significant predictors of the data, along with an interaction between speaker sex and birthdate.

Figure 6.48 shows the clear difference between male and female speakers' use of /hw/ in the speaker analysis data set. Female speakers used /hw/ significantly more often – over twice as frequently as the male speakers. This figure also shows the overall effect of time; unexpectedly, the use of /hw/ *increases* over the period of the corpus, both for men and for women.

The change over time is shown more precisely in Figure 6.49. Because of the finding of a significant interaction between gender and birthdate, separate

[28] It should be noted that there was not such a strict binary distinction between /hw/ variants; rather, realisations occurred along a continuum, with varying degrees of aspiration. We are currently working on an analysis of this data that treats aspiration as a continuous factor.

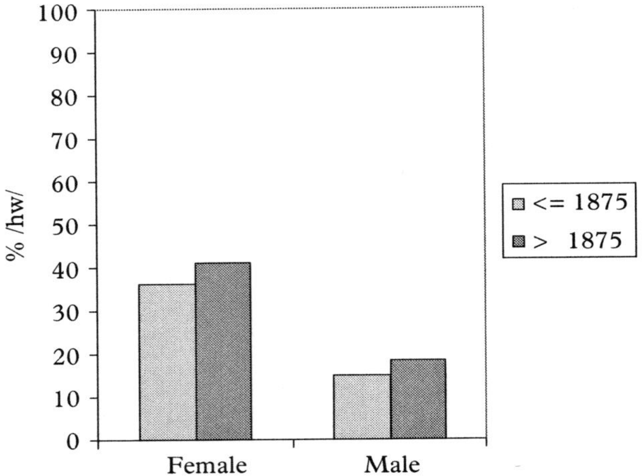

Figure 6.48 Percentage /hw/, by gender and birthdate

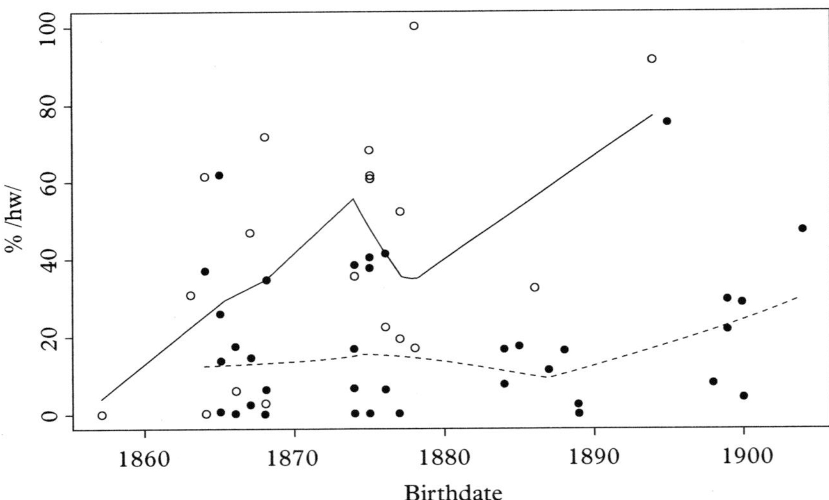

Figure 6.49 Change in /hw/ over time (The x-axis indicates the birthdate of the speaker; the y-axis indicates that speaker's percentage /hw/. Each point represents a single speaker – solid points for male speakers, unfilled points for female speakers. The lines represent a non-parametric scatterplot smoother (Cleveland 1979) fit through the points. The solid line is fit through the female speakers; the dashed line is fit through the male speakers.)

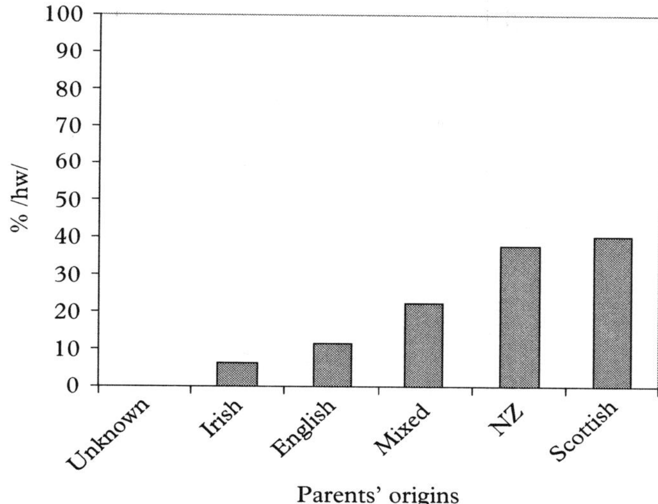

Figure 6.50 Percentage /hw/, by origin of parents

lines are fitted through male and female speakers. As stated, the use of /hw/ is increasing over the period we have analysed; this increase is markedly sharper for female speakers. Note that the technique used to fit the lines through the graph is highly sensitive to local variation in the data. Thus, the particularly sharp increase seen in the last decade for the female speakers is unlikely to be reliable; rather, it is strongly influenced by a single speaker. What is statistically reliable, however, are the results that /hw/ is increasing over time, that women are using more /hw/ than men, and that women are increasing their /hw/ usage more quickly than men.

Figure 6.50 shows the effect of parental origins. Those with Irish and English parents show the least use of /hw/, whereas those born of Scottish or New Zealand parents show the greatest /hw/ usage.

In Figure 6.51, we see the effect of settlement type, which displays a similar pattern. It is in the Scottish settlements that the use of /hw/ is most prevalent.

A CART analysis of the degree to which individual speakers display /hw/ retains parents' origins, date of birth, and speaker sex as important predictors. The resultant tree is shown as Figure 6.52.

18.3.2 Token analysis. A token analysis was conducted to investigate the possible effect of linguistic environment on the likelihood of /hw/ use. Five factors were investigated: lexical frequency; whether the word was a content word (e.g. *wheat*) or a function/question word (e.g. *why*); whether the variable occurred word initially (e.g. *where*), or was embedded (e.g. *somewhere*); and the preceding and following environment.

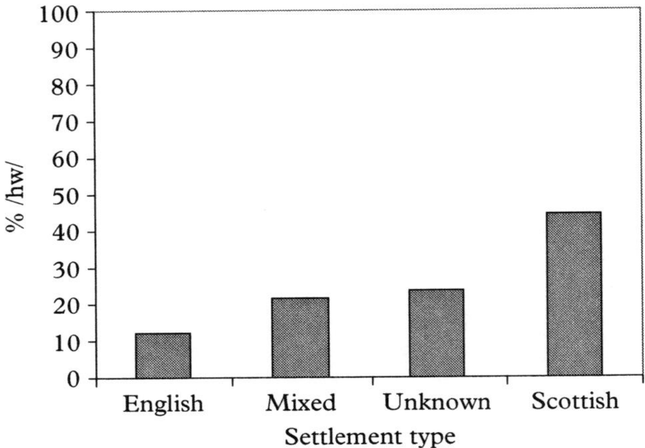

Figure 6.51 Percentage /hw/, by settlement type

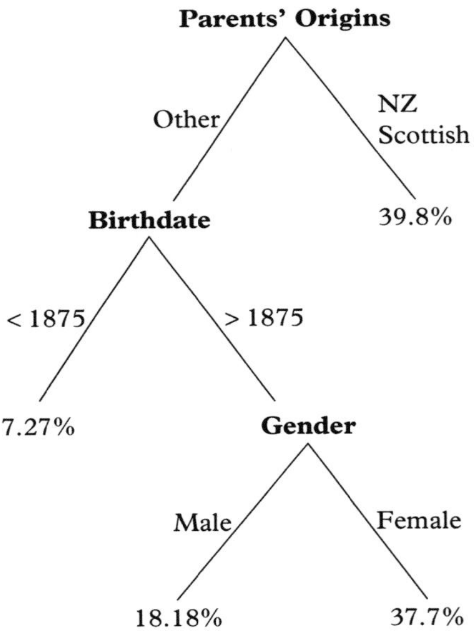

Figure 6.52 CART regression tree predicting individuals' percentage /hw/

The inclusion of both frequency and function/content in the same statistical model is problematic, as the two factors are clearly correlated with one another and therefore introduce collinearity into the data set, violating the assumptions of logistic regression modelling. When independently included (together with the other factors) in a binomial logistic regression model, both frequency and content/function were found to be statistically significant predictors of the data.

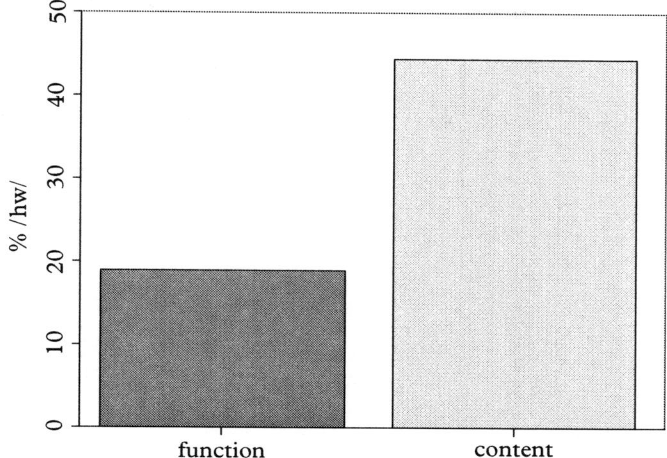

Figure 6.53 Percentage /hw/ for function/question words and content words

In order to disentangle the effects of frequency and word type, the data set was divided into two parts: a content-word part and a function-word part, and these were tested for an effect of frequency within each of the sets. No significant effects emerged, and therefore frequency as a factor was discarded, as it is likely to be an artifact of a strong effect of word type.

A stepwise logistic regression containing content/function, embeddedness, following environment, and preceding environment retained the first three factors as significant predictors of the patterns in the data. Preceding environment is significant in any model that does not also contain following environment, that is, the effect of the following environment is sufficiently strong that any effect of the preceding environment becomes insignificant.

Figure 6.53 shows that content words, such as *wheel*, are more than twice as likely as function words like *where* and *why* to be produced with /hw/. High frequency function words are often prone to effects of articulatory reduction.[29]

Embeddedness is also an extremely important factor in predicting the token analysis data. /hw/ is much more likely to be realised when word-initial than when embedded inside a word, as shown in Figure 6.54. In general, word-initial position is in a class of its own, and tends to receive extra articulatory effort (see, e.g., Byrd 1994; Keating, Wright, and Zhang 1999). On top of this, while some embedded words in the data set were stressed (e.g. *worthwhile*), and some

[29] For example, van Bergem (1993) demonstrates that function words contain vowels that are more reduced, and Jurafsky (in press) summarises a range of evidence that high probability function words tend to have greater vowel reduction, higher rates of coda-deletion, and are produced more quickly.

Table 6.15 *Linguistic constraints on /hw/*

	Facilitation of /hw/
Preceding environment	plosive >> fricative > sonorant consonant > vowel > pause
Following environment (environments with less than 20 tokens not shown)	FLEECE > PRICE > SQUARE > KIT > LOT > DRESS

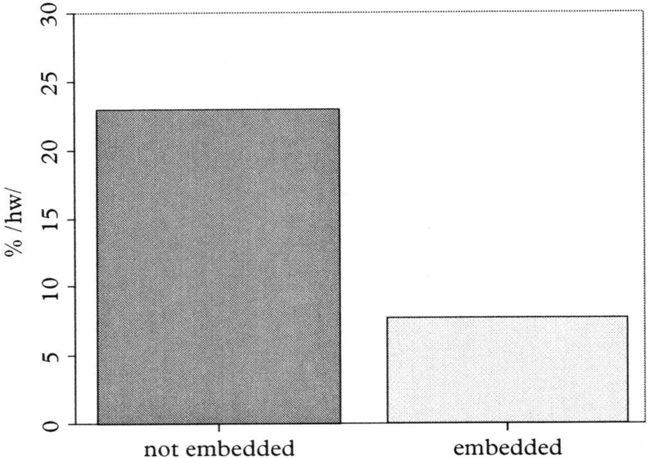

Figure 6.54 Percentage /hw/ for embedded and non-embedded words

non-embedded words contained /hw/ in an unstressed position (e.g. *whenever*), the great majority of embedded /hw/ tokens are not stressed, and the great majority of non-embedded /hw/ are in stressed syllables. The overlap between embeddedness and stress is so strong that it is impossible to untangle their effects statistically.

The final factor significantly involved in the production of /hw/ is the following environment, as shown in Table 6.15. Following close (high) vowels appear to encourage /hw/ more than open vowels, which is not surprising, as neighbouring close vowels will facilitate the production of frication. Long vowels facilitate /hw/ more than short vowels, possibly because long vowels will be more robust in the face of coarticulatory effects of voicelessness, that is, if the initial part of the vowel is devoiced, no information will be lost.

One factor that may be relevant to the production of /hw/ is the preceding environment; however, this failed to reach significance in any model that also included following environment. The directionality of the possible effect is shown in Table 6.15. Preceding plosives appear to facilitate /hw/; other classes of sounds behave fairly similarly to one another, though the minor differences in rate of /hw/ do suggest a possible sonority hierarchy at work.[30] A larger corpus would reveal whether this patterning is due completely to chance, or is a robust effect, which is simply overwhelmed by the significance of the other factors at work in this data set.

18.4 Discussion of the increase in /hw/ over time

Given that the /w/ ~ /hw/ distinction is still made in Scotland today, it is unsurprising that our results show that Scottish parents and Scottish settlements facilitated its retention in New Zealand. The difference found between female and male speakers is also to be expected if /hw/ was the more prestigious variant in late nineteenth-century English (see Sections 18.1, 18.2), given the overwhelming sociolinguistic evidence that women attend more to overt linguistic norms than men do (see Labov 2001).

What is unexpected about these results is that use of /hw/ increased with time in the corpus, particularly since modern New Zealand English has all but lost the /hw/ variant. However, this pattern agrees with the apparent anomalies in the data sets reported by Woods (2000b) and Bayard (1991c, 1995a), both of whom found high levels of /hw/ used among speakers born in the 1930s. Bayard's finding that speakers born in the 1920s used rather less /hw/ suggests that perhaps the increase in use of /hw/ we have documented here continued up until the 1930s, at which time the trend reversed, and /hw/ began to disappear. Bayard reported about 90% /hw/ usage for speakers born in the 1930s, which is certainly much higher than the level observed in our data set at the turn of the century. Clearly an extension of the current analysis to speakers born during the first half of the twentieth century is required in order to clarify the trajectory of this variable, and pinpoint the time at which the trend we observe in this data set reversed.

Why was the usage of /hw/ increasing in the late nineteenth century in New Zealand English? This increase could potentially be attributed to the influence of education (and spelling), as mentioned in connection with British speech in Section 18.1. About 31% of school-aged children in New Zealand attended school in 1858, 54% in 1871, and compulsory schooling was introduced in 1877 (Belich 1996: 381). We may be seeing here the influence of the norm advocated in schools and an increased awareness of spelling, resulting in an increased use

[30] The facilitating effects of some preceding environments on the production of /hw/ could be explained in articulatory terms, relating to availability of airflow. When the preceding consonant is a plosive, then the articulators are in a good position to provide strong aspiration. This makes post-plosive /hw/ tokens particularly prone to aspiration. The differences amongst the non-plosive categories are relatively minor, but nonetheless ordered in a suggestive manner – Table 6.15 contains a perfect sonority hierarchy. We can conceive of this organisation purely in terms of available airflow. The less sonorous the preceding segment, the more airflow is available for aspirating the consonant.

of the aspirated /hw/. The prestige associated with the /hw/ variant may help therefore to explain both the increased use of /hw/ and the marked difference between male and female speakers.

19 L-vocalisation

The most significant feature in the /l/ variable in modern New Zealand English is l-vocalisation, which has now reached 70% occurrence in reading list style for young working-class speakers, both male and female (Maclagan 2000).

19.1 British historical antecedents to variation in /l/

The pronunciation of /l/, and in particular the distribution of 'clear' and 'dark' allophonic variants, is in many forms of New Zealand English very similar to British RP pronunciation. In modern RP, /l/ is normally 'clear' [l] before a following vowel or /j/, but 'dark' (velarised) [ɫ] before a consonant, including /w/, or a pause, regardless of word boundaries. The process of l-vocalisation affects only dark /l/ (e.g. 'kill' as [kɪ̞ ɤ] or [kɪ̞ ʊ]). It is generally said to be a recent occurrence even in London, where it is most advanced today. Wells (1982: 259) points out that there is no reference to it in descriptions of Cockney until the early twentieth century.[31] However, there are indications of its presence in regional dialects in England. For example, Wright (1905: 216–17) found loss of /l/ after 'guttural vowels' in words such as *all*, *ball*, *awl*, *fall*, *fool*, *foul*, *full*, *pool*, *pull*, *school*, and so on, and in *bold*, *gold*, *old*, *bolster*, *false*, *bolt*, *colt*, *fault*, and so on in numerous dialects, including some in the south. He mentions 'vocalisation of l' specifically, which he recorded as, for example **biȯ** *bill*, **tuȯ** *tool*, **tweȯf** *twelfth*, and **seŋgȯ** *single* in mid-east Wiltshire (p. 217). L-vocalisation is normal in the SED records only in south-eastern Essex, southern Hertfordshire, north-western Kent, Surrey, Middlesex, and Sussex, that is, the areas immediately to the south, east, and north of London.

It is also often argued that even the clear~dark /l/ allophony – a necessary prerequisite to l-vocalisation – appears to be a recent addition to English phonology and does not seem to reach back further than the late nineteenth century. The SED materials show that in the traditional dialects of the 1950s/60s, dark /l/ was found only south of a line passing between Shropshire and Hereford and proceeding more or less due east to pass between Norfolk and Suffolk. However, its modern distribution notwithstanding, dark /l/ was probably a significant trait in the earlier history of English. Old English breaking (diphthongisation) took place before clusters of /l/ + obstruent (e.g. *eald* 'old'), and the dark allophone persisted into Middle English, later vocalised before an obstruent, as in, for example, *talk* and *chalk* (Hickey 2000: 106). In modern dialects dark /l/ is now found everywhere except in the north-east (Trudgill 1999d). No form of Irish

[31] Wells (1994: 202) suggests that l-vocalization is now found in RP.

English has dark /l/, clear /l/ being usual in all environments, as it is in the Scottish Highlands. In the Lowlands, on the other hand, dark /l/ is usual in all phonological environments.

We can assume that the mid-nineteenth-century input to New Zealand English included a significant number of varieties without dark /l/. It would also appear from the chronology that l-vocalisation in British dialects was sufficiently late that most if not all l-vocalisation in New Zealand is the result of independent parallel development from the dark /l/ in both locations.

19.2 Early New Zealand commentaries on l-vocalisation

There are no early comments in New Zealand to reflect the now far-reaching effects of l-vocalisation. This means either that it was late in developing or that it was not considered worthy of comment. The results from the Mobile Unit (see next section) would appear to suggest the former explanation is correct. The first written comments we have found were reported in a letter to the editor of a Christchurch newspaper in 1995, where the writer complained of hearing the phrase 'a drink of mook' and seeing a notice offering 'warnuts' for sale (*The Press*, 10 September 1995).

19.3 Results from the Mobile Unit speakers for /l/

Three-quarters of the 95 Mobile Unit speakers in the auditory perceptual analysis have both clear and dark allophones of /l/ as in modern New Zealand English. Eleven speakers always use clear /l/ and a further nine speakers sometimes have syllable final clear /l/. Only three speakers, all with Scottish parents, have dark /l/ in all environments. In a separate analysis, a random sample of thirteen speakers from Otago in the South Island was checked for l-vocalisation, and two speakers were found to use this feature (Gordon and Trudgill 1999): Mrs Annie Hamilton (b. 1877) from Arrowtown, with Irish parents, and Mr Robert Templeton (b. 1887) from Waikouaiti, with an Irish mother and an Australian father. A third speaker, Mr George Firth (see Appendix 4), who was born in Australia and came to New Zealand in his early twenties (for whom we have no details of parentage), also uses some vocalised /l/.

20 Interactions between the variables studied

20.1 Relationship between the quantified consonantal variables h-dropping and /hw/

Given that h-dropping and /hw/ both involve aspiration (at least in the view of some scholars) and have even been said to be part of the same phenomenon (Wells 1982: 228; J. Milroy 1983: 38), it is reasonable to question whether these two variables are correlated for individual speakers. That is, if we know how much

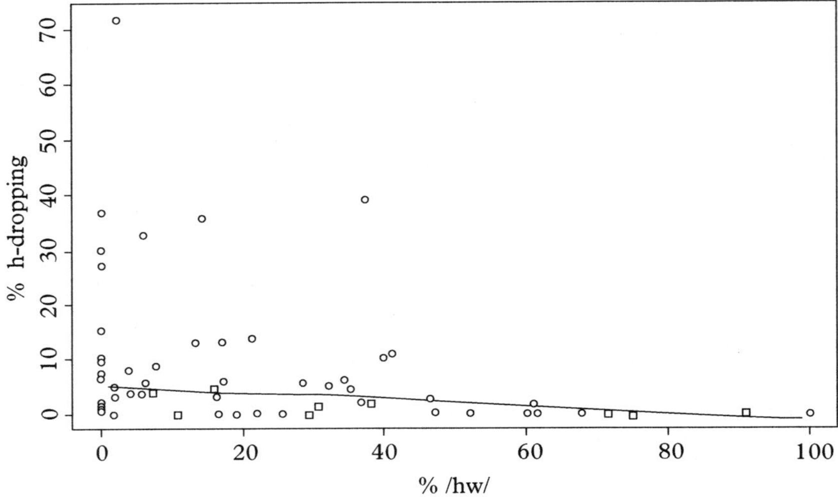

Figure 6.55 Correlation between percentage /hw/ (x-axis) and rate of h-dropping (y-axis) (Spearman's correlation, rho = 0.49 p<.00001)

someone h-drops, is it possible to make a reasonable prediction about their rate of /hw/? Trudgill (1997b: 201) writes of an implicational scaling relationship between /hw/ loss and h-dropping, such that 'loss of /h/ before vowels implies loss [of /h/] before /w/, but where the reverse is not the case'. However, Trudgill et al. (2000a) find both h-dropping and /hw/ together in one of the Mobile Unit speakers, Mr Malcolm Ritchie. This combination is said to be unknown in the British Isles, and to be possible in New Zealand only because of the extreme variability and mixing that occurs during new-dialect formation.

The auditory quantified analyses for /h/ and /hw/ reveal that in fact a non-trivial number of individual Mobile Unit speakers display both some h-dropping, and some /hw/-retention. Figure 6.55 shows the rate of /hw/-retention and h-dropping for the 59 speakers analysed. All the points that do not lie along one of the axes of the graph represent speakers displaying some degree of both. As expected, there is a negative correlation between frequency of h-dropping and frequency of productions of /hw/ – or, viewed differently, there is a positive correlation between presence of aspiration in both these variables. The less likely individuals are to pronounce /hw/ (unmerged with /w/), the less likely they are to use the aspirate /h/. Thus, while there is no absolute implicational scale at work with this set of speakers (perhaps due to the variability associated with dialect contact, as Trudgill et al. 2000a argued), there is still a clear statistical relationship in the predicted direction: the upper right hand quadrant of the graph (high h-dropping and high /hw/ usage) is empty. To conclude, both h-dropping and /hw/ are variable, and as a result some individuals do have a

Table 6.16 *Spearman's correlation coefficients, showing degree of correlation between vowel index scores for* KIT, DRESS, TRAP, *and* START *(Note: 'ns' indicates non-significant correlations.)*

	KIT	DRESS	TRAP
DRESS	0.26, $p < 0.05$	–	
TRAP	ns	0.64, $p < 0.0001$	–
START	ns	ns	0.28, $p < 0.05$

certain amount of both h-dropping and /hw/ unmerged with /w/ simultaneously, in the ONZE corpus (see the further discussion in Chapter 7).

It remains an open question whether the correlation observed between /h/ and /hw/ is due to an interdependence of /h/ and /hw/, or whether it is a simple statistical reflection of the fact that what we are witnessing is two co-evolving sound changes. Use of /hw/ is increasing over time in the corpus, and is more frequent in Scottish settlements, in the speech of women and of individuals with Scottish parents. H-dropping is decreasing, and is more frequent in English settlements, and in the speech of men. Given that complementary populations favour these two variables, it may not be surprising that the two are negatively correlated. In New Zealand in the late nineteenth century, the more deeply entrenched speakers were in the community, one that favoured /hw/, the less likely they were to participate in h-dropping.

20.2 Interactions between quantified vocalic variables

This section examines the degree to which the front vowels are correlated with one another, a matter highly relevant for interpreting claims about vowel shifts in New Zealand English. We examine these correlations by taking the speaker indices for each of the vowels that have been quantified and examining the degree to which an individual speaker's productions of one vowel can predict their production of a second. In order to investigate this question, we conducted Spearman's correlations on pairs of vowels from the set: KIT, DRESS, TRAP, and START. Three of the correlations proved significant; START is correlated with TRAP, TRAP is correlated with DRESS, and DRESS is correlated with KIT. All other correlations are non-significant. The results are summarised in Table 6.16.

The correlation between START and TRAP is shown in Figure 6.56. The degree of scatter on this graph is high. There are individuals with very fronted START and not particularly raised TRAP (bottom right). And there are individuals with not particularly fronted START who nonetheless have quite raised TRAP (top left). Thus, there is a large degree of independence between these two vowels. Nonetheless, the Spearman's correlation does show a low but significant relationship between the two. The fronter an individual's START vowel tends to

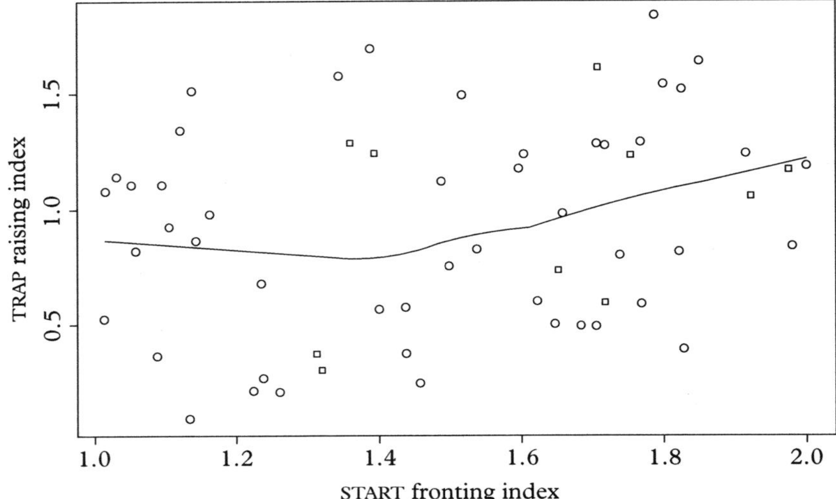

Figure 6.56 START fronting index and TRAP raising index (Spearman's correlation $r = 0.28$, $p < 0.05$) (Every point represents an individual speaker. The line represents a non-parametric scatterplot smoother, showing the line of best fit through the data.)

be, the higher his or her TRAP vowel is likely to be. This relationship is shown by the line fit through the graph, which represents a non-parametric scatterplot smoother, showing the line of best fit through the data. We see a weak, positive relationship between the two indices.

Figure 6.57 shows the relationship between TRAP and DRESS. Here we see a much tighter correlation. There is no speaker who has a significantly raised DRESS vowel without also having raised TRAP, and everyone who has fairly extreme TRAP raising also shows a significant degree of DRESS raising. The degree of scatter on this graph is markedly reduced, relative to Figure 6.56. The more raised TRAP, the more raised DRESS is likely to be.

The final significant correlation is seen in Figure 6.58, which shows the correlation between degree of DRESS raising and KIT centralisation. The range in the realisation of KIT is much smaller than in the other variants, hence the shallower slope. The positive slope of the line (together with the significant Spearman's correlation) shows that KIT centralisation is not independent of DRESS raising. While relatively few individuals show KIT centralisation, those who do usually also display DRESS raising.

The overall body of evidence indicates that a chain shift was in action. The positions of adjacent vowels are predictive of one another, whereas the positions of non-adjacent vowels are largely independent. Table 6.17 shows, for each of these four vowels, the proportion of variants that are highly conservative,

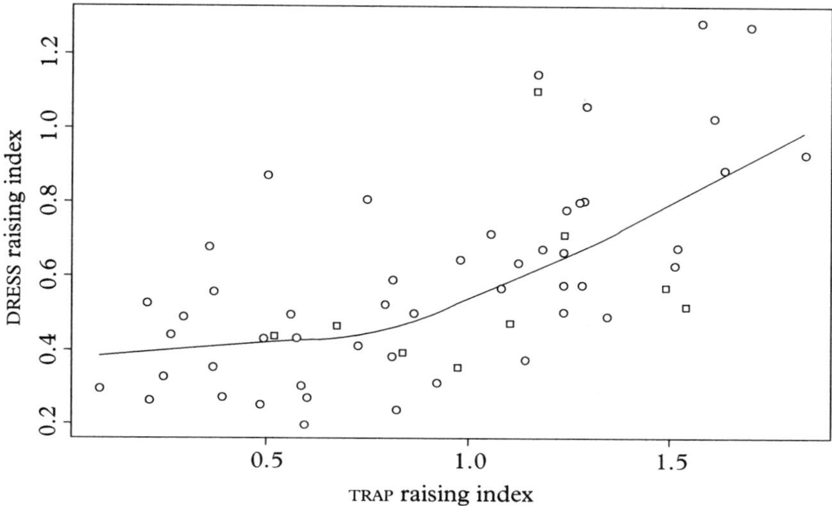

Figure 6.57 TRAP raising index and DRESS raising index (Spearman's correlation, rho = 0.68, p < 0.0001)

'non-shifted' variants. Also indicated, for each variable, is whether the variable is changing significantly over the time period we have analysed.

At the time analysed, START was already considerably front, and becomes more front with time in these data. TRAP is also considerably raised (though there are not as many raised TRAP tokens as there are fronted START tokens). We know that some tokens of raised TRAP arrived in New Zealand with the early immigrants. However, TRAP also appears to have continued to raise further over the time analysed, and the degree of raising is at least partially predictable from the degree of START fronting. This could be taken to indicate that START fronting was the first step in a push chain of the New Zealand English front vowels. A raised TRAP would certainly have provided greater auditory contrast with a fronted START. However, START is part of the long vowel system, which is generally considered to be independent of the short vowel system. This, together with the fact that the correlation between START and TRAP shows a high degree of scatter, suggests that caution is advisable in interpreting the relationship between these two vowels. We have no clear-cut way of knowing whether the long vowel START initiated the movement of the front vowels TRAP, DRESS, and KIT, whether START moved forward as TRAP rose, or whether the correlation found between START and TRAP does not in fact actually indicate any true causality in their relationship.

While some degree of raising of DRESS was among the variants brought to New Zealand (see Section 2), it is clear that a majority of early DRESS tokens were not raised (as seen here in Table 6.17 and earlier, in Section 3). The fact

Table 6.17 *Proportion of 'non-shifted' variants, and patterns of change over time*

Variable	'Non-shifted' variant	Percent of total variants represented by 'non-shifted' variant	Changing with time? *significant on at least one test **definitively significant
KIT	[ɪ]	95	Yes*
DRESS	[ɛ]	59	Yes**
TRAP	[æ]	40	Yes*
START	[ɐ̞]	[52]	Yes**

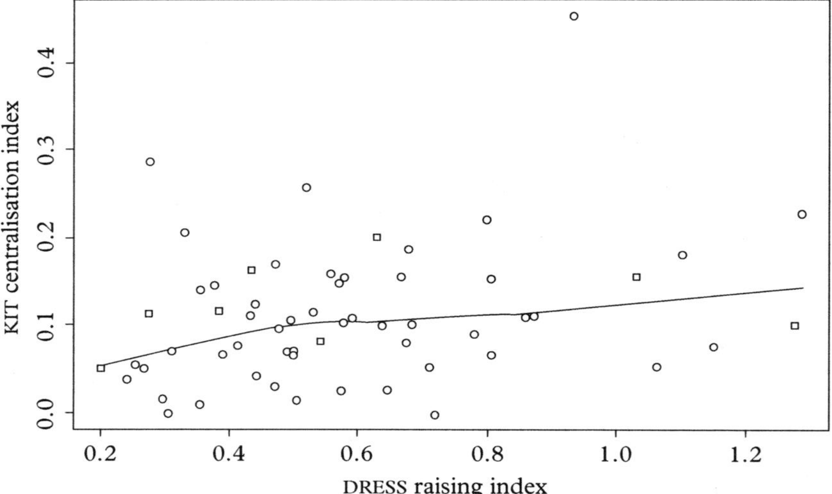

Figure 6.58 KIT centralisation index and DRESS raising index (Spearman's correlation, rho = 0.26, $p < 0.05$)

that we see a very significant increase in raised DRESS tokens over the duration of our corpus, together with the tight correlation between raised TRAP and raised DRESS, suggests that DRESS raised largely as a result of the force of TRAP raising and encroaching on its territory. Furthermore, the tight correlation between TRAP and DRESS, together with the fact that it is for DRESS that we have the most conclusive evidence for change over the period of our corpus, suggests that it is the raising of DRESS that is the step in the push chain most active during this time period.

The final step is the effect of DRESS on the centralisation of KIT. The vast majority of KIT tokens are non-centralised, suggesting that centralised KIT in

New Zealand English is not the result of a significant amount of centralisation in the original input. The main motivation for centralised KIT appears to be the force of the raising DRESS vowel. The significant correlation between DRESS raising and KIT centralisation, together with the indication that centralised KIT is very infrequent but appears to be increasing in frequency over the duration of the corpus, suggest that this step of the push chain was initiated during the end of the nineteenth century, but that it was not until some years later that it firmly began to take hold.

Thus, taken together, our data suggest that the front short vowels of New Zealand English are the result of a push chain, which in the late nineteenth century had the most primary effect on DRESS. It could be argued that the seeds of this vowel shift were inherited in the varieties of English first brought to New Zealand, with raising of TRAP and a certain degree of DRESS raising, and even perhaps a very small amount of KIT centralisation; however, there is little doubt that the vowels shifted or continued to shift in New Zealand English, seen in the much greater degree of raising and centralisation and in the much higher incidence of raised and centralised variants of these vowels. This is further considered in Chapter 8 where the principles of vowel shifting in general are discussed together with the relevance of this New Zealand chain shift for general claims about vowel movements.

Figures 6.59 and 6.60 show the vowel indices for KIT, DRESS, TRAP, and START for the seven oldest and the seven youngest speakers included in the auditory quantitative analysis. Inspection of these graphs demonstrates that, while there are some exceptions, the majority of speakers are most advanced in START, and least advanced in KIT, with DRESS and TRAP somewhere in between. Of course, these graphs should be interpreted with appropriate caution, as the index scores are calculated on different scales for each of the variables, and so cannot be straightforwardly compared. However, these figures appear to provide evidence of the beginnings of a vowel shift in New Zealand English.

20.3 Interactions between non-quantified vocalic variables

In the acoustic analysis we considered the whole vowel system for ten speakers, five men and five women, who were chosen in order to be representative of the corpus as a whole (their individual vowel charts are presented in Appendix 5). Although many fewer speakers are available in the acoustic analysis than in the auditory quantified analysis, the acoustic analysis can give important information because the whole of the vowel system was analysed. The acoustic analysis agrees with the auditory quantitative analysis in terms of the front vowel movements, that is, acoustic analysis shows that TRAP is relatively further raised than DRESS and that KIT is hardly centralised at all (see Figure 6.5 in Section 2.3.2). It also confirms that diphthong shift took place in the following order: MOUTH followed by PRICE then GOAT and finally FACE (see Figure 6.30 in Section 12.2.3).

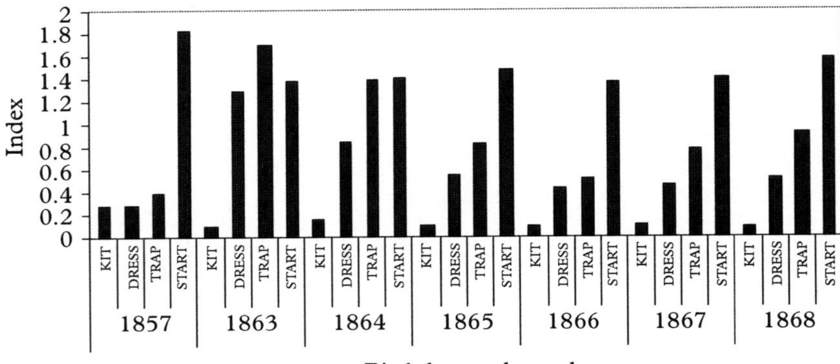

Figure 6.59 Vocalic index scores for seven early speakers

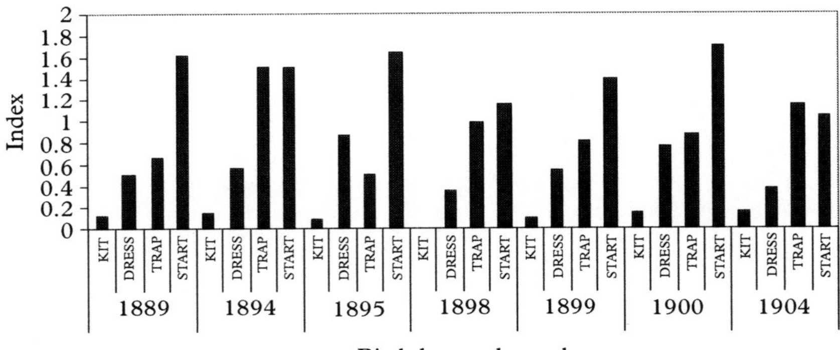

Figure 6.60 Vocalic index scores for seven late speakers

For the other vowels, the acoustic analysis shows that the back vowels are raising in parallel with the front vowels. As TRAP raises, so does LOT, and as DRESS raises, so does THOUGHT. Given the small number of speakers, we cannot perform a correlation analysis in order to determine the correlation between the raising of the front and back vowels, nor do we have enough data to consider change over time. However, by considering the relationship between the various vowels for both men and women, we can make a tentative suggestion as to the mechanism involved. The women have fronted GOOSE significantly more than the men[32] – for the women, but not the men, GOOSE is significantly farther

[32] T-tests with Bonferroni correction (because of multiple use of the data) were used to determine the level of significance of differences between vowel formant frequencies. All results presented are significant at least at the 0.01 level.

forward than START. The women have raised THOUGHT significantly more than the men. They have also raised LOT significantly more than the men, but the level of significance is lower. The women have also lowered STRUT more than the men, but the difference is not significant. For both men and women, contrary to the situation in modern New Zealand English, STRUT is significantly closer than START.

It is possible that GOOSE is leading a pull chain movement of the back vowels that is operating in parallel to the push chain raising the front vowels. STRUT lowering, which is barely visible in the ten speakers analysed acoustically, may also become caught up in this movement. In the period studied, NURSE has started to raise towards a closer position for the women but not yet for the men. It is not clear what other vowels are influencing the movement of NURSE.

The acoustic analysis confirms that diphthong shift and glide weakening are working together in the closing diphthongs (see Section 12.1). The first element of MOUTH has fronted and the first element of PRICE has backed through diphthong shift. With glide weakening, the second elements of both these diphthongs have lowered. The first elements of FACE and GOAT are lowering and centring (diphthong shift), with GOAT having moved somewhat more than FACE. The second element of GOAT is not yet showing the centralisation that can be seen for modern New Zealand English (see Chapter 2, Figure 2.2). The acoustic analysis confirms that the closing diphthongs moved in the order MOUTH then PRICE then GOAT and FACE.

21 Effects of gender

In all of the vowel analyses carried out on the Mobile Unit speakers, women are leading men in terms of moving towards modern forms. Women are leading men in TRAP and DRESS raising in the front vowels and also in raising LOT, THOUGHT, and NURSE. Women have fronted START and GOOSE and lowered STRUT more than the men. Although there is little centralisation of KIT, women are in the lead. They also lead in the use of schwa rather than KIT in unstressed syllables. They display significantly more diphthong shift and glide weakening for the closing diphthongs. As yet, there is no sign of the women pulling back with the closing diphthongs MOUTH and PRICE, which are strongly stigmatised class markers in modern New Zealand English (see Maclagan et al. 1999). Woods (1997) found that daughters of some of the speakers analysed here had not continued to raise the first element of MOUTH, perhaps showing an awareness of its developing stigmatisation. The vowel plot for modern New Zealand English (Chapter 2, Figure 2.2) shows the women's MOUTH rising towards FOOT, in contrast to Figure 6.30 (in Section 12.2.3), where MOUTH hardly rises at all. The women analysed for the modern data were all middle class, in contrast to the Mobile Unit speakers, who were more working class. Because of the already mentioned stigmatisation of MOUTH and PRICE, the middle-class speakers presented in Chapter 2, Figure 2.2 demonstrate a more conservative version of MOUTH than do the Mobile Unit speakers, with the first element somewhat retracted and the second element closer.

For the consonants that were analysed quantitatively, women showed less rhoticity and less h-dropping than the men, and more /hw/-retention. It is unlikely that loss of rhoticity was stigmatised, and it may even have carried prestige in the input dialects that formed New Zealand English. With rhoticity, as with the vowels, women are ahead in the ongoing sound change. Both h-dropping and /hw/-retention do have social connotations, with h-dropping being stigmatised and /hw/-retention potentially having positive connotations (see Sections 18.1ff. and 20.1). In these two cases, the Mobile Unit women are demonstrating conservative behaviour that is now regarded as commonplace (see Labov 1994, 2001; Chambers and Trudgill 1998 for examples).

22 Social influences

In this chapter the focus has been on the overall average development shown by the speakers in the Mobile Unit database. However, although the overall patterns are clear, there are individual speakers who do not fit the expected patterns. In many cases, not enough is known about them to be able to explain why they do not fit, but where more information on their backgrounds is available, there are usually social explanations for the differences. For example, Mr Charlie Hovell (born in 1855) had a number of Irish features in his speech, though neither of his parents was Irish – his mother was born in England, probably in Kent, and his father came from Suffolk. However, further investigation revealed that his mother died following a fall from a horse when Charlie was a small child, and he was cared for by an Irish washerwoman, explaining his Irish linguistic traits that had initially seemed odd.

Just as we can find unexpected features in the speech of some individuals, so we also find some settlements that differ linguistically from other settlements. There are settlements where New Zealand English appears crystallised at a considerably earlier date than in others, and settlements where speakers retain some British dialectal features into the second and even third generations. A study of rhoticity in speakers born at the same time, all with Scottish parents, in several towns in Otago demonstrates these differences. Speakers born in Kaitangata and Milton are highly rhotic. For example, Mrs Christina Bisset, born in Kaitangata in 1875, is 47% rhotic and Mr James Stewart, born in Milton in 1876, is more rhotic still – he was found in a separate study to be 53% rhotic. Speakers born in settlements like Arrowtown are considerably less rhotic. Mrs Jane Reid and Mrs Alice Mackie were both born there in 1877; Mrs Reid is only 3% rhotic, and Mrs Mackie is not rhotic at all. If other speakers are added, a similar pattern emerges. These patterns can be correlated with the different patterns of settlement in the towns (see Chapter 3 and Appendix 2 for details). This is seen in a comparison

Table 6.18 *Population statistics for Milton and Arrowtown (NZ Census Reports, 1879)*

Place of birth	Milton	Arrowtown
New Zealand	544	150
Scotland	293	49
England	178	34
Ireland	77	49
Australia		33
China		20
Other origins	69	15
Total	1,161	350

of the population of Milton and Arrowtown, as given in the 1879 census, in Table 6.18.

These figures show that, of those born outside New Zealand, Milton has a much larger number of people from Scotland. Since the New Zealand-born would be mainly made up of children, that number would include a majority who were children of the Scottish immigrants.[33] Arrowtown, on the other hand, is very mixed, with no other country of origin dominating. Being a goldmining town, it also includes a number of Australian-born settlers.

Significant for the question of individuals who do not fit expectations, the figures for rhoticity in Arrowtown reveal speakers who do not fit the general pattern. Two speakers have a much higher degree of rhoticity: Mr David Mackie (born 1871) has 24% and Mrs Ellen Dennison (born 1874) has 56%, which is much higher than the other speakers from Arrowtown, and as high as the Milton speakers. Once again, further investigation explains the anomaly. David Mackie and Ellen Dennison (née Mackie) are brother and sister. A local account written about Ellen Dennison's life reveals that her father died when she was four and her mother when she was eight. She was then taken in by a farming family who were most likely Scottish, and from the age of ten she worked for them as a nurse-maid, until at the age of fifteen she left and moved to nearby Macetown, where she worked as a cook in a hotel kitchen, until she married. From this it is clear that from the age of eight Ellen Dennison did not actually live in Arrowtown, but on a farm that, at that time, would have been relatively isolated. Information about her brother David is not available, but we know he was seven when his father died and eleven when his mother died. It is possible that he also was taken in by a family with Scottish origins.

[33] This is confirmed in Appendix 2, where figures for church membership in Milton are given. In 1881 there were 642 Presbyterians, 344 Anglicans, 137 Roman Catholics, and 81 Wesleyan Methodists.

The implications of these results, including the atypical individual speakers, are considered in the following chapter, where we return to the question asked in Chapter 4, concerning how New Zealand English came to be the way it is today. In the light of the data from the Mobile Unit speakers reported in the present chapter, we take the proposed explanations for the development of New Zealand English outlined in Chapter 4 and evaluate them along with other more general explanations for the development of new dialects.

7 The origins of New Zealand English: reflections from the ONZE data

More nonsense has been spoken and written and there is generally more misinformed opinion about pronunciation in this country than about our indigenous slang – which is saying a lot.

(Sidney Baker 1941b: 93)

1 Introduction

In his discussion of dialect levelling and homogenisation, Chambers (1995: 58) writes:

> We would like to understand precisely how this homogenisation takes place. Which features of constituent accents are retained, and which ones are lost? In other words, what are the dynamics of homogenisation? Since no sociolinguists were present – or even existed – during the European imperialist era, we will probably have to wait for the planting of colonies in outer space for large-scale studies of the dynamics of homogenisation.

The ONZE data and analyses (in Chapter 6) contribute to answering Chambers' questions without awaiting the colonisation of outer space.

The goal of this chapter is to assess critically the various proposed explanations of and approaches to the origins of New Zealand English that were introduced in Chapter 4. We also consider other sociolinguistic explanations for new-dialect development in the light of the results of this research. Where possible, we measure the degree to which the frameworks and proposals live up to the results from the data analysis presented in Chapter 6 and to newly available background material we present here.

For ease of reference, we utilise as far as possible the same numbering of sections in this chapter as in Chapter 4.

2 What needs to be explained?

Before we turn to assessing the proposed explanations for the origins of New Zealand English summarised in Chapter 4, it is worth recapping the facts that need to be explained. We focus here on the quantified variables – that is, those for which we have the most information (see Chapter 6 for details). Table 7.1 summarises the variables, indicating for each one which factors were involved in predicting that variable's usage during the second half of the nineteenth century in New Zealand.

This table reveals that all four of the social variables that were found relevant have a pervasive effect. The birthdate of speakers, their sex, where their parents came from, and the type of settlement in which they lived all played an important role in the formation of New Zealand English.

The first of these variables should not surprise us. In a variety that is undergoing fairly rapid change, the year of birth will inevitably go some way towards predicting usage of certain variables. Overall, we have seven quantified variables that show signs of increasing in frequency over the period of the corpus (1–7), three variants that are disappearing (8, 9, 10), and just one variable (11) that appears to be relatively stable over the time period analysed.[1]

In general, we also see the common pattern in which gender and direction-of-change are non-randomly intertwined. For those variables that increase in frequency, females appear to be in the lead. This is true for all variables except the long vowel in the *dance* lexical set (6). Here we have an exception to the overall rule. Later-born speakers use more long vowels in such words, and the overall usage of these long vowels is increasing. Moreover, as was shown in Chapter 6, the men increased their usage, whereas the use of long vowels by women in fact remained fairly stable across the time period analysed. Here, then, we have an exception to the general pattern – a change towards the modern New Zealand English realisation being led by male speakers.

Similarly against the grain is the example of raised KIT (8). This variant is used more by the female speakers than male speakers, and is clearly decreasing during the period of the corpus. It is important to keep in mind with this variable, however, that the overall number of tokens involved is extremely small. Raised KIT never had a convincing foothold in New Zealand English. However, there were some early speakers – more female than male – who used some raised variants.

It may not be coincidence that both raised KIT (8) and short front *dance* (6) are the two variables that show considerable influence from Irish parents. Speakers with Irish parentage averaged roughly 70% short front *dance*, which is considerably higher than any other group. And the proportion of raised KIT

[1] Of course, some of the terms used here are a matter of how you look at it. For example, the rhoticity variant in Table 7.1 is defined as the preservation of non-prevocalic /r/. This is disappearing as 'r' ceases to be pronounced by older people; alternatively, one can say that loss of /r/ is increasing in the speech of younger people.

Table 7.1 *Summary of facilitating factors for quantified variables (Note: factors are shown if identified as significant by at least one statistical test. Some of these results are therefore more robust than others.)*

	Tokens with feature (%)	Birthdate	Sex	Origin of parents	Settlement type	Linguistic factors
1 START fronting	47	Later born	Female	Non-English	Unknown	Preceding Following
2 TRAP raising	60	Later born	Female	NZ, Scottish, English	Mixed	Preceding Following
3 DRESS raising	41	Later born	Female	Scottish	Mixed	Preceding Following
4 KIT centralisation	5	Later born	Female	NZ	Scottish	Preceding Following
5 Unstressed vowel centralisation (Weak Vowel Merger)[2]	49 (16% centralised to /ə/)	Later born	Female	NZ, Irish, Mixed	Mixed	Preceding Following
6 Long vowel in the *dance* lexical set	51	Later born	Male	NZ, mixed	ns	Preceding Following
7 /hw/	20.5	Later born	Female	NZ, Scottish	Scottish	Preceding Following Content words Not embedded
8 KIT (raising)	2	Earlier born	Female	Irish, Australian	English	Preceding Following
9 h-dropping	9	Earlier born	Male	ns	English	Preceding Following Lexical frequency
10 Rhoticity (preservation of non-prevocalic /r/)	9	Earlier born	Male	Scottish, NZ	Mixed, Scottish	Preceding Following Stressed Prosodic Boundary Semantic domain
11 Long vowel in BATH	93	ns	Female	NZ, Irish, Mixed	English, mixed	Preceding

[2] As noted in Chapter 6 we analysed the unstressed vowels in *rabbit* class words but not in *abbot* class words

variants in speakers with Irish parentage is almost double that present in other groups. It is curious that these two variables, which reflect Irish background, are the two in which the women display uncharacteristically conservative behaviour.

In general, it is clear that both parental origins and settlement type are important. These data provide strong evidence that New Zealand English initially developed differently (or at least at different rates) in different parts of New Zealand. They also provide strong evidence that the language of individuals during this period of new-dialect formation was influenced significantly by the language used by their parents.

Three of the variables (2, 3, 5) appear to change most convincingly in the mixed settlements. This provides some evidence for the levelling effect of such communities. As we saw in Chapter 4, some people expect that mixing of a larger variety of dialects may lead to faster levelling. It is notable that this is true of TRAP raising (2) and DRESS raising (3), changes that we argue are partially driven by internal factors (i.e. a chain-shift – see Chapter 6, Section 20.2, and Chapter 8). Mixed communities may be less strongly influenced by any single majority dialect and so more susceptible to the force of internal factors in the process of levelling and dialect formation.

The facts that parental origins and settlement type played a strong role are themselves of considerable theoretical interest, but they are also interesting in that they provide us with evidence about the origins of variants in early New Zealand English that may otherwise be controversial. The strong influence of Scottish parents and settlements on rhoticity, for example, suggests that this was the main source of /r/, rather than any strong rhotic input from parts of England, as has previously sometimes been suggested (Trudgill et al. 2000b).

Two variables are demonstrably influenced by Scottish origin: /hw/ (7) and rhoticity (10). These two variables show clear evidence of Scottish input into the early forms of New Zealand English, though neither of these variables has really survived into modern New Zealand English. TRAP and DRESS raising ((2) and (3)) also show some indication of being associated with Scottish parents.[3]

There are some difficulties with the categorisation of English settlements because, even though the majority of immigrants in these towns were English, they could have come from different regions within England. Nevertheless, it is interesting to note that for none of the variables that increase in frequency over time are the English settlements in the lead. That is, the Scottish settlements or the mixed settlements appear to have been more like modern New Zealand

[3] For KIT centralisation ((4) in Table 7.1), it may appear possible that a small number of partially centralised tokens came to New Zealand English via Scotland, though we do not see this as especially significant. There are speakers in the corpus who had Scottish parents but who do not have KIT centralisation, and others in the sample who had parents from various places other than Scotland (Australia, Norfolk, France, etc.), from both North Island and South Island towns, who have some centralised KIT tokens. (See Gordon and Trudgill 1999 for arguments and detail.) However the degree of centralisation found did not begin to approximate to that found in modern New Zealand English. The modern New Zealand English central KIT is a result of continued centralisation of KIT under the chain-shifting influence of DRESS.

English during this time than the English settlements. This is a curious finding, given the pervasive influence of the English south-east on New Zealand English (see Section 6.1). In fact the only variable for which English settlements were ahead is the use of the long vowel in BATH – a variable that remained stable throughout the period covered by the ONZE corpus.

The fact that the variables are further ahead in mixed rather than English settlements calls for an explanation. On the one hand, it suggests that it is not only the English origin itself that facilitated the survival of English variants, but also the effect of contact with other varieties that may have facilitated the levelling process. On the other hand, because the mixed settlements such as Arrowtown, Queenstown, and Bannockburn came about because of goldmining or military recruitment, where a higher proportion of the immigrants came from Australia (see Chapter 3), the early advance towards New Zealand English in these towns could possibly have been further facilitated by Australian influence (see Section 5.4).

We now return to the various proposed explanations of New Zealand English that were set out in Chapter 4, and consider these in light of the results summarised in Table 7.1 and detailed in Chapter 6.

3 Lay theories and language contact

Lay approaches to explaining the origins of New Zealand English, along with the theory of language contact, were discussed in Chapter 4 and found not to be relevant; therefore they are not taken up here in detail. Although a number of the speakers recorded by the Mobile Unit had considerable interaction with Maori and many acquired considerable fluency with the Maori language, none of the speakers recorded shows any evidence of influence from Maori grammar or pronunciation in their recordings. Most of the Maori placenames used show thoroughly Anglicised pronunciations, using, for example, /æ/ rather than /a/ in names such as Rangiaowhia.

4 The Cockney explanation

The frequent comments about similarities between New Zealand English and Cockney need to be put into perspective. The first question to consider is what Cockney was like in the mid to late nineteenth century. McBurney (1887) quoted Ellis' own description of the features of Cockney:

> The modern Cockney, according to A. J. Ellis, the leading authority on dialects, is of comparatively recent date, and is, I think, not to be found in Dickens. Its leading features are:
>
> (1) The omission of the aspirate and its occasional wrong insertion [h-dropping, with h-insertion by hypercorrection in inappropriate contexts];
> (2) clipping *ing*, as *singin'*, *shillin'*;

(3) alteration of *a* in *fate* to nearly *i* in *bite*;
(4) alteration of *o* in *hope*, to nearly *ow* in *how*;
(5) alteration of the first factor *ow* in *cow*, so it is written *kyow*, or *caow*;
(6) a general drawling of the vowels, so that dog becomes *dawg*, coffee *kawfy*
(7) insertion of r between vowels, *I saw-r'im*.

(McBurney 1887, quoted in Ellis 1889: 238)

Note that none of these traits is limited exclusively to London in its distribution within dialects of Britain. McBurney made this point as he compared these traits to antipodean usages:

> (1), (2) and (7) are of frequent occurrence, as in all parts of England, but they are decidedly less frequent in New Zealand where (1) and (7) are rarely to be met, at least in flagrant positions.
>
> (3) and (4) are to be heard pretty often in Australia, but seldom in New Zealand.
>
> (5) has nearly naturalised itself in Australia, and is extremely hard to express or to get rid of. The first part of the diphthong is often so short it is difficult to fix it. The ordinary English *ow* begins with the *a* of *sofa, u* of *nut* or *a* of *father*, tapering off to *oo* of *woo*. The Australian begins with *a* of *cat* or *e* of *get* prolonged, while New Zealanders give all sorts of varieties, but are, I think, settling down to a sharp *a* of *father*, followed by *oo*. One has only to hear 'down town' or 'around and around' said by Scotchmen, Englishmen and Colonials, to notice that at least there is a difference.
>
> One thing in common with Australia is the broadening of i in *die*, which is a diphthong formed by a very broad ah, tapering to ee. This in Tasmania and parts of New Zealand even approaches *oi, I die* sounds like *oi doi*. (McBurney 1887, quoted in Ellis 1889: 238)

Thus, the main features said to reflect 'Cockney' are h-dropping, diphthong shift, and *in'* for *-ing*. All the features are much commented on in the New Zealand written records, and McBurney's descriptions have their parallels in later school inspectors' reports (see Chapter 6). However, *in'* for words spelled in *-ing* is a general pattern of vernacular English everywhere except in South Africa (Wells 1982: 263), while h-dropping and diphthong shift extend far beyond London and Cockney (again, as seen in Chapter 6).

4.1 The demographic argument for Cockney

Arguments in support of Cockney (Wall 1939, 1951b) were that large numbers of 'pioneers' and school teachers came from the London area and would have spoken Cockney. An examination of immigration figures shows that this was not true. The percentage of Londoners coming to New Zealand was about the same as the percentage of Londoners in England as a whole, around 15%. Bauer

(1994: 421) pointed out, 'there is little, if any, evidence that [the European settlers in the early period] were Cockneys. Indeed, what we know of their social class suggests not only that they were not Cockneys, but that they would have despised a Cockney accent.' As described in Chapter 3, immigration to New Zealand came from many regions in the British Isles, though immigration from the south-east (with London) was high – 36% of immigrants for 1840–52, and 30–31% for 1853–80.

Wall's claim of a preponderance of Cockney-speaking teachers in New Zealand is also not true. McGeorge's (1984) dispute with Wall's view that New Zealand school teachers were largely Cockney is revealing:

> This seems quite implausible . . . Of the seventy-six men in the Wellington [school] district whose birthplaces are given, only nine came from London and of those only some were likely to have spoken with anything like a Cockney accent. One of them was educated at Rugby, for example, and another in private schools; one's father was a doctor and another was educated at Canterbury University College. If sheer weight of numbers had counted, then pupils at Otago and Southland should have spoken with marked Scottish accents, for twenty-three of the fifty-six headmasters whose birthplaces can be ascertained were born in Scotland – and there were more Australians (10) than Londoners (4). (McGeorge 1984: 17)

Since the possible connection with London and especially with the dialects from the south-east of England comes up very frequently, it is important to provide some additional perspective on how these are related. The varieties of London and the south-east were far from homogeneous or even completely focused, though many traits were held in common, particularly among working classes. Ellis (1889: 225) described his 'South Eastern' dialect region in the following way: 'the population is so shifting, that it would be misleading to suppose that there was any real hereditary dialect or mode of speech. But there is a decided tendency to E[ast] as distinguished from S[outh] feeling, and hence the district is considered to be a mixture of Metropolitan and Eastern.' He spoke of 'the two halves of the Metropolitan [London] area, n[orth] and s[outh] of the Thames R[iver], where the enormous congeries of persons from different parts of the kingdom and from different counties, and the generality of school education, render dialect nearly impossible' (p. 225). After discussing a series of traits of London English presented by D'Orsey, Ellis (p. 227) concluded that 'Mr D'Orsey's examples [of London], therefore, do not seem to characterise a peculiar mode of speech, but merely show a grafting of some E[astern] habits on our received speech'. He goes on to say, however, 'almost all the so-called "vulgarisms" of London are E[astern] and more especially metropolitan E[astern] origin. And this form of speech has become prevalent also in Australasia' (p. 225).

In similar vein, Wright (1905: viii) insisted that the material he had collected had 'proved to be valueless, especially such as related to dialects spoken within twenty-five miles of London. In these regions the dialects are hopelessly mixed and are now practically worthless for philological purposes.'

Ellis' declared connection between London and the south-east, and of Australasian English to both, makes it important to keep this dialect area in clear focus as we consider various other arguments for the origins of New Zealand English and the evidence upon which they are based.

Other reasons offered for why some claimed New Zealand English originated in Cockney are the following:

(1) New Zealand English came from or was influenced by Australia. It is possible that some of the traits attributed to Cockney in New Zealand English came through Australia, where many of the early settlers, convicts, and their keepers had come from London and spoke an early version of Cockney.

(2) Diphthong shift was an independent series of sound changes, already underway in England (see Chapter 6), which affected London speech and later English in Australia, New Zealand, South Africa, and so on. The early colonists brought a variety already in the process of changing, which then continued to change in the same general direction in the new countries. (See 'drift', Section 10.)

(3) A combination of (1) and (2). The diphthongs were undergoing change and were already in a variable state in England at the time of colonisation. In New Zealand this was reinforced by the Australian connection.

(4) What is thought to be Cockney simply reflects the south-east and London dialects, and it was these that eventually won out in the formation of New Zealand English.

The most likely account is that in New Zealand, the Cockney traits are only apparent; that is, the traits are indeed from the south-east of England, but it is not necessary to associate them directly with Cockney and thus with London.

Cockney has always been evaluated negatively by other British English speakers, even though the exact meaning of 'Cockney' is not clear. It can be taken as the speech of members of the lower socioeconomic classes of London, and features negatively evaluated in other varieties, particularly if they bear any similarity to the non-standard variety of London, were also labelled 'Cockney'. The comments of D. M. S. [Dorothy M. Stewart] (in the *Education Gazette*, 1 October 1924: 160–1) give an idea of what some people understood by Cockney and what their attitudes towards it were:

> First, Cockney is intrinsically ugly, and offends the cultured ear; second, it indicates slovenly vocal habits, and suggests equal carelessness in other respects; and, third, it is associated with the uneducated, even the vulgar, and stamps with the brand of inferiority – more or less deservedly – even men of the highest training, ability and character.
>
> The dialect of the London slum, composed as it is chiefly of standard English carelessly pronounced, may be heard with minor variations almost all over the English-speaking world . . . In Australia there never existed this strong determination to break away from the English tradition . . . in many – though not all – highly educated Australians one meets with the same peculiarities of speech as issue from the mouth of the London newspaper-boy.

> Attempts at reform have come too late, and have, it appears, been lacking in organisation and scientific method. Thus we have the spectacle of an immense continent, destined probably to a glorious future, speaking the language of the London Cockney.
>
> And what of New Zealand? Is she to let her language develop along the line of least resistance, or is she to set up artificial control? . . . Even the most conservative of us must differ in vowel and accent subtleties from our grand-parents. Granted, then, that the language of New Zealand must alter, we cannot help asking ourselves in which direction changes are likely to take place. We have already seen that the natural tendency is to take the line of least resistance – to make many assimilations, to place the tongue laxly, producing indistinct consonants, to shape the lips feebly, moulding ill the vowels. Add to this natural tendency the neighbourhood of a great continent already far advanced in the direction and the result is obvious. New Zealand will, if unrestricted, become a Cockney-speaking nation.

Baker (1986: 434) questioned the theory of a Cockney origin for Australian English and insisted that a group of diphthongs does not make a dialect. Like others after him, he showed that the Australian and New Zealand dialects may have some points in common with Cockney, but they have many differences. The closing diphthongs carry a great deal of social-class information in varieties of English. It is not surprising, therefore, on the basis of these diphthongs that people made the association between New Zealand English and Cockney.

Because Cockney was considered socially inferior and greatly disliked, this could also explain the adverse tone to the early comments on the New Zealand accent among the school inspectors and others who had a vested interest in 'correctness'. McGeorge (1984: 16) also made this point and suggested that the adverse comments on the New Zealand accent were an example of 'cultural cringe':

> What the controversy clearly demonstrates, however, is . . . 'cultural cringe', a belief that no good thing could come out of New Zealand and the best we could hope for was to meet someone else's standards. With this went the view that New Zealand's chief claim to fame was being more like Britain than any other country, in speech as in other things. Those who thought that New Zealand speech was notably 'pure' and those who fulminated against the 'colonial twang' shared the assumption that educated English speech, or Received Pronunciation, set the only conceivable standard and that any departure from it could only be a degeneration as a result of laziness carelessness or sheer incompetence ('the incorrect use of the vocal organs'). New Zealand English was only English defaced or soiled; it was 'impure', 'degraded', 'defiled'. **'Cockney' was thus a convenient summary term of abuse**; it was the speech of working-class people, unredeemed by any suggestion of bucolic charm, and it smacked of urban squalor left behind in the Old World [our emphasis].

5 The 'New Zealand English as Australian' hypothesis

5.1 The emergence of Australian English

For Australian English to have had a serious impact on the origin and development of New Zealand English, a distinctive form of Australian English would have had to exist at the appropriate time. We first ask whether Australian English already existed at a time early enough to have been able to influence New Zealand English. As there is no recorded evidence of early Australian speech, speculation about the emergence of a distinctive Australian accent can only be based on contemporary comment and demographic factors.

Australian commentators vary in their estimates of the time when the Australian English variety emerged as distinctive. Mitchell (1995) initially suggested a date as early as 1831 but finally decided that 1861 was the most likely time, and quotes Bernard (in the *Macquarie Dictionary* 1981: 19):

> There are persistent references from about the end of the Macquarie era [Governor of New South Wales, 1810–21] to a distinctive manner of speaking among the Australian born. Some scholars, notably Bernard favour the view that a distinctive Australian style of speech emerged quite early among the young, and hold that the peer group is the most powerful agent of language change and transmission from one adult generation to another. 'The great likelihood is that it was the children of the first convicts and colonists generally, taking their speech variety from the community about them, who generated the first Australian pronunciation' (Bernard 1981). (Mitchell 1995: 25)

Mitchell arrived at the 1861 date because that is when the number of native born was approaching being half the total population (p. 26). If Bernard's earlier date for the emergence of Australian English is accepted, Australian English was firmly established at the time of the first European settlement of New Zealand. Moreover, Mitchell's later date of 1861 still allows the possibility of an already focused variety of English in Australia affecting the newly forming variety in New Zealand after 1860.

5.2 Pervasive similarities between the varieties

Arguments supporting the Australian connection mentioned in Chapter 4 included the similarities between the two varieties. Unfortunately, Australian data from the appropriate time is not available to compare with the Mobile Unit data, so we cannot say categorically that the two varieties were similar. Nevertheless, we have some indirect evidence.

There are five Australian born speakers in the Mobile Unit archive, four of whom came to New Zealand very young (aged five or younger). However, one speaker, Mr George Firth, born in Tasmania in 1875, came to New Zealand in his early twenties and therefore probably spoke an Australian variety of English. Mr Firth's speech does not stand out from that of other Mobile Unit speakers of comparable age. Like the New Zealand-born at this time, Mr Firth has some relatively advanced features. He uses close DRESS and TRAP vowels and diphthong-shifted MOUTH and PRICE vowels. He is non-rhotic and has the Weak Vowel Merger (schwa) in unstressed syllables. He also has some relatively conservative features such as the use of the THOUGHT vowel in *off*, *across*, and so on. Like half of the Mobile Unit speakers, but unlike most modern Australians, he uses the START vowel in the *dance* lexical set. So we have reason to suspect from the evidence of this one speaker that the English of Australia and New Zealand was not strongly differentiated during the second half of the nineteenth century.

5.3 The demographic argument

Demography is a crucial consideration and is the basis of the arguments for both those who support the Australian connection and those who reject it. The figure given for the Australian-born resident in New Zealand varies: from 7% in 1881 (McKinnon 1997: 42), to 4.8% in 1871, reducing to 3% in 1881 (Belich 1996). Such low percentages would support those who, like Trudgill et al. (2000a), argue against the influence of Australia on New Zealand English on the grounds of the small number of Australian-born immigrants. Those who argue in support of the Australian influence cite historians (Arnold, Belich, Carmichael, Sinclair) who argue that the small percentage of Australian-born in New Zealand conceals the constant interchange between the two countries. As Carmichael (1993: 517) explains, 'few trans-Tasman migrants were native-born and . . . birthplace data greatly underestimate transfers of population between the two countries'.

Belich (1996) elaborated on the nature of the immigration from Australia:

> Most Australians (especially adult males, who were the most common crossers of the Tasman) were not native-born in this period; those who were native-born were disproportionately inclined to stay in Australia, and until the 1900s they were only a fraction of the people with significant Australian experience living in New Zealand. It is also possible that the number of Australian arrivals has been substantially underestimated. Another somewhat deceptive statistic is *nett* migration – those who came minus those who left. In the 1870s for example, when gold had ceased to be the main magnet and when most immigration from Britain came direct, nett migration from Australia to New Zealand was only 7,000 – a pale reflection of the 50,000 who went one way and the 43,000 who went the other. Sojourners can be as important as settlers, and in any case people who came from Australia to New Zealand were not always those who went the other way. (Belich 1996: 316–17)

Belich (p. 117) suggested that 'New Zealanders' may have made up as much as 17% of the 1880s immigration to Victoria (Australia) and that 20% of the founding pakeha population (in New Zealand) was born or bred in, or substantially influenced by, Australia.

Sinclair (1986a: 109), in his work on national identity, observed the lack of distinct identities for nineteenth-century New Zealand and Australia. He described 'inter-colonial' ocean mail services, cable services, tariffs and tariff preferences, trade unions (shearers, miners, seamen, wharf labourers), and church connections. The association between the two countries was so close that in the 1880s the question of federation between Australia and New Zealand arose (see Chapter 3).[4]

Immigration statistics, in Table 7.2, also show the strength of the Australian connection, though we do not know how many of these people were only in transit and how many spent a longer time in Australia. The figures in Table 7.2 also show that people were travelling in both directions across the Tasman Sea.

These figures show a relatively steady pattern of immigration from the United Kingdom, with occasional increases (1863–5), and a very sharp increase in 1874–5 reflecting the programme of assisted immigration under the Vogel administration (see Chapter 3). Relatively few people emigrated from New Zealand to the United Kingdom. The years 1861–3 show a very large number of men arriving in New Zealand from Australia, but also a considerable number leaving for Australia. In some years, emigration from Australia was much greater than from the United Kingdom: 1861–3, 1866–71. In the years 1868, 1871, 1872, and 1877, more people went to Australia than came from Australia. The figures support the historians' interpretation that there was a significant amount of two-way traffic across the Tasman.

5.4 The influence of children

Another argument for an Australian influence on New Zealand English is that it could have come through children. Mitchell (1995: 25, 26) emphasised the influence of children in the emergence of Australian English:[5]

> In 1821 there were 7,568 children in the mainland colony in a population of 29,783. That is over 25%, not an insignificant proportion, particularly when one notices that the proportion for 1805 was already at 22%.
>
> One would at first doubt whether this minority style of speech could hold against the speech of the greater number of convicts coming in and the flood of free migrants, who brought children with them, that began in

[4] For further information on the Australasia common heritage, see Borrie 1987.

[5] See Berthele 2000 and Kerswill and Williams 2000 for studies showing the extent to which children are able to accommodate and what they are able to do in situations of dialect contact; see below for discussion of accommodation theory; cf. Kerswill 2002.

Table 7.2 *New Zealand immigration and emigration figures, 1861–1880*[6] *(From Statistics of New Zealand (1890), p. 23)*

	Immigration to New Zealand from:				Emigration from New Zealand to:			
	United Kingdom		Australia		United Kingdom		Australia	
year	male	female	male	female	male	female	male	female
1861	2,350	1,597	17,454	829	140	113	5,490	311
1862	5,318	3,429	21,598	3,845	238	133	12,394	458
1863	8,247	6,131	26,164	5,059	316	141	9,268	787
1864	6,187	4,455	6,570	3,574	418	168	10,363	1,337
1865	5,473	4,368	7,647	1,315	309	200	4,861	1,032
1866	2,404	1,878	8,464	2,003	313	187	5,373	1,018
1867	2,372	2,088	4,936	1,348	417	221	4,224	814
1868	1,742	1,280	3,909	1,230	302	198	5,865	852
1869	1,587	1,190	4,518	1,351	451	289	3,423	910
1870	2,266	1,749	3,526	1,127	384	212	3,275	1,012
1871	1,768	1,368	5,313	1,111	413	264	3,108	815
1872	3,067	2,324	2,842	1,028	371	257	3,470	873
1873	4,682	4,240	2,744	1,224	272	184	2,831	929
1874	20,197	16,203	5,002	1,625	555	312	3,538	1,070
1875	12,547	9,311	4,428	1,900	443	356	3,255	1,085
1876	6,433	4,699	3,963	1,566	645	465	3,865	1,264
1877	4,308	3,327	3,414	1,441	585	407	3,876	1,412
1878	5,216	3,993	5,045	1,469	504	334	3,289	1,154
1879	9,863	6,872	4,878	1,759	423	234	3,195	1,053
1880	4,675	3,839	4,492	1,639	383	300	5,083	1,686

1831. From 1831 to 1851, the 124,458 assisted and unassisted immigrants included 10,963 children under 14 (that is 9% of the total). Though these migrant children were not in quite the same position as the native born in their language behaviour, they were similar in their youth and in their responses to the peer group. From Robinson's (1985) study, it is clear that the migrant children were capable of exercising a strong influence on the transmission of language and were certainly not merely, 'a tribe of untutored convict bastards'. (Mitchell 1995: 25, 26)

Chambers (2002: 122) argues for an 'innate accent filter', which is 'active in dialect convergence as well as language convergence'. Observing in what he calls the 'Ethan Experience' that children of immigrant parents do not acquire their

[6] In the original table, the column we have labelled here 'Australia' was headed 'Other British Possessions', but in reality these immigrants were almost all from Australia – only one or two came from India or South Africa.

parents' non-native accents and furthermore are often even unaware of the differences, Chambers concludes that 'the innate accent-filter appears to function as a subconscious guide to phonological acquisition . . . smoothing the process of screening out non-native elements. As an attribute of sociolinguistic competence, it follows that it will be activated by accent variation of all kinds, whether interlanguage or interdialect' (p. 122). If Chambers' observation is correct, then we can expect children in a situation of dialect mixture to acquire what they perceive to be the principal dialect of the community, thus further driving focusing on that accent (see Section 11).

We notice that the non-native-born Australians coming to New Zealand had children born in or influenced in Australia, who would have brought the Australian English of the period with them to New Zealand. Information on the number of children among those coming from Australia is not readily available, but we can get a good idea from the shipping records that are accessible. We examined the passenger lists on sailings from Victoria (capital city, Melbourne) to New Zealand over the periods 1852–60 and 1866–70.[7] (This is only a sample because for some sailings passenger information is missing; ships with only one or two passengers are not included.) Between 1852 and 1861, from the sample of 245 sailings, it is clear that there was a continuous stream of children arriving in New Zealand from (or via) Australia. With figures for children and infants combined,[8] in this period there was approximately one child for every four adults. Some individual ships regularly carried numerous children and infants on their trans-Tasman sailings, for example *The Marchioness*:[9]

December 1854:	57 adults; 28 children; 5 infants
February 1855:	34 adults; 15 children; 4 infants
January 1858:	20 adults; 9 children; 3 infants
March 1858:	17 adults; 12 children

The passenger lists for 1866–70 show many more ships leaving Victoria for New Zealand than in the earlier period, with some carrying two to three hundred passengers, including numbers of Chinese. In the sample of 335 sailings, there was still a steady stream of children arriving, but there were proportionately more adults than in the earlier period, with a ratio of approximately one child to ten adults.[10] When the figures are examined for the ships in 1866–70 that did carry

7 Passenger lists, Victoria, Australia, outwards to New Zealand, 1852–1870, microfiche, compiled by Gaynor Kirkby, in the Macmillan Brown Library, University of Canterbury, Christchurch. Shipping records from other Australian states were not kept or do not contain the information we need.

8 Children are classified as twelve years and under, infants as two years and under.

9 Only 4 out of the 245 ships were reported as carrying no children. Many ships in this period carried fewer than twenty passengers and only four ships had over a hundred.

10 Ninety-six sailings carried no children or infants at all, compared to only four in the earlier period. In general the ships carried more people, too, with fifty sailings carrying over a hundred passengers each.

children, the average number of children and infants combined is 6.2 per sailing. In the earlier period 1852–61 it was 6.1 per sailing, showing a similar number of children arriving in New Zealand in both periods. The difference in the 1866–70 period is the increased numbers of adults, caused by the goldrush in Otago, and the recruitment of men to join the North Island militia.

Given the large numbers of children among immigrants coming via Australia (see also Chapter 3), some accommodation to Australian English was quite likely. Indeed, people did comment on the fact that the new colonial accent was especially noticeable in children. For example, at a meeting of the National Council of Women in Wellington in 1898, Mrs Sievwright spoke out about 'parental responsibility':

> [D]o not let your child unlearn at school the mother tongue which it has lisped at your knee. A lady just come from England, said to me the other day 'Men and women here – parents – speak like other people, but the children! Well I really can scarcely understand a word they say'. (Quoted in Sinclair 1986a: 88)

A number of the Mobile Unit speakers report that their families came to New Zealand via Australia. For example, Mrs Annie Hamilton (née Cotter), encountered in Chapter 1, tells that her parents went from Ireland to the Australian goldfields, where the older children were born, and then came to New Zealand (to Arrowtown), where more children (including Annie) were born. In families such as hers, it is possible that the older children developed an Australian accent and influenced the younger children.

New Zealand English may be more than simply a transported version of Australian English, but these figures show that the possibility of Australian influence cannot be overlooked. Australian immigration was greatest in the goldfields, but also many were recruited from Australia into the military during the New Zealand wars in the 1860s. One explanation for the earlier manifestation of a New Zealand accent in precisely these goldmining and military settlements (see Section 22 in Chapter 6 for a discussion of goldmining settlements) could be that they had more people who had come from or via Australia, where the 'accent' was essentially already established.

5.5 Summary of the 'New Zealand English as Australian' hypothesis

The ONZE data cannot confirm or refute the possibility of an Australian input into early New Zealand English. Responses by students to some Mobile Unit speakers 'that they sound Australian' could be a response to certain variables (such as the use of the TRAP vowel rather than START in the *dance* lexical set), which today are associated only with speakers of Australian English. However, even though Mr Firth, the adult Australian in the Mobile Unit archive discussed earlier, is only one speaker, the evidence from his speech suggests that the two varieties were very similar. Demographic evidence, which shows that there was constant interchange between Australia and New Zealand and that many immigrants to New Zealand came via Australia, is strongly suggestive. The figures do not tell us the length of time the immigrants to New Zealand had spent in Australia, but many young children came to New Zealand from or via Australia. It is possible that they might have picked up Australian English on the way and spread its influence in New Zealand.

While it is unlikely that New Zealand English is purely a transported version of Australian English, evidence in favour of Australian input into and influence on New Zealand English as it was forming comes from a combination of demographic information showing the contact between New Zealand English and Australian English, and from the probability that an Australian English was already well formed at the appropriate time. Taken together, this body of evidence suggests that the Australian influence should not be ignored.

6 Transplanted dialects and their level of impact on New Zealand English

6.1 New Zealand English as transplanted south-east / London dialect

To the extent that New Zealand English is similar to south-east English of England, it would simply seem to be conforming to Lass' claim referred to in Chapter 4 that, 'there is no ETE [Extra-territorial English] that is not a dialect of Southern English' (1990: 247).[11] Bauer believes that 'phonologically speaking, New Zealand English is a variant of the southeast England system' (Bauer 1994: 388).[12] In his survey of eighteen phonological traits of New Zealand English that are not RP, not independent developments within New Zealand, and are widespread features of New Zealand English, Bauer (1999: 298) found them 'to be based firmly on the southern rather than the northern varieties of British English'. His investigation led him to conclude that 'the much-discussed south-eastern bias of New Zealand English is not entirely a myth' (p. 300). He also believes south-western features are more important than generally acknowledged, and therefore concluded that 'New Zealand English pronunciation comes through as

[11] As noted in Chapter 4, Newfoundland English is an exception.

[12] Bauer reports, 'the two systematic differences between the vowels of New Zealand English and those of RP are (1) the lack of a phoneme /ə/ contrasting with the vowel of KIT in unstressed syllables and variable merger of /ɪə/ and /eə/'. In fact, as seen in Chapter 6, the lack of contrast in unstressed vowels, though not RP, was nevertheless a variable feature of the southern dialects of England, found in particular in the speech of lower social classes. The merger of /ɪə/ and /eə/ in the NEAR and SQUARE lexical set is a fairly recent development in New Zealand English (Gordon and Maclagan 1985, 1989, 2001; Maclagan and Gordon 1996a), but even so it is not without parallels in various dialects of south-east England and elsewhere (see Wright 1905: 41, 43, 48, 68, 323, 366, 427, 560, 593, 669–70, etc.).

being much more a mixed dialect than is often recognised' (p. 300).[13] This is the very issue addressed (below) by theories of new-dialect formation, the question of dialect mixture and its outcome. However, Bauer's conclusion may not be completely warranted by the data, and his study, though in the right direction, does not necessarily demonstrate that the input to New Zealand English,[14] whatever it may have been, produced results that combined features from various regions. The south-east traits clearly dominate in the result, and the question remains open whether or to what extent significant phonological traits from any other areas may have made their way into modern New Zealand English (see Gordon and Trudgill forthcoming).

As mentioned above, the results of the quantified variables (shown in Table 7.1 above) give an indication as to whether New Zealand English is simply transplanted from the south-east of England and London. We also noted above that

[13] For example, Bauer (1994: 386) reports that 'about 10% of the assisted immigrants came from Cornwall', but this is from 1874, too late to have had a very significant impact on the development of New Zealand English.

[14] Some of the eighteen traits cited by Bauer need to be adjusted, since some may not be independent of one another (diphthong shifts), some were not in fact absent from nineteenth-century RP (e.g. the raised TRAP vowel, see Chapter 6), and the area of some is not correct. Bauer's New Zealand English traits that coincide with those of the south-western areas, and not the south-east, may not be as significant as his numbers suggest. Devon has nine of the eighteen, Cornwall six – all six of the Cornwall traits are also in Devon (fronted BATH, fronted and raised start of MOUTH [counted as two traits], DRESS-TRAP neutralisation [only in southern Devon and Cornwall], /i/ in *happy*, and /t/-voicing); Devon in addition has GOOSE-fronting, schwa in unstressed syllables, some yod-dropping (e.g. *nude* as [nu:d] not [nju:d]), and the FOOT vowel in *women* [only in north Devon] (Bauer 1999: 298–9). Some of these, of course, are not limited to these south-western areas, but are found in several other southern and southeastern zones:

fronted BATH: Hampshire, southern Suffolk, Bedfordshire, Huntingdonshire, Cambridgeshire, parts of Northampton, Dorset, and north-west Warwickshire;
DRESS-TRAP neutralisation: Dorset.
/i/ in happY: as mentioned earlier (also see Chapter 6, *happY*-tensing) was broader than just the south-west areas mentioned by Bauer.
/t/-voicing (intervocalic flapping): Hampshire, Dorset.
schwa in unstressed syllables: Essex–London area, southern Suffolk, Dorset.
yod-dropping: northern Kent, eastern Berkshire, north-west Warwickshire.

Of these, fronted BATH, *happY*-tensing, and unstressed syllable schwa have figured in the discussion of the origins of New Zealand English (see Chapter 6), the others less so. As seen here and in Chapter 4, all three of these features were more widespread than just the south-west and were salient in traditional dialects. Of the others, FOOT in *women* is found only in north Devon. It is probable that New Zealand English underwent this change independently and late in its history. It appears correlated with centralised KIT, where the centralised first vowel of /wɪmən/ 'women' is easily rounded in the environment between labial consonants, after /w/ and before /m/. Since the centralisation of KIT is largely late in New Zealand, this change in *women* must have been even later. Yod-dropping, which is not a particularly salient feature of New Zealand English either, is also found in the south-east of England. GOOSE-fronting, as seen in Chapter 6, was found in a wide variety of traditional dialects in England, and was not limited to Devon.

care is needed in interpreting the quantified results from 'English' settlements. Taking these cautions into account, it can still be seen that the quantified variables are more advanced in the Scottish or Mixed settlements than in the 'English' settlements. This result would argue against New Zealand English simply being a transplanted variety from the south-east of England.

6.2 Why the lack of Irish impact on New Zealand English?

Demographically, Irish-born immigrants made up about 20% of the New Zealand population in 1871, but there were no settlements planned for Irish immigrants like those established to maintain and improve English and Scottish religion and life. One account has it that the Irish 'were under-represented for the first fifty years of settlement – dramatically so among those given free passages by the New Zealand Company' (nzhistory.net.2002). 'The bulk of the Irish community of New Zealand is descended from those who arrived in the twenty years 1860–1880 – either as miners in the 1860s or as assisted immigrants in the 1870s' (nzhistory.net.2002). Galbraith (2000: 43) suggests that the social status of Irish immigrants would have been affected by strong anti-Irish prejudice directed at immigrants from the predominantly Catholic south of Ireland, and also suggests (p. 53) that Irish Protestants assimilated much more easily to colonial society than the Irish Catholics, because of shared religious traditions with the Scots Presbyterians and the Anglican English.

Hearn, using an analysis of immigration in the 1870s, explains that Irish immigration was dominated by single people: 'If accompanying children are excluded from the total, 77.5% of the adults were single and single males alone accounted for 45%. This high proportion reflected a decline in the emigration of Irish families to New Zealand after 1875' (2000: 65). Hearn also points out that the Irish men who had already married before arriving in New Zealand did so largely in Australia, and the same was true for Irish women (p. 84).

As Hickey (2002) points out, more than twice as many Irish immigrants were unmarried upon arrival than English immigrants, and this means that a high proportion of the Irish had their children in New Zealand, where they would be exposed to the developing variety of New Zealand English and thus not acquire Irish linguistic traits to the same degree that they would acquire traits of the emerging dialect. For example, Corbyn (1854) observed strong Irish accents in Australia, but noted that the children did not adopt the pronunciation of their parents (cf. Chambers 2002). This means that the Irish segment of the late nineteenth-century New Zealand population had less influence on the formation of New Zealand English than their proportion of the population would suggest.

In short, for social and demographic reasons, Irish English, in spite of the number of Irish immigrants to New Zealand, had no lasting significant impact on New Zealand English phonology (cf. Bauer 1999: 291). This is consistent with the lack of visible Irish influence in a number of other colonial settings that had sizeable numbers of Irish immigrants but no significant impact from Irish English (see, for example, Bernard 1969: 65).

The data discussed in Chapter 6 provide some evidence for linguistic effects of Irish parentage over the time span of the Mobile Unit Archive. However, this appears to have been an effect only on individuals, and not a lasting one. For example, significantly more individuals with Irish parents used TRAP vowels in *dance* words (variant (6) in Table 7.1) and raised variants of KIT ((8) in Table 7.1), but these variants have not survived into modern New Zealand English.

In fact, of the four phonological features found throughout Ireland, which Hickey (1999: 42–3) characterises as 'uncontroversial' and which can be heard in the speech of some Mobile Unit speakers, three did not survive into modern New Zealand English, and the fourth is now uncommon:

1. Use of clear /l/ in all positions in a word.
2. Retention of syllable-final /r/.
3. Distinction of short vowels before /r/.
4. Retention of the /w/~/hw/ distinction.

Eleven speakers in the Archive use substantial amounts of clear /l/ in all positions in a word, but only two of them have Irish parents. A further nine sometimes use syllable final clear /l/, but only one of them has an Irish father. So, even though the first of Hickey's uncontroversial Irish features can indeed be found among speakers in the Mobile Unit Archive, its presence does not represent a clear Irish influence, and, of course, it did not survive.

The last trait, retention of the distinction between /w/ and /hw/ ((7) in Table 7.1), survived to some degree in the Mobile Unit speakers, but is now uncommon. However, as argued in Chapter 6, it would be difficult to attribute this primarily to Irish influence, since it was retained by most speakers of educated southern English until into the second half of the nineteenth century, was prominent in Scottish English, and was the prestige variant for many. Also, having Scottish or New Zealand-born parents favours wh-retention in the data, but having Irish parents does not (see Table 7.1).

6.3 The influence of the Scottish immigrants on New Zealand English

In Chapter 3 we saw that 21% of the non-Maori population in 1881 were born in Scotland (see Chart 3.1 in Chapter 3). Tables 3.2, 3.4, and 3.5 (in Chapter 3) show that the Scottish immigrants were not evenly distributed around New Zealand; the majority of them settled in the south of the South Island, in Otago and Southland, where 50–60% of the immigrants came from Scotland. With 21% of the original population coming from Scotland, we might expect there to be discernible Scottish influences on the pronunciation of modern New Zealand

English, since there are Scottish influences on the vocabulary with words such as *wee* (see Bauer 2000).

However, the only obvious Scottish influence on Modern New Zealand English pronunciation is the rhoticity that still persists in Southland and parts of Otago. This is now receding, to the extent that it is only retained by younger speakers in words of the NURSE lexical set, and only at low levels of frequency (see Bartlett 1992, 2003). It appears that, apart from this one trait in this one area, the early Scottish settlers, like the Irish, left no obvious phonological effects on modern New Zealand English. This, however, may be open to some interpretation.

As demonstrated in Chapter 6, New Zealand English appears strongly to reflect the input from the south-east of England, from where the largest number of settlers came. Even so, it is possible that the Scottish immigrants may have had an influence in the overall mixture, but that their influence is now less visible (see Trudgill, Maclagan, and Lewis 2003). In particular, the dialect input of the Scottish immigrants, together with that of the Irish, lent support to the retention of /h/ (loss of h-dropping, (9) in Table 7.1). Although h-dropping was common in the dialects from the south-east of England, it was correlated with lower social classes. The presence of /h/ (lack of h-dropping) in the speech of the Scottish immigrants could have contributed to the loss of h-dropping in New Zealand English, even though the school inspectors were still complaining about h-dropping around 1900 (see Chapter 6). Scottish influence, however, may not be necessary for h-dropping to be lost. For example, Kerswill and Williams (2002: 94) found h-dropping to be receding in the south of England, that is, that /h/ was reinstated 'by southern working-class teenagers' (for example, 83% of the time in Milton Keynes, where elderly speakers in the southern towns they investigated 'used /h/ only between five and twelve per cent of the time'). Similarly, the presence of /hw/ in the speech of the Scottish immigrants would have added to the numbers of early speakers who retained the /w/~/hw/ distinction, even though many of the speakers from the south-east of England had already merged the two sounds (see Chapter 6). Indeed our data demonstrate that the observed increase in /hw/ over the time period analysed was greater in Scottish settlements, and strongly facilitated by Scottish parents. Our analysis of the late nineteenth-century data, then, suggests this is one realm in which Scotland had an impact. However, we also know that the trajectory of change for this variable reversed during the twentieth century, and that /hw/ is now not common in modern New Zealand English.

It has also been suggested that Scottish speakers are the source of the centralised KIT vowel in New Zealand English (Trudgill 1986b, but see Trudgill et al. 1998). The data presented in Chapter 6 indicate that only 5% of the KIT tokens analysed were coded as being centralised, and none were coded as the Scottish [ɜ], even though many of the Mobile Unit speakers had Scottish parents and lived in predominantly Scottish settlements. The statistical analysis showed that the very slight number of centralised KIT tokens increased over the period of time analysed, but Scottish speakers per se do not seem to have been the source of this typical New Zealand English pronunciation.

7 The mixing bowl (or 'melting pot') approach

As noted in Chapter 4, Bauer (1994: 424) believes that the mixing bowl approach is unable to explain the loss of rhoticity in New Zealand. Our analysis (see Chapter 6 and later) showed that, overall, there were low levels of rhoticity. The loss of rhoticity in modern New Zealand English could, in fact, be accounted for in a straightforward fashion by the mixing bowl approach (though other factors may also have been involved, as we discuss later in Sections 9 and 10.3).

Another result that lends support to the mixing bowl theory is the finding that mixed settlements appear to be ahead in the change for a number of the variables (in Table 7.1). This, together with the fact that change appears often to have moved more rapidly in these mixed settlements (see, for example, rhoticity – (10) in Table 7.1, the unstressed vowel – (5)), provides evidence suggesting that mixing was involved in the formation of New Zealand English. Interestingly, it is in the communities where there was *no clear majority* that change often took hold faster.

8 Stages of new-dialect formation

As described in Chapter 4, Trudgill distinguished three chronological stages, seen as corresponding roughly to generations, in new-dialect formation (Trudgill 1986b; Trudgill 2001: 43; Trudgill et al. 1998: 38; cf. Britain 1997a: 41; Kerswill and Williams 2000), and he has applied these to interpreting the formation of New Zealand English.

8.1 The first stage: rudimentary levelling

The first stage of new-dialect formation involves the initial contact between adult speakers of different regional and social varieties in the new location, and involves rudimentary dialect levelling.

The majority of the ONZE speakers analysed were born in New Zealand. They therefore do not give information about the first stage of rudimentary levelling, which in Trudgill's approach would have taken place in the speech of their parents. Nevertheless, that rudimentary dialect levelling did occur in New Zealand can be inferred indirectly from the data. There are, for example, features of nineteenth-century British Isles traditional dialects (see Wells 1982) that are not even vestigially present in the ONZE corpus data, though it can be assumed that some of them were present in the speech of at least a few of the immigrants; for these it can be assumed that they were levelled out very early on because of their extreme minority and/or regionally marked and/or sociolinguistically low status. For instance, a widespread nineteenth-century British feature that is absent from the recordings of the New Zealand-born (but variably present in one speaker, Mr John Prendergast, who was born in Ireland around 1857 and came to new Zealand aged about twenty) is the merger of /v/ and /w/ giving *village* as 'willage', which was a feature of many south-of-England dialects at this time (see Trudgill et al. 2003). This feature did make it into a number of other colonial varieties such as those of Tristan da Cunha (see Schreier 2003: 212) and the Bahamas, presumably because of the earlier date of formation of these varieties.

8.2 The second stage: extreme variability

The second stage of the new-dialect formation process, as described by Trudgill, is characterised by considerable variability.

One kind of variability, where it is believed that there is no single peer-dialect for children to acquire, may be exemplified by the speech of some of the oldest Mobile Unit speakers. For example, the auditory perceptual analysis of Mr Malcolm Ritchie, who was born in 1866 in Cromwell (in Otago in the South Island, a goldmining settlement) of parents who came from Perthshire, Scotland, showed that his phonological system combined features of Irish or Scottish origin with features of English English origin. For example, he often pronounces /θ/ and /ð/ as dental stops [t̪] and [d̪], as in Irish English, and /t/ is often dental [t̪ʰ] before /r/, as in *tree*. He also has cases of clear syllable-final /l/, as in Irish English. On the other hand, he also has variable instances of h-dropping, which is not a trait of Scottish or Irish English, and, even more unusual, his h-dropping is combined with the presence of the distinction /hw/~/w/, as in *whine*, *wine*. The quantitative analysis revealed that Mr Ritchie has 13% h-dropping and 17% /hw/-retention. Although these percentages are not large, it would be unusual to find this much h-dropping in a speaker of a Scottish or Irish variety of English, and certainly unusual to have a degree of h-dropping combined with a degree of /hw/-retention.[15] Mr Ritchie's pronunciation appears to reveal a mixed dialect input.

Mr Ritchie also pronounces *wasn't* as *wadn*. This trait is associated with the south-west of England, and there was an area of Cromwell that was known at the time as 'Cornishtown' because of the many Cornish miners who lived there; nevertheless, it is also known from other dialects in England (cf. Britain 2002: 35, for example).

The question of whether 'extreme variation' is present in the data is an important one in this context. This may be even more difficult to determine than it

[15] In drawing attention to the presence of h-dropping and /hw/-retention in Mr Ritchie, we are *not* claiming that his phonological system is in violation, for example, of the universal that the presence of /hw/ presupposes the presence of /h/ in the phonemic inventory. Given the predominance of tokens (87%) in this variable where /h/ was pronounced, it is not so surprising to find Mr Ritchie has preserved the /hw/~/w/ phonemic contrast.

might at first seem, given that rather extreme variation is also possible in other kinds of situations (as argued by Dorian 1994, 2001, see later, Section 14). If many situations have considerable variation, even when no new-dialect formation is involved, then how does one know how much variation constitutes 'extreme variation'?

8.3 *The third stage: focusing*

8.3.1 Third-stage levelling: the survival of unmarked forms. In Trudgill 1986b, it is suggested that in certain circumstances unmarked forms, even if they are in a slight minority, may survive rather than marked forms in new-dialect formation (see discussion also in Kerswill 2001: 674–5; Kerswill and Williams 2000; also Mufwene 2001: 5–31). At an earlier stage of the ONZE analysis it appeared that Weak Vowel Merger (Wells 1982: 167) (variant (5) in Table 7.1) was not the majority form in the unstressed syllables of words like *David*, *hundred*, *wanted*, *naked*, *horses* (that is, that the contrast between the closer vowel of the *rabbit* class of words and the more open vowel of the *abbot* class was maintained in New Zealand English as in varieties in England, in particular in RP; see Chapter 6). Trudgill et al. (2000a: 311) noted that only 32% of the Mobile Unit informants analysed to that point had Weak Vowel Merger. This seemed to support the notion of the survival of unmarked forms, where schwa is the unmarked vowel *par excellence*. It was thought that the large minority figure of 32% of informants with Weak Vowel Merger at the second stage of new-dialect development was high enough for it to replace other (non-merged) forms at the third stage on the grounds of its unmarkedness. Further auditory perceptual analysis including seventy-five speakers divided into earlier and later periods, indicated that just over 50% of the speakers at both time periods had Weak Vowel Merger (centralised vowels in unstressed syllables) most of the time; however, the auditory quantified analysis indicates that not all of the centralised tokens could be classified as [ə]. In summary, although fully centralised schwa-like vowels were not used in the majority of unstressed syllables, and were only used by just over 50% of the ONZE speakers, their unmarked nature would have helped them to survive into the third stage of new-dialect development.[16]

Questions that need to be addressed with respect to unmarkedness concern how large the unmarked minority must be and how markedness/unmarkedness is determined. These considerations are important, since it has been claimed that in some instances a minority marked feature can nevertheless survive (for examples, see Siegel 1993: 116). Some of the 'embryonic variants' cited by Gordon

[16] As pointed out in Chapter 6, the Weak Vowel Merger had begun in 'vulgar' (lower-class) speech or in the 'regions' (regional dialects), according to Wyld (1920: 258–82), before the Mobile Unit speakers' parents left for New Zealand, and because many of the early settlers in New Zealand came from the working classes or 'the regions', we would expect that the clear distinction between [ɪ] and [ə] in unstressed syllables was not present in the speech of many of them.

and Trudgill (1999) and Trudgill (1999d), fit here, instances that had extremely few tokens when first detected in the past, but that came to be much more dominant later in time (see also Trudgill 1988). For example, Trudgill (1999d: 41) says of the rounded NURSE vowel, 'our studies show that this was absent from earlier forms of NZ English – except that perhaps as many as 10 per cent of the nineteenth-century-born ONZE speakers have at least some tokens of this type' (see Chapter 6).[17] In short, even a marked variant in a minority can nevertheless survive and even grow in strength. Questions, then, for further research, concern the conditions under which a minority unmarked variant might win out, and when a minority marked variant might survive and even increase in frequency.

8.3.2 Third-stage reallocation and the survival of variation. 'Reallocation occurs where two or more variants in the dialect mix survive the levelling process but are refunctionalised, evolving new social or linguistic functions in the new dialect' (Britain and Trudgill 1999: 245). Variants originally from different regional dialects may become social-class, stylistic, or allophonic variants (see Britain 1997a: 35–8; 2002: 36; Britain and Trudgill 1999; Trudgill et al. 1998: 38; cf. Siegel 1993: 110; Sudbury 2000: 54–7). For example, formerly words of the class *dance*, *ample*, *plant* characterised different regional dialects of England; the 'northern' /æ/ and 'southern' /aː/ variants were both in the original dialect input to Australian English. Now, however, the two survive in some parts of Australia as social-class and stylistic variants, the latter associated more with cultivated speech and contexts. That is, 'the northern and southern regional variants have been reallocated roles as low and high status variants respectively' (Britain and Trudgill 1999: 248; cf. Wells 1982: 134–5). Modern-day New Zealand English no longer exhibits significant examples of reallocation; however, Britain and Trudgill (1999: 248) argue that 'the reallocated Australian pattern [for *dance* class words] was also present in late 19th and early 20th century New Zealand English (NZE), but . . . today this reallocation is no longer found there, with the prestigious lengthened variant having completely taken over the less prestigious short one'. The Mobile Unit speakers do demonstrate variability between TRAP and START in the *dance* word class, with 49% of the tokens being realised with TRAP rather than START (see Chapter 6). However, except for the indication that women used more short variants (the variant that has not survived into modern New Zealand English), there is no evidence to indicate that the choice of variable was or was not influenced by stylistic or social factors, and Wall (1936: 29) who was the arbiter of 'correct' usage in New Zealand, says that both variants are 'equally good'.

Although not reallocation, nevertheless, the vowel variants in the CLOTH set of words (*off*, *froth*, *cross* etc.) illustrate the survival of variability into modern

[17] In the later analysis based on more speakers, this figure turned out to be 20% of speakers with variants of NURSE that are lip rounded, with three speakers using variants that are both lip rounded and raised, as reported in Chapter 6.

New Zealand English, with a few older speakers still using the THOUGHT vowel (/ɔː/) rather than LOT (/ɒ/) for some of these words. The Mobile Unit speakers pronounce words in this set predominantly with /ɔː/; in fact, nearly half of the informants (excluding the eight speakers who have the Scottish system, which does not distinguish between the vowels of the LOT and THOUGHT lexical sets) use this pronunciation at least sometimes. This variability must have been a feature of New Zealand English from the outset, including variability among speakers *and* among lexical items. Thus, both variants survived the levelling process, presumably because the number of relevant lexical items involved was small and because the proportion of those who actually had the short vowel in the relevant set was almost half of the total number of informants.

8.4 Summary of new-dialect formation

Because the majority of the ONZE speakers were born in New Zealand, we can only make limited inferences about Trudgill's proposed first stage of rudimentary dialect levelling from the Mobile Unit data. We are dealing only with the children of the first immigrants and therefore have no direct evidence of the parents' speech. These Mobile Unit speakers do give evidence of Trudgill's stage 2 variability, even though in some cases, the percentages are not large. The Mobile Unit corpus also gives some evidence for focusing, thus proving consistent with the stages of the theory of new-dialect formation as presented in Trudgill 1986b and elsewhere.

9 Determinism in new-dialect formation

When Trudgill et al. (2000a) published their work on determinism in new-dialect formation (see Chapter 4), adequate historical information about early immigrants and settlement patterns in New Zealand was not available to support the hypothesis categorically. With the more recent historical information presented in Chapter 3 (in particular from nzhistory.net 2002), it is now clear that the south-east of England did contribute the majority of immigrants and hence the often noted south-eastern nature of modern New Zealand English is consistent with determinism, based on the larger numbers of immigrants representing that dialect. A more recent analysis of the Mobile Unit data shows that some cases that originally seemed to be inconsistent with determinism turn out not to be.

Determinism aims to predict which variant of a particular variable will emerge in the output when a new dialect is formed, based on which variant is in the majority in the input. However, there are different ways in which a variant can be in the majority: it can be used by a majority of speakers, or it can be the variant with the majority of occurrences among the tokens of the variable. Since earlier ONZE work was not based on a token-by-token analysis, the notion of majority used was the former, that of the majority of speakers. However, now that quantified analysis of a number of these variables is complete, the picture is clearer. Table 7.3 shows the percentage of speakers and the percentage of tokens for each of the quantified consonantal variables (the variables with just two variants). From this we see that it is possible for a variant to be to be found in the speech of a majority of speakers, but nevertheless not occur in a majority of tokens. A moment's reflection reveals that the opposite is not true. With an equal number of tokens collected from each speaker, if a variant is used by only 49% of speakers, it is impossible for it to be the majority variant – even if those speakers each used it 100% of the time. Therefore, if a variant constitutes a majority of tokens, it is also used by a majority of speakers, but if it is in a minority of tokens, it may be used by a minority or a majority of speakers.

So the relevant question is, does the number of tokens matter? It seems clear that the 'majority wins' claim does not work in any of these three cases if we consider the number of speakers alone. Neither h-dropping nor rhoticity has survived into modern New Zealand English, and /hw/ is not common, yet all were used (at least to some degree) by a majority of speakers in the early corpus. Trudgill et al. (2000b) had argued that rhoticity is a counterexample to determinism because it was used by a majority of speakers and yet it disappeared. They attributed this to 'drift' (see later, Section 10). However, if we consider the notion 'majority' to be based on the percentage of tokens from among the total number of tokens possible, then loss of rhoticity is not a counterexample – rhotic tokens were only a small proportion of the total tokens for this variable (9%), though used by 98% of speakers. Indeed, determinism holds much better when we consider the number of tokens – all three of these variants occurred in only a small minority of the total tokens of the variable during the period analysed; two of the variables (h-dropping and rhoticism) have not survived into modern New Zealand English, and the third is uncommon.

When we consider the numbers in Table 7.3, it could be argued that both tokens and speakers are important. These variants also disappeared at different rates. H-dropping disappeared quite early, rhoticity took somewhat longer, and /hw/ is still found in some older speakers today – and still lingers as a residual class marker. As /hw/ was represented by twice as many tokens in the Mobile Unit data as the other two variables, a deterministic approach would predict that it would stay around longer. It was in a minority – but a less restricted minority. H-dropping and rhoticity were represented by a similar proportion of tokens but a larger number of speakers used these tokens in the case of rhoticity than in the case of h-dropping. So if the proportion of speakers using a variant also plays some role, then this could go some way to explaining the faster disappearance of h-dropping.[18]

[18] Of course other views are also possible. Others would argue that social factors played a large role, that it is the social value of /hw/ which both contributed to its continued use and to its growth in percentage of tokens for a period in its history in New Zealand English (see Chapter 6); the negative status of h-dropping would have worked in the opposite direction. It is also possible, of course, that determinism and other factors worked in concert to produce these results, that is, multiple causation.

Table 7.3 *Percentage of tokens and speakers for quantified consonantal variables*

Variable	% tokens	% speakers
h-dropping	9.0	71.0
/hw/	20.5	80.0
rhoticity	9.0	98.0

In short, the data here provide preliminary support for determinism, provided that the notion 'majority' is considered token-wise, rather than (or at least, as well as) speaker-wise. It seems clear that it is not enough only to consider how many speakers use a particular variant. We also have to consider the degree to which they use it.

10 Drift

Trudgill et al (2000b) proposed 'drift' – inherited propensities for change – as a subsidiary principle to account for cases that did not fit well with new-dialect formation approaches. Drift in this view can refer both to inherited variants in the speech of arriving immigrants, which then go on to change further after arrival, and to independent but parallel developments which take place after separation of dialects. We consider the most salient examples that have been proposed as examples of drift involving New Zealand English.

10.1 Diphthong shift as drift

From the ONZE data we observe that 'diphthong shift' (Wells 1982: 256, see Chapter 6) occurred in the following order: /au/ then /ai/, followed by /ei/ and /ou/ (or/ou/and/ei/) (we did not treat /iː/ or /uː/ as part of the closing diphthong series). That is, speakers who have shifted /ou/ will necessarily have shifted /ai/ but not necessarily /ei/. This follows the chronological and geographical pattern in England, seen in Maps 3a–3d (Appendix 3). It also tallies with early New Zealand commentaries on these pronunciations, and the acoustic analyses of Mobile Unit speakers. The acoustic analyses show that, for the youngest of the ten speakers investigated, the starting points of /ei/ and /ou/ have moved together (i.e. /ou/ has become more fronted and /ei/ further back), while this has not occurred in the speech of the oldest speakers, who demonstrate shift only in /au/ and, to a lesser extent, /ai/. The clear conclusion is that diphthong-shifted vowels – at least to a certain extent – were inherited by New Zealand English from English English varieties. Since diphthong shift can be seen to increase with time throughout the ONZE data and the extent of the shift in New Zealand English today has gone farther than in English English, this supports the suggestion that it was the ongoing process of diphthong shift that was inherited rather than the shifted vowel qualities themselves.

10.2 Fronted and lowered STRUT *as drift*

Another possible example of drift is the vowel /ʌ/ (the development of which is discussed in Chapter 6; see also Britain and Sudbury 2002: 211). In the ONZE corpus materials, fronted and lowered vowels beyond [ɐ] are not common for most of the oldest speakers, although such pronunciations are attested; however, they become more common during the forty-year period represented in the Mobile Unit recordings. Of the informants born between 1850 and 1869, 35% have some fronting and lowering, while the figure for those born between 1870 and 1889 is over 60%. These numbers, however, conceal the fact that the degree of fronting also increased during this period and that STRUT became more open (lower) during the same time. The acoustic analyses confirm this. The two oldest speakers in the group of ten analysed acoustically both have relatively close (high) productions for STRUT, whereas the younger speakers produce a range of variants.

Clearly, then, in some sense a trend to fronting and lowering movement of this vowel came from England and continued in New Zealand (see Map 5, Appendix 3). Today, the most advanced varieties of English so far as this vowel is concerned have continued the fronting and lowering process to reach a point around [a] (as in 'Broad New Zealand English'). These 'most advanced' varieties are precisely the Englishes of New Zealand, Australia, South Africa, and London (see Wells 1982: 305, 599). Developments concerning this vowel in the three major southern hemisphere varieties appear to be independent events that happened in parallel. The same can be said for the development in London. Trudgill et al. (2000b) conclude that these events represent continuations of a long ongoing process of change involving the STRUT vowel.

10.3 Loss of rhoticity as a case of drift

A very notable finding that emerged from the analyses of the speech of the ONZE speakers concerns rhoticity. As mentioned earlier, there is in New Zealand today a well-known but small area in Southland, in the lower South Island, which has traditionally been rhotic. Bartlett (2003) accounts for this regional difference by the heavier proportion of Scottish immigrants to this area of the country (see Chapter 3). The rest of New Zealand English today, however, is non-rhotic, though, as seen in Chapter 6, this was not always the case.

In view of the expectations from new-dialect formation, Trudgill et al. (2000b) asked why rhoticity – a majority variant in terms of speakers – was levelled out in koinéisation, with the result that modern New Zealand English is now non-rhotic. At that stage in the ONZE work, the data did not seem to support determinism or new-dialect levelling for this feature, and it was thought to be an example of drift (see also Britain and Sudbury 2002: 211). As shown above, further analysis of the data, including the quantitative analysis, shows that loss of rhoticity is not in fact a counterexample to determinism, to the principle 'majority wins'. It can be explained deterministically; rhoticity was a small minority of the total number of tokens of this variable, and therefore appeal to drift is unnecessary to explain its loss.[19]

11 The role of children in new-dialect formation

Approaches to new-dialect formation emphasise adult linguistic accommodation in the levelling of variants. The acquisition of language by children is also considered important, though its role is less developed in this literature. In the case of the founder effect (see below), it is different; it is assumed that there is a peer-dialect in place which influences strongly the variety acquired by children, especially adolescents. Kerswill and Williams (2000) see children as the primary agents of koinéisation. As they point out, in most cases of new settlements, there are children among the arrivals as well as children born to the adult immigrants:

> These youngsters will quickly form a new 'native' speech community; and the degree of focusing they achieve as the first generation of natives will depend on a wide range of linguistic and demographic factors, especially the proportion of children to adults in the earliest years of settlement. (Kerswill and Williams 2000: 69)

They argue that 'the presence of a high proportion of children and young people in a new town accelerates the process of koinéisation' (p. 74, cf. Sudbury 2000: 62).

The impact of children and their different role in the process is reflected in Kerswill and Williams' principles, namely that 'adults, adolescents, and children influence the outcome of dialect contact differently', and that 'because of sociolinguistic maturation, the structure of the new speech community is first discernible in the speech of native-born adolescents, not young children' (2000: 84, 90, 102). Mitchell (1995) argued in a similar way for the role and importance of children in the development of Australian English (see Section 5.4). Because only adults were recorded, the Mobile Unit data can say nothing directly about the role of children in new-dialect formation in New Zealand. Nevertheless, the figures given in Section 5.4 provide concrete evidence that the number of children in the early years of settlement in New Zealand was sufficiently great to have a marked effect on the development of the new variety. In Chapter 3 we

[19] Other examples in New Zealand English earlier thought to be due to independent parallel drift (for example, some of those mentioned by Britain and Sudbury 2002: 212) turn out not to be; that is, the variation was extant already in the input dialects brought to New Zealand from England. Thus *happ*Y-tensing, for example, was not independent in New Zealand but rather, as seen in Chapter 6, was variably present already in the Mobile Unit data.

cited Sinclair (1986b: 2) who pointed out that in 1896, when 62% of the Europeans in New Zealand were born in New Zealand, 330,000 of these were under twenty-one and only 11,600 of the native-born (less than 5%) were over twenty.

We also note that, with the introduction of free compulsory education in New Zealand in 1877, large numbers of children were brought together in contact with one another (see Chapter 3). Compulsory schooling could have accelerated the already existing processes of new-dialect formation. Speakers in the Mobile Unit database who were born in the 1880s or later have fewer traditional dialect features than those born earlier, or none at all (though of course it is possible that focusing could have taken place by then without the boost from compulsory education). At the same time, these later-born speakers manifest more examples of New Zealand features, such as diphthong shift.

12 Founder effects and colonial lag

The *founder principle* (see Mufwene 1996, 2001)[20] holds that 'the structural peculiarities of a given dialect have their root in the varieties spoken by the population(s) that originally introduced the language to the region' (Wolfram and Schilling-Estes forthcoming). This is essentially the same as Zelinsky's (1992) 'doctrine of first effective settlement', which 'limits the influence of new groups entering an established community, in asserting that the original group determines the cultural pattern for those to follow, even if these newcomers are many times the number of the original settlers' (Labov 2001: 503). Applied to new-dialect formation, this principle would mean that the dialects spoken by the early settlers should be more predictive of the new dialect than are the varieties spoken by individuals or groups who arrive subsequently. The idea is not new; even before recent literature on the founder principle, this was Turner's view (cited in Chapter 3):

> When a new form of language develops, the study of that language must give a disproportionate attention to the first generation of settlers, new things are named early and new ways of speech develop from a linguistically mixed community. Later arrivals, even if numerous, are less important because they are absorbed as newcomers and learn to conform, and indeed wish to conform. (Turner 1996: 6)

Bernard (1969) also argued a version of what is in effect the founder principle to explain the lack of Irish imprint upon Australian English (see the discussion of Irish influence on New Zealand English in Section 6.2).

[20] Mufwene's (1996: 84) original formulation was for Creoles: 'The term *Founder Principle*, also identified as *Founder Effect* . . . is used here, along with *founder population*, to explain how structural features of Creoles have been predetermined to a large extent (but not exclusively!) by characteristics of the vernaculars spoken by the populations that founded the colonies in which they developed'. (See also Rickford 1997.) The principle was formulated in Creole studies earlier also by Sankoff (1980) as 'the first past the post' principle; cf. Labov 2001: 504.

Founder effects can be likened to long-term persistent substratum influence, where the language of the founders persists in spite of the onslaught of later varieties. Later immigrants are less influential as a result of the founder effect if at any given time they are insufficiently numerous to influence significantly the speech of those already established in the country. Crucial is the claim that it is difficult for traits of the founders' speech to be overridden by different traits typical of the speech of later arrivals (see 'swamping', in Section 13). This makes it important to know what linguistic traits the founders had, in what measures they had them (that is, if they were variable, how frequent was their occurrence), and to what social and linguistic constraints they were subject.

An important question is: How strong is the founder principle? While evidence of the principle has been observed in many situations, it is also clear that its effects should not be overestimated. There is now considerable evidence that the long-term impact of founder effects must be qualified (Sellers 1999; Wolfram and Thomas 2002; Wolfram et al. 2000; Schreier 2001). Many dialect contact situations exhibit levelling and independent change that override and obscure any founder effect (Schreier 2002b).[21] As Wolfram and Schilling-Estes (forthcoming) found in their study of several coastal dialects of the eastern US, 'issues of donorship [dialect origin] can also be quite complex and may require the consideration of several layers of dialect transportation' to sort out the influence of 'various dialect groups at various points in time'. Both the bulk of the evidence and common-sense intuition support Labov's (2001: 504) reading that 'in any one generation, if the numbers of immigrants rise to a higher order of magnitude than the extant population, the doctrine may be overthrown, with qualitative changes in the general speech patterns'.[22]

As seen in Chapter 3, the number of established settlers in New Zealand was exceeded many times over by the number of new arrivals up to the crucial years for the formation of New Zealand English. In the early period of organised settlement (1840–53), about 30,000 people arrived in New Zealand; between 1861 and 1867 net migration exceeded 105,000, and between 1871 and 1880 there was a net population gain through immigration of nearly 137,000 (Hearn 2000: 56). Studies elsewhere have found that immigrant speakers have influenced the direction of phonological change in some communities (e.g. in Sydney, see Horvath 1998). Thus, given the very large numbers of later immigrants, it is

[21] Labov (2001: 503) believes that the principle of 'first effective settlement' (founder principle) is consistent with what we know of New York City, Philadelphia, Boston, and Chicago, whose dialects 'show only slight influences' from the languages of the ethnic groups who came to these cities later in numbers. This is not the same thing, though, as a massive influx of later immigrants speaking the *same* language, albeit different varieties thereof.

[22] Kerswill and Williams (2000: 84, 95) appear to take the opposite view from that of the founder principle, based on their survey of dialects in contact, that 'most first and second generation speakers are oriented towards language varieties that originate elsewhere' (see the discussion of swamping, in Section 13.)

quite possible that the founder effect in New Zealand, at least for some traits, was overridden. We also note that the case histories of selected towns visited by the Mobile Unit (see Appendix 2) show that the early histories of many New Zealand settlements were marked by constant change and mobility. This too would impede any lasting founder effect.

Related to the founder principle is the notion of *colonial lag* (see Marckwardt 1958), which refers to the retention, in colonial varieties, of earlier linguistic features that are no longer found in mainstream British dialects (cf. Görlach 1987; Trudgill 1999a; 1999b: 227; Sudbury 2000: 63; Woods 2000a). The idea is that the new varieties somehow lag behind the original varieties from which they come, as in American dialects that retain the TRAP vowel in words like *path*, *dance* and *can't* (Wolfram and Schilling-Estes 1998: 93). Trudgill (1999b: 227) explains how this might come about in new-dialect formation:

> A lag or delay in the normal progression and development of linguistic change which lasts for about one generation and arises solely as an automatic consequence of the fact that there is often no common peer-group dialect for children to acquire in first generation colonial situations involving dialect mixture.

Because of the fragmentation of transplanted speech communities, the children of colonial founding populations may lack well-defined peer groups and the models they provide; in such an event, the influence of the dialects of the parents' generation would be stronger than in more typical linguistic situations. This is especially true of more isolated settlers' children. As a result, the dialect that develops in such situations largely reflects the speech of the previous generation, thus lagging behind.

The results presented in Chapter 6 show that parental origin is often an important predictor of aspects of individuals' speech. This provides some support for the notion of colonial lag. In fact, it appears that the parents play a stronger role even than initially argued for by Trudgill (1986b; Trudgill et al. 2000a). He distinguished between children in fairly isolated settlements, who acquire their parents' dialects, and those in mixed, non-isolated communities. Of the latter, he claimed, 'there seems to be no particular connection between their speech and that of their parents' (Trudgill 1999b: 230). The findings relating to parental origins, however, extend well beyond the speakers in isolated communities (who would be classified as being in 'unknown' settlement types according to our census-based classification scheme, as reported in Chapters 5 and 6). The significant effect of parental origins pervades the data. Thus, while Trudgill et al. (2000a) see such speakers as choosing more or less randomly from forms available from their parents' generation, the data in Chapter 6 suggest that the selection may not be so random after all. There is a clear link between parental origin and linguistic behaviour in this period of New Zealand English, thus providing insights on the nature of 'colonial lag' in this variety.

13 Swamping

Lass' (1990; 1997: 206) term *swamping* is applied to two types of situations. The first is where the dialect of the majority of speakers is accepted and thus causes variants from minority dialects that are not shared with the majority dialect to be overcome and suppressed. (In this sense, swamping is like levelling in the determinism model, see Section 9.) A second swamping situation is where the cumulative weight of the speech of subsequent immigrants is so great that it takes over and pushes out, or 'swamps', traits from earlier varieties that are not found in the dialect of the new incoming majority. In a sense, then, swamping is the antithesis of founder effect.

For the sake of illustration we can consider as a case of swamping the replacement of monophthongal [aː] in words such as 'pie' in Texas dialects with the diphthong variant more common elsewhere in the US, though it is important to keep in mind that other accounts of its history could also be put forward (see in particular 'levelling' and 'focusing'). Thomas (1997: 328) found that the monophthongal [aː] variant, stereotypic of Anglo-Texan dialects, is being driven out in urban centres due to the large-scale immigration of 'Northerns' from outside Texas (cited in Gordon and Trudgill 1999: 118; see also Kerswill and Williams 2000: 72–3), that is, the older, more traditional Texan variant is being swamped by the later-arriving diphthongal variant that is the predominant pronunciation of the new settlers.[23]

One of Lass' examples of swamping is relatively straightforward and illustrates the claim very well:

> Of course Mainland features, bolstered or not by population movements, can enter an ETE [Extraterritorial English] at a relatively advanced stage of its evolution, and even override features already present. The New England and southeastern U.S. 'broad <u>a</u>' in <u>bath</u>, etc. is a case in point. The settlements that show [æ] in <u>cat</u> vs. [aː ~ äː] in <u>bath</u> are all generally at least half a century too early for this to have been part of the input; the first Mainland testimony in the late 1670s suggests that lengthening (not to mention quality change) could not have occurred in the inputs to coastal settlements like Jamestown (1607), Plymouth (1620), etc. This must be an 18th-century feature superimposed on areas that had developed their own regional character much earlier.[24] (1990: 267–8)

[23] It could be objected, as Ray Hickey does (personal communication 2002), that in this instance it is not entirely a matter of the mass of later immigrants, but rather involves also their status, representing what is urban, modern, outside, and probably prestigious. We believe status and numbers of speakers both enter the picture; indeed, multiple causation is not uncommon in situations of linguistic change.

[24] The lengthening in the BATH lexical set in this variety of American English is an example of what Hickey (2002) calls supraregionalisation, where in his view what took place here is that speakers came to adopt a later pronunciation which they realised was different from their own and more contemporary (Hickey, personal communication).

Facts such as the swamping of Texas monophthongal [aː] and the replacement of the US 'broad a' in 'bath' have important implications for thinking about the strength of the founder principle, and about new-dialect formation. Such examples may show that the founder principle does not always hold, since in these instances the variants of the founders did not survive.

Bauer (1999) used the concept of swamping to explain the development of the /r/ of modern New Zealand English. New Zealand English had numerous kinds of /r/ from different dialects in its original inputs (the founding populations), including Scottish, Irish, and regional English English varieties (Chapter 6 Section 16.3, Bauer 1999: 303); however, the only one to survive is the pronunciation from the south-east of England, which includes non-rhoticism in non-prevocalic position. Bauer (1999: 304) argues that this can be interpreted as an instance of swamping:

> [T]he use of [ɹ] in New Zealand in pre-vocalic position and the lack of non-pre-vocalic /r/ over the largest part of New Zealand becomes less odd. It must . . . have been the case that New Zealand English was affected by English norms well after the time of first settlement for this to have become such a widespread pronunciation, otherwise the current lack of rhoticism would not have developed. This extended influence of English norms, which may no doubt be seen as part of the swamping process, may simply be due to the continued immigration from England in the relevant period, though another possible source is the emotional links with 'home', which were undoubtedly strong at the time.

Bauer (1994: 424) says, to explain the loss of non-prevocalic 'r' in New Zealand, 'we need a particularly strong form of "swamping" (Lass 1990) which obliterates non-southeastern forms in mixed dialects despite their prevalence in the input dialects'. Following Lass (1990: 269), Bauer (1999: 300) explicitly links the notion of swamping to the south-east features in colonial Englishes: 'swamping, whereby colonial varieties of English, when faced with alternative pronunciations for a particular feature, tend to choose the south-eastern variant, with the result that the south-eastern variants swamp other potential variants in the colonial varieties'. However, Bauer (1999: 300) argues from his results that 'swamping may not be such an important force in the formation of New Zealand English as is sometimes supposed: there are many variants surviving in New Zealand English where the south-eastern variant has not swamped the opposition'.

In fact swamping may not be the only possible explanation for the loss of non-prevocalic /r/. In the results reported in Chapter 6 we saw that, while the majority of speakers analysed quantitatively did use this feature, most used it sporadically, and over the entire data set only 9% of tokens were rhotic. That is, non-prevocalic 'r' was a minority feature – and as such was a target for levelling (see Sections 9 and 10.3 above). That is, it is possible that it could have been levelled without the impact of masses of later non-rhotic immigrants, though, again, it is a good possibility that both these factors worked together, another case of multiple causation.

Kerswill and Williams (2000: 84, 95) propose a principle of dialect contact which, though perhaps not intended by them, provides support for swamping: 'There is no normal historical continuity with the locality, either socially or linguistically. Most first and second generation speakers are oriented towards language varieties that originate elsewhere.' They point out 'the disappearance, within one generation, of several salient features' originally present in the variety spoken in the original villages where the new town of Milton Keynes came into being, bringing in a massive number of immigrants from outside the area (Kerswill and Williams 2000: 95–6). This is, then, not unlike the large-scale later immigration seen in some colonial settings.

It is possible to make a circumstantial case for swamping in New Zealand English, based on the immigration records. As Gardner (1999: 71, cited in Chapter 3) said, 'there are good grounds for asserting that the most important social episode in New Zealand history was the great immigration of the 1870s', and 'immigration doubled the colony's population in a decade [1870–80]; it *strengthened the British culture* in the colony' (our emphasis). Also, as seen in Chapter 3, immigration from the south-east of England dominated from the beginning, and even more so in the 1870s. Among the New Zealand Company 1839–50 immigrants, 25.9% were from London, 20.8% from the south-east of England, with 26.4% from the south-west, and only 3.4% from Lancashire – that is, 46.7% from London and the south-east, the largest number for an area represented in New Zealand by a commanding margin. In Britain itself, the people in London and the south-east constituted only 26.1% of the overall population in the 1871 census. The place of birth of the foreign-born in New Zealand in the 1881 census reveals 119,224 born in England, but only 52,753 in Scotland and 49,363 in Ireland (Wales, with 1,963, is separated from England in this figure). If the English of London and the south-east had not gained an advantage through majority influence earlier (determinism), it might well be argued that any existing resistance was levelled out (swamped) in the great numbers entering from there in the 1870s.

However, it could also be pointed out that, at the time of the immigration of the 1870s, more than half the New Zealand population was native-born. According to McKinnon (1997: 49) the percentage of immigrants was not large; at no stage during the 1870s did the total population increase more than 20% because of immigration. We must also remember that the number of immigrants themselves is less important for new-dialect formation than what happened to their children. Such children would have grown up in an environment where there was already an existing variety of developing New Zealand English.

Still, a number of sound changes which had the effect of increasing the south-east-of-England appearance of New Zealand English appear to intensify greatly at precisely this period of the 1870s' wave of immigration from England. CART modelling repeatedly identified the mid-1870s as a relevant transition point for the quantified variables. In part, this may simply be the result of the mid-1870s being the position of the median birthdate. If the model identifies age as a relevant variable, and if change is fairly constant, it may just split the data in half. However, it is worth entertaining the possibility that the identification of the mid-1870s is more than just a statistical artifact. This is, after all, exactly the period of 'the most important social episode in New Zealand history' (Gardner 1999: 71) – large-scale immigration from Britain. Did the 1870s see a linguistic reaction to this new wave of immigration, and the concurrent increased proportion of people from the south-east of England?

The variables that CART modelling split between 1875 and 1877 are TRAP raising, START fronting, loss of rhoticity, increase in /hw/ and loss of h-dropping (see Chapter 6 for details). All but the last are consistent with the increased influence of England. We might expect that h-dropping, if it was affected by new immigrants in the mid-1870s, would conceivably have received a boost in the opposite direction from the actual one taken, that is, rate of h-dropping should have increased if we focus on sheer numbers of speakers. It should be recalled again that this was the minority variant in terms of numbers of tokens and its social status has not been factored in. Overall, the facts are largely consistent with continued immigration playing a role in the formation of New Zealand English.

The mid-1870s were, after all, not only a time of increased immigration, but also the time when a second generation of New Zealanders would have been born, and the time when groups of children would have been coming together on a regular basis, with the advent of compulsory education. All this could perhaps have led to an acceleration of change, possibly with several factors working together.

14 Questions about the role of different settlement types

A question not so far considered is: What is the impact of nucleated settlement vs rural dispersal? For Trudgill et al. (2000a: 305) the greatest degree of variability from multiple input dialects was found in the 'linguistic melting pots' of the towns and urban centres, and of the goldmining settlements, Arrowtown in particular, and it is in these that new-dialect formation was more advanced. This suggests that new-dialect formation is essentially a phenomenon of nucleated settlements, requiring a density of speakers from different dialect backgrounds. The results of Chapter 6 provide multiple examples of how the early dialect developed quite differently across different settlement types. (See Wolfram and Beckett 2000, and Schilling-Estes 2002 on variability in isolated communities; see also Dorian 1994, 2001.)

Correlated with this is a second question: How dense must the communication networks in the formation of a new dialect be? (See L. Milroy 1980, 2001, 2002; Milroy and Milroy 1985; J. Milroy 1992.) That is, if new-dialect formation is seen as essentially a matter of nucleated settlement, how is the focused dialect transferred to the rural populations, how long does this take, and how dense must the network connections to the towns and cities be for the development to take place in rural places, particularly if the founders and the dialect mix in some rural regions are significantly different from that of the nucleated settings? (Cf. Britain 1997a and Woods 2000a for views on the role of networks in explaining new-dialect formation.)

This recalls Bloomfield's 'principle of density', which simultaneously anticipates network theory, the role of variation in language change, and accommodation theory:

> The reason for this intense local differentiation [in local European dialects] is evidently to be sought in the principle of density. Every speaker is constantly adapting his speech-habits to those of his interlocutors; he gives up forms he has been using, adopts new ones, and perhaps oftenest of all, changes the frequency of speech-forms without entirely abandoning any old ones or accepting any that are really new to him. The inhabitants of a settlement, village, or town, however, talk much more to each other than to persons who live elsewhere. When any innovation in the way of speaking spreads over a district, the limit of this spread is sure to be along some lines of weakness in the network of oral communication, and these lines of weakness, in so far as they are topographical lines, are the boundaries between towns, villages, and settlements. (Bloomfield 1933: 476; cf. also Labov 2001: 19)

J. Milroy (1992, 1993) has argued that a distinction must be made between the speaker and the language system in order to explain language change, and by extension dialect change. It has been argued that the relatively strong (dense, multiplex) networks that are possible in nucleated settlements can act as norm-enforcement mechanisms. In the Milroys' approach (see J. Milroy 1992; L. Milroy 2001), the stronger the network ties, the less likely an individual member is to accept variants used by individuals without strong ties to themselves, meaning that strong-tie networks tend to preserve the status quo and resist changes that may be going on elsewhere in a language community. However, at the same time, it is also in urban settings that new norms can emerge relatively quickly because there is greater opportunity for multiple networks, each with their own norms, to co-exist, and for certain individuals with weaker ties to bridge these networks. (Weak-tie individuals may have contacts in more networks but their ties are not as strong as for strong-tie individuals.) Thus the existence of weak-tie speakers can lead to the introduction into strong networks of innovations from outside. In this function, J. Milroy (1992: 184) calls such speakers 'innovators'. By this theory, innovations are resisted by members of (norm-enforcing) strong networks, but if they are taken up by core members of these networks – Milroy calls such speakers 'early adopters' (ibid.) – this leads to fairly rapid change in the speech of strong-tie, not just weak-tie, individuals. In an immigrant setting, many individuals will be seeking to fit in, and new immigrants, at least initially, tend to have weak ties and therefore to have marginal connections in more than one network. This can lead to situations where new norms would form quickly. The rapidity of such developments across weak-tie urban networks is particularly plausible when we consider children, as the main agents of new-dialect formation, forming new networks and accommodating to one another.

Conversely, new dialects that are more rural can take much longer to focus. Rural networks have fewer participants and they are less dense, but each small rural settlement tends to have relatively strong ties; therefore, there are fewer weak-tie members who might have contacts with outside networks with other language norms. Thus variants from outside are slow to be brought in because of Bloomfield's 'lines of weakness in the network of oral communication' between one settlement and the next.

One of Kerswill and Williams' (2000: 84, 92) principles of dialect contact reflects the role of network ties: 'The adoption of features by a speaker depends on his or her network characteristics' (see also Britain 1997a; Sudbury 2000: 61). Woods (2000a: 143) connects weak-tie networks directly to the patterns of change in early New Zealand, claiming that 'weak-tie networks are more likely to favour change than close-knit communities', and she quotes J. Milroy's (1993: 228) observation that situations '"clearly amenable to weak-tie explanations . . . appear as essentially language-contact situations"' (in Woods 2000a: 143). She relates weak-tie network explanations to the 'particular patterns of linguistic change' that often result in the mixing, levelling, and simplification called koinéisation (p. 143); she concludes that 'patterns of dialect contact and weak-tie networks which characterised early New Zealand society are known to favour linguistic innovation' (pp. 144–5). The results of Chapter 6 provide multiple examples of how the early dialect developed quite differently across different settlement types (see also Table 7.1 earlier). Our finding that mixed towns tended to be more advanced in the koinéisation process provides support for this argument that 'weak-tie networks are more likely to favour change than close-knit communities' (Woods 2000a: 143; cf. J. Milroy 1992, 1993).

The questions about the actual process whereby change is incorporated into rural communities, raised earlier in this section, cannot be answered by the ONZE data at present.

15 The impact of standardisation, education, and social factors

It is argued that standardisation, norming, and education can have an impact on the outcome when speakers of different dialects mix together in a new location. As Labov (2001: 512) points out, 'Whether we are studying stable sociolinguistic variation or change in progress, the attitudes that emerge from the speech community almost always reinforce the prestige forms taught in schools and the older forms of the language'. L. Milroy (2002: 8) describes straightforward instances of normalisation in dialect contact where, by levelling, 'socially marked or stigmatized elements are eliminated from the pool of variants' (see also Yoneda 1993). Dorian (1994, 2001) argues that uniformity would not come about without 'the effects of a tradition of standardisation and norming'; she does not believe that homogeneous results are due only to koinéisation (Dorian 2001: 389). She cautions that, 'the effects of a tradition of standardisation and norming should not be underestimated in the New Zealand case' (p. 389). At the same time, she is not surprised by the variability reported for early Arrowtown (Trudgill 1997b: 204; Trudgill, Gordon, and Lewis 1998). She found the 'Scottish Gaelic spoken by isolated, deeply interrelated, socially homogeneous, and fully fluent residents of the East Sutherland village of Embro, Scotland, established around the first decade of the nineteenth century, to show still more variability than the Arrowtown speakers' (Dorian 2001: 389). She writes:

> A good part of the Embro Gaelic variability shows no signs of moving toward regularity, a fact that suggests that the subsequent reduction of variability in the new settlement area of Otago [where Arrowtown is located], in the generations following the [Mobile Unit] interviewees, reflects an English-language tradition of strong standardisation rather than koinéisation that arises naturally in monolingual settlements whose early residents came from diverse backgrounds. (Dorian 2001: 389)[25]

Sudbury's (2000) study found a similar lack of focusing in the English of the Falkland Islands. These cases show, among other things, that focusing is not a necessary outcome of dialects in contact.[26] Scholtmeijer (1992, 1997) claims the 'strong impact of schooling in the standard' as an important contributing factor to the absence of new-dialect formation in new settlements in the Dutch polders (land reclaimed from the sea in the Netherlands) (quoted in Kerswill and Williams 2000: 74). This shows both the powerful effects of standardisation and the fact that new-dialect formation is not a necessary outcome of dialects being thrown together in new settlements. In the cases cited

> there was a distinct break between the settlers' strongly regional dialectal speech and the speech of their children, who came to speak a highly standardized form of Dutch, with relatively few traces of the dialect/accent of the older generation . . . the parents' speech is irrelevant for the

[25] It should be pointed out that it is not necessary and probably not wise to separate 'norming' and 'standardisation' from other social factors. Thus, in New Zealand, it is possible that the 'norming' that occurred was based in part on the vernacular south-east English variety, where concerns were more with social status of these speakers than with bookish dictates of standard English.

[26] Nor is new-dialect formation the only way by which focused varieties can come into existence. Hickey (2002: 214) shows that both new-dialect formation and language shift (as in the case of Irish English) can lead to focused varieties that are distinct from 'mainland British English'. Clearly, language shift does not apply to New Zealand.

> development of the children's speech . . . there is no question of any new dialect in the polders which might be an amalgam of the varieties from the 'old land'. (Kerswill and Williams 2000: 74)[27]

There can be little doubt that education and spelling can have an impact in language change, as evidenced by the many well-known examples of spelling pronunciations in English. This raises the question: To what extent may the prestige of the standard language, reinforced through education, have impacted on the development of New Zealand English? There is some evidence in Chapter 6 that education and social value influenced the erratic trajectory of the /hw/~/w/ merger, while the suppression of h-dropping and non-prevocalic 'r' (rhoticism) are other likely candidates that may have been influenced in this way. Of course, while many changes appear concurrent with the introduction of compulsory schooling, it can be difficult to disentangle the effects of the explicit instruction given in the classroom from the effects of a structured environment being provided, in which children could interact with one another on a regular basis.

Another approach to new-dialect formation calls upon speakers' motivations. Hickey (2002) makes reference to the notion of supraregionalisation, by which he means a process where dialect speakers progressively adopt more and more features of a mainstream, non-regional variety with which they are in contact. Trudgill et al. (2000a: 307) see the lack of regional variation in modern New Zealand English as the result of focusing; Hickey sees supraregionalisation as a possible alternative explanation for the lack of regional dialect differences. 'Supraregionalisation is a process of direct substitution: a local realisation X for a feature is replaced by a mainstream realization Y, irrespective of its formal proximity to X' (Hickey 2000: 123). It was noted in Chapter 3 that there was a movement of people from the countryside to the towns in the 1870s; the process of supraregionalisation would have been aided by this tendency and so also would the new-dialect formation process of levelling. Adopting a non-regional variant need not be the same as focusing in dialect mixture. One difference involves the kinds of choices, overt or otherwise, that speakers make, and in particular their motivations. Dorian (1994, 2001), considers that the focused dialect that emerged in New Zealand is not the result of the koinéisation process itself; rather, she brings in standardisation and 'norming', somewhat akin to supraregionalisation, driven in part by acts of identity. We are unable to either support or refute these ideas from the ONZE data.

Another consideration, not emphasised in most accounts, is mobility (see Chambers 2002). Lack of significant regional variation in Australia (until quite recently) has been attributed to the high mobility of early settlers, with extensive internal migration. The highly mobile society could be the means through which

[27] The situation in these Dutch polders, however, is not comparable to that of New Zealand, since the polders are adjacent to the rest of Holland and were formed much later, in the twentieth century, with different kinds of contact possible due to modern transportation and media.

emerging Australian English traits spread quickly and widely (Horvath 1985: 33), a driving force in supraregionalisation (and also in dialect mixture). As Chambers (2002: 117) puts it, 'mobility is the most effective leveller of dialect and accent'. Early New Zealand society also exhibited extensive mobility, particularly in the goldrush years. As Gardner (cited in Chapter 3) described the situation:

> In New Zealand we are not dealing with communities established on the same ground over millennia, with age-old dialects, customs, symbols and family names. Our society has included many rising and falling towns and districts; there has been a large mobile element, and the 'stable' proportion in any given region or centre may have fallen as low as 10% or even less. This is our untidy past, a game of regional snakes and ladders, and we have to accept it. Historical community in New Zealand may mean a rather small solid core, and a large fluid overlay. (1999: 50)

It is uncertain whether this mobility was sufficient, without the need to appeal to supraregionalisation and associated motives of identity-seeking, to generate the modern focused, non-regionalised variety in New Zealand.

Britain (1997b: 160) and Kerswill and Williams (2000; 2002: 83, 89) also bring social and psychological motivations to inform explanations of new-dialect formation. Britain suggests that from a socio-psychological perspective, salient forms may focus more quickly in dialect contact, particularly if they are seen to act as markers of local identity (see Sudbury 2000: 62; see Kerswill and Williams 2000: 101 and Downes 1984: 216 for similar views; cf. Kerswill and Williams 2002). Given that there are instances of new settlements with dialect mixture where no new or focused dialect emerges (Mæhlum 1992, 1996; Sudbury 2000: 70–1), there needs to be more than just the right linguistic situation for a new dialect to form – the social conditions and psychological motivation to establish a new focused dialect within the community must also be favourable. Britain (1997a: 38) holds that network theory (L. Milroy 1980; Milroy and Milroy 1985; J. Milroy 1992) is a significant part of the answer to the question of why 'dialect contact scenarios typically result in the focusing and koinéization of language'. He couples this with the role of 'routinisation': 'routines (like strong networks . . .) lead to system preservation . . . it is through routines that norm-enforcement is achieved' (Britain 1997a: 39). He believes that when routines are disrupted (as in economic migration to colonial settings) 'humans will seek to re-routinise their lives' (p. 39), and 'those involved in such regrounding are likely to be convergent, rather than divergent linguistic accommodators – reducing and simplifying marked linguistic differences between each other . . . and in situations where no one variety is dominant, they rationalise [reduce] the linguistic resources of the community around them' (p. 40). Wolfram and Schilling-Estes (forthcoming) find that 'community attitudes, in the final analysis, may play a far greater role in guiding the directionality of change in interdialect contact than levels of contact'. (See also Kerswill and Williams 2000: 101.) Many connect this motivation with LePage and Tabouret-Keller's (1985) 'acts of identity' (e.g. Britain 1991,

1997a; Mæhlum 1992, 1996; Sudbury 2000). (This topic receives more attention in Chapter 8.)

The results from our study of the Mobile Unit speakers does not tell us anything about the extent to which they may have been 'predisposed to selecting innovative variants because these represent the vanguard of change in a developing society' (Hickey 2002: 215). The earliest immigrants to New Zealand would not have had ready-made varieties of a local language with which to identify. Nevertheless, comments such as the following from William Swainson, quoted in Chapter 3, suggest the possibility of emblematic identity via means of a newly arising variety:

> A new comer is still immediately recognised: an air of conscious superiority not infrequently betrays itself in every look and gesture. But the new arrival is not long in finding his true level; for in apprehension of character the people of New Zealand are marvellously clear-sighted – quick in detecting it, and just in appreciation: no one can long pass for what he is not; and if not distinguished by some useful or agreeable quality, the new arrival soon finds his level in a modest insignificance; and many who, on landing, move confidently on with buoyant step and lofty mien, may soon be seen passing modestly along, undistinguished from the common crowd. (Swainson 1859: 230–1)

16 Conclusions

We end this chapter with the question we asked at the start of Chapter 4: How did the distinctive variety that is modern New Zealand English come into being? We can eliminate the Cockney hypothesis once and for all; anything similar to the English of the south-east of England and London, about which negative judgements were expressed, was typically called 'Cockney' or likened to it. As for the other proposed explanations we have examined, the ONZE data do not allow us to confirm or deny categorically that New Zealand English came about in any of these particular ways. The final result clearly owes much to south-eastern English English, but this could have come about in a number of ways. It could have arisen through:

1. the founder effect, because the majority of the early immigrants came from the south-east of England;
2. the Australian connection, because the majority of immigrants to Australia came from the south-east of England and many immigrants to New Zealand came via Australia;
3. swamping, because, during the Vogel immigration period of the 1870s, the majority of the immigrants again came from the south-east of England;
4. a combination of these, the product of all three working in concert, each later one reinforcing the earlier ones.

However, the ONZE findings show that some of these are more likely than others. The notion of 'founders', for example, is problematic given the mobile and fluid nature of the early population (see Chapter 3 and Appendix 2), and the cumulative weight of the evidence indicates that New Zealand English owes some of its character to Australian input. It is possible that all these factors had some influence on the final outcome to a greater or lesser extent.

What the ONZE data do provide is information about the processes through which the final focused dialect emerged. The data conform to aspects of the processes of new-dialect formation (as originally formulated in Trudgill 1986b), seen in the examples discussed here of variability, levelling, and focusing. However, claims about the role of markedness and reallocation in new-dialect formation cannot easily be assessed against the New Zealand English data, since the examples of these in the data are not clear-cut. The ONZE findings support determinism, the principle whereby majority variants in the input survive into the final output: the largest group of immigrants was from the south of England (more specifically, from the south-east and London), and it is features of their dialect that predominate in modern New Zealand English. The type of 'drift' involving sound changes already begun in England and transported to New Zealand, where they continued, is supported by several examples (see Section 10). However, cases of drift of the sort involving independent but parallel developments in England and New Zealand are less clear (i.e., changes *not* already underway in England and brought here with the immigrants, but which started up independently in the two varieties). Most of the possible candidates for this type of drift turn out to have been variable already in England, for example loss of rhoticity, so that it is not possible to show that the developments are fully independent in the two locations or that the variation (possibly ongoing change) was not brought with the settlers rather than begun in New Zealand.

It seems that some social factors need to be taken into account. They affect the process of development, especially the rate at which the focused dialect emerged. The ONZE results show that women are in the lead in almost every change that continues into modern New Zealand English. Mixed towns lead over more homogeneous towns such as the Scottish settlements, where forms like rhoticity survived longer. The fact that the New Zealand dialect appeared earlier in towns such as Arrowtown, where the population was made up of a balanced mixture of immigrants from England, Ireland, Scotland, and Australia, could indicate that a mixed environment possibly contributed towards more speedy development of the new variety. However, because Arrowtown was a goldmining town, almost all of the inhabitants came to New Zealand via the Australian goldfields, so that an Australian influence cannot be ignored. Again we cannot state categorically that the earlier development of the New Zealand dialect was caused by one factor and not the other, but it was in such places that New Zealand English first began to appear as a distinct variety, and we have to allow for the possibility of multiple influences. The ONZE findings do not confirm or deny other social influences, and therefore they require caution. From the ONZE data it is not possible to say to what extent factors such as education, standardisation, and acts of identity may have influenced the final outcome, but neither can they be eliminated; that we cannot confirm them does not mean that they had no effect.

Overall, we consider it most likely that the origins and development of New Zealand English were affected by multiple factors, bringing about similar results. The findings of the ONZE project on New Zealand English have implications beyond New Zealand. The data archive on which this work has been based may well be unique, but the processes upon which it has thrown light are not unique at all. That is, it should be possible to generalise from this work on New Zealand English to new-dialect formation and other forms of linguistic change generally. Since the ONZE data extend over a period of more than 150 years, moreover, they shed light also on a number of other issues in historical linguistics. We treat some of these issues in Chapter 8.

8 Implications for language change

I have crossed an ocean I have lost my tongue from the root of the old one a new one has sprung.

(Grace Nichols 1983, Guyanese poet: i is a long memoried woman)

1 Introduction

In this chapter we consider the implications of the ONZE findings for the study of language change generally. In particular we use these results to test or clarify a number of general claims that have been made about change in sociolinguistic contexts. Some of these claims are verified or strengthened further by these results, some are challenged, and a few are shown to be wrong. The ONZE results reveal that some claims are in need of significant modification. In Section 2, we discuss difficulties with apparent- vs real-time studies of linguistic change, and in this connection we consider the question of accommodation by adults and the possibility of change in the vernacular later in life. Section 3 is concerned with the finding that speakers' families also can play an important role in influencing the variables they use. Sections 4 and 5 examine claims about vowel shifting and mergers. In Section 6, we take up the role gender plays in linguistic change. Section 7 is dedicated to the possibility of lexically conditioned sound change and lexical diffusion. Section 8 examines the question of whether linguistic change reflects speakers' 'acts of identity' and the possibility generally that certain social variables may condition aspects of sound change.

2 Apparent-time versus real-time studies of change in progress

The methodology utilised in the ONZE project uses the apparent-time approach to the study of change extensively (cf. Bailey 2001; Bailey et al. 1991) – people of different ages are recorded during a single time period, and differences in their speech that correlate with age are assumed to reflect changes at different times and are used to draw inferences about language change. A crucial supposition in the apparent-time construct is the assumption that people's basic phonology is stable and does not change significantly during adulthood. It is assumed that the difference between the speech of older speakers and younger speakers represents change that has taken place in the language since the older speakers acquired their vernacular.

There is no shortage of anecdotal evidence involving dialect shift – particularly where one speaker moves to a new community (e.g. a New Zealander moving to Chicago, or an Alabaman to Australia) – which shows that speakers can and do change their speech at least to some degree later in life. Munro, Derwing, and Flege (1999) provide empirical evidence for shift in the speech of Canadians living in Alabama. Such shift occurs as a result of long-term accommodation on the part of the individual (cf. Giles 1973, 1977), and 'If a speaker accommodates frequently enough to a particular accent or dialect . . . then the accommodation may in time become permanent, particularly if attitudinal factors are favourable' (Trudgill 1986b: 39; see Sudbury 2000: 44). While such shifts clearly take place, the question of dialect stability for individuals who have not changed their environment is slightly less clear cut. However, most evidence does seem to point to some limited shifting.

Sankoff et al. (2001) studied production of (r) (with uvular versus alveolar variants) in Montreal French, in twenty-five speakers, twelve of whom were recorded three times over a twenty-four-year period – 1971, 1984, 1995. They found that a not inconsiderable number of people had significantly adjusted their pronunciation over this time, concluding that 'apparently, in a change from above, there is a minority of atypical people who can modify their phonetics in later life, pushing the limits of the possible and challenging us for explanations' (Sankoff et al. 2001: 154). Yoneda (1993) conducted dialect surveys at twenty-year intervals – 1950, 1971, and 1991 – in Tsuruoka, Japan, which was relatively isolated in 1950, but has since undergone rapid social change, with many of the regional forms being replaced by standard forms. The study provided conclusive evidence for standardisation: the results showed that individual groups must have increased their use of standard variants during adulthood. Cedergren's study of Spanish in Panama City, conducted in 1969 and 1982–84 (Cedergren 1973, 1984), and Trudgill's revisiting of Norwich (Trudgill 1974, 1988) together reveal a lack of stability in the systems of individual speakers.

Labov (1994: 98) points out that changes from above inevitably involve instability – the individual acquires such features late, and gradually improves in ability to produce the particular features. The issue of stability, then, claims Labov, is only relevant for changes from below. This is consistent with evidence from migrant speech, where individuals clearly adjust more 'salient' features earlier (Auer et al. 1998; Trudgill 1986b).

Labov reported on an ongoing longitudinal study of the effects of normal aging on language use in Philadelphia. The general pattern that emerged is that, while many variables remain stable, variables undergoing extreme change in the community tend to show 'older speakers influenced slightly by the changes taking place around them' (1994: 105). This pattern is reinforced by studies such as Prince (1987), who tracked the speech of a single speaker for an extended period of time, and Yaeger-Dror (1994) who analysed speakers of Montreal French, demonstrating that they continue to advance toward a newer phonology well into middle age. Bauer (1985), in his study of RP speakers recorded on separate occasions seventeen years apart, concluded that individuals do tend to shift: 'Individuals change their pronunciations with time. It seems likely that descriptions of phonetic change based on change in apparent time can be extremely misleading, and in some cases may severely underestimate the amount of change that has taken place' (Bauer 1985: 80). Labov echoes this conclusion, but with some reservation: 'From present indications, apparent-time studies may understate the actual rate of sound change, since older speakers show a limited tendency toward communal change, participating to a small extent in the changes taking place around them' (1994: 112). Recently, Harrington, Palethorpe, and Watson conducted a study of Queen Elizabeth II's production of monophthongs, which reveals that she has changed pronunciation over the course of her lifetime. The analysis was based on her Christmas broadcasts from the 1950s, late 60s/early 70s, and 1980s. Harrington et al. conclude that there is good evidence for accent change over this time, with the Queen's vowels shifting in the direction of a more mainstream form of Received Pronunciation. They add their voice to the warning about apparent-time methodology, pointing out that the findings of such projects 'may well be distorted by underestimating the influences of community changes on an adult's vowel space' (2000: 927). We have conducted similar work on the speech of Sonja Davies (a well-known New Zealand trade union leader and politician). Davies was interviewed seven times in the twenty-four years spanning 1976–2000. Analysis of these interviews shows considerable shift in her vowels during this time – in the direction of modern New Zealand English.

Thus, there is good evidence of quite extreme shifting when adults are placed in a community that speaks a second dialect, and evidence of moderate shifting even within a single dialect area, with individual speakers shifting at least somewhat in the direction of new norms throughout their adult life.

For many of the ONZE speakers, we are in fact dealing with a third situation, somewhere between exposure to a new dialect and remaining in a single location which has a relatively stable linguistic system. Some of these speakers were not exposed to any particularly focused variety of New Zealand English when they were children. However, a focused dialect emerged during their lifetime – a dialect to which they would have been heavily exposed as adults. Exposure to this dialect is likely to lead to accommodation, especially as there may have been good social and attitudinal reasons for such accommodation to occur. Sufficiently large numbers of individuals were speakers of this focused dialect at the time of the Mobile Unit recordings so that it is hard to imagine that individual older speakers would not have accommodated towards these new norms to some degree. Thus, we should expect that, whatever the degree of shift that occurs in normal, non-dialect-contact situations, a greater degree is likely to have occurred in the speech of the speakers analysed here.

Therefore, some of our results may inaccurately estimate the degree and rate of change of the variables in question. For variants that have since disappeared (e.g. h-dropping, rhoticity [non-prevocalic /r/]), the apparent-time approach may underestimate the degree to which these pronunciations were present in the input to New Zealand English. For variables that show shift towards modern New Zealand English (diphthong shift, for example), the approach may well overestimate the degree to which these were present in the earliest stages.

In many cases we have independent corroborating evidence that convinces us that our interpretation is correct. For example, it is likely that the tokens of centralised KIT in the ONZE data are in fact the result of accommodation later in life to a centralised KIT that was emerging in the early twentieth century. This is strengthened because, although there are significantly more centralised KIT tokens in Scottish settlements, they are produced predominantly by speakers with New Zealand-born rather than Scottish parents. Labov's (1994, 2001) distinction between change-from-above and change-from-below leads us to exercise more caution with some of the variables we treat than others.

The evidence relating to dialect contact points to some features being more frequently subject to accommodation than others – it may be fruitful to explore the hypothesis that variables may be placed in a type of hierarchy, with 'easier', more natural processes more likely to be accommodated (Trudgill 1986b; Kerswill 1996). The more natural processes are not necessarily (or even likely) to be the same as those involved in 'change from above'. Here, the literature on linguistic change within a single speaker in a single community (cf. Labov 1994, 2001) does not make exactly the same predictions as the literature on accommodation in cases of dialect contact.

Unfortunately, we are not in a position to untangle the intricacies of these questions, as our data were all recorded at approximately the same time. Given the data available, all we can do is study how speakers of different ages speak. The fact that normal speakers do adjust their phonology during adulthood, together with the fact that the new-dialect formation environment is not a normal one, means that it would be unwise to take the apparent-time hypothesis as completely reliable. Caution is required.

We are limited by having a body of recordings made in the mid 1940s, ninety years or so after the time period that we are attempting to understand. We must work within the restrictions that this imposes. Given this, it is in fact remarkable that the patterns of change that emerge are, in most cases, clear and clean. Despite all these limitations, we have been able to use this data set to make considerable inroads into the understanding of the input to New Zealand English, and the processes through which it came into its own.

3 The role of the family

For all but one of the quantified variables (in Chapter 6), parental origin played a significant role in predicting the linguistic behaviour of individual speakers. As mentioned in Chapter 7, Trudgill (1999b) had suggested that parental influence would be important, and that it would be most significant for children who were raised in isolated situations (such as Mrs Catherine King, mentioned in Chapter 3, whose family lived largely out of contact with other people). However, the results of the quantitative analysis show that parental origins were an important predictive factor for more than just children raised in isolated situations. Our analysis therefore adds to the growing body of literature that demonstrates the importance of parental influence, and the strong role of the family unit as a community of practice (see Eckert 2000). Hazen (2001) provides a comprehensive overview of the literature, which demonstrates conclusively that there can be an effect of the family on the language variation patterns of a speaker. Such a result should not be surprising, though it is significant in that the family's role has not received much attention in sociolinguistic investigation. Of course, this influence is most profound upon children, who first acquire patterns from their immediate caregivers; however, it can also extend into adulthood, especially for features that are non-salient or non-stigmatised (see Payne 1980; Deser 1990; Kerswill and Williams 2000).

Summarising the literature on this topic, Hazen concludes:

> [I]t appears that the input variation from the home does have an influence on what quantitative rates of variation are attainable for some variables. Perhaps the family has a more predominant influence on the rates of variation rather than the establishment of language variation patterns not found in the wider community. (2001: 511)

Hazen suggests that family variation patterns may be noticeable to the extent that they differ from established community norms. If patterns acquired from parents are not social markers, there is no reason to assume that peer group influence will necessarily counteract those traits. However, as noted in Chapter 7, where family patterns are contrary to the emerging norms, the innate accent-filter posited by Chambers (2002: 122) as part of the 'Ethan experience' will help children to focus on the principal emerging dialect.

The large degree to which parental influence has proven significant in our data may well be due to a lack of peer-group influence that might have been quite common. However, we maintain that there were still other social influences. Perhaps, for example, it is no accident that the only variable for which no significant parental influence was found is h-dropping. This feature is likely to have been highly salient and stigmatised, and, moreover, was a clear minority feature from the beginning. This would seem to make it a prime candidate for a feature that, even if acquired from the parents, could be counteracted later by peer-group influence.

4 Vowel shifting

4.1 Push chains versus pull chains and teleological explanations

In the literature on chain shifts there has been considerable debate about their nature, about pull (or drag) chains versus push chains. In particular, some have argued that push chains are illegitimate for philosophical reasons, namely, because they typically appeal to the teleological motivation of the language needing to preserve phonemic contrasts or striving to avoid masses of homonyms. A pull chain is not seen as problematic in this way: a segment moves to some other location in phonetic space, leaving a gap where its original location was, whereupon in time some other segment moves into this now vacated gap, an opportunity provided by the movement of the first segment but not caused by it. The gap could have remained empty, and in fact in may such shifts the gaps do remain empty for long times before later shifts take place and fill them. There is nothing especially teleological about this pull-chain scenario, there is no 'need' to maintain phonemic contrasts driving the second change.[1] A push chain, on the other hand, is seen as a situation in which one segment begins to move towards the phonetic space of another segment, and this segment that is encroached upon moves away in turn *in order to* avoid merger and thus to prevent the loss of a phonemic contrast that distinguishes numerous words from one another. It is important, though, to point out that claims about chain shifts have not always taken the care necessary to show that stages of a putative chain are actually interrelated. That is, it is important to distinguish between a situation in which one change leaves a gap that triggers another change to fill the gap (for phonological symmetry, naturalness, or whatever) – a true pull chain – and another situation in which the changes just happen independently of one another and are not causally connected at all (cf. M. Gordon 2001: 255).

Citing Martinet (1955), Labov (1994: 117) writes, 'chain shifts reflect the functional economy of the vowel system: vowels move together [i.e. with one another at the same time] to avoid merger and preserve their capacity to distinguish words'. Those opposed to teleological explanations in linguistics object to the appeal to a need or intention to maintain distinctions which is assumed to be behind a push chain.[2] However, whether push chains exist or not is an empirical matter, and cannot be resolved by philosophical debate, as we shall see presently.

[1] Of course, it is possible to see the later shifts in a pull chain as teleological in Martinet's (1955) sense of fulfilling needs of symmetry and the like in the phonological inventory (cited in Labov 2001), but not in the more immediate sense of being needed in order to preserve phonological distinctions, as is claimed for push chains.

[2] Functional motivations involving the overall configuration of phonemic space are often seen in both pull chains and push chains. As Labov (2001: 498) says, 'the principle of functional economy outlined by Martinet (1955) may be considered to apply to any situation where the movement of one phoneme is dictated by the configuration of neighboring phonemes'. However, it is the push chains that are seen as most directly teleological, and for that reason have received the most sceptical assessment.

In this regard, Labov, who in general opposes functional explanations, is compelled to admit from his survey of vowel shifts:

> the study of chain shifting does not provide many examples of unexpected mergers; examples of unexpected avoidance are easier to locate. This situation reinforces the case for a functional interpretation of chain shifting. But it does not resolve the question of how such functional effects take place.[3] (Labov 1994: 270)

In the chain shift involving the short front vowels in New Zealand English, we now have, apparently, empirical confirmation that what took place was indeed a push chain and not a pull (drag) chain. Both a push-chain and a pull-chain account have been proposed to account for these changes. At an earlier stage of analysis of the ONZE data, Trudgill et al. (1998: 38) had argued for a drag chain in which the short front vowels were assumed to have been raised already in England, before the European colonists' arrival in New Zealand, and then subsequently lowered in the British Isles varieties. Bauer (1979), on the other hand, had argued for a push chain, triggered by movement of the STRUT vowel into the front vowel area. Later, Bauer (1992) withdrew this suggested explanation, since there are varieties of English that have the short front vowel shift but no STRUT fronting and there are other varieties that have fronted STRUT but no short front vowel shift, suggesting that, 'the quality of the TRAP vowel . . . does not appear to depend in any way on the quality of the STRUT vowel' (1992: 254).

As seen in Chapter 6, the vowel-shift sequence in New Zealand was thus: Firstly, already raised TRAP impinged further upon DRESS; secondly, as a consequence DRESS began to raise; and, thirdly, raised DRESS crowded KIT, which in reaction began to centralise. (That is, while a somewhat raised TRAP, plus some tokens of raised DRESS and a very few tokens of centralised KIT, arrived with the colonists, the movement has continued and gone much further in New Zealand English.) What changed, when it changed, and in what sequence the changes took place are now quite clear in the evidence involving these vowels in New Zealand English (Chapter 6) – KIT centralisation was last and late, much after TRAP raising, for example, and thus it is impossible to maintain that KIT centralisation left a gap in the inventory into which DRESS was pulled, and so on down the chain, in pull-chain fashion. Even if KIT centralisation were set aside from this series of changes, DRESS raising is also documented as later and less complete than TRAP raising, meaning that it would still be impossible to see the series of shifts as anything other than a push chain.[4] The New Zealand

[3] We note that Labov's final position on functional explanations for vowel shifts and sound change states that 'the relative progress of sound change is determined by phonetic factors alone, without regard to the preservation of meaning' (1994: 603).

[4] In Chapter 6, Section 20.2, it was noted that there is a significant correlation between the degree of START fronting and TRAP raising. This could be taken to indicate that START fronting was the first step in the push chain of the New Zealand English front vowels. However, see Chapter 6, Section 20.2 for arguments against this interpretation.

English shifting vowels are not subject to the problem encountered in some work on vowel shifts, namely, failure to show that the sound distinctions are actually being preserved. It is not the case here, as in some instances elsewhere, that a shift may appear to preserve some distinctions but not others, as a vowel may move to avoid an encroaching vowel only to end up in the phonological space of another, endangering or losing that contrast (cf. M. Gordon 2001: 253–5).

This makes it very difficult to escape the conclusion that the New Zealand vowel shift offers empirical confirmation of the existence of a push chain. To put it slightly differently, there is a tight correlation among these vowels and among their movements in the vowel systems of the different ONZE subjects: there is no significant degree of DRESS raising without also TRAP being raised, and there are very few speakers with KIT centralisation who do not also have raised DRESS, but there are speakers who have close TRAP but not close DRESS and speakers with close DRESS who do not have centralised KIT. These correlations point to a causal connection, a push chain.

The argument that push chains exist, in turn, bears significantly upon the issue of whether teleological explanations are ever appropriate. While we do not insist on seeing things as teleologically explained, we do argue that teleology cannot be set aside completely as an inappropriate form of explanation, at least not for the commonly offered reasons. That is, we wish to make a case for keeping the question open and encouraging further research.

Philosophers distinguish 'teleology of purpose' – the intentionality, purposiveness, or goal-directedness exhibited in the behaviour or actions of people, other organisms, or machines – from 'teleology of function', which refers to the contribution that the presence or absence of some object makes to some state of affairs being attained or maintained (Campbell and Ringen 1981: 57). In spite of the sometimes vigorous opposition to teleological explanations of linguistic change, we take it that at least some changes explained by 'teleology of purpose' are really not controversial: Language is, after all, used by humans, who, through intention and intervention, bring about some purposive changes in language. The sociolinguistic literature on language change offers abundant examples where attempts to attain prestige, show local identity, identify with a particular group, and so on lead to purposeful selection of certain variants over others that condition change in language, for example, centralisation of diphthongs on Martha's Vineyard, the Northern Cities Vowel Shift, presence or absence of non-prevocalic 'r' in New York City, and so on. (For other examples, see Campbell and Ringen 1981; see also the discussion of social factors and linguistic acts of identity later in this chapter.)

One of the frequent objections to teleological explanations involves the claim that teleology reverses the normal order of cause before effect (that is, that it is post hoc); however, there is nothing in an appeal to goals, functions, motives, purposes, aims, drives, needs, or intentions that requires inversion of the normal cause-before-effect order. The problem is not so much about reversal of cause and effect, as about the proper identification of the cause. In the cases just mentioned, it is clear enough that the intentions, desires, beliefs (to affiliate with some group, to attain higher social status, etc.) precede the linguistic behaviour, and the selection of linguistic traits (variables and variants of variables) is in order to attain these ends.

Chain shifts, however, are more appropriately seen as instances where the teleology of *function* is involved, where the presence or absence of some object contributes to some state of affairs being attained or maintained. To say that the chain shift changes take place in order to preserve phonemic contrasts or to maintain lexical distinctions by avoiding the many homonyms that would result from merger is not the same as saying that the preservation of these distinctions causes chain shifting. Preservation is not the cause, but the goal. The cause is the state of affairs in which such changes are required or helpful in maintaining the distinctions, and this state of affairs existed prior to the chain-shifting changes (the effect).

Another common objection to teleological explanations is the claim that they inappropriately attribute human characteristics to other things. One answer to this objection is that indeed language is used by humans and some linguistic changes are clearly due to human intentions (teleology of purpose), as seen in the discussion above. In these sorts of changes, the objection of 'anthropomorphism' does not hold. In the examples involving teleology of function, again, no misguided anthropomorphism need be involved. These examples do not refer to any intentions, beliefs, or desires of the language or the vowel system in question, but rather refer only to some state of affairs in which certain events or entities would in fact contribute to maintaining the goal of keeping distinctions. So long as the states of affairs can be identified reliably, there can be no objection on this basis to the teleology of function explanation offered (Campbell and Ringen 1981: 63–4).[5]

In short, then, the teleology of function – to maintain distinctions – is not an illegitimate form of explanation for chains shifts in vowels, and indeed there is considerable empirical evidence in the ONZE results in support of a push chain in the raising of the short front vowels.

The question of teleology comes up again below in the discussion of merger.

4.2 Principles of vowel shifting

Hawkins (1973b: 7, mentioned in Chapter 2) likened the New Zealand ongoing vowel changes to the Great Vowel Shift:

> Let me conclude, however, by dipping into my crystal ball and pulling out one more prophecy: the changes currently taking place in the diphthongs [of New Zealand English] strongly suggest that the Great English Vowel Shift . . . is happening all over again, in exactly the same way.

[5] For more discussion of these and answers to other, lesser, objections to teleological explanations of linguistic change, see Campbell and Ringen 1981.

Discussions of vowel shift have played a significant role in work on New Zealand English (cf. Maclagan 1975; Bauer 1979, 1982, 1992; Matthews 1981; Trudgill 1986b; Woods 2000a: 136), and New Zealand shifted vowels have figured in theoretical discussions of vowel shifting in general (see Bauer 1992; Labov 1994: 138, 201–2, 209, 212, 285; and 2001: 187, 421). Nevertheless, we believe that the ONZE findings contribute new insights into the New Zealand changes, which in turn have important implications for claims about vowel shifts in general. In this section, we evaluate some of those claims, based on the ONZE findings.

Labov has proposed a number of general vowel-shift principles. One early formulation was: 'in chain shifts, short vowels fall' (see Labov 1994: 116; cf. Labov 1994: 31, 'short nuclei fall'). Clearly, however, New Zealand was an exception to this, where the short front vowels TRAP and DRESS have risen, not fallen (as Bauer 1992: 260 showed). As Labov (1994: 116–7) points out, 'Principle II [that in chain shifts, short vowels fall] applies generally to most of the available examples, but the historical record does contain exceptions'. Labov's (1994, 2001) proposed revisions of his principles rely crucially on the notion of 'peripherality', the feature [±peripheral]. There may be, however, problems in this formulation. We consider first the exit principles proposed by Labov to explain chain shifts, and then discuss the notion of 'peripherality' and its attendant problems.

Labov (1994) postulates 'exit principles' that operate in chain shifts. These include:

1. The *Lower Exit Principle*: 'In chain shifts, low nonperipheral vowels become peripheral.' This principle 'governs the tensing of low vowels as they reach the lower perimeter of phonological space' (pp. 601–2).
2. The *Upper Exit Principle*: 'In chain shifts, the first of two high morae may change peripherality, and the second may become nonperipheral.' This principle 'registers two *possibilities* for tense monophthongs as they are raised to the least open [highest] position, developing into upgliding or ingliding diphthongs' (p. 602).
3. The *Mid Exit Principle*: 'In chain shifts, peripheral vowels rising from mid to high positions develop inglides.' This *principle* 'concerns the shift of monophthongs to ingliding diphthongs as they move from mid to high position' (p. 602).

The principles, however, would not explain the New Zealand short front vowel shifts, as they fit none of these exit principles, which relate only to tensing of the lowest vowels, diphthongisation of long high vowels (of two morae), and the diphthongisation of mid vowels as they rise to be high. Specifically, in the case of the raised short vowels in New Zealand, (1) does not apply because the vowels are not low, and neither are (2) and (3) relevant, since the changes do not primarily involve diphthongisation, nor are the vowels long (as those of (2) would require). There seems, for example, to be no provision for a mid vowel to continue to raise without diphthongisation as New Zealand English DRESS is currently doing.[6]

Labov appears to confirm this. He says:

> London working-class speech shows [i], [e̝], [ɛ] for the front short vowels /i/ [i.e. /ɪ/], /e/, /æ/ (Sivertsen 1960). In this case, there are no entering and leaving phonemes that would define a vowel shift. One might say instead that it represents an upward compression of the phonological space used by the short vowels. But if /i/ [i.e. /ɪ/] had not moved to an upper-mid position, its margin of security with /e/ would have been seriously endangered. The same upward shift appears in Australian English . . . The New Zealand version of this short vowel perturbation . . . is much more clearly a chain shift. Instead of moving farther up, the high front short vowel /i/ [i.e. /ɪ/] moves to the back, becoming a lower high central vowel, while /e/ moves to replace it, and /æ/ moves up behind /e/.
>
> This clearly violates both Principle III (since a front vowel is moving to the back in a chain shift) and Principle II (since short vowels are rising together). It is possible that there are no general constraints on the movement of short vowels: we must end the survey of completed changes by concluding that this is a possibility. (1994: 138)

The New Zealand short front vowel shift then is an exception to the original vowel shift principles, and they must either be abandoned or stated as tendencies that permit exceptions; Labov appeals to the notion of peripherality to explain the New Zealand vowel shift and avoid its being an exception.

Labov's proposed principles of vowel shifting depend heavily on the notion of 'peripheral'. He explains thus:

> the term *peripherality* was introduced to describe the path of the high vowels in the Great Vowel Shift . . . I will use the term *nonperipheral* and the feature [−peripheral] to describe any type of vowel nucleus that is plainly more distant from the periphery in its mean and distribution than another vowel of the same height. (1994: 172)

A central principal he proposes is: 'In chain shifts, peripheral vowels become more open [lower] and nonperipheral vowels become less open [higher]' (p. 601) (though we note that this is a typographical error; from the context it is clear that Labov means that peripheral vowels are raised and non-peripheral vowels are lowered).

Of the reasons for introducing the notion of peripherality, Labov says, 'a new conception of the feature *peripherality* shared by other Germanic and Baltic languages . . . [is] proposed to modify the basic principles of chain shifting to assert that tense vowels rise along the peripheral path, and lax vowels fall along

[6] At one stage it seemed as though DRESS was diphthongising, but this tendency seems to have ceased (see Maclagan 1998).

the nonperipheral path' (1994: 32). He notes that the principle that peripheral vowels become less open and nonperipheral vowels become more open rests upon the definition of peripherality, 'a definition which holds for articulatory position as well as acoustic properties' (p. 601). This gives the impression that there is a precise physical definition of peripherality, which can be called upon to determine directions of change in vowel shifts. However, in characterising peripherality, different statements by Labov (1994) reveal that it not a precise concept with inherent phonetic content; it is somewhat vague and imprecise in this regard, as seen in, for example:

> Peripherality is not an absolute location in phonological space but, like height or frontness, a relationship determined by the elements of the system as a whole. A peripheral element is closer to the outer envelope of the vowel system than a nonperipheral element . . . It follows that a set of vowels may be assigned to another subsystem without any shift in their position, as a result of the shift of other vowels. The Redefinition Principle [note that peripherality is defined relative to the vowel system as a whole] is so named because it governs change induced by the redefinition of one or more vowels as peripheral or nonperipheral . . . It is even more apparent in the Southern Shift. The laxing of the nuclei of the upgliding diphthongs, and their subsequent centralization and lowering, leads to a redefinition of the originally short vowels as lax. In British, Australian, and New Zealand English, this leads to an upward movement of short tense vowels. (p. 285)

> At the level at which sound change takes place, there is no direct relationship between length and peripherality in English vowels. (p. 173)

> In London, Norwich, the Outer Banks, and other areas of the Southern United States, the originally short, lax vowels become [+peripheral]. In London, Australia, and New Zealand, they remain phonetically short, so that they are clearly short, tense [+peripheral] vowels.[7] (p. 212)

[7] Acoustic analysis gives some support to the notion that modern New Zealand English DRESS and TRAP are relatively tense. In a comparison of the speech of four of the youngest ONZE speakers with speakers of modern New Zealand English, Watson, Maclagan, and Harrington (2000) showed that modern New Zealand English DRESS and TRAP are actually longer than might be expected if they were fully short, lax vowels. Vowel height is inversely related to vowel length so that higher (closer) vowels are generally shorter than more open (lower) vowels (see Maddieson 1997). This relationship holds for the ONZE speakers, for whom KIT is shorter and higher than DRESS, which is shorter and higher than TRAP, which in turn is shorter and higher than STRUT. The relationship no longer holds in modern New Zealand English. As DRESS and TRAP rose, their length did not change. For modern New Zealand English, therefore, DRESS is higher than KIT, but longer than KIT, and TRAP is higher than STRUT, but longer than it. DRESS and TRAP are thus phonologically short (because they cannot occur in open syllables) but phonetically relatively long. This, however, does not affect their phonemic analysis nor the contrasts among them. Modern New Zealand English KIT remains a lax vowel.

Clearly, whether tied to the overall system of a given language or whether connected abstractly with tense/lax or long/short, peripherality is nevertheless imprecise. As Bauer (1992: 261) points out, a problem with determining peripherality is that its definition 'demands comparisons between "neighbouring" vowels', but it is often not clear what comparisons should be made in order to determine whether a given vowel is [+peripheral] or [−peripheral]. This becomes even clearer when the New Zealand shift in short front vowels is taken into account. We believe that the imprecision in the definition of peripherality has allowed it to be used inappropriately, defined after the fact to deal with certain situations. A short or lax vowel that does not seem to be behaving according to the principles may be redesignated [+peripheral], seeming to explain why it rose; however, even if the vowel in question has become somewhat longer (see n. 7) and hence somewhat more tense, what is missing is a solid basis (independent of its exceptional raising behaviour) for labelling the vowel [+peripheral], when such short vowels are typically considered [−peripheral]. Bauer (1979: 64) writes that 'synchronically there is now no distinction between so-called "tense" and "lax" vowels' in English, and thus where the fifteenth-century Great Vowel Shift involved only long ('tense') vowels, both 'long' and 'short' alike participate in the twentieth-century shift. Even with the notion of peripherality, the principles cannot explain why similar vowels (such as KIT in Australia and New Zealand) can move in opposite directions.

We suggest that this is confirmed in Labov's own view of this change; he says:

> In the clearest exemplars of Pattern 4, in London, Norwich, the Outer Banks, and other areas of the Southern United States, the originally short, lax vowels become [+peripheral]. In London, Australia, and New Zealand, they remain phonetically short, so that they are clearly short, tense [+peripheral] vowels. (1994: 212)

It is not immediately clear why these vowels are 'clearly short, tense [+peripheral]' in New Zealand (particularly since the same ones are short and lax in other varieties exhibiting Labov's Pattern 4, mostly characterised by a number of diphthongisations that are missing in the New Zealand case), other than that they rise unexpectedly, rather than fall, as predicted by the principles (but see n. 7). In any event, the New Zealand English short front vowels are not treated consistently, since apparently the KIT vowel is not thought to have become tense and peripheral as the others are assumed to have done;[8] rather, the KIT vowel is said to conform to the principle that 'in chain shifts, tense vowels move to the front along peripheral paths, and lax vowels move to the back along nonperipheral paths' (Labov 1994: 200), and 'the same [backward movement of lax vowels along nonperipheral paths] can be said for the backing of /i/ [i.e. /ɪ/] in New Zealand English' (p. 201). It is difficult to avoid the conclusion that peripherality for these vowels has been determined after the fact: TRAP and DRESS are

[8] However, the raised KIT vowel in Australia is said to have become tense in the process.

designated as tense and peripheral because they did rise – rising is along the peripheral track according to the proposed vowel-shift principles; likewise KIT is labelled nontense and nonperipheral because it centralised – the centralisation is following a nonperipheral track in this model.

Not only is the notion of 'peripherality' in question, the principles themselves do not apply universally. However the short front vowels are stated (in terms of 'short' or 'lax' or '[±peripheral]'), caution is needed in applying the vowel-shifting principles to them. Not only do the principles as they stand not handle the outcomes when the KIT vowel can centralise in New Zealand English (towards [ɘ]), but raise in Australian English (to [i̞]), but neither do they explain how the originally somewhat raised TRAP and DRESS vowels can continue to rise in New Zealand, but go in the opposite direction in major varieties of the South of England, that is, reverse their trajectory and lower (see Chapter 6, Sections 2.1 and 3.1; cf. Bauer 1992; Trudgill 1986b). Thus, the results of the ONZE research reveal that the vowel-shift principles affecting these vowels do not work fully without exception.[9]

5 Mergers and other linguistic constraints on change

Considerable attention has been dedicated to merger in the sociolinguistic literature on language change. Claims range from, essentially, that mergers are preferred to that mergers tend to be avoided. As M. Gordon explains:

> Chain shifts and mergers can be seen as alternative outcomes of a change situation. Both involve the encroachment of one phoneme into the phonological space of another. If the second phoneme changes so that the distinction between the two is maintained, then the result is a chain shift. If, however, the second phoneme does not change, the distinction is lost, and a merger occurs. (2001: 244)

Some statements on this matter, if accurate, would predispose us to believing the avoidance of merger, as in vowel shifts, should not exist or at least should be very rare; for example: 'The relative progress of sound change is determined by phonetic factors alone, without regard to the preservation of meaning' (Labov 1994: 603) and 'mergers are, in general, much more common than chain shifts' (M. Gordon 2001: 253). Nevertheless, as seen in the previous section, vowel shifts in which mergers are avoided are reasonably common, and the overwhelming majority of changes affecting New Zealand English vowels are shifts in which meanings are preserved. The only significant vowel mergers in New Zealand English are of the contrast in the NEAR and SQUARE diphthongs, a very recent change (Maclagan and Gordon 1996a; Maclagan and Gordon 1996b;

[9] Hickey (2000) believes that one reason for this reversal of vowel movement for these short front vowels in southern England is that the lowering is a dissociative reaction to the raising of pre-war generations, i.e., a social rather than an asocial reason.

M. Maclagan 1998; Maclagan and Gordon 1998; Maclagan and Gordon 1999; Maclagan, Gordon, and Lewis 1999; Maclagan 2000; Gordon and Maclagan 2000; Maclagan and Gordon 2000; Gordon and Maclagan 2001), and the Weak Vowel Merger (of the unstressed vowels, where the lack of contrast between the last vowels of *rabbit* and *abbot* class words was a variable feature in the south-east English dialects brought to New Zealand) (see Chapters 6 and 7). In short, from the New Zealand English data, it is not possible to argue for the dominance of merger over shift. This is apparently true generally, not just for New Zealand English. As cited already, Labov concedes that 'the study of chain shifting does not provide many examples of unexpected mergers; examples of unexpected avoidance are easier to locate' (1994: 270). He says, 'there is no doubt that in some way or other, linguistic systems respond to change in ways that maintain meaning – more or less' (p. 569).

Claims about mergers have also figured in approaches to new-dialect formation. For example, in Trudgill's (1986b: 105) discussion of koinéisation, levelling that involves mergers wins out over distinctions, but, nevertheless, speakers avoid accommodations that merge phonological contrasts (Trudgill 1986b: 17; cf. also Bauer 1994: 423). This seeming contradiction may not be real. That is, however adults behave when phonemic contrasts are potentially merged, mergers may spread at the expense of contrasts because children acquiring their language in a diffuse situation where a choice between merged and non-merged contrasts is available may opt for the merged variant. Where relevant, we use material from the ONZE findings as we now consider claims about mergers.

The general principle that, in contact situations, mergers are preferred over distinctions (cf. Hickey 2002; Trudgill 1986b: 105) appears to be connected with what Labov (1994: 35) calls 'Herzog's Principle', the rule that 'mergers expand at the expense of distinctions' in dialect geography (see also Labov 1994: 602; 2001: 498). From the point of view of child language acquisition, there is no compelling reason why mergers should necessarily be preferred and should thus expand their geographical territory; that is, if there is a non-merged variant in the dialect mix that has a considerable edge over the other variants in terms of numbers or social advantage, then it is predictable that children acquiring their language in that setting will favour and acquire the non-merged variety.

However, Labov (1994, 2001) brings up two reasons for why mergers might win out in dialect contact situations. The first involves his claim (1994: 324) that 'mergers rarely rise to the level of overt social consciousness', that 'mergers are almost invisible to social evaluation, and it is difficult to think of them as diffusing under the social pressures of social imitation and association' (2001: 27). He finds that 'the evidence for the absence of social affect of splits and mergers is massive and overwhelming' (1994: 343), and relates this to the claim that

> For the most part, linguistic structure and social structure are isolated domains, which do not bear upon each other . . . those sound changes with clear structural consequences – mergers – are almost entirely without

> social evaluation. The force of social evaluation, positive or negative, is generally brought to bear only upon superficial aspects of language, the lexicon and phonetics. (2001: 28)

While not part of Labov's exposition, it could be extraploated from this that, if indeed mergers are almost invisible to social evaluation, it is wrong to imagine, as hypothetically argued above, that children in a contact situation might give preference to a non-merged form because of dominance of numbers or social advantage for identity among their peers. However, this does not mean that in such a situation only the merged versions will ever win – in fact there are numerous instances where non-merged variants have won out (as we discuss below). Moreover, it is possible to accept the social invisibility of mergers per se and still have recourse to social explanations when non-merged variants triumph over merged ones in dialect contact. That is, child language acquirers could perhaps place no social significance on a merger or non-merger itself, but nevertheless could come to select a particular variety wholesale, including its non-merged variants, for its overall dominance or social advantages.

Whether one takes the view that mergers are invisible to social evaluation or not, it is relatively easy to point to a number of clear examples of variables involving a merged and non-merged variant in which social factors have influenced the trajectory of change and favoured the non-merged variant. To mention just a few: (1) The socially more stigmatised variant of non-rhoticity (merger of 'r' with 'zero' non-prevocalically) in New York City has reversed, moving towards the more prestigious general American model so that the incidence of 'r' as opposed to non-'r' is much higher now than in the past. (2) The stigmatised /v/~/w/ merger of areas of southern England has been reversed so the contrast is again firmly established in locations that formerly had the merger (see Trudgill, Schreier, Long, and Williams in press). (3) In New Zealand, the once more prevalent though socially stigmatised h-dropping (merger of /h/ with zero) has been entirely eliminated so the contrast remains. (4) The historical trajectory of the /hw/~/w/ merger (of *which* vs *witch*) in New Zealand English shows that the merger at one point had progressed further but at a later point in time had been turned back considerably in terms of percentage of occurrence, only later in time to move ahead again (see Chapter 6), showing that this merger may have been sensitive to social factors. In short, social factors have had an impact on the fate of several mergers, including some in New Zealand English. This means that it is not safe to assume that mergers have an automatic advantage in dialect contact situations.

Labov's second reason for believing that mergers win in dialect contact relates to strategies from cross-dialect communication. He cites Herold (1990), who used data from eastern Pennsylvania to formulate a mechanism for the expansion of mergers, as a gain of information – not a loss – on the part of speakers who use the two-phoneme, non-merger variety. In Labov's words, 'they learn that there are speakers who do not make the distinction, and they cease to misunderstand those speakers by adjusting their own system accordingly' (Labov 1994: 324). It is said that speakers representing the non-merger variety 'may continue for some time to produce the distinction [but] without using it for semantic interpretation' (ibid.). In the end, according to Herold and Labov, neither the speakers who make the phonemic contrast nor those who do not make it attempt to use the contrast to understand; instead they rely on semantic, pragmatic, and syntactic (non-phonetic) clues to interpret cases of homonymy. Hence Herold's claim, again in Labov's words, 'that merger represents the acquisition rather than the loss of information' (1990: 35), that is, the new information in the form of the realisation that, to understand, one needs to ignore the merged phonetics and look elsewhere for clues. This, then, is used to support the belief that mergers are preferred in situations of dialect contact.

This line of thought is indeed interesting, but questions arise. For example, to what extent does this strategy for understanding interlocutors who use merged forms hold for settings other than eastern Pennsylvania? What numbers of speakers of the respective dialects might be required? To what extent do social factors condition what occurs? Clearly, as Labov (1994: 325–7) shows, in many situations, people without a merger continue to misunderstand those with a merger. Is it not just as possible that the children of parents who merge could grow up in a community where the non-merged variety has the numerical or social advantages and as a consequence they acquire a non-merging variety of their own, even if their parents' generation no longer listen for the relevant phonetic contrasts? Obviously, if the people after whom children and adolescents model their language do not make the contrast, the merger could win out; however, if in the broader context (of supraregionalisation, swamping, founder effect, new-dialect formation on the majority wins principle, or whatever) the variety with merger does not have numbers or social advantage or something to bolster it, this particularly local strategy for interdialectal comprehension may have little or no lasting effect.

Whereas Labov and Herold have each argued that in contact situations the homophony resulting from mergers comes to be ignored and the strategy of not attending to such phonetic distinctions in comprehending meaning encourages the spread of the merger, others argue that meaning distinctions can carry so much weight that mergers can tend to be avoided in new-dialect formation. This raises the questions of functional load and numbers in a very explicit way.

Thus, for example, Hickey places a 'significant homophony' rider on the principle that prefers mergers in dialect contact:

> Two further aspects, over and beyond numerical considerations, should be added here. The first is that /h/-dropping, like the /v/ to /w/ shift . . . is a feature which results in considerable homophony in English so that while the general principle that mergers are preferred over distinctions in contact situations holds, this is not so when significant homophony arises as a result. (2002: 218–19)

In this view, the amount of homophony that would have resulted was sufficient to cause these mergers ultimately to be suppressed. Hickey clarifies this further, giving examples of mergers that succeed due to low functional load and examples of others that fail because the level of homophony would be much higher:

> [M]ergers are only preferred if the functional load of the distinction realised in the non-merged situation is *low*. This is clearly the case with short vowels before tautosyllabic /r/. The distinction between /i/ and /u/ has a minimal pair *fir* vs. *fur* and for the mid front vowel one of the few pairs is *tern* vs. *turn*. The homophony is nothing near that resulting from /h/-dropping or the merger of /v/ with /w/. (2002: 220)

It is difficult to use the ONZE data to argue for or against Hickey's significant homophony rider. As noted near the beginning of this section, the existence of chain shifts, particularly push chains, makes a good case against mergers necessarily being preferred in dialect contact. If this were not the case, we might expect, for example, the TRAP and DRESS vowels to have merged, rather than to have moved in concert, maintaining their distinction, as they did in New Zealand English (see Chapters 6 and 7). From Hickey's perspective, functional load could also have helped to keep them distinct. There are no clear examples of vowel mergers in the ONZE materials; this, however, while suggestive, does not allow us to completely reject the idea that mergers are necessarily preferred in dialect contact.

6 Gender

Our results are broadly consistent with a host of previous results relating to gender and language change. For all but one change, the women are ahead in the changes that we have documented that are leading towards modern New Zealand English. In particular we note that the women are ahead of the men in the diphthong-shifted variants of the closing diphthongs that later came to be stigmatised in New Zealand (suggesting that diphthong-shifted pronunciations were not perceived as stigmatised when the Mobile Unit speakers were growing up, even though they attracted negative comments from school inspectors by 1900, and the daughters of some of the speakers analysed here did not continue to advance in the same direction as their mothers (see Woods 2000b)). We do not intend to enter the debate about why women should tend to lead language change. For extensive discussion of this topic see Labov 2001, Cheshire 2001, and Chambers 2003, among others. The clear gender-based patterns that emerge from the analysis of the Mobile Unit speakers strengthen our contention that social factors may also have been involved in the variants concerned (see Chapters 6 and 7).

7 Lexical diffusion

An ongoing debate in the literature on sound change relates to the question of whether sound change spreads regularly (mechanistically to change a sound in all words that happen to contain it in the relevant phonetic environment, simultaneously), or whether lexical diffusion occurs (with a change spreading across the lexicon, reaching some words before others, and some perhaps not at all). One group of researchers has said that 'words change' and another that 'phonemes change'. Labov (1994) has reviewed this literature at length and attempted to reconcile the differences; he concluded that there is strong evidence for the occurrence of both types of change, but identified the precise delineation of when each occurs as a project for future research. From his survey of the literature he locates regularity in 'low level output rules' (in phonetic detail), and lexical diffusion in 'the redistribution of an abstract word class into other abstract classes' (1994: 541, 542). Thus, in Labov's view, certain types of sound changes are predicted to be fully regular, and others prone to lexical effects.

In the analysis of the ONZE data, the quantified variables were subject to different degrees of analysis. In terms of linguistic conditioning, the vocalic variables were tested just for preceding and following phonetic environment. The focus with these variables was on establishing the degree of advancement of the vowels, and how this correlates with other vowels in the speech of the same speakers. In all cases, we found strong evidence for phonetic conditioning. However, because we did not test for any word-specific effects, we are not in a position to comment on the degree to which the diffusion across the lexicon could have been involved in these vowel shifts. Labov's analysis would position 'vowel shifts in place of articulation' (1994: 543) clearly within the realm of regular sound change – change that is below the level of consciousness and is associated with low-level output rules. That is, Labov predicts that such changes will be regular. We have not investigated whether counterexamples might be found in our data.

We did conduct more elaborate tests of linguistic conditioning on the three consonantal variables that have been quantified: /hw/, h-dropping, and /r/. For all three of these, we found some evidence of the involvement of the lexicon, though not all the evidence is equally convincing. For the three consonantal variables analysed quantitatively, there are different types of word specific effects at play, effects relating to frequency, word type (function versus content), and semantic field. We consider each in turn.

7.1 *Lexical frequency*

As reported in Chapter 6, Section 17.3.2, lexical frequency was a significant predictor of /h/ in our data; the more frequent a word is, the more prone it was to h-dropping.

It should not surprise us to find effects of word frequency in language change – especially involving h-dropping. Lexical frequency has a pervasive effect throughout the system, affecting both speech perception (Connine, Titone, and Wang 1993; Grosjean 1980; Balota and Chumbley 1984) and speech production (see, e.g., Levelt 1983; Dell 1990). High-frequency words tend to be produced more fluently and to undergo greater reduction in speech (Fidelholz 1975;

Whalen 1991; Wright 1997; Jurafsky et al. 2001). Because high-frequency words tend to be more prone to reduction in speech, it is often argued that they lead leniting changes (Hooper 1976; Krug 1998). Bybee explains this line of thinking:

> If sound changes are the result of phonetic processes that apply in real time as words are used, then those words that are used more often have more opportunity to be affected by phonetic processes. If representations are changed gradually, with each token of use having a potential effect on representation, then words of high frequency will change at a faster rate than will words of low frequency. (2001: 11)

Disentangling the reductive effect of frequency on production from its potential role in sound change is rather complicated. For example, one of the well-documented frequency effects relates to *t-d* deletion in varieties of spoken English (Bybee 2000; Jurafsky et al. 2001). Word-final /t/ and /d/ are demonstrably more often deleted in high-frequency words than low-frequency words. This has been taken to be evidence in favour of the involvement of frequency in sound change, with words of high frequency changing at a faster rate than words of low frequency. However, just because more frequent words show greater rates of reduction does not mean that frequency is necessarily involved in sound change. Such effects can exist for stable variables (not apparently undergoing change) as well (see, e.g., Wright 1997). What is needed is diachronic evidence to show that frequent words were in fact changing at a different rate – that is, that change occurred faster in these words – than in non-frequent words. Documentation of rates of reduction at a single slice of time is not sufficient to demonstrate the involvement of frequency in sound change.

While it may be likely that frequency can be involved in sound change (as it is involved in many other aspects of speech), we are not in a position to document such an effect with h-dropping in New Zealand English. Interestingly, the direction of change here is unusual – h-dropping is on its way out. The less reduced form is the preserved one (/h/ is fully restored), due presumably to the small frequency of h-dropped forms in the input and perhaps social influences on how the variable was evaluated. Thus, it is the *most frequent* forms that are most reduced. If we were to interpret this as significant in terms of sound change, we would be forced to conclude that the frequent forms are lagging in the change towards restoring h-fulness. In fact, it is probably the case that lexical frequency is involved in dialects with stable /h/ variation – with frequent words tending to display more h-dropping, the pattern we see in Chapter 6. This is not about lexical diffusion; rather, it is about economy of articulation.

7.2 Open versus closed class

A second apparently lexical result involves function and content words and the production of /hw/. Note that lexical frequency may also be involved here, but to a much lesser degree (see Chapter 6, Section 18.4). However, a very robust result is that function words such as *where* or *why* are significantly less likely to be produced with /hw/ than content words such as *wheel* – content words are more than twice as likely to be produced with /hw/. Other researchers have found a distinction in production between content and function words. Van Bergem (1993), for example, has demonstrated that function words tend to be more reduced, and Jurafsky (in press) summarises a range of evidence that high-probability function words tend to have greater vowel reduction, higher rates of coda-deletion, and are produced more quickly. These results are consistent with lessened production of /hw/ in function words. However, they also make it plausible that in dialects that are fairly stably /hw/-producing, the /hw/ may be heavily reduced in function words. Thus, again, we have to question whether what we are seeing really relates to sound change per se, or whether it is an artifact of a fairly stable force of articulatory reduction.

The rate of /hw/ production in function words in the Mobile Unit speakers is strikingly low and this, combined with the set-like quality of the question words, makes /hw/ a more plausible case for the involvement of the lexicon in sound change than the frequency effect with h-drop. In addition, the change involving /hw/ was probably a salient one in the community (see Chapter 6), a factor that is argued to increase the involvement of the lexicon. In her study of the Yiddish folksinger Sarah Gorby, Prince (1987: 110) finds that salient socially prestigious variants are maintained more successfully in open-class words, arguing that 'the most consciously aimed-at target is reached more successfully in open-class items, the items to which speakers are better able to attend'.

While there is some evidence that the lexicon is involved in the change in /hw/, the most interesting case for lexical diffusion in our data comes from the behaviour of /r/.

7.3 Semantic domain

In Chapter 6 we reported that the semantic domain of some words significantly affected the likelihood that they would be realised rhotically. Farming words and mining words, in particular, were much more resistant to /r/-loss than other types of words for a number of the Mobile Unit speakers. For example, if we consider the two speakers with the highest incidence of rhoticity in the quantified analysis, Mrs Ellen Dennison and Mr Tony Tweed, we see that they are 56% and 42% rhotic, respectively. However, if we confine the analysis to just those words in the semantic domain of farming, we find that these words have significantly more rhoticity, 75% rhotic for Ellen Dennison and 66% rhotic for Tony Tweed.

This is more convincing than the frequency-based or function-based cases for lexical diffusion, as there is no synchronic force (such as articulatory economy) that could possibly support such a system in a stable manner. It seems that this should be attributed to the change-in-progress involving /r/. However, the existence of such a word-based effect could be controversial, and so it is worth examining the degree to which this result is truly lexical.

One possible interpretation of this result is that it may not be a case of lexical diffusion, but rather a type of topic-based style shifting (see, e.g., Rickford and McNair-Knox 1994). Perhaps speakers shift into a more rhotic style when discussing certain topics – most notably farming and mining. Of course a speaker is likely to use more farming words when talking about farming, so this type of topic-based shifting would lead to the type of result reported here. Coupland (2001: 198) discusses how style unfolds as 'persona-managmement': 'individuals, within and across speaking situations, manipulate the conventionalized social meanings of dialect varieties – the individual through the social'. It could be the case that discussions involving farming, for example, cause a shift to a style associated with 'the old days' (which would lead to greater rhoticity, since the less /r/-ful style would be due to the change-in-progress away from /r/-fulness). In this case, we would not be dealing with lexical diffusion, but rather with the intricacies of style.

This hypothesis is easily tested by examining the excerpts where the speakers discuss farming topics. If the increased rhoticity is due to style shift, all words with 'r' in appropriate contexts in such passages should show increased rates of rhoticity – not just those related to farming. However, if the result is genuinely lexical, then, while the farming words should show high rates of /r/-production (in whatever style they may occur in), the non-farming words should not.

We present an excerpt from an interview with Tony Tweed; it includes a small excerpt of concurrent speech (the ellipses represent interviewer speech or speech of other participants). The topic relates to farming, and so there are several farming words in the passage (*horse*, *farm*, *farmer*). If the result that farming words tend to be more rhotic related to style shifting, then all appropriate words in this passage should show increased rates of rhoticity, relative to rhoticity rates in the rest of Tony Tweed's speech. In this excerpt of an orthographic transcription, the tokens of /r/ that were included in the analysis are shown in bold (one example each of *horses*, *according* and *or* [marked with *] were not analysed).

Key:
small caps R = 'r' tokens in words classified as non-farming
non-italic r = 'r' tokens in words classified as farming
underlining = 'r' tokens for which /r/ was actually pronounced rhotically

Mr T: a horse poweR drove a small mill. the horse. went walked round and round and drove this horse poweR. that was the poweR that was used to drive the small mill. that was the next. and it. completed the whole job of thrashing [threshing] and dressing

. . . .

Mr T: but then lateR you came on to what was called a poRtable engine. it drove a mill. and both the mill and the poRtable engine weRe drawn

> round the countryside by teams of horses. farmers owned teams of horses* with his neighbouR to help him. fouR six eight ten horses according* to the weatheR conditions had to be used. and it was a most difficult job
>
> . . .
>
> Mr T: and those days theRe'd be twelve or* fouRteen men going round with this threshing outfit. and they had to be all fed on the farm that was. quite a hectic time

Overall, Tony Tweed is 42% rhotic. This particular passage contains eight tokens of (r) in farming-related words, and twelve tokens in non-farming words. Seven out of the eight tokens in farming words were realised rhotically (87.5%), compared with only one out of the twelve tokens in non-farming (8.3%). That is, the behaviour of 'r' in this passage suggests that what we are dealing with here is a genuinely lexical effect. For Mr Tweed, for example, all instances of *horse* tend to be realised with /r/, while *portable* does not.

While we have not conducted such an analysis systematically across all our speakers, the cursory investigation that we have done provides no evidence for a stylistic account of this result.[10]

There is evidence also from Montreal French that semantic gangs of words can be 'left behind', or be the last to change in a historical phoneme shift, if they are used predominantly in a certain social circle or type of situation, or have connotations of 'the old days' (Yaeger-Dror and Kemp 1992; Yaeger-Dror 1996). This is certainly the case with the mining and farming words in the speech of these Mobile Unit speakers, which have strong associations with early pioneering days and settlement, and which were probably used more by the speakers during their childhood and early adulthood than in the time period immediately prior to recording.

7.4 The domain of lexical diffusion

Labov carefully delineates the domains of lexical diffusion versus regular sound change as follows:

> **Regular sound change** is the result of gradual transformation of a single phonetic feature of a phoneme in a continuous phonetic space. It is characteristic of the initial stages of a change that develops within a linguistic system, without lexical or grammatical conditioning or any degree of social awareness ('change from below').

[10] One thing that we are not able to test for is the possibility that Mr Tweed may have been more fully rhotic earlier in life but, except in old-fashioned farming and mining words, has accommodated to the later focused non-rhotic variety that developed. If this were the case, it would be consistent with Labov's claim about lexical diffusion being possible only in changes from above, since such accommodation would be below the level of awareness.

Table 8.1 *Regular sound change versus lexical diffusion (from Labov 1994)*

Regular sound change ('from below') i.e. *when sounds change*	Lexical diffusion ('from above') i.e. *when words change*
– Vowel shifts in place of articulation	– Shortening and lengthening of segments
– Diphthongisation of high vowels	– Diphthongisation of mid and low vowels
– Consonant changes in manner of articulation	– Consonant changes in place of articulation
– Vocalisation of liquids	– Metathesis of liquids and stops
– Deletion of glides and schwa	– Deletion of obstruents

> **Lexical diffusion** is the result of the abrupt substitution of one phoneme for another in words that contain that phoneme. The older and newer forms of the word will usually differ by several phonetic features. This process is most characteristic of the late stages of an internal change that has been differentiated by lexical and grammatical conditioning, or has developed a high degree of social awareness or of borrowings from other systems ('change from above'). (1994: 542)

Based on a review of the literature, he provides a table (reproduced in Table 8.1) indicating the types of sound changes that should be expected to display regularity versus lexical diffusion.

Consistent with this analysis is our finding that, in the ONZE data, /hw/ tokens occurred significantly more often in function words, compared with content words, which tended to have the merged form /w/. We also noted in Chapter 6 (Section 18.4) that /hw/ could well have been socially marked, and the limited use of /hw/ that remains today in New Zealand is still sensitive to social influence (see Gordon and Maclagan 2000). Thus it is plausible to conclude that this variable is situated above the level of consciousness. Labov lists 'deletion of obstruents' as prone to lexical diffusion, which is also consistent with this account (where the /h/ that is lost in the /hw~w/ merger – as some see it – can be viewed as an obstruent).

However, the status of /r/ is not so clear. Labov situates the 'deletion of glides' together with the types of sounds that display regular sound change. It is certainly true that the loss of /r/ in New Zealand shows many hallmarks of regularity, including very precise phonetic conditioning. However, there appears to be a clearly lexical element to the change as well. It seems plausible that the loss of 'r' in New Zealand English carried with it some social prestige, and so would have come to some extent 'from above'. /r/-loss does not fall cleanly into either camp. It is consistently affected by environmental factors and thus demonstrates features of regular sound change, including prosodic position and lexical stress, and is more advanced in some parts of the lexicon than others thus also exhibiting traits associated with lexical diffusion.

8 Can speakers' choices affect the direction of linguistic change?

Linguists have been conditioned at least since Labov's (1963) Martha's Vineyard study to believe that speakers' attempts to signal their own identity can condition pronunciation, and hence linguistic change. In the Martha's Vineyard case, speakers who identified locally with the island had more centralisation of diphthongs than other residents of the island who did not have such a strong sense of local identity. Given this tradition of thought, it is surprising that the possibility that speakers can identify themselves with particular social groups and thus contribute to linguistic change has been questioned, even by Labov (2001) himself, while at the same time evidence supporting speakers' acts of identity influencing change continues to accumulate in other quarters (see Schilling-Estes 2002; Trudgill 1986b: 66–78; Wolfram, Hazen, and Schilling-Estes 1999). We survey some of the debate here, since such notions have played a role in attempts to explain the origins and development of New Zealand English (see Chapter 7).

According to Giles' accommodation theory (Giles 1973, 1977; Giles and Coupland 1991) from social psychology, speakers may modify their speech in order to sound more like interlocutors in order to achieve greater social integration with them. This is what lies behind 'accommodation' in approaches to new-dialect formation (Chapters 4 and 7). Not so often cited, however, is the part of Giles' approach that deals not with convergence through accommodation, but with divergence, where a group can deliberately employ linguistic differences as a symbolic act of asserting or maintaining their distinct identity. Both notions have been mentioned with respect to New Zealand English: accommodation in connection with levelling in new-dialect formation, and divergence in the deliberate attempt by colonials to establish a local identity distinct from Britain (Hickey 2002). In this section, we examine claims concerning accommodation and acts of identity and their possible impact on linguistic change.

In works on new-dialect formation (see Chapters 4 and 7), the process that leads to a new dialect is not generally thought to be under the control of speakers. That is, the construction of the new variety is not motivated by speakers' desire to have a distinct form of a language emblematic of their own identity, to match and reinforce non-linguistic differences found in the new society. Trudgill (2001: 44) argues explicitly against social factors of prestige, stigma, and identity; he says, 'it [is not] at all necessary to call on social features like "prestige" or "stigma" as explanatory factors, nor to have recourse to notions such as "identity"'. As seen in Chapters 6 and 7, with the advantage of further information and further analysis, it appears that for some traits it is not possible to divorce social factors entirely from the picture that emerges, and other scholars bring social and psychological motivations into attempts to explain new-dialect formation (see Britain 1997b: 160; 2002; Hickey 2002; L. Milroy 2002: 4, 9; Kerswill and Williams 2000, 2002; Sudbury 2000: 62). Given that there are instances of new settlements with dialect mixture where no new or focused dialect emerges (Mæhlum 1992, 1996; Sudbury 2000: 70–1), it is clear that, for a new dialect to form, more is needed than just a linguistic situation with more than one variety present – the social conditions, attitudes, and other psychological motivation to establish a new focused dialect within the community must also be favourable. Wolfram and Schilling-Estes (forthcoming) find that 'community attitudes, in the final analysis, may play a far greater role in guiding the directionality of change in interdialect contact than levels of contact'.

Hickey argues that the form the new variety assumes is a product of unconscious choices made in a new society to create a distinct linguistic identity. He argues that speakers are 'unconsciously aware of the linguistic relationship between old and new variants . . . and they are predisposed to selecting innovative variants because these represent the vanguard of change in a developing society' (2002: 230). At first glance, it would seem doubtful that speakers would somehow subconsciously know the direction of linguistic changes and make choices accordingly. However, recent work by Eckert (1988, 2000) and Labov (2001) lend some credence to the claim. For example, Eckert shows that adolescents in Detroit high schools engage in linguistic 'acts of identity', selecting linguistic variables specifically to fit the social groups with which they want to be associated. Labov shows how, by subconsciously selecting the most advanced tokens of a variable correlated with a group, speakers, though unaware that their behaviour is leading to such results, can bring about change in the perceived core of the target.[11] That is, if initially most of an adolescent group's tokens of DRESS cluster on, say, a somewhat centralised variant, but some overshoot the centralisation occasionally, giving a few outlier tokens of an even more centralised pronunciation – such as schwa – it can happen that people trying to identify themselves with the group with whom they associate this new development may overshoot the target even more, producing more tokens of the centralised sort, making them no longer the infrequent outliers, but leaving them the predominant representatives of the sound in question, thus producing a new core for the tokens of this sound which thus results in a sound change of a particular sort.

Many connect this sort of motivation with LePage and Tabouret-Keller's (1985) 'acts of identity' (mentioned above; see, e.g., Britain 1991, 1997b; Mæhlum 1992, 1996; Sudbury 2000). LePage and Tabouret-Keller (1985) defined acts of identity as follows: 'the individual creates his systems of verbal behavior so as to resemble those common to the group or groups with which he wishes from time to time to be identified' (quoted in Labov 2001: 505). They find 'positive and negative motivation to identify with groups' as 'by far the most important' of their constraints governing linguistic behaviour (Le Page and Tabouret-Keller 1985: 184; see also Denison 1997: 65–6; Hickey 2000; Tabouret-Keller 1997). This suggests that sheer weight of numbers in new-dialect formation is not enough (cf. Kerswill and Williams 2000: 66), that we must also allow for the possibility

[11] We note that, unlike the situation in early New Zealand English, speakers in these cases have already established varieties with which to identify, even as their pronunciations contribute to the ongoing changes of these varieties.

that social factors and speakers' choices also play a role, such as the selection of variables to show group membership, identity, and so on. Thus, Kerswill (2001: 673) believes 'that, for a koiné to form, the speakers must waive their previous allegiances and social divisions to show mutual solidarity'.

As seen in Chapter 7, 'supraregionalisation' has also been called upon to attempt to explain aspects of new-dialect formation. Supraregionalisation is defined as 'a process where dialect speakers progressively adopt more and more features of a non-regional variety which they are in contact with' (Hickey 2002: 236). Thus, where Trudgill et al. (2000a: 307) see the lack of regional variation as the result of focusing, Hickey (2002) sees supraregionalisation as a potential alternative explanation for the lack of regional dialect differences. Adopting a non-regional variety need not be the same as focusing when dialects come into contact. A difference is the assumed motives of speakers (whether above or below the level of consciousness).[12]

An opposing view comes from Labov (2001: 191–2; 1994: 549–50). He is sceptical of claims that 'acts of identity' and 'attitudes' motivate change or the acceptance of change. As he points out:

> [Such views] attribute linguistic change to: (1) the association of positively regarded traits and social privileges with membership in a given social group, and (2) the association of a linguistic form with membership in that social group. If such attitudes are to be used to account for linguistic diffusion [spread of innovations], it is necessary to posit a covert belief structure: that speakers feel that their adoption of the linguistic form will lead others to attribute to them the positive traits of the given group and allow them to share in the privileges of that group . . . such covert attitudes and beliefs . . . are not usually supported by material evidence . . . language change may simply reflect changes in interlocutor frequencies which are in turn the result of changes in social preferences and attitudes . . . The . . . pattern of a sound change from an originating group to neighboring groups may then be the simple product of frequencies of interaction. The account based on covert attitudes is redundant to the extent that the network of daily interaction brings people into contact with the new form in proportion to their distance from the originating group. (Labov 2001: 191–2)

These important sociolinguistic matters, concerning speakers' choices and attitudes, deserve particular attention in the further investigation of how and why languages and dialects diversify or consolidate. It is not entirely clear whether these theoretical outlooks considered in this section may inform us with respect to

[12] Recent work from several independent quarters appears to converge as different scholars investigate the relationship of speakers' choices with apparent reasons for language consolidation or diversification (see Thurston 1987, 1989; Ross 1996, 1997, 2001; Golla 2000; Hill 2001; Schilling-Estes 2002). These considerations intersect with social network theory (J. Milroy 1992; Ross 1997) and 'communities of practice' (Eckert 2000). Much of this work deals with multilingual settings, but the discussion has relevance for issues in new-dialect formation.

how New Zealand English came into being or whether the events in New Zealand English are able to tell us more about the theories, or possibly both. Given that it is not necessary for dialects in contact to focus and form a new dialect, as seen in Chapter 7 and above, it would appear plausible that there was some additional reason for why dialect differences were levelled out in New Zealand over and beyond dialect contact. It is therefore very possible that some insight from current work that focuses on speakers' choices may help us understand the historical development of New Zealand English. For the most part, the situation in New Zealand is not clear enough categorically to support or deny speakers' choices and the social factors that influence them in new-dialect formation here.

9 Conclusions

It is not surprising that a study of the magnitude of the one presented in this book should have some major implications for a number of claims about linguistic change that have been made in the sociolinguistic literature. And, indeed, this is what we have seen in this chapter. Not only does the analysis of the invaluable Mobile Unit corpus – which represents the development of New Zealand English almost from its earliest years – add greatly to what we know about this variety, but also, in one way or another, it provides data that can invigorate the study of linguistic change in general. The ONZE data add to our knowledge about complications with apparent and real time studies of linguistic change, and whether adults may accommodate and change their vernacular later in life. The findings show that speakers' families can have a highly influential role. The understanding of the part that gender plays in linguistic change is amplified. The possibility of lexically conditioned sound change receives some support. Some important general claims about vowel shifting and merger are challenged, while others are refined. Where the data are inconclusive, we hope that the study nevertheless makes a contribution by identifying matters for further investigation.

Appendix 1 Mobile Unit speakers

Speaker name	No.	Sex	DoB	Town	Region	Island	Mother	Father	Interviewed
Cross, Mrs Hannah Jane Campbell (née Peterson)	1	F	1851	Anderson's Bay nr Dunedin	Otago Peninsula	S.I.	Scotland	Scotland	Dunedin
Barr, Mr David	2	M	1853	Wanganui	Wanganui	N.I.	Outside NZ	Outside NZ	Wanganui
Hovell, Mr Charles Woodward*	3	M	1855	Howick	South of Auckland	N.I.	England	England	Coromandel
Barraclough, Mr Lawford Stroud	4	M	c 1856	Patea/Hawera	Nelson	S.I.	Unknown	Unknown	Patea
Knight, Mr Fred William	5	M	1856	Waipori	Tuapeka Dist., Otago	S.I.	England	England	Waipori
Gratton, Mrs Helen (née Gorton)	6	F	1857	Hamilton	Waikato	N.I.	Outside NZ	Outside NZ	Te Aroha
Haylock, Mr Arthur Lagden	7	M	1860	Christchurch & Dunedin	Canterbury & Otago	S.I.	England	England	Wellington
Riddle, Mr Bob	8	M	1860	Palmerston	Coastal Otago	S.I.	Outside NZ	Outside NZ	Palmerston
Butler, Mr Kingsley*	9	M	1861	Arrowtown	Central Otago	S.I.	Outside NZ	Ireland	Arrowtown
Bennetts, Mr John	10	M	1862	Roxburgh	Central Otago	S.I.	England	England	Roxburgh
Flannery, Mr James	11	M	1862	Waikouaiti	East Otago	S.I.	Australia	Ireland	Waikouaiti
St Omer, Mr Frank	12	M	1862	Queenstown	Central Otago	S.I.	Outside NZ	Other	Queenstown
Wyllie, Mr W. J.	13	M	1862	Oamaru	North Otago	S.I.	Unknown	Unknown	Oamaru
Fuller, Mrs Eleanor (née Vaughan)*	14	F	1863	Hamilton	Waikato	N.I.	England	England	Ngaruawahia
Ritchie, Mrs Helen Davidson (née Elliott)	15	F	1863	Arrowtown	Central Otago	S.I.	Scotland	Scotland	Arrowtown
Fullerton, Mrs	16	F	1864	Port Chalmers	Otago	S.I.	Scotland	Scotland	Port Chalmers
Hollis, Mrs Sarah Margaret (née Compston)	17	F	1864	Waihi	Lower Coromandel	N.I.	Ireland	Ireland	Waihi
Ritchie, Mr Robert	18	M	1864	Bannockburn (Nevis)	Central Otago	S.I.	Scotland	Scotland	Arrowtown

Cameron, Mrs (née McGregor?)	19	F	1865	Wanganui	Wanganui	N.I.	Scotland	Scotland	Wanganui
Crosby, Mr Patrick Cornelius (Paddy)	20	M	1865	Kirikiriroa/ Pukekohe	Waikato	N.I.	Ireland	Ireland	Hamilton
Dufty, Mr William*	21	M	1865	Parawai/Thames	Coromandel	N.I.	England	England	Thames
Forrester, Mr John Meggett	22	M	1865	Oamaru	North Otago	S.I.	Scotland	Scotland	Oamaru
Paul, Mr George	23	M	1865	Auckland city, rural Waikato	Auckland, Waikato	N.I.	Unknown	Scotland	Te Awamutu
Tweed, Mr Anthony	24	M	1865	Lovell's Flat/Milton	Coastal Otago	S.I.	Scotland	Scotland	Milton
Betts, Miss Rachel Florence Ward*	25	F	1866	Rangiora	North Canterbury	N.I.	England	England	Okaiawa
Harris, Mr James Bassiere	26	M	1866	Huntly	Waikato	N.I.	Other	Ireland	Huntly
McKearney, Mrs Susan Sarah (née Hooey)	27	F	1866	Patumahoe, Mauku	South of Auckland	N.I.	Outside NZ	Ireland	Cambridge
Ritchie, Mr Malcolm	28	M	1866	Dunedin	Otago	S.I.	Scotland	Scotland	Cromwell
Algie, Mr David Greenfield	29	M	1867	Balclutha	Clutha Dist., Otago	S.I.	Scotland	Scotland	Balclutha
Dixon, Mr Chris (Charles)	30	M	1867	Naseby	Maniototo, Otago	S.I.	Scotland	England	Naseby
Rigby, Mrs Frances C. J. (née Goullet)	31	F	1867	Te Awamutu	Waikato	N.I.	Outside NZ	Other	Hamilton
Drinnan, Mrs Jessie (née Adam)	32	F	1868	Clarksville nr Milton	Coastal Otago	S.I.	Scotland	Scotland	Milton
German, Mrs Edith Anne (née Steel)	33	F	1868	Kurewa Station nr Clinton	Southland	S.I.	England	England	Balclutha
Gray, Mr Robert T.	34	M	1868	Blue Spur, near Lawrence	Otago	S.I.	Outside NZ	Outside NZ	Lawrence
King, Mrs Catherine Maria (née Pipson)	35	F	1868	Makarora	Lakes Dist., Otago	S.I.	Scotland	Scotland	Wanaka

(*cont.*)

(*cont.*)

Speaker name	No.	Sex	DoB	Town	Region	Island	Mother	Father	Interviewed
Rivers, Mr George	36	M	1868	Manuherikia, near Alexandra	Central Otago	S.I.	Ireland	England	Alexandra, Central Otago
Shepherd, Mr Henry Franklin (Frank)	37	M	1868	Thames & North Shore	Coromandel & Auckland	N.I.	England	NZ	Thames
Strange, Mr Frederick Marychurch*	38	M	1868	Thames & Te Aroha	Coromandel & Piako Dist.	N.I.	England	England	Te Aroha
Temple, Mr Samuel Edwin	39	M	1868	Kihikihi, nr Te Awamutu	Waikato	N.I.	Ireland	Australia	Te Awamutu
Falconer, Mr David Charles	40	M	1869	Milton area	Clutha Dist., Otago	S.I.	Scotland	Scotland	Milton
Gifford, Mr James Gavin Bradshaw	41	M	1869	near Rangiaowhia (farm)	Waikato	N.I.	Ireland	Scotland	Te Awamutu
Gilchrist, Mr George Bowton	42	M	1869	Hyde, Cromwell, Roxburgh	Maniototo & Central Otago	S.I.	Outside NZ	Scotland	Roxburgh
Hammond, Mr Thomas (William) G. H.	43	M	1869	Thames	Coromandel	N.I.	England	England	Thames
Lawrence, Mr William C.*	44	M	1869	Lawrence	Central Otago	S.I.	Scotland	Scotland	Lawrence
Park, Mr Abraham Yueddle*	45	M	1869	Waikouaiti	Coastal Otago	S.I.	Scotland	Scotland	Waikouaiti
Schnackenberg, Mr Edward Henry	46	M	1869	Raglan, Auckland, Kawhia	King Country & Auckland	N.I.	England	Other	Kawhia
Von Tunzelmann, Mr W. J. Nicholas	47	M	1870	Queenstown	Central Otago	S.I.	England	Other	Queenstown
Mackie, Mr David	48	M	1871	farm near Arrowtown	Central Otago	S.I.	Scotland	Scotland	Arrowtown

Hanrahan, Mr Moses Halord	49	M	1872	St Bathans	Central Otago	S.I.	Ireland	Ireland	Ranfurly
Noble, Mr James Robert	50	M	1872	Thames/Waihi	Coromandel	N.I.	Ireland	Ireland	Waihi
Duigan, Mr Charles Lowther	51	M	1873	Wanganui	Wanganui	N.I.	Australia	Ireland	Wanganui
Hill, Mr James	52	M	1873	Hamilton	Waikato	N.I.	Ireland	England	Hamilton
Mason, Mr Peter	53	M	1873	Balclutha	Clutha Dist., Otago	S.I.	England	Scotland	Balclutha
Morrison, Mr William Gillies	54	M	1873	Palmerston	Coastal Otago	S.I.	Scotland	Scotland	Palmerston
Day, Mr Reginald*	55	M	1874	Christchurch? New Plymouth?	Canterbury/ Taranaki	N.I.	England	England	New Plymouth
Dennison, Mrs Ellen (née Mackie)	56	F	1874	Arrowtown/ Macetown	Central Otago	S.I.	Scotland	Scotland	Arrowtown
Edgar, Mr John William	57	M	1874	Tokotea & Coromandel	Coromandel	N.I.	England	England	Coromandel
Fell, Mr Ben Witt	58	M	1874	Waikouaiti	Coastal Otago	S.I.	Scotland	Scotland	Waikouaiti
Steel, Mr Thomas	59	M	1874	Pirongia nr Te Awamutu	Waikato	N.I.	Scotland	England	Te Awamutu
Warren, Mr William	60	M	1874	Queenstown	Wakatipu, Central Otago	S.I.	Ireland	England	Queenstown
Bisset, Mrs Christina	61	F	1875	Kaitangata	Clutha Dist., Otago	S.I.	Scotland	Unknown	Kaitangata
Mason, Miss Margaret Strachan	62	F	1875	Balclutha	Clutha Dist., Otago	S.I.	NZ	Scotland	Balclutha
McKinlay, Mr James Bryce	63	M	1875	Lawrence	Central Otago	S.I.	Scotland	Scotland	Lawrence
McLew, Mr John	64	M	1875	Shag Valley nr Palmerston	Coastal Otago	S.I.	Scotland	Scotland	Palmerston
Miller, Mr James S.	65	M	1875	Shag Valley	Otago	S.I.	Scotland?	Scotland	Palmerston
Paterson, Mr William McDonald	66	M	1875	Auckland & Ngaruawahia	Auckland, Waikato	N.I.	NZ	Scotland	Ngaruawahia

(cont.)

(*cont.*)

Speaker name	No.	Sex	DoB	Town	Region	Island	Mother	Father	Interviewed
Turnbull, Miss Mary Ann	67	F	1875	Morrinsville	Waikato	N.I.	Scotland	Scotland	Morrinsville
Cannon, Mr Thomas	68	M	1876	farm near Milton	Clutha Dist., Otago	S.I.	Unknown	Ireland	Milton
Cruickshank, Mrs Emily Woodley (née Bertram)	69	F	1876	Rangiaowhia nr Te Awamutu	Waikato	N.I.	England	Other	Te Awamutu
Michelle, Mr Thomas Philip Harvey	70	M	1876	Coal Creek Flat nr Roxburgh	Central Otago	S.I.	Australia	England	Roxburgh
Stewart, Mr James Armstrong	71	M	1876	Milton	Clutha Dist., Otago	S.I.	Scotland	Scotland	Milton
Hamilton, Mrs Anne Elizabeth (née Cotter)	72	F	1877	Arrowtown	Central Otago	S.I.	Ireland	Ireland	Arrowtown
Kenny, Mr Courtenay	73	M	1877	Thames & Paeroa	Coromandel	N.I.	England	Burma	Paeroa
Mackie, Mrs Alice (née McPherson)	74	F	1877	Arrowtown	Cental Otago	S.I.	Australia	Scotland	Arrowtown
Reid, Mrs Jane Elizabeth (née Shiels)	75	F	1877	nr Lumsden & Balfour	Northern Southland	S.I.	Scotland	Scotland	Arrowtown
Aitcheson, Miss Ada	76	F	1878	Kaitangata	Otago	S.I.	Outside NZ	NZ	Kaitangata
Little, Mr John (Jack)	77	M	1878	Ngaruawahia	Waikato	N.I.	Ireland	Ireland	Ngaruawahia
McConachie, Mrs Kathleen (née Barrett)*	78	F	1878	Paeroa	Coromandel/Thames Valley	N.I.	Ireland	Ireland	Paeroa
North, Mrs Emma Elinor (née Mainwaring)	79	F	1878	Kihikihi nr Te Awamutu	Waikato	N.I.	NZ	England	Te Awamutu
Ross, Mr George	80	M	1878	Patearoa	Central Otago	S.I.	Unknown	Scotland	Palmerston
Bertram, Mr Francis John (Frank)	81	M	1879	Rangiaowhia nr Te Awamutu	Waikato	N.I.	England	Other	Te Awamutu

McCullough, Mr Frank Errington	82	M	1879	Auckland & Thames	Auckland & Coromandel	N.I.	England	Ireland	Thames
Reilly, Mr Louis	83	M	1879	Waipori	Otago	S.I.	Australia	Australia	Alexandra
Strong, Mr William	84	M	1879	Naseby	Maniototo Dist., Otago	S.I.	Ireland	England	Naseby
Bell, Miss Iris (Brenda)	85	F	1880	Shag Valley Station nr Palmerston	Coastal Otago	S.I.	NZ	NZ	Palmerston
Reid, Mrs Olive Mildred (née Burnett)	86	F	1880	Ngaruawahia	Waikato	N.I.	England	England	Ngaruawahia
Welsh, Mr Robert (Bob)	87	M	1880	Kaitangata	Clutha Dist., Otago	S.I.	?Scotland	?Scotland	Kaitangata
Weatherall, Mr John Thomas	88	M	1883	Roxburgh	Central Otago	S.I.	England	Australia	Naseby
Douglas, Mr John H.	89	M	1884	rural (Douglas Vale) Wakatipu	Otago	S.I.	Australia	Scotland	Arrowtown
Wishart, Mr George	90	M	1884	Cromwell	Otago	S.I.	Scotland	Scotland	Cromwell
Luckie, Mr T. R.	91	M	c 1885	Queenstown	Wakatipu, Central Otago	S.I.	Scotland	Scotland	Queenstown
Young, Mr Vivian (Raupo)	92	M	1885	Otakeho & Paeroa	Taranaki & Coromandel	N.I.	Scotland	NZ	Paeroa
Dudley, Mrs Catherine Dolena (née Austin)	93	F	1886	Cardrona & Arrowtown	Central Otago	S.I.	Scotland	Ireland	Arrowtown
Templeton, Mr Robert	94	M	1887	Waikouaiti	East Otago	S.I.	Ireland	Australia	Waikouaiti
Ellery, Mr James Yeoman (Jim)	95	M	1888	Te Aroha	Lower Coromandel	N.I.	NZ	England	Te Aroha
Wood, Mr Allie*	96	M	1888	New Plymouth	Taranaki	N.I.	NZ	NZ	New Plymouth
Lillis, Mr Thomas	97	M	1889	Coromandel	Coromandel Peninsula	N.I.	Ireland	Ireland	Coromandel

(*cont.*)

(*cont.*)

Speaker name	No.	Sex	DoB	Town	Region	Island	Mother	Father	Interviewed
Magner, Mr Cornelius	98	M	1889	Te Kowhai	Waikato	N.I.	Ireland	Ireland	Ngaruawahia
Swarbrick, Mr Henry	99	M	1889	Kirikiriroa	Waikato	N.I.	Holland	England	Te Awamutu
Symons, Miss Marguerite	100	F	1894	Alexandra	Central Otago	S.I.	NZ	England	Alexandra
Partridge, Mr William	101	M	1895	Cromwell	Central Otago	S.I.	NZ	Australia	Cromwell
Ritchie, Mr George	102	M	1898	Bannockburn	Central Otago	S.I.	Unknown	NZ	Arrowtown
Bannatyne, Miss E.	103	F	1899	Waikouaiti	East Otago	S.I	NZ	Scotland	Waikouaiti
Munro, Nr James	104	M	1899	Evans Flat	Central Otago	S.I.	NZ	Scotland	Cromwell
Scott, Mr Thomas	105	M	1899	Milton	Central Otago	S.I.	NZ	NZ	Milton
Drinnan, Mr Nelson	106	M	c 1900	Milton	Central Otago	S.I.	NZ	NZ	Milton
Gray, Mr James B.	107	M	c 1900	Milton	Central Otago	S.I.	Unknown	NZ	Milton
Sumpter, Mr Dennis	108	M	1904	Oamaru	North Otago	S.I.	Unknown	NZ	Milton

N.I. = the North Island, S.I. = the South Island * = not born in NZ; details as follows:

Mr Hovell, born in Kent, came to NZ aged approximately 7 years
Mr Butler, born in Ballarat, Australia, came to NZ as a baby
Mrs Fuller, born in England, came to NZ aged 13–14 years
Mr Dufty, born in Australia, came to NZ aged 2 and a half years
Miss Betts, born in England, came to NZ aged 8 years
Mr Strange, born in Northampton, England, lived in Australia, came to NZ in 1872, aged 4 years
Mr Lawrence, born in Edinburgh, Scotland, came to NZ as a baby
Mr Park, born in Scotland, came to NZ aged 4–5 years
Mr Day, born in Dorset, England, came to NZ aged 1 year
Mrs McConachie, born in Ireland, came to NZ aged 6 years
Mr Wood, born in Kent, England, came to NZ aged 7–8 years

(*cont.*)

Non NZ-born speakers	No.	Sex	DoB	Birthplace	Age when came to NZ	Island	Mother	Father	Interviewed
McFarlane, Mrs Susan	109	F	c 1845	Scotland	33	Unknown	Unknown	Unknown	Unknown
Prendergast, Mr John	110	M	c 1857	Ireland	approx. 20	N.I.	Unknown	Unknown	Ngaruawahia
Cullinan, Mr Tom**	111	M	c 1860	Ireland	'young man' (1875)	N.I.	Unknown	Unknown	Patea
Thompson, Mr John (Jack)	112	M	1870	Ireland	approx. 20	S.I.	Ireland	Ireland	Queenstown
Eccles, Mr Alfred	113	M	c 1880	England	approx. 20	S.I.	Waikouaiti	Unknown	Waikouaiti
Firth, Mr George***	114	M	c 1875	Australia	approx. 20	N.I.	Outside NZ	Outside NZ	Te Aroha
Benham, Rev. Noel	115	M	c 1900	England	approx. 21	S.I.	Unknown	Unknown	Waikouaiti

** Mr Cullinan came to N.Z. via Australia.

*** The interviewer refers to him as Mr Frith, but his tombstone says Firth.

Appendix 2 The historical background of some settlements visited by the Mobile Unit

In this appendix, we describe the historical background of some of the towns visited by the Mobile Unit. We do this to demonstrate the amount of variation within settlements and among settlement types in different parts of the country and to provide a context for the Mobile Unit speakers, whose speech is analysed in this book. We make use of various historical sources including census reports.[1]

1 North Island

The North Island settlements chosen are Wanganui, representing an early settlement and part of the New Zealand Company efforts; the Waikato towns, established in connection with military occupation at the time of the New Zealand Wars; and Thames, which began as a goldmining town.

1.1 Wanganui

Wanganui, 150 miles north of Wellington at the mouth of the Wanganui River, was founded in 1841, one year after New Zealand became a British colony, as an off-shoot of the New Zealand Company's first settlement in Wellington. Its development into a market town with a port depended to a large extent on the growth of the economy of the wider region. The district had a considerable Maori population, and trade in potatoes, fruit, wheat, and pigs for Wellington gave the settlement its early start – a trade described in several of the Mobile Unit interviews. Up to 1846, the settlement had about 200 people, with hotels, small schools in private homes, and an Anglican church (Smart and Bates 1972: 81). Nevertheless, in spite of these promising beginnings, there were major problems

[1] As was pointed out in Chapter 3, details of individual boroughs appear in the New Zealand census reports only when they have a population of over 500, so in our discussion here we have had to use other sources on some of the towns. We note also that population figures from census material are always exclusive of Maori, so it is difficult to know what the total population of New Zealand was at any time.

for the European settlement: the land purchase was faulty and colonists faced being evicted from the land by the Maori owners. In 1846, a military garrison was stationed at Wanganui, and in the following year fighting broke out between British soldiers and Maori from the upper Wanganui River (Smart and Bates 1972: 65–77).

When Wanganui was besieged in 1847, the European population took shelter in stockades, farms were deserted, and settlers did not dare to work in areas outside the protection of the military. The majority of the 'respectable' settlers were reported as 'wanting to try their fortunes elsewhere, while the working class were content to live "on and by" the troops' (Wards 1968: 346). In any event, the settler population dropped from 215 in 1846 to 110 in 1847 (Reid 1940: 41). After hostilities ended, the land purchase was completed in 1848 and Wanganui began to consolidate and grow once more. The civilian population reached 432 by 1852 (Reid 1940: 43), and it was 1,324 in 1858, of whom 600 were under fifteen years of age (Chapple and Veitch 1939: 267).

Over the next twenty years, the military gave an impetus to the economy as well as providing new settlers when those soldiers who obtained their discharge locally began a new life as settlers (Smart and Bates 1972: 78; Wards 1968: 378). After fighting ceased, a smaller permanent garrison of some 300 remained until the outbreak of war in Taranaki in 1860 brought a major influx of British and colonial troops to Wanganui. British troops were withdrawn from New Zealand in 1870. In regional composition, the army did not differ significantly from the general population of the British Isles.

In 1862, a town board was established, and in 1872 Wanganui was constituted a borough. The population rose steadily, rather than rapidly. In addition to farm labourers, there were merchants and tradesmen, and more well-to-do people settling in the coastal lands adjoining the town (Volkerling and Stewart 1986: 99–100). The first newspaper was issued in 1853, and a second one appeared in 1867 (Smart and Bates 1972: 177–8). A Mechanics' Institute existed from the early 1850s, and a Druids' Hall was another public amenity to appear in the following decade. Churches of all the major denominations went ahead in the course of the 1850s, and by 1867, Anglican, Presbyterian, and Roman Catholic churches stood in Victoria Avenue, the principal street, with the Methodist chapel nearby (Taylor 1868: 285–6).

In 1855 a Common School was set up, with the Wellington provincial government paying half of the cost of buildings and salaries, the remaining half being paid for by voluntary donation. A report on the school in its second year, when the total number on the roll was 75, records the religious denominations of those who were attending the school: 34 Presbyterians, 21 Catholic, and 20 Church of England (Smart and Bates 1972: 211). The first Catholic School, which started in 1858, also attracted students of all denominations in the 1860s (p. 215). With the abolition of provincial government and the passage of the 1877 Education Act, a much larger number of single-teacher schools appeared in and around Wanganui.

Table 1 *Birthplaces of the population of Wanganui (from Census Reports, years stated)*

	NZ	England	Scotland	Ireland	Australia
1874	1,269	598	264	237	129
1878	1,689	955	311	375	153
1881	2,280	1140	371	454	185

The borough of Wanganui had reached a total population of 2,390 by 1871 (*NZ Census* 1871, Table 3), and by 1874 its population, whatever its historical antecedents, matched the national pattern for the proportions of English to Scots to Irish for New Zealand (see Table 1). (In 1874, the national percentages from the three major sources in the British Isles were England 24.92%, Scotland 12.83%, and Ireland 10.10% (*NZ Census*, 1874: 79).)

Unlike many other places, Wanganui did not receive a large influx of government-assisted immigrants in the 1870s, and Table 1 shows that, in common with the national trend, the numbers of Irish-born immigrants began to overtake those born in Scotland. Railway construction linked Wanganui to New Plymouth in 1885 and Wellington in 1886 (McLintock 1966, vol. 3: 546–7). The advent of the frozen-meat trade and the growth of dairy farming in the wider region led to further economic expansion in the later 1890s.

1.2 Ngaruawahia, Te Awamutu, and the Waikato military settlements

The Mobile Unit travelled around townships in the Waikato, a large fertile plain south of Auckland, which is now home to extensive dairy farming. They interviewed people in Ngaruawahia, Te Awamutu, Hamilton, and Cambridge. These were all towns that came into being with the military advance into the Waikato in 1863–4, either as bases for British and colonial troops or as military settlements set up by the New Zealand government.

Waikato Maori took advantage of the markets offered by European settlement and from the 1840s on were trading with Auckland settlers. The Europeans, especially those in Auckland, wanted to settle the fertile land between the Waipa and Waikato rivers and they were frustrated by Maori refusing to sell. Maori resistance to the selling of land gave rise to a political movement with pan-tribal and separatist aspirations under a Maori ing. In 1863, the British army advanced into the Waikato, and by 1864 there were 12,000 British and colonial troops, as well as approximately 1,000 Maori allies, fighting against the Maori King Party and their allies (about 4,000 men) (Bassett et al. 1985: 89). The Waikato campaign was the largest and most 'successful' British military operation in the colony. It defeated the Maori king's supporters and led to the confiscation of large areas of Maori land; the Waikato was largely depopulated of Maori as the supporters of the king withdrew (see McKinnon 1997: plate 38). In 1881 the Maori King leaders made their peace with the government.

At this time, much of the North Island was only sparsely peopled by Europeans. In Ngarauwahia, initially the army's headquarters, the military were among the buyers when 'sections' of land were auctioned (Latta 1963: 48). Te Awamutu also began as an army base (Barber 1984: 40–52). The fortunes of both of these towns were to be bound up with an ambitious policy of creating a buffer zone by the use of militia. In 1863, the colonial government promoted the occupation of confiscated Maori land by recruiting regiments of armed settlers. But few were able to establish themselves on the land that had been allotted to them. Of the 2,056 soldier-settlers who had been encouraged to farm the Waikato and Waipa in the 1860s, only 214 still owned farm sections in 1880, indicating a very high degree of mobility (McGibbon 2000: 327; see also Norris 1963). Gardner (1999: 50) points out that this was 'colonial mobility of a sort, but certainly not the upward mobility which new societies of the nineteenth century afforded to many of their citizens'.

Some officers, acting as recruiters, secured commissions by raising a company of one hundred men from the Australian colonies and the South Island. Others, more enterprising, brought boatloads of immigrants from their homelands – the founder of the Ohaupo settlement, halfway between Hamilton and Te Awamutu, recruited his company from Bohemia (Barber 1978: 31). According to the most recent account (McGibbon 2000: 325), 'most of those who enlisted were young, single men born in Great Britain and from the lower stratum of Victorian society, labourers and semi-skilled workers attracted by the promise of a free farm'. In addition, there were European peasant farmers and men who had formerly served either in the Royal Navy or in the army in the Crimea or in India. From a census taken at the end of 1864 showing the birthplaces of both men and their wives, it appears that while the English-born were the most numerous nationality in this region, there were relatively high numbers of Irish in comparison to the general population of New Zealand (*NZ Census* 1864, Appendix, Table B).

The government laid out town allotments of one acre, and rural sections of various sizes, depending on rank, ranging from 50 acres for an army private to 400 acres for field officers. Many settlers were young and inexperienced and lacked sufficient capital to succeed. There was little infrastructure, and isolation made goods and transport expensive, and settlers were vulnerable to attack from the dispossessed Maori. When the government cut pay for active service in 1865 and curtailed public works spending, there was no alternative employment available, and these settlements collapsed.

Those who stayed on the land for three years were able to claim a title, which many then sold, mostly to Auckland businessmen, bankers, and farmers with capital. McGibbon (2000: 327) concludes that the idea of creating instant military settlements in the Waikato that would be able to both economically support and defend themselves was, in the end, a failure, but it did have the effect of ensuring that large portions of land were now under European occupation. The departure of the British regiments from the Waikato in 1867 and the disbanding of the militia in the same year left the little settlements in a depressed state with greatly reduced populations. Yet core communities began to develop around a stable element of the pioneering small farmers who survived, along with newcomers. In the 1870s, Ngaruawahia was overtaken by Hamilton, and the advance of the railway into the Waikato brought further redistribution of population.

1.3 Thames

Thames is on the south-east coast of the Firth of Thames, on a narrow coastal strip of flat land at the western end of the Coromandel Peninsula. It is 78 kilometres north-west of Auckland by sea, though further by road and rail. Thames was settled first in the 1860s, though in a process that was dramatically different from the settlement of Wanganui.

The European population arrived suddenly and rapidly after the discovery of reefs of gold in 1867. This was still a frontier area, and infringing on Maori land was dangerous while fighting was still going on in the Bay of Plenty. Mining was held back until the Civil Commissioner for the Hauraki district purchased goldmining rights from three Maori chiefs early in 1867. The Commissioner also laid out the town of Shortland, which was to merge with a further settlement called Grahamstown developed by an Auckland businessman. Together the two townships became known as Thames (McLintock 1966, vol. 3: 386–7). The town of Shortland sprang up suddenly, and by 1868, according to the enthusiastic anonymous writer of *The Thames Miner's Guide* (Anon. 1868: 69), it had well laid out streets, a court house, custom house, post office, four banks, a theatre, five hotels, five restaurants, four churches and chapels, and several small schools. The only drawback, the writer admitted, was the mud.

Those who went to the goldfields at Thames were, by and large, people who already resided in New Zealand, especially in the Auckland province. The late 1860s were years of economic recession, and the withdrawal of imperial troops and the transfer of the seat of government to Wellington added to economic stagnation in Auckland. 'Many of the early miners were unemployed urban workers from Auckland. These men, rather than the independent alluvial miners, stayed on to provide labour as the field was converted into a capitalist industry' (Salmon 1963: 191). Transport from Auckland was cheap. Among the early miners at Thames were also many of the military settlers, from the Waikato and elsewhere, who had left their unprofitable lands. Many of the experienced alluvial miners who flocked to Thames did not stay. Quartz-crushing to extract gold required companies and investment, rather than the independent miner with a gold pan. Company mining began almost at once, in 1868, and this saw the end of the influx of itinerant miners from Westland.

Different sets of geographical boundaries used in the various estimates make it difficult to establish the population of Thames during the boom years, but there are other indications of the scale of the population increase. According to

Table 2 *Birthplaces of the population of Thames (from NZ Census, years stated)*

	NZ	Australian	English	Scots	Irish
1874	3,479	442	2,223	569	996
1878	2,588	208	1,456	355	586

the contemporary *Thames Miner's Guide* (Anon. 1868: 70), the population could 'not be less than 18,000 souls, men, women and children'. The Warden's 1870 report of the population in the field gives the figure of 15,000 (Weston 1927: 59). In 1871, the combined figures for Shortland and Grahamstown (the Thames urban township) totalled 5,789, which put it behind the five large provincial capitals, but well ahead of all other towns in the country (*NZ Census* 1871: Table 3). The historian of New Zealand goldmining, J. H. M. Salmon, concluded that:

> The expansion of the Thames goldfield had no lasting demographic effect on Auckland Province comparable with the provincial consequences of the Otago and West Coast rushes. A European population of little over 48,000 in 1867 had increased by 4,000 by 1869 and by 14,000 in 1871. General immigration was a more important factor in this growth than the settlement of experienced gold-miners from other provinces. The sudden expansion in population in the Thames area, and the decline in numbers there throughout 1869 and 1870, should be seen partly as a redistribution of provincial population and partly as evidence of the discontent of visiting alluvial miners. (Salmon 1963: 200)

Because transport from Auckland was cheap and easy, there were more commercial and business ventures in Thames than in other goldrush towns, though in other respects it was a frontier town, exhibiting the ethics of the goldfields and surrounded by hostile Maori. Table 2 shows the large drop in population in Thames between 1874 and 1878. In the 1874 Census, the total population of Thames was 8,073, but by 1878 it had fallen to 5,424. In 1878 the New Zealand-born component, at 2,588 was nearly half the total. The numbers of Australian, English, Scots, and Irish were roughly the same pattern as that of the Auckland province.[2]

The figures for religious denominations in 1874 also are informative: 3,424 Anglicans, 1,205 Presbyterians, 969 Methodists, and 1,459 Roman Catholics. The number of Irish is interesting because there is evidence from other sources to suggest that a number of immigrants came from Ulster, and several histories of Thames refer to the battles between Protestant Orangemen and the Roman Catholic population.

[2] *NZ Census*, p. 241; Auckland Province p. 228.

2 South Island

The three towns chosen to represent the South Island tour of the Mobile Unit are Arrowtown, a goldrush town; Milton, a larger farming town; and Kaitangata, a small farming and coalmining settlement.

2.1 Arrowtown

Arrowtown is situated on the banks of the Arrow River, 20 kilometres north-east of Queenstown (which is now a major tourist resort) in Central Otago. The town was founded with the discovery of gold, in either 1861 or 1862 (a matter of dispute). The effect of the goldrush was that the few pastoralists who had arrived in the Wakatipu area after 1859 were dramatically outnumbered. The *Cyclopedia of Otago and Southland* gives these details:

> By the end of January 1863 the population of Arrowtown and the gorge had swelled to 3,000. In February, 9,000 ounces were taken out by the gold escort. A calico ['canvas' or 'tent'] town was quickly established . . . By the end of 1864 Arrowtown had 19 stores and shops, ten hotels and a number of private dwellings. Gradually the town settled down and more amenities were introduced. A borough council was formed in 1874 and churches were constructed at about the same time. Avenues of trees were planted and more houses built. Schools were established and the Arrow District Hospital and a doctor's residence were constructed on the outskirts of town. (Sorrell 1999: 419)

In 1863 the Arrowtown Public School was opened (Thomson 1972: 17). We cannot ascertain what the school roll was, but Thomson says that in a 'comparatively short time a second room of wood was added'.

As the gold became exhausted, the population declined. Some families among the early arrivals settled in the town. Those singled out by the centennial history of the Lake District came from different parts of the British Isles, all via Australia (see Miller 1949: 103–11). What remained after the goldrush was over – hotels, stores, banking and postal services – reveal Arrowtown's continuing role as a town servicing the rural area. In contrast with the bustling population of some

Table 3 *Birthplaces of the population of Arrowtown (from NZ Census, years stated)*

	NZ	Australia	England	Scotland	Ireland	China
1878	150	33	44	49	49	20
1881	188	18	65	68	52	18
1886	238	37	48	39	50	21
1891	259	20	43	30	49	19

Table 4 *1891 – overseas-born males and females in Arrowtown (from NZ Census)*

Place of birth	Total	males	females
England	43	28	15
Scotland	30	21	9
Ireland	49	27	22
Australia	20	6	14
China	19	19	

Table 5 *Census returns for religion in Arrowtown (NZ Census reports, years stated)*

	Anglican	Presbyterian	Methodist	Rom. Catholic	Pagan[3]
1878	106	96	32	81	20
1881	160	106	30	81	18
1886	173	105	27	82	21

thousands in evidence during the gold days, the 1871 Census gives a total of only 208 for Arrowtown; the imbalance between sexes, 155 males to 53 females, shows that it was still a frontier town (*NZ Census* 1871: Table 3). The Census figures for 1874 and 1878 show a slow population rise from 259 to 363. In 1881, the total was 418. Men continued to outnumber women considerably, though the gap was less than in the earliest years. In 1886, of a total population of 440, 252 were male and 188 female. By 1891, with a total population of 426, the figures of 224 males to 202 females suggest that Arrowtown was becoming a settled community.

Tables 3–5, reveal the mixture of immigrants from Australia, England, Scotland, and Ireland that settled in Arrowtown, with no one group seeming to predominate.

Mobile Unit speakers from Arrowtown have figured in a number of publications on New Zealand English (for example, see Trudgill et al. 1998; Woods 1997).

2.2 *Milton*

Milton is located in the centre of the Tokomairiro plain, 57 kilometres south-west of Dunedin and 27 kilometres north-east of Balclutha. In 1856, land in the vicinity of the present town began to be settled, a flour mill was built in 1857, and 'Milltown' came into being after 25 acres was cut up into town lots in 1860

[3] The term 'Pagan' was used in the Census for 1886 and 1891. In 1896 it was changed to 'Buddhists, Confucians and etc.'

(McLintock 1966, vol. 2: 558). When the town was surveyed, streets were named after Scottish and English poets, and in this naming a link was made with the poet John Milton. The official name was changed to 'Milton' in 1872.

According to the centennial history of Tokomairiro, 'by far the greater majority of settlers in the district were of Scottish descent, possessing those characteristics of the Scot which have made history throughout the world' (Sumpter and Lewis 1940: 13). The authors of this work suggested that these characteristics possibly accounted for 'a reluctance to put all the eggs in one basket', with mixed farming and some industry providing a basis for 'solid, unspectacular prosperity'. In the pioneering period, the town 'was a place of sawmills, a flour mill, and shopkeepers, while most settlers were small holders and part-time labourers' (Sorrell 1999: 547).

There is evidence that communal activities were under way in 1856 when an early ploughing contest took place: 'The pride of the Scottish ploughman and his natural love of animals was not long in showing itself in the early pioneers of the Tokomairiro district to whom must go the honour of instituting the first ploughing match in Otago' (Sumpter and Lewis 1940: 24). Almost every Mobile Unit speaker from Milton described these annual ploughing matches. A Farmers' Club was formed in 1866.

The predominantly Presbyterian district was initially part of the extensive parish of Dr Thomas Burns of Dunedin, and the first service was held in 1851. In 1854, with the arrival of two more Scottish ministers, regular services were held every three weeks and the first church was built. Milton became a parish in 1859 (Milton Borough Council 1966: 'Churchlife'). In 1856, the first school was established; this early development was seen by local historians as typically Scots: 'With their predominant Scottish background, the pioneers on the Plain, having established their religion, showed a characteristic zeal for education' (Milton Borough Council 1966: 'Education'). Church and school were associated; the first schoolmaster was also the Sabbath schoolteacher and the precentor.

In the 1860s with the Otago goldrush, prosperity grew out of providing the goldfields with goods and services. A post office was opened about 1862, as was a branch of the Bank of New Zealand, and then a branch of the Bank of Otago in 1863. Milton became an incorporated town in 1866, with an elected mayor and council. By 1871, the population of Milton was recorded as 797, the most substantial town south of Dunedin (*NZ Census* 1871: Table 3). This figure had grown to 977 in 1874 (*NZ Census* 1874: 96).

To what extent did the goldfields also bring new arrivals from a wider background than the predominantly Scots community of the earliest years? Government-assisted immigration of the mid-1870s brought higher numbers of Irish to New Zealand. Birthplaces of persons in the borough of Milton given in the New Zealand Census in 1878 show that the total population had risen to 1,161 but, as Table 6 shows, despite the borough's association with the goldfields, only 77 of the population were of Irish birth, compared with almost four times as many (293) born in Scotland, and 178 born in England. Almost all the others

Table 6 *Birthplaces of the population of Milton (from NZ Census, years stated)*

	NZ	Scotland	England	Ireland	Australia
1874	432	254	141	57	58
1878	544	293	178	77	46
1881	676	251	179	116	42
1886	716	215	127	85	20

Table 7 *Census returns for religion in Milton (years stated)*

	Presbyterian	Anglican	Roman Catholic	Wesleyan Methodist
1878	567	398	87	30
1881	642	344	137	81
1886	550	340	122	98
1891	572	245	118	136

were of New Zealand birth (544). According to the Mobile Unit speakers, the goldfields attracted some people from Milton, but many miners, including the Chinese, came to Milton for supplies. Some men recorded by the Mobile Unit described this trade in enthusiastic detail.

The 1881 Census shows a population of 1,287 in Milton. The New Zealand-born component had risen further, but people of Scottish birth still outnumbered the combined number of those born in England and Ireland. The next Census, in 1886, shows a slight decline in the total population but the basic pattern of an increasing New Zealand-born component, with Scots predominating among the foreign-born, still prevails.

Judging by church membership, local historians have good reasons for continuing to stress Milton's link with Scotland. In 1863, a new and larger Presbyterian church was built. The Anglicans replaced their small chapel, built in 1860, with a church dedicated by Bishop Selwyn in 1866. A priest with a very extensive district held services for Roman Catholics, initially in a store, with no church being built until 1869 (Sumpter and Lewis 1940: 52). Table 7 gives the census figures for religion from 1878 to 1891, and shows that, of the three major denominations, Presbyterians still predominated, followed by members of the Church of England and Roman Catholics. Wesleyan Methodists were well behind the other three.

The old school became the Tokomairiro Grammar School in 1869, making Milton an early centre for secondary education in the region. The name was changed to Tokomairiro District High School in 1877. The birthplaces – all in Scotland, of masters and headmasters for the first fifty years are worth noting:

Alexander Ayson (1856–66) born in Glenshee in Perthshire; David Ross (1866–74), from the Highlands, educated in Edinburgh as a teacher in English and Gaelic; William A. McD. Malcolm (1874–80), born at Stromness in Orkney; and James Reid (1880–1906), born at Carmylie, Forfarshire (Scholefield and Forsyth 1956: 23–6).

In the 1880s and 1890s, some of the town's long-standing architectural features appeared. The substantial stone District High School was built in 1880. A Catholic convent school opened for some ninety children in 1890 (Sorrell 1999: 547). The large stone Presbyterian church was built in 1889. The *Cyclopedia of New Zealand*, published in 1905, lists Presbyterian, Anglican, Roman Catholic, and Wesleyan churches, and two public halls, as well as woollen mills, flour mills, a brewery, a fellmongery, brick works, pottery works, and a bacon factory. Milton is described in the *Cyclopedia* as a prosperous town, which had never fallen into debt, but 'all along made steady progress'; it was known to be 'one of the cleanest and most complete towns in New Zealand' (vol. 4: 662).

2.3 Kaitangata

Kaitangata is located 13 kilometres south-east of Balclutha, in the lower Clutha basin. The land where the town is located was marked as 'Site for a Village' when the land in the Otago Block between the Clutha and Tokomairiro rivers was surveyed in 1847. European settlement in the district began at Port Molyneux in 1849 and continued at Inch Clutha, with the first settler taking up land at Kaitangata in 1855 (McLintock 1966, vol. 2: 201).

Kaitangata does not appear in the tables of boroughs summarised in the New Zealand Census until 1891; the major source for information given here is Bamford (1982). One difficulty is that data from the early years come from different sources so the various figures are not comparable. In 1854, Inch Clutha and the north bank of the Matau River, the site of the future town of Kaitangata, had a population of 75. The region was mostly agricultural, the population widely dispersed, and there was the two-to-one male-to-female ratio characteristic of pioneering settlements (Bamford 1982: 89). The development of the goldfields at Gabriel's Gully stimulated the district's growth, and in 1862, the first sale of Kaitangata town sections took place. In 1864, the Electoral District of Matau, Kaitangata, and Inch Clutha had a population of 656, made up of 403 males and 253 females. A primary school opened in a former storeroom in 1866, with a roll of about 40. This was replaced by a new school room and teacher's residence in 1872 (Rutherford 1966: 7–9). The earliest Presbyterian services were held in 1856, according to the centennial history of the Kaitangata Presbyterian Church, and in 1863 a church was opened in the charge of a minister newly arrived from Scotland (Anon. 1960: 27). Growth was slow; it is estimated that the population of the town of Kaitangata in the early 1870s was less than one hundred.

This was to change rapidly when coalmining came into full force in the area. Although coal had been reported in the locality as early as 1844, it was some time

Table 8 *Birthplaces of the population of Kaitangata in 1891 (from NZ Census)*

	NZ	Scotland	England	Ireland	Australia
1891	639	300	133	45	11

before communications were sufficiently developed to make transportion of the coal possible. Coalmines were opened near the town in 1869 and 1870. In 1872, the Kaitangata Coal Company was set up, to become the Kaitangata Railway and Coal Company in 1875, with a branch line built to link the mine with the main railway line in 1876. The population grew rapidly, though by goldfields' standards, this was only a minor boom: 1878, 135; 1881, 394; 1886, 925; 1891, 1145; 1896, 1362 (Bamford 1982: table).

Two hotels and several stores were built in the 1870s. In 1882, the Kaitangata Town District was formed, and Kaitangata was proclaimed a borough in 1887 (Sorrell 1999: 502).

The 1891 Census is the first one to give detailed information about the origins of the population of Kaitangata (see Table 8).

Religious affiliations recorded by the 1891 Census in Kaitangata were: Presbyterian, 669; Wesleyan Methodist, 73; Roman Catholic, 69; Baptist, 68; Church of England, 156; Church of Christ, 52; and Christadelphian, 28. The very high number of Presbyterians support the categorisation of Kaitangata as a Scottish town.

Two of the Mobile Unit speakers from Kaitangata were grandchildren of the first settlers in the 1850s. Miss Aitchison's grandfather, William Aitchison, was the first permanent European settler in the area. It was also on his property that coal was first discovered. Mrs Christina Bissett's grandfather, Mr Darling, befriended Mr Smaill, another immigrant from Edinburgh, on the ship to New Zealand. They bought land together at Kaitangata and the families worked closely together on this land.

3 Works consulted for this appendix

Anon. 1868, *The Thames Miner's Guide: with Maps*, Auckland: E. Wayt (reprint by Capper Press, Christchurch, 1975).

Anon. 1960, *Kaitangata Presbyterian Church, 1860–1960*, Balclutha: Clutha Leader Print.

Bamford, Tony 1982, '*Black Diamond City': A History of Kaitangata Mines, Miners, and Community 1860–1913*, BA Hons Thesis, University of Otago, Dunedin.

Barber, L. H. 1978, *The View from Pirongia: The History of Waipa County*, Te Awamutu: Ray Richards Publisher and Waipa County Council.

1984, *Frontier Town: A History of Te Awamutu, 1884–1894*, Te Awamutu and Auckland: Ray Richards Publisher and Te Awamutu Borough Council.

Bassett, J., Sinclair, K., and Stenson, M. 1985, *The Story of New Zealand*, Auckland: Reed Methuen.

Chapple, L. J. B. and Veitch, H. C. 1939, *Wanganui*, Hawera Star and Wanganui Historical Committee.

Cyclopedia of New Zealand, Vol. 4: *Otago and Southland Provincial Districts* 1905, Christchurch: Cyclopedia Co.

Cyclopedia of New Zealand 1897–1908, Wellington: Cyclopedia Co.

Gardner, W. J. 1999, *Where they Lived: Studies in Local, Regional and Social History*, Christchurch: Regional Press.

Gibbons, P. J. 1977, *Astride the River: A History of Hamilton*, Hamilton: Whitcoulls and Hamilton City Council.

Latta, A. M. 1963, *Meeting of the Waters: The Story of Ngaruawahia, 1863–1963*, Ngaruawahia: Ngaruawahia Borough Council.

McGibbon, I. (ed.) 2000, *The Oxford Companion to New Zealand Military History*, Auckland: Oxford University Press.

McKinnon, Malcolm (ed.) 1997, *New Zealand Historical Atlas*, Auckland: Bateman.

McLintock A. H. (ed.) 1966, *An Encyclopedia of New Zealand*, 3 vols., Wellington: Government Printer.

Miller, F. W. G. 1949, *Golden Days of Lake County*, Dunedin: Whitcombe and Tombs.

Milton Borough Council, Centennial Historical Subcommittee 1966, *Milton Borough Centenary, 1866–1966*, Milton: Milton Borough Council.

Norris, H. C. M. 1963, *Armed Settlers: The Story of the Founding of Hamilton, New Zealand, 1864–1874*, 2nd ed., Hamilton: Paul's Book Arcade (1st ed. 1956).

Reid, V. H. 1940, *A Short Historical Account of Wanganui, Wellington Province*, MA Thesis, Canterbury College, University of New Zealand, Christchurch.

Rutherford, Alma 1966, *From Humble Beginnings: The Story of Kaitangata, Wangaloa and Matau Schools, 1866–1966*, Balclutha: Centennial Celebrations Committee of the Schools.

Salmon, J. H. M. 1963, *A History of Goldmining in New Zealand*, Wellington: Government Printer.

Scholefield, Guy and Forsyth, David (eds.) 1956, *The History of the Tokomairiro District High School, 1856–1956*, Milton: Bruce Herald.

Smart, M. J. G. and Bates, A. P. 1972, *The Wanganui Story*, Wanganui: Wanganui Newspapers.

Sorrell, Paul (ed.) 1999, *The Cyclopedia of Otago and Southland*, Vol. 1, Dunedin: Dunedin City Council.

Sumpter D. J. and Lewis, J. J. 1940, *Faith and Toil: The Story of Tokomairiro*, Dunedin: Whitcombe and Tombs.

Taylor, R. 1868, *Past and Present of New Zealand*, London: William McIntosh; Wanganui: Henry Ireson Jones.

Thomson, John Bell 1972, *Swiftly Flows the Arrow: The Story of Arrowtown and its District*, Dunedin: J. McIndoe.

Trudgill, Peter, Gordon, Elizabeth, and Lewis, Gillian 1998, 'New dialect formation and Southern Hemisphere English: The New Zealand short front vowels', *Journal of Sociolinguistics* 2.1: 35–51.

Volkerling, R. H. and Stewart, K. L. 1986, *From Sand to Papa: A History of the Wanganui Country*, Wanganui: Wanganui County Council.

Wards, Ian 1968, *The Shadow of the Land: A Study of British Policy and Racial Conflict in New Zealand, 1832–1852*, Wellington: Department of Internal Affairs.

Weston, F. W. 1927, *Diamond Jubilee Souvenir, The Thames Goldfields: A History from Pre-Proclamation Times to 1927, Gathered from Authentic Documents and Living Witnesses*, Thames Star.

Woods, Nicola 1997, 'The formation and development of New Zealand English: Interaction of gender-related variation and language change', *Journal of Sociolinguistics* 1: 95–125.

Appendix 3 Maps

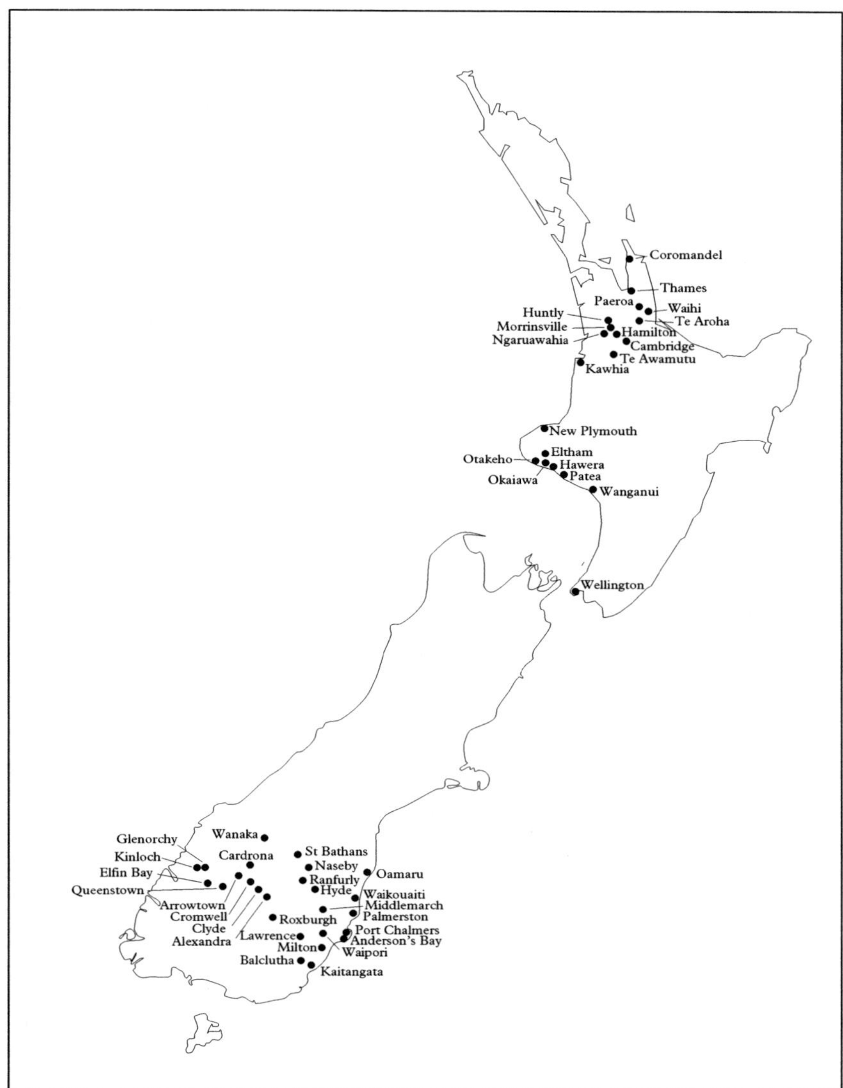

Map 1. Locations visited by the Mobile Unit

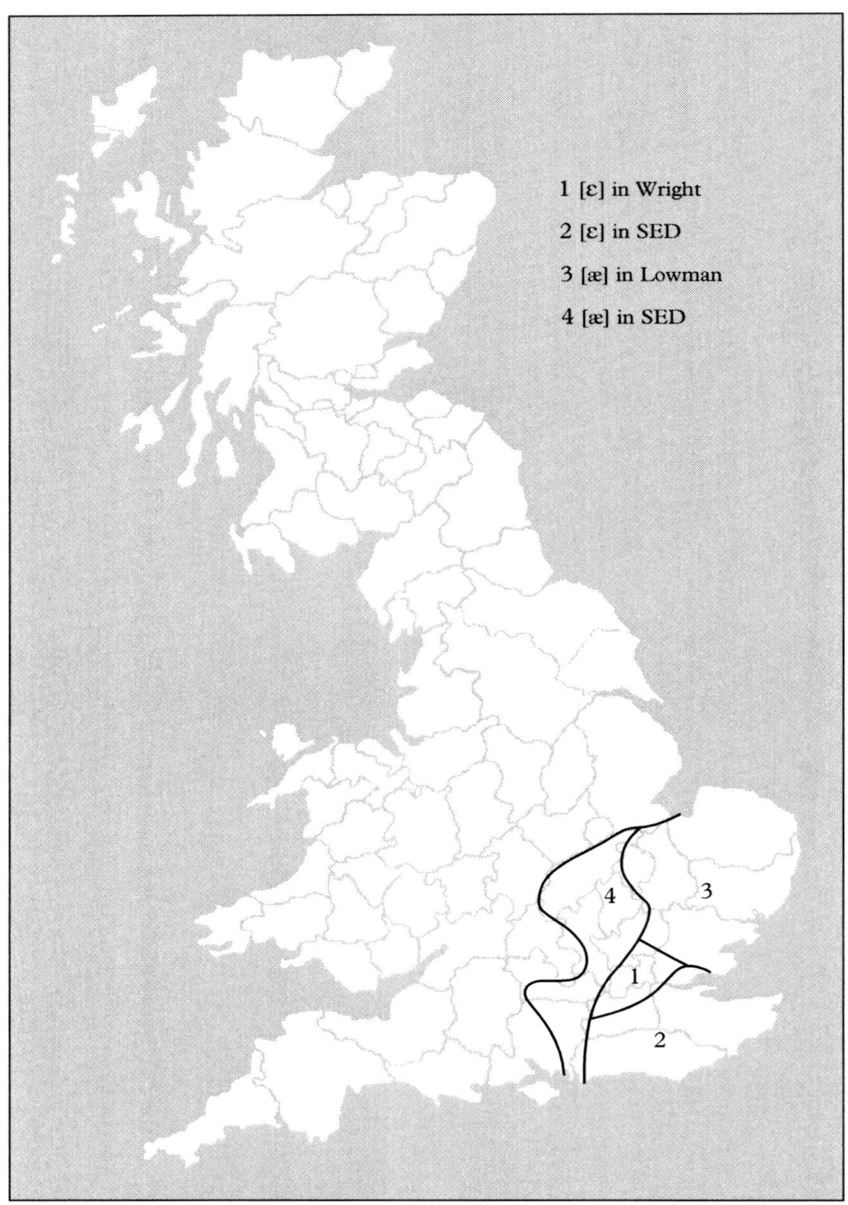

Map 2. The TRAP vowel

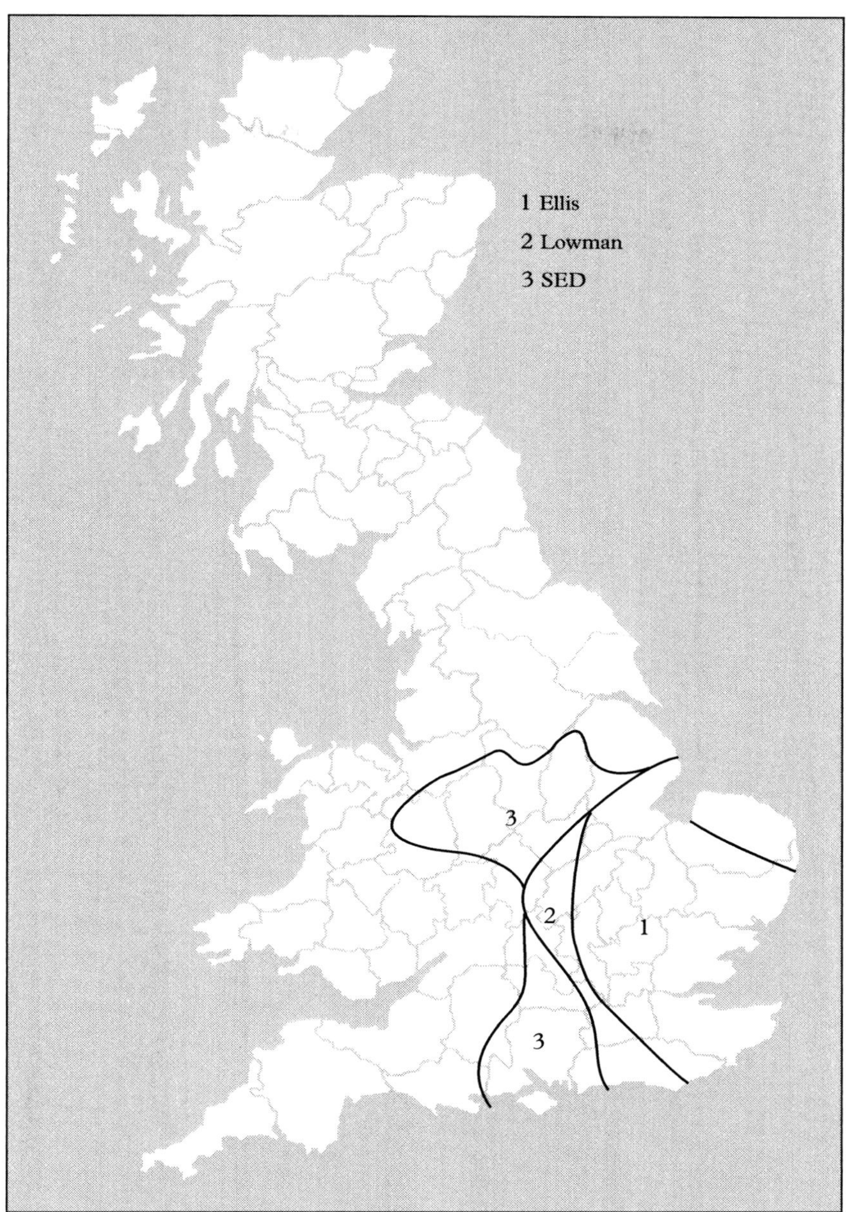

Map 3a. Diphthong shift in MOUTH

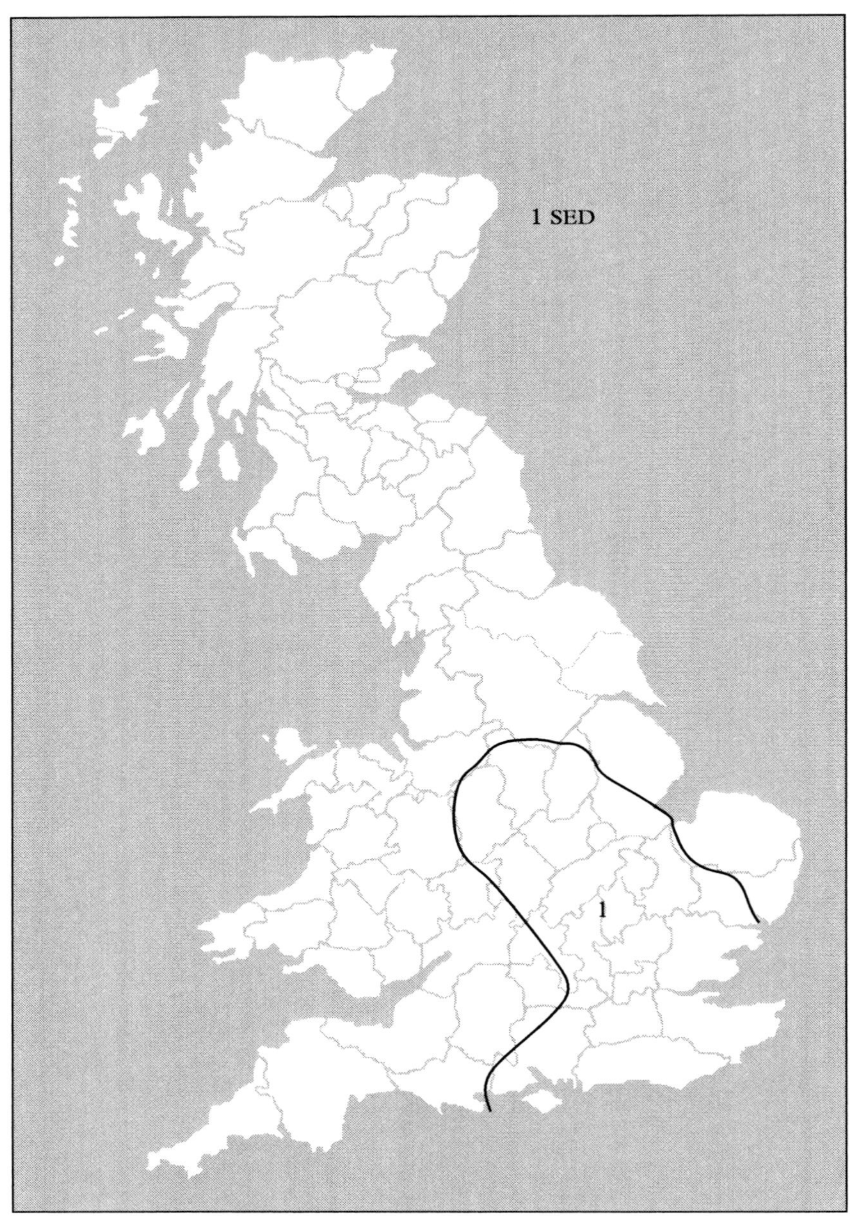

Map 3b. Diphthong shift in PRICE

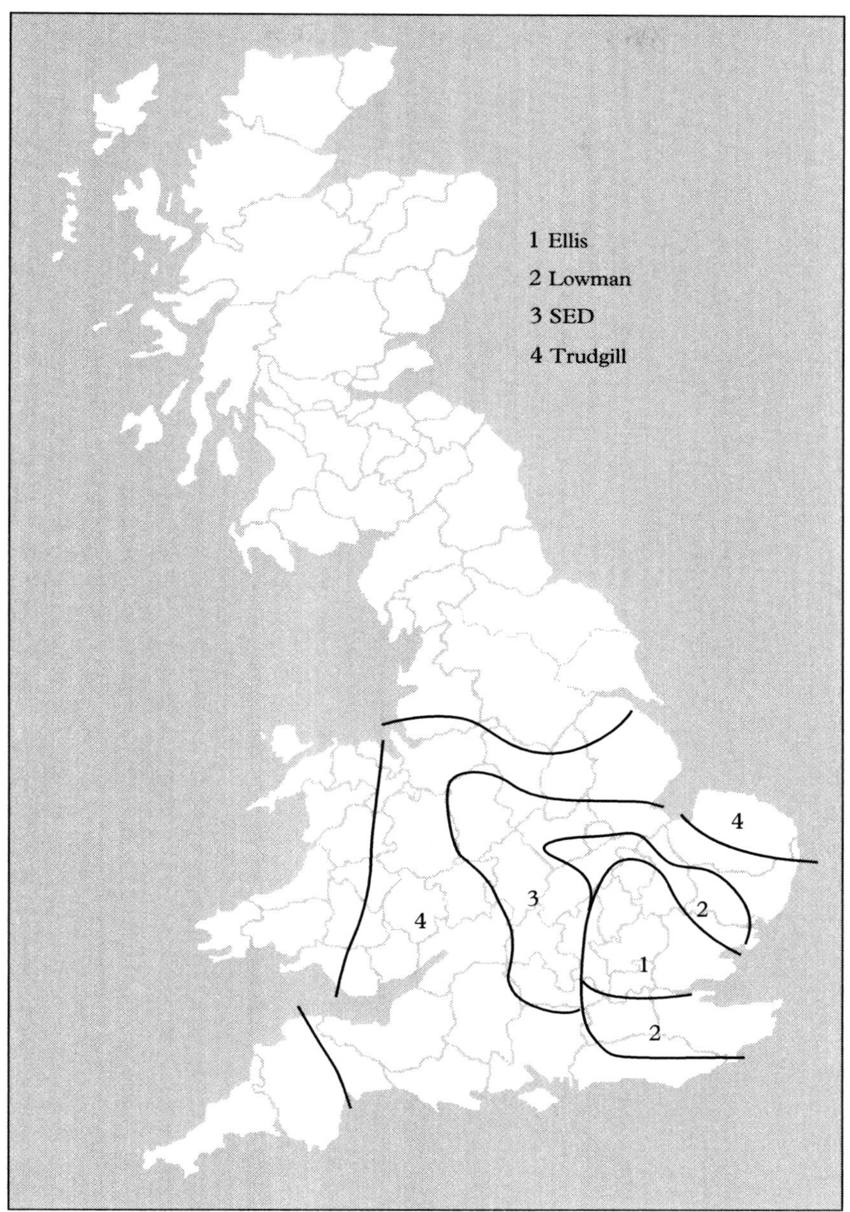

Map 3c. Long Mid Diphthonging in FACE

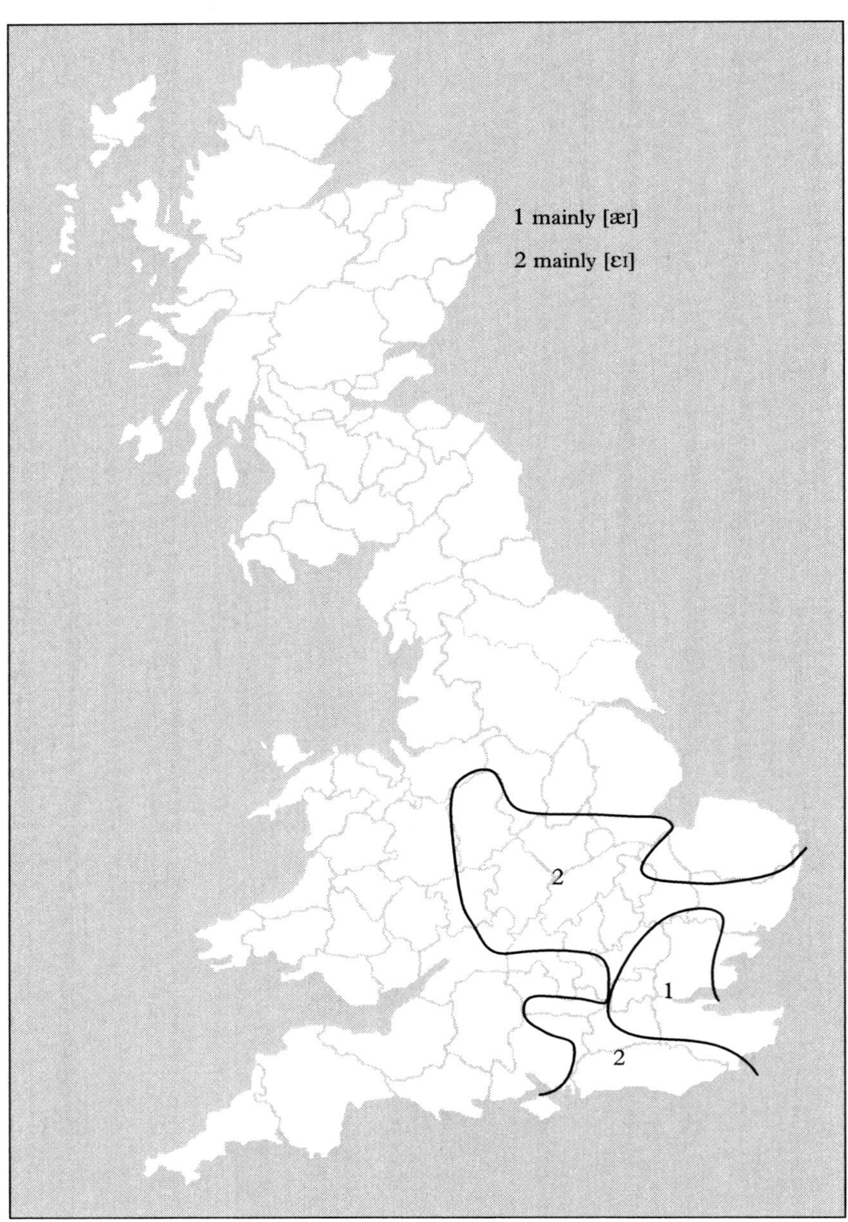

Map 3d. Diphthong shift in FACE

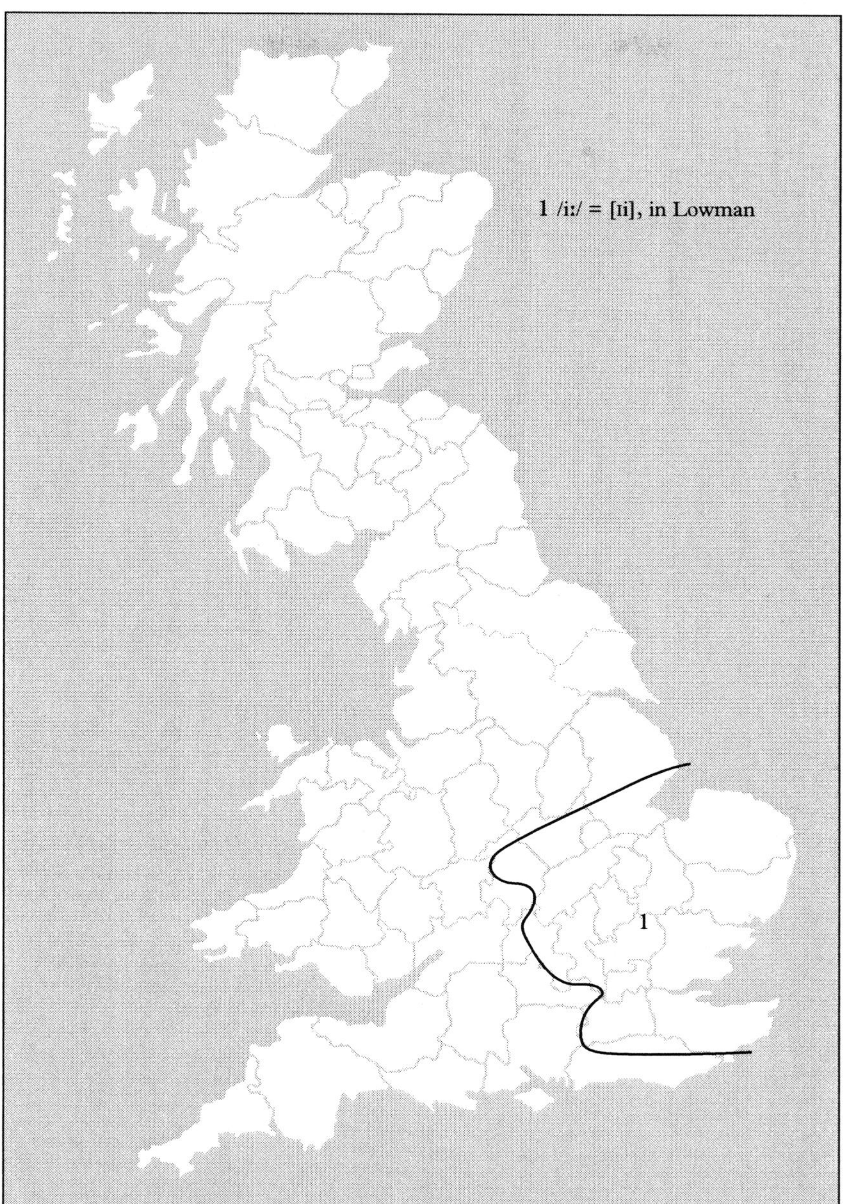

Map 3e. The FLEECE vowel

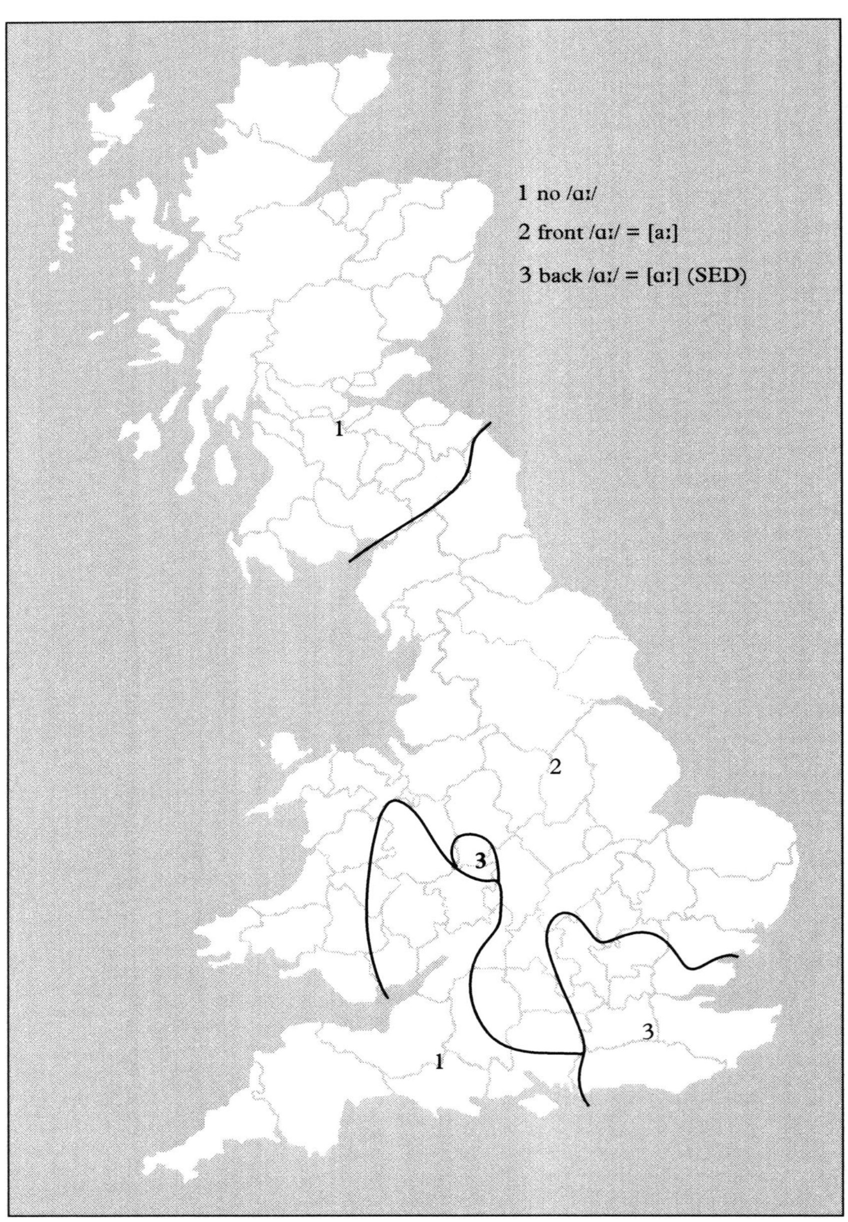

Map 4. The START vowel

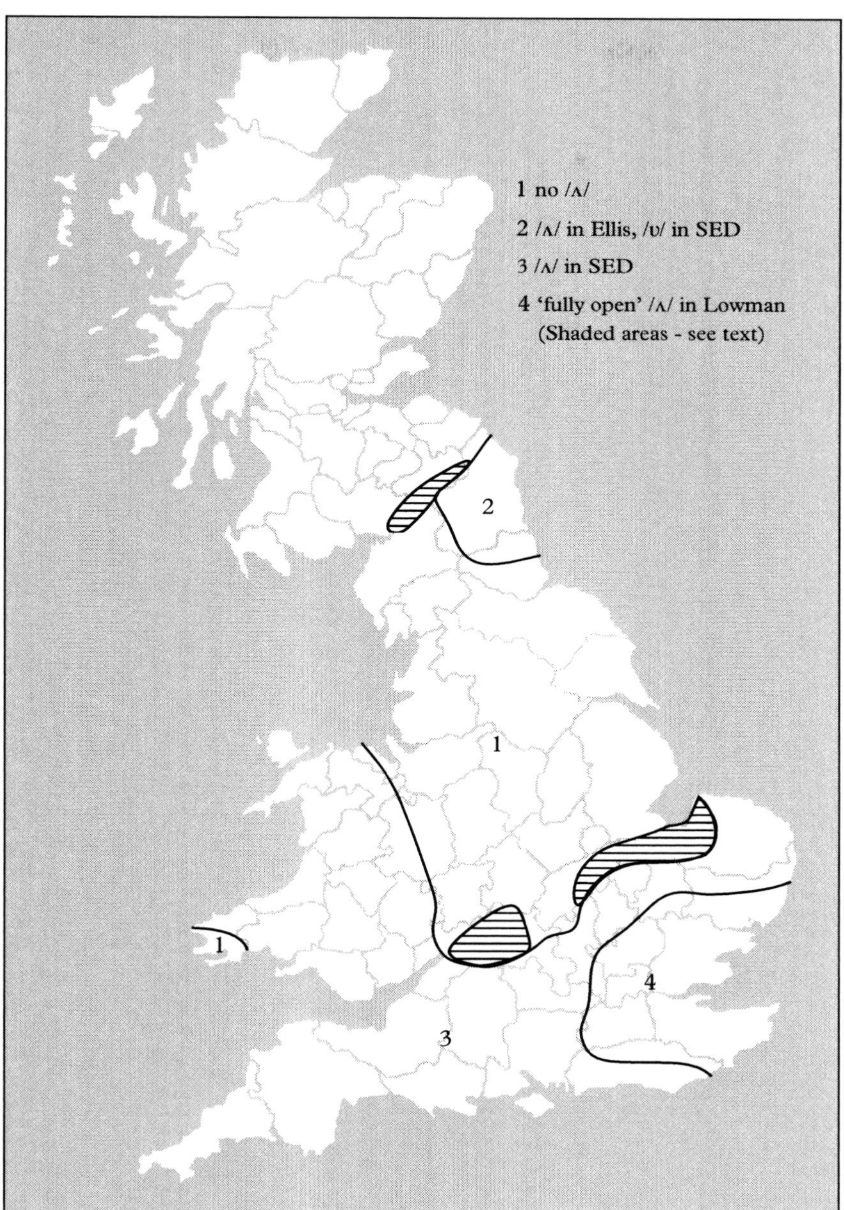

Map 5. The STRUT vowel

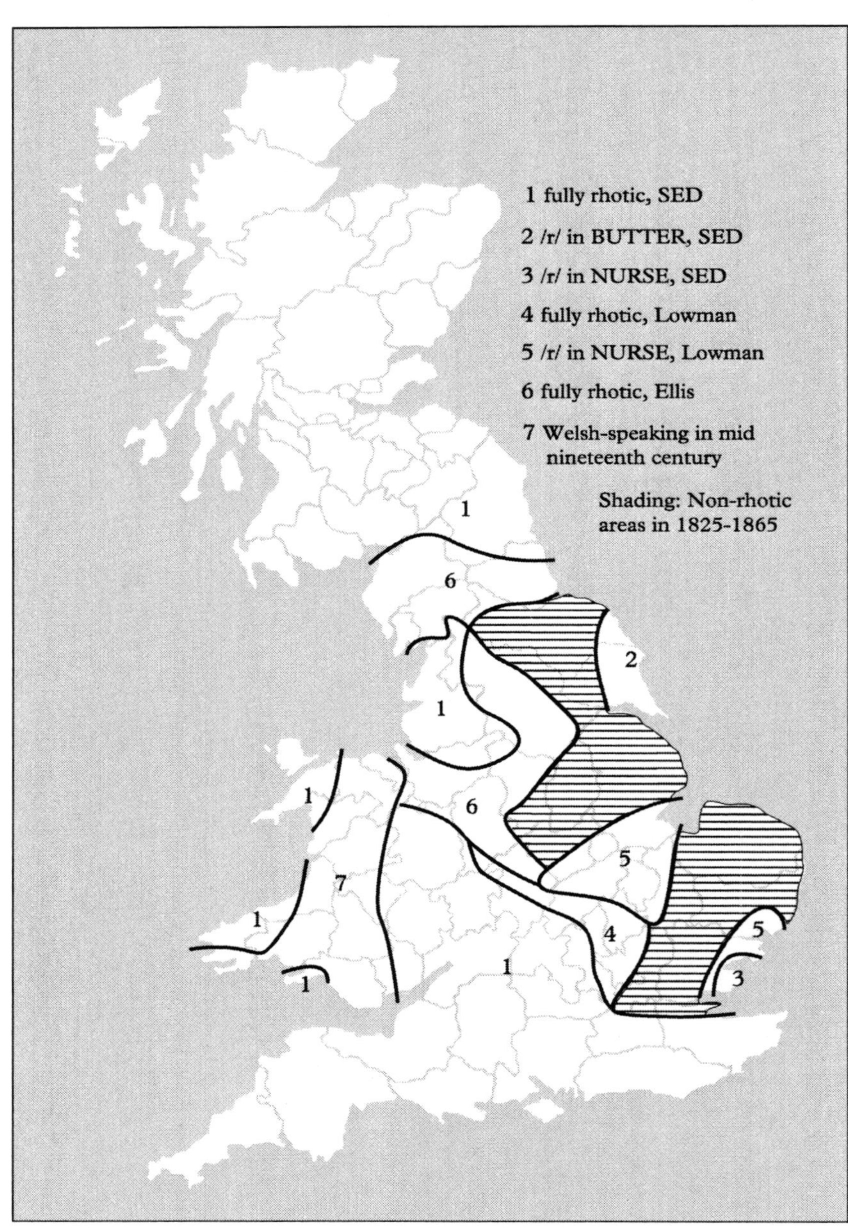

Map 6. Rhoticity

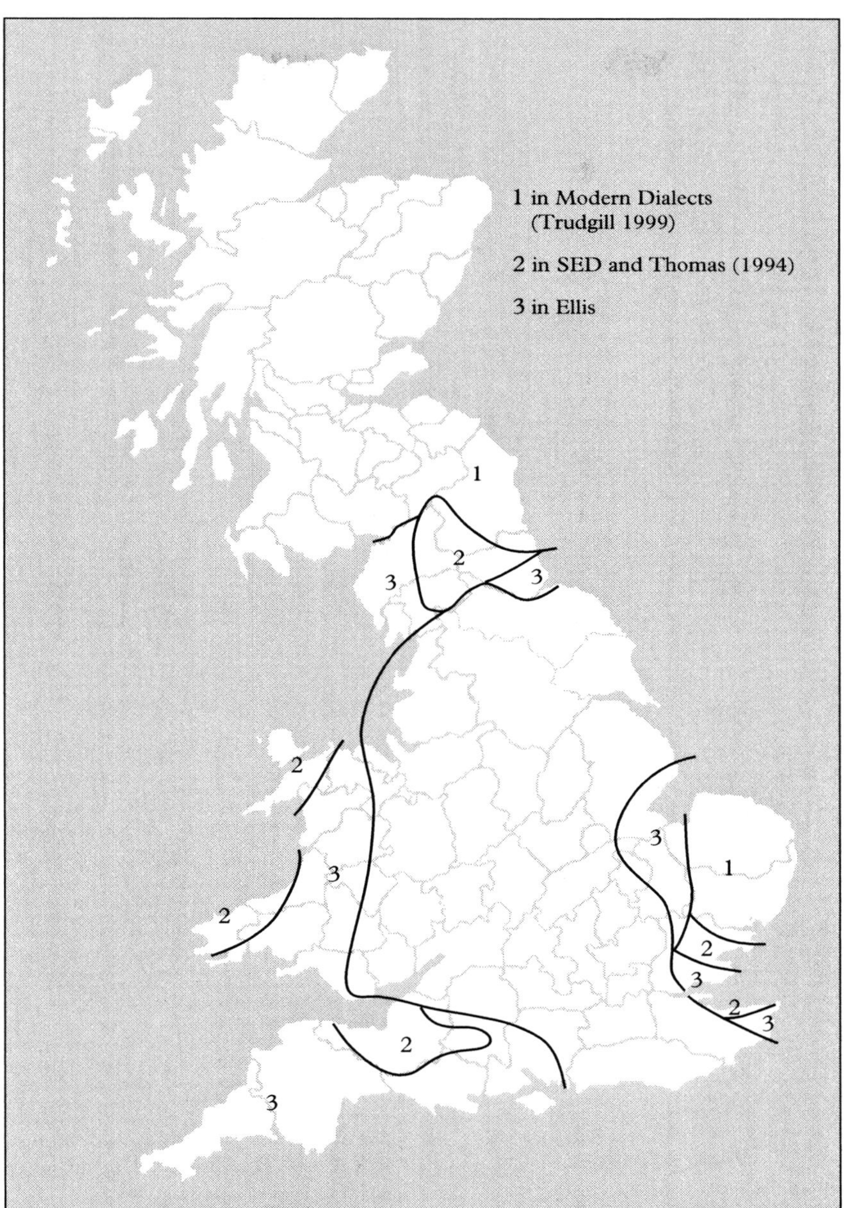

Map 7. h-retention

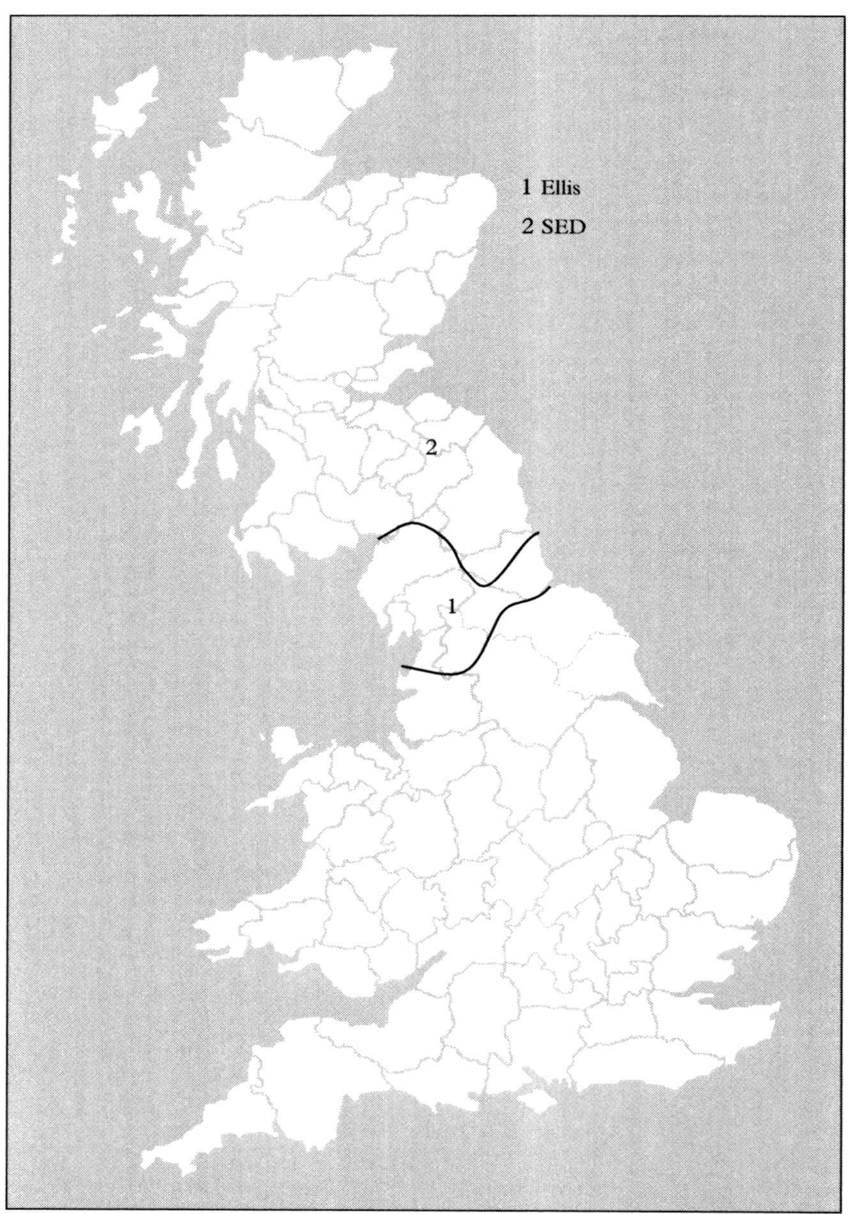

Map 8. /hw/-retention

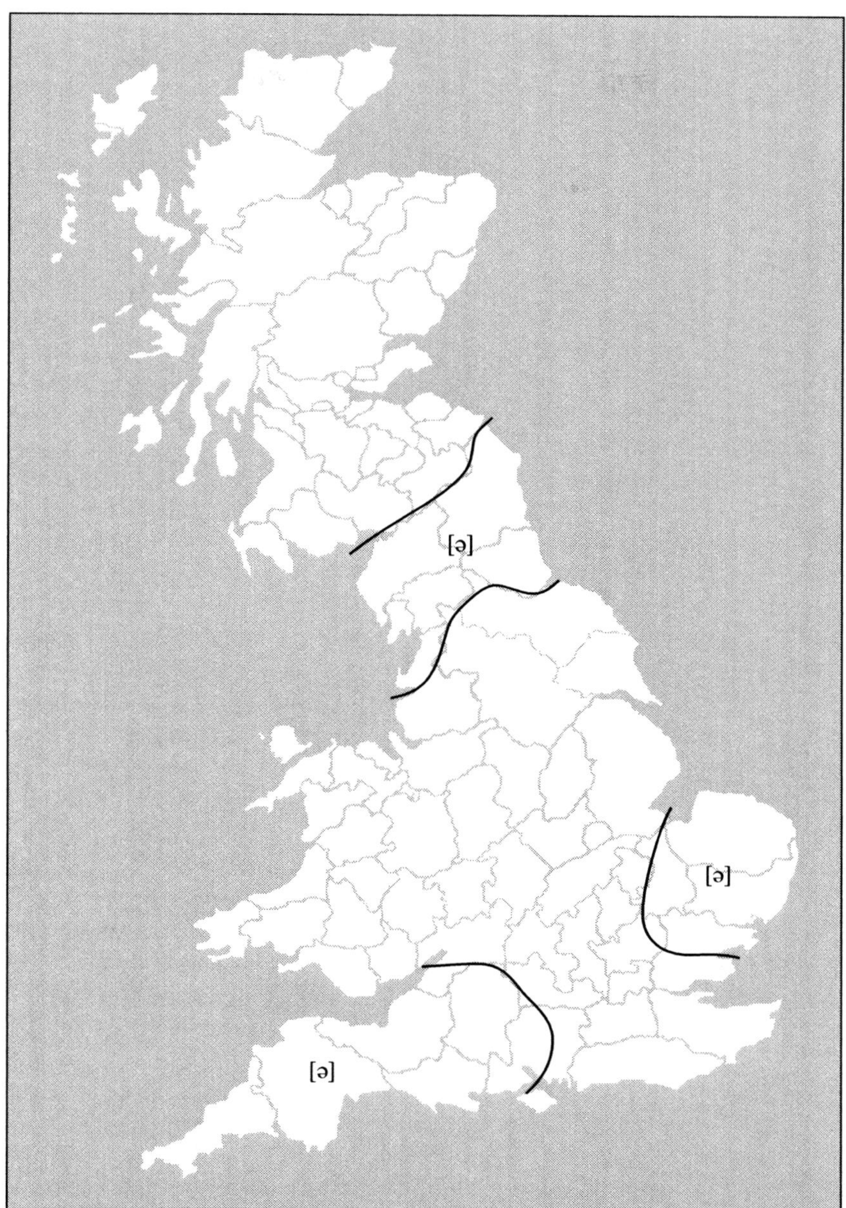

Map 9. Weak Vowel Merger

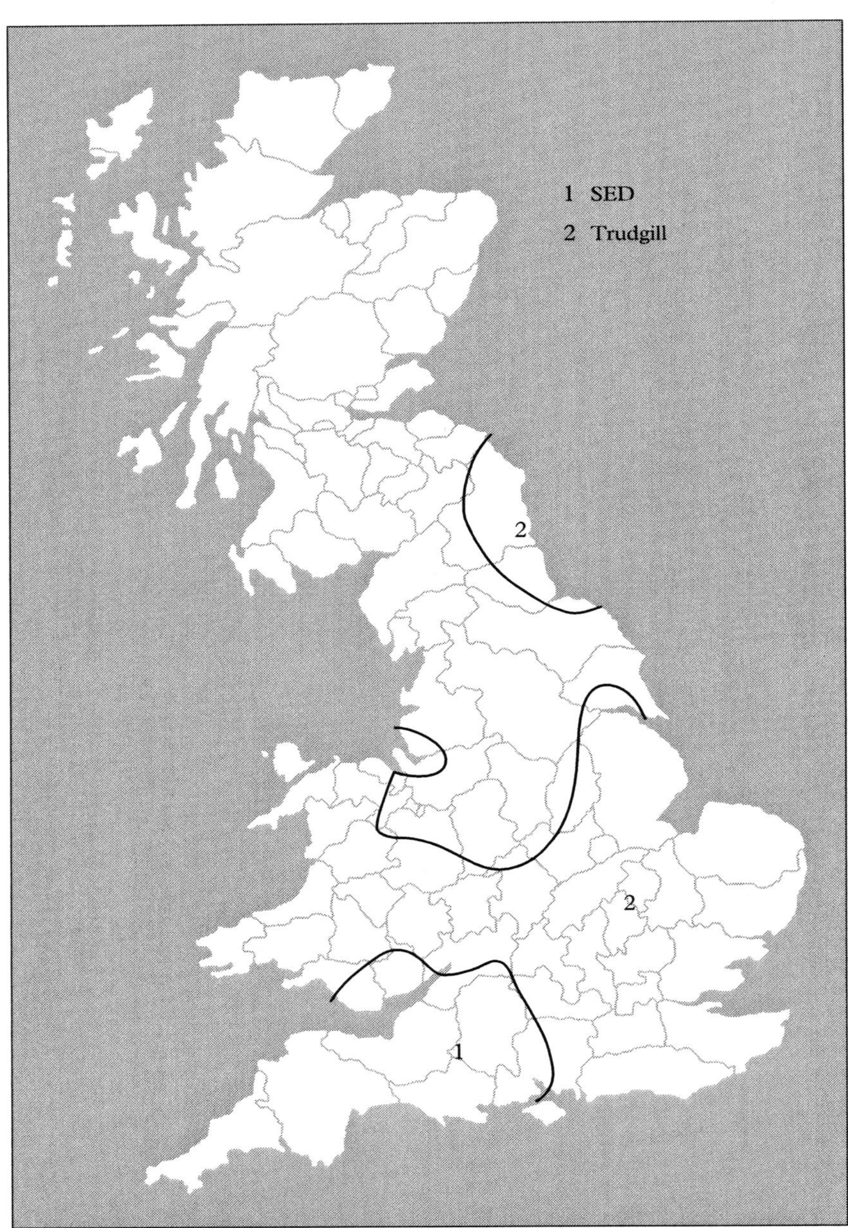

Map 10. *Happ*Y-tensing

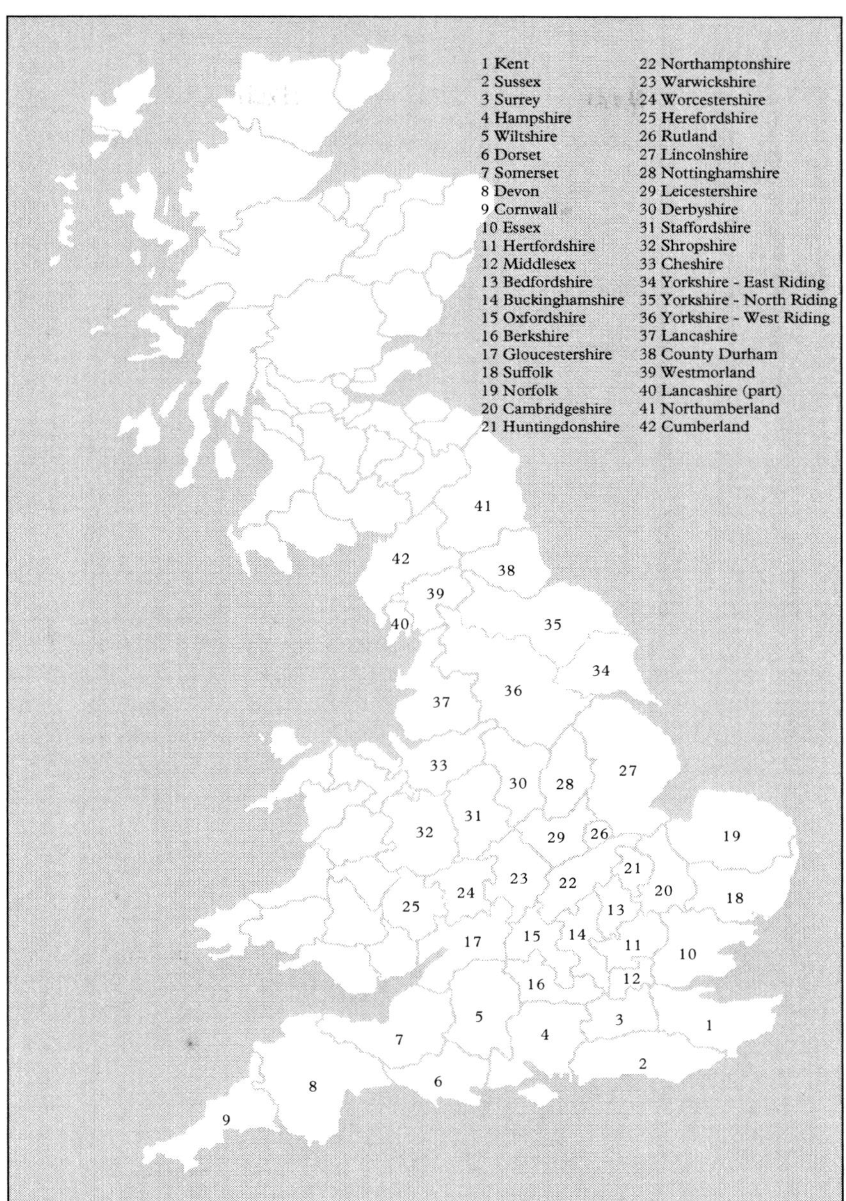
1 Kent
2 Sussex
3 Surrey
4 Hampshire
5 Wiltshire
6 Dorset
7 Somerset
8 Devon
9 Cornwall
10 Essex
11 Hertfordshire
12 Middlesex
13 Bedfordshire
14 Buckinghamshire
15 Oxfordshire
16 Berkshire
17 Gloucestershire
18 Suffolk
19 Norfolk
20 Cambridgeshire
21 Huntingdonshire
22 Northamptonshire
23 Warwickshire
24 Worcestershire
25 Herefordshire
26 Rutland
27 Lincolnshire
28 Nottinghamshire
29 Leicestershire
30 Derbyshire
31 Staffordshire
32 Shropshire
33 Cheshire
34 Yorkshire - East Riding
35 Yorkshire - North Riding
36 Yorkshire - West Riding
37 Lancashire
38 County Durham
39 Westmorland
40 Lancashire (part)
41 Northumberland
42 Cumberland
41
42
38
39
40
35
34
36
37
33
27
30
28
31
32
29
26
19
21
23
22
24
20
18
25
13
15
14
17
11
10
12
16
5
3
1
7
4
2
8
6
9

Map 11. The traditional counties of England

Appendix 4 Seven Mobile Unit speakers born outside New Zealand

Data from these speakers are not included in the various analyses reported elsewhere in this book. For an explanation of terms used and a fuller description of the variables, see Chapter 6.

1 Australia

Mr George Firth was born in Tasmania in 1875 and came to New Zealand in his early twenties. His speech does not stand out from that of other Mobile Unit speakers of comparable age. Like the New Zealand-born, Mr Firth has some relatively advanced features; he uses raised DRESS and TRAP vowels and diphthong-shifted MOUTH and PRICE vowels, he is non-rhotic and uses schwa in unstressed syllables. Like some New Zealand-born speakers, he also has some relatively conservative features, such as the THOUGHT vowel in *off*, *across* and so on. Unlike most modern Australian speakers, but like other New Zealand-born Mobile Unit speakers, he uses the START vowel in the DANCE class of words.

2 Scotland

Mrs Susan McFarlane was born in Scotland around 1845 and came to New Zealand aged thirty-three. Her speech differs considerably from that of the New Zealand-born Mobile Unit speakers of comparable age (see Trudgill, Maclagan and Lewis 2003). Unlike the New Zealand speakers, she has a fully centralised KIT vowel, realised as [ɜ ~ ɘ ~ ə], she uses [x] in words like *wrought* (= *worked*) rather than only in proper names like *Cochrane*, and her START and TRAP vowels are not distinct (only three other Mobile Unit speakers have this feature, all with Scottish parents). Like fourteen of the New Zealand-born speakers, all but one with Scottish parents, she has a three-way split in the NURSE vowel (so that *fir*, *fern*, and *fur* all have different vowels), but unlike most of the other speakers with this feature, she is consistent in making the three-way distinction; and, finally, like a significant minority of New Zealand-born speakers (mostly with Scottish parents), her FOOT and GOOSE vowels are not distinct.

3 Ireland

Mr John Prendergast was born in Ireland around 1857 and came to New Zealand aged twenty. Unlike other speakers in the Mobile Unit archive, he has the /w ~ v/ merger variably, pronouncing *volunteer* as 'wolunteer', he does not distinguish STRUT and FOOT, has a very back pronunciation of START and uses [ɔɹ ~ ʌɹ] for the NURSE vowel. He uses clear /l/ in all positions (like some of the other Mobile Unit speakers of Irish parentage) and dental /t/ and /d/.

Mr Tom Cullinan was also born in Ireland and came to New Zealand as a young man in 1875. We do not have a birthdate, but he was probably born in the very early 1860s. His speech sounds very Irish, but his phonology has more in common with the New Zealand-born Mobile Unit speakers than does Mr Prendergast's. Like Mr Prendergast, he uses dental /t/ and /d/, but unlike him he variably produces MOUTH and PRICE with diphthong shift.

Mr John (Jack) Thompson was born in 1870, the youngest of the Irish-born Mobile Unit speakers. He came to New Zealand aged approximately twenty, having spent time in Tasmania. His DRESS vowel is much less raised than New Zealand-born speakers of comparable age and, unlike the New Zealand speakers, he has a fully back GOOSE vowel. His START vowel is fronter than the New Zealand speakers. He has a high degree of h-drop and does not distinguish /w/ and /hw/; neither of these features is compatible with his Irish origins. He has diphthong shift and glide weakening to a degree similar to his New Zealand-born peers and is overall less different from the New Zealand born than are the other two Irish-born speakers.

4 England

Mr Alfred Eccles was born in England (in Torquay, Devon) in 1880 and came to New Zealand aged twenty. He retains no trace of a Devonshire accent, but rather has an old-fashioned near Received Pronunciation (RP) accent. Unlike most New Zealand-born Mobile Unit speakers of comparable age, he has a fully back GOOSE vowel and retains KIT in unstressed syllables and in the final syllable of *happ*Y words. He displays much less diphthong shift and glide weakening in his closing diphthongs than his New Zealand-born peers.

Rev. Noel Benham was also born in England, twenty years later than Mr Eccles, in 1900. He also came to New Zealand aged twenty. He is one of the youngest speakers we have analysed. Unlike Mr Eccles, he has some tokens of schwa in unstressed syllables and uses FLEECE in the final syllable of *happ*Y (*happ*Y-tensing). He also has some centralisation of KIT. However he still uses less diphthong shift and glide weakening than his New Zealand-born peers, and his STRUT vowel is less fronted than theirs.

Appendix 5 Acoustic vowel charts for the ten speakers included in the acoustic analysis

Speaker	Birthdate	Birthplace	Island
Mrs Sarah Hollis	1864	Waihi	North Island
Miss MaryAnn Turnbull	1875	Morrinsville	North Island
Mrs Emily Cruickshank	1876	Rangiaowhia	North Island
Mrs Annie Hamilton	1877	Arrowtown	South Island
Mrs Catherine Dudley	1886	Cardrona/Arrowtown	South Island
Mr William Dufty	1865	Parawai/Thames	North Island
Mr Peter Mason	1873	Balclutha	South Island
Mr John Edgar	1874	Tokotea/Coromandel	North Island
Mr James McKinlay	1875	Lawrence	South Island
Mr Frank Bertram	1879	Rangiaowhia	North Island

Mrs Hollis normalised, 1864

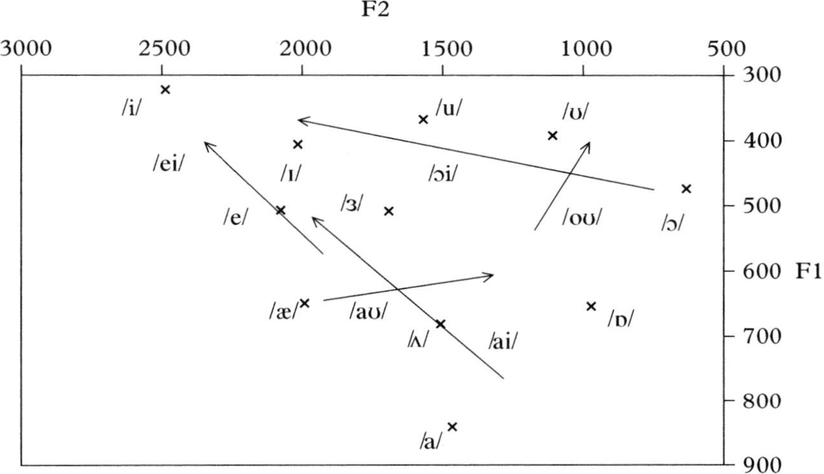

Miss Turnbull normalised, 1875

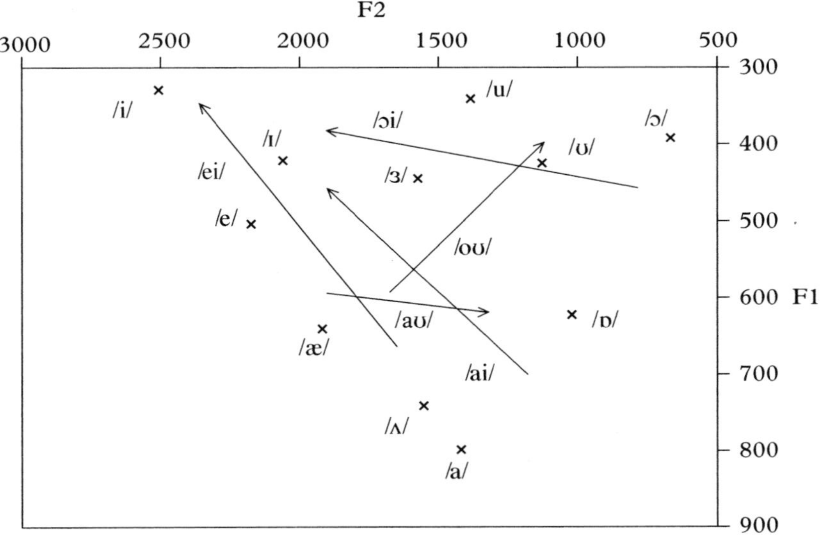

Mrs Cruickshank normalised, 1876

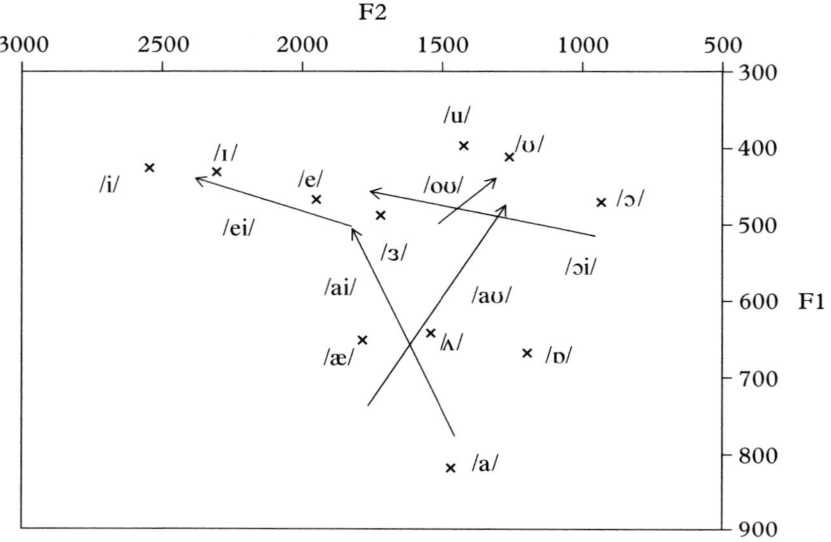

Mrs Hamilton normalised, 1877

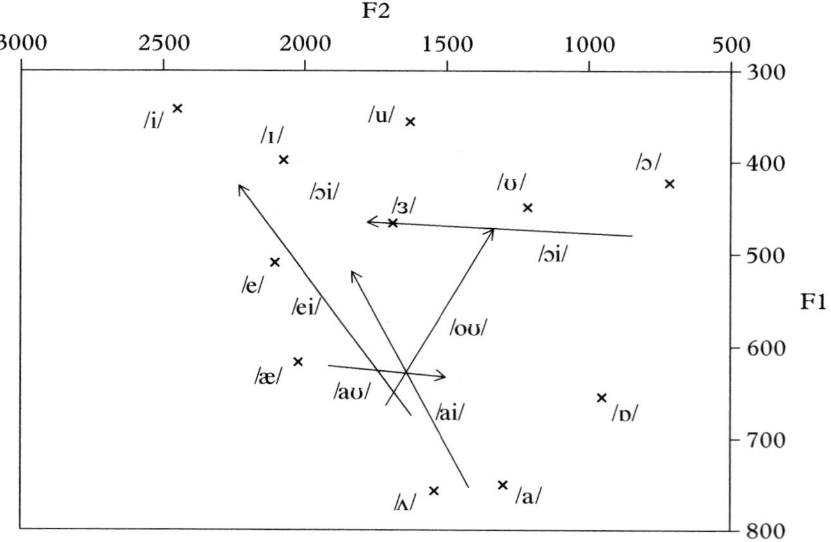

Mrs Dudley normalised, 1886

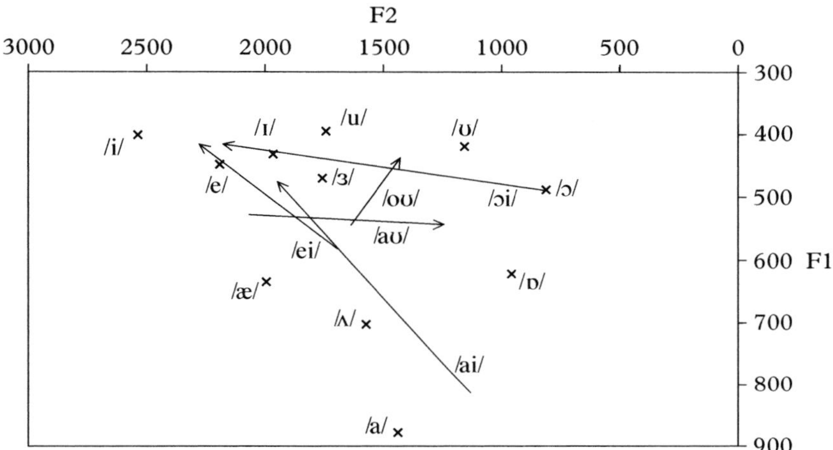

Mr Dufty normalised, 1865

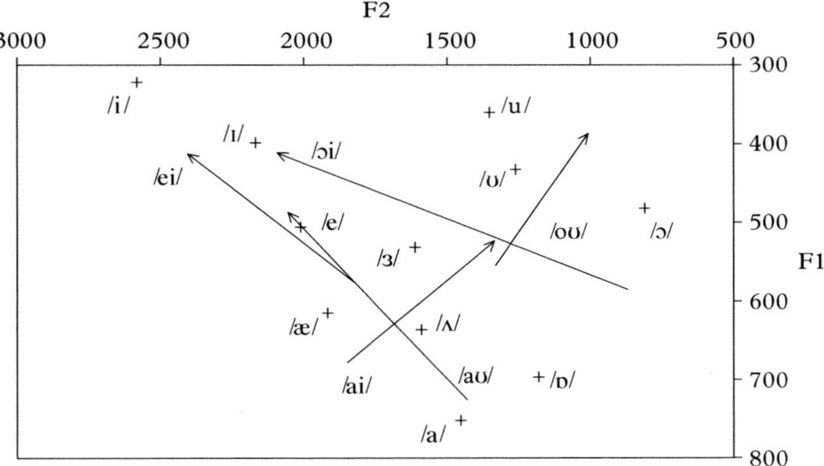

Mr Mason normalised, 1873

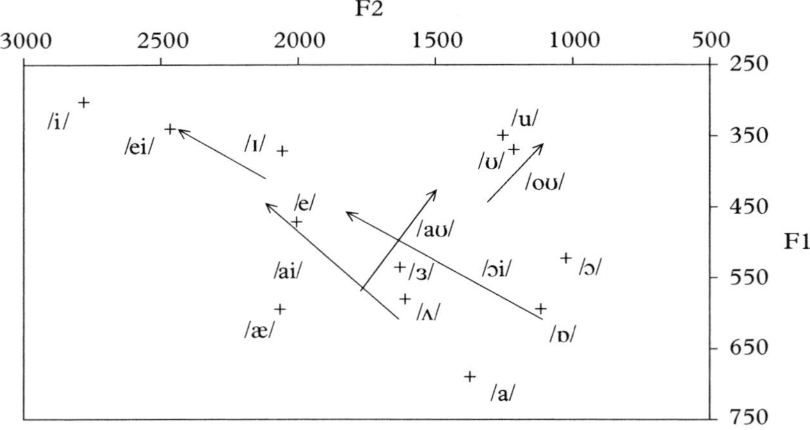

Mr Edgar normalised, 1874

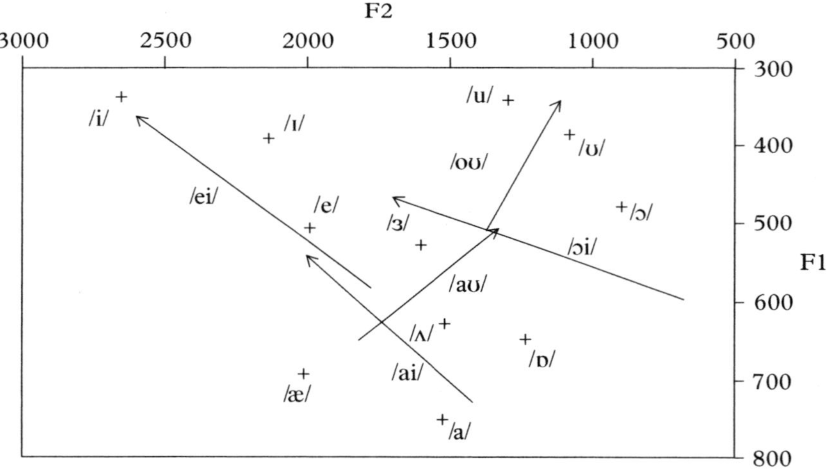

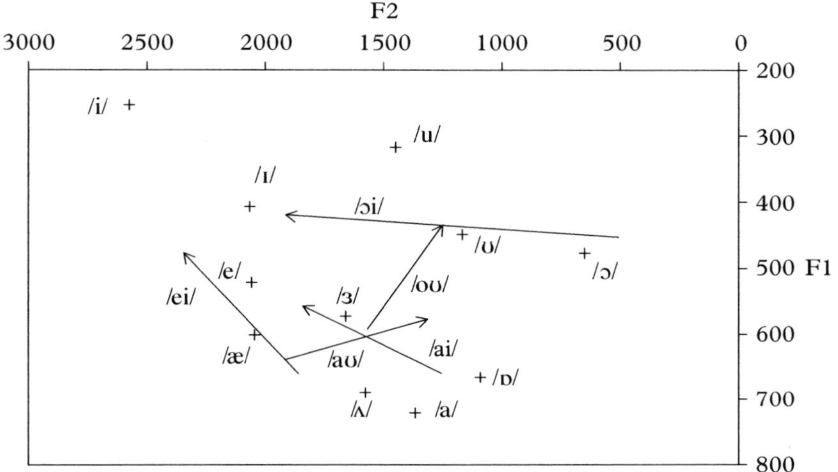
Mr McKinlay normalised, 1875
F2
3000
2500
2000
1500
1000
500
0
200
300
400
500 F1
600
700
800
/i/
/u/
/ɪ/
/ɔi/
/ʊ/
/ɔ/
/e/
/ei/
/ɜ/
/oʊ/
/æ/
/aʊ/
/ai/
/ɒ/
/ʌ/
/a/

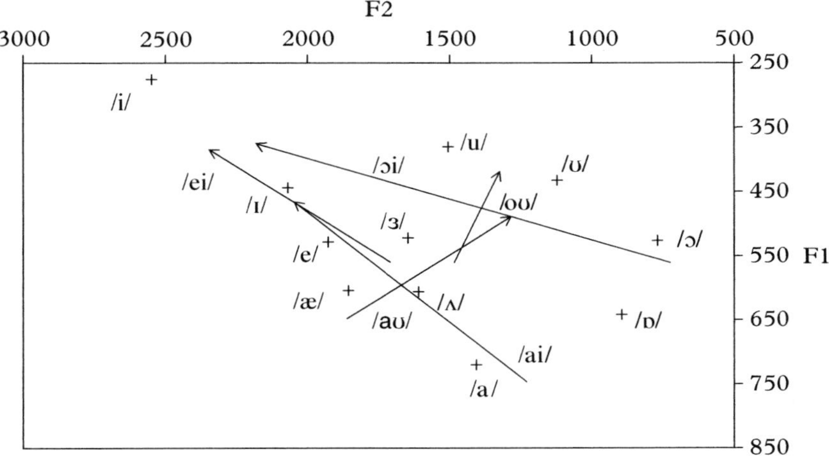
Mr Bertram normalised, 1879
F2
3000
2500
2000
1500
1000
500
250
350
450
550 F1
650
750
850
/i/
/u/
/ʊ/
/ɔi/
/ei/
/oʊ/
/ɪ/
/ɜ/
/ɔ/
/e/
/æ/
/ʌ/
/aʊ/
/ɒ/
/ai/
/a/

Appendix 6 Speaker indexes for quantified variables, together with relevant social information

	Speaker Number	KIT (centralisation)	DRESS (raising)	TRAP (raising)	START (fronting)	UNSTRESSED (centralisation)	rhoticity	/hw/	h-drop	date	sex	parents	Town type
Aitcheson, Ada	76	0.453125	0.931818	1.83333	1.78788	1	0.59	100.0	0	1878	F	N	S
Algie, David	29	0.115385	0.384615	0.813559	1.82143	0.36	5.85	14.29	35.5	1867	M	S	U
Bisset, Christina	61	0.114035	0.529412	0.203125	1.26087	0.318182	46.58	60.87	1.75	1875	F	M	S
Cannon, Thomas	68	0.096774	0.47619	1.10638	1.09524	0.5	17.7	41.18	10.71	1876	M	M	S
Crosby, Paddy	20	0.112245	0.275	0.6	1.62366	0.614458	17.0	13.33	13.0	1865	M	I	U
Cruikshank, Emily	69	0.153846	0.806452	0.75	1.5	0.272727	0	22.0	0	1876	F	E	U
Day, Reg	55	0.123457	0.440678	0.520833	1.01493	0.44	3.67	16.67	0	1874	M	E	U
Dennison, Ellen	56	0.162602	0.435185	0.493151	1.68571	0.931034	56.13	35.29	4.35	1874	F	S	M
Dixon, Chris	30	0.07	0.5	0.864706	1.14286	0.865854	0.67	2.04	5.0	1867	M	M	E
Douglas, John	89	0.050251	0.71	1.23871	1.39175	0.79	1.0	16.4	3.0	1884	M	M	E
Drinnan, Jessie	32	0	0.305556	0.586207	1.76923	0.588235	25.37	71.43	0	1868	F	S	S
Drinnan, Nelson	106	0.111111	0.433333	0.575758	1.4375	0.238095	34.34	28.57	5.71	1900	M	N	S
Dudley, Catherine	93	0.076142	1.15	1.17355	1.59677	1.02778	12.3	32.1	5.0	1886	F	M	M
Dufty, William	21	0.076142	0.413174	0.731092	1.65116	0.618182	0.33	1.0	72.0	1865	M	E	E
Edgar, John	57	0.070352	0.489011	0.297468	1.31944	0.608247	4.0	0	30.0	1874	M	E	E
Fell, Ben	58	0.066667	0.804598	1.28814	1.36	0.795918	6.25	38.1	1.89	1874	M	S	U
Forrester, John	22	0.028571	0.470588	1.10465	1.05263	0.392405	1.68	25.71	0	1865	M	S	S
Fullerton, Mrs	16	0.228395	1.28676	1.57534	1.34328	0.872727	2.67	61.11	1.77	1864	F	S	U
German, Edith	33	0.090452	0.78	1.2459	1.91398	1.04255	1.33	2.13	3.0	1868	F	E	U
Gratton, Helen	6	0.285714	0.276316	0.390625	1.82857	0.378378	4.61	0	27.12	1857	F	U	E
Gray, Mr	107	0.18	1.10169	1.17073	1.97561	0.558824	2.88	4.0	4.0	1900	M	M	S
Hamilton, Annie	72	0.2	0.63	1.515	1.1383	1.24	3.0	19.0	0	1877	F	I	M
Harris, James	26	0.139535	0.355932	0.366667	1.4386	0.794118	4.56	0	9.5	1866	M	M	U
Hollis, Sarah	17	0.186916	0.676471	1.52239	1.82609	0.74359	5.15	0	6.39	1864	F	I	U

(*cont.*)

	Speaker Number	KIT (centralisation)	DRESS (raising)	TRAP (raising)	START (fronting)	UNSTRESSED (centralisation)	rhoticity	/hw/	h-drop	date	sex	parents	Town type
Kenny, Courtenay	73	0.111675	0.882682	1.63522	1.85	0.94898	0	0	1.45	1877	M	M	U
King, Catherine	35	0.221311	0.798246	1.27586	1.71875	0.55	17.51	34.48	6.25	1868	F	S	U
Lillis, Thomas	97	0.08	0.673469	1.1875	2.0	0.47619	0	0	1.79	1889	M	I	E
Mackie, Alice	74	0.152941	0.578125	1.2381	1.91667	0.666667	12.38	0	2.17	1877	F	M	M
Magner, Cornelius	98	0.206186	0.33	0.245	1.45745	0.41	10.67	0	1.0	1889	M	I	U
Mason, Margaret	62	0.25641	0.519231	1.54167	1.8	0.454545	12.0	60	0	1875	F	M	U
McKearney, Susan	27	0.037879	0.240876	0.823529	1.53731	0.85	7.89	5.88	3.64	1866	F	M	U
Mclew, John	64	0.026042	0.643939	0.98	1.65789	0.2	20.26	37.3	39.02	1875	M	S	U
Michelle, Thomas	70	0.107143	0.589744	0.814815	1.05882	1.04878	13.33	6.02	32.59	1876	M	M	E
Miller, James	65	0.099237	0.637168	1.125	1.48718	0.454545	10.1	40.0	10	1875	M	S	U
Munro, James	104	0.081871	0.525424	0.796992	1.73913	0.98	4.3	29.3	0	1899	M	M	M
North, Emma	79	0	0.717949	1.05556	1.92308	0.785714	0	16.7	0	1878	F	M	U
Partridge, William	101	0.111111	0.87234	0.5	1.64706	0.836957	5.36	75.0	0	1895	M	M	E
Paterson, William	66	0.053571	0.254717	0.485714	1.70588	0.545455	0.46	0	8.89	1875	M	M	U
Paul, George	23	0.052632	1.0625	1.29231	1.76744	0.761194	0.39	0	36.76	1865	M	M	U
Reid, Jane	75	0.155779	1.03	1.61176	1.70732	0.48	3.33	52.08	0	1877	F	S	U
Rigby, Frances	31	0.168224	0.471154	0.672414	1.23529	1.09091	2.94	46.43	2.66	1867	F	M	U
Ritchie, George	102	0.01	0.35443	0.97619	1.16279	0.24	17.07	7.89	8.64	1898	M	M	M
Ritchie, Helen	15	0.101523	1.275	1.69531	1.38776	0.26	25.0	30.61	1.11	1863	F	S	M
Ritchie, Malcolm	28	0.101523	0.68	0.360406	1.08889	0.37	22.33	17.17	13.0	1866	M	S	E
Ritchie, Robert	18	0.025126	0.572864	1.07874	1.01613	0.176471	22.0	36.71	2.0	1864	M	S	M
Scott, Thomas M.	105	0.15544	0.665	1.23636	1.75281	0.52	39.47	21.43	13.64	1899	M	N	E
Shepherd, Frank	37	0.105528	0.495	1.345	1.12121	0.94	4.0	3.95	8	1868	M	M	E
Steel, Thomas	59	0.015873	0.29771	0.086022	1.13462	0.511628	0	0	7.41	1874	M	M	U
Sumpter, Dennis	108	0.144231	0.376812	1.14286	1.03125	1.07692	0.62	47.1	0	1904	M	M	S

Swarbrick, Henry	99	0.065657	0.5	0.56051	1.4	0.62	1.3	2.0	0	1889	M	M	E
Symons, Marguerite	100	0.147959	0.57	1.49153	1.51685	0.79	7.33	91.0	0	1894	F	M	U
Temple, Sam	39	0.049296	0.267123	0.210145	1.22388	0.491228	5.33	0	15.15	1868	M	M	U
Templeton, Robert	94	0.014815	0.504202	1.2381	1.60377	1.0	1.91	11.11	0	1887	M	M	U
Turnball, Mary Ann	67	0.103825	0.57732	1.28421	1.70588	0.583333	7.87	67.69	0	1875	F	S	U
Tweed. Anthony	24	0.158273	0.558824	0.369565	1.3125	0.883721	41.67	61.54	0	1865	M	S	S
Warren, William	60	0.041237	0.442748	0.265957	1.2381	0.8	2.6	6.45	5.77	1874	M	M	M
Wishart, George	90	0.070352	0.311765	0.923469	1.10606	0.916667	5.69	7.35	4.0	1884	M	S	E
Wood, Allie	96	0.050505	0.2	0.59375	1.71698	0.3	8.6	16.1	4.35	1888	M	N	U
Young, Vivian	92	0.06599	0.39	0.836735	1.98	0.67	3.33	17.35	6.0	1885	M	M	U

KEY for mother, father, parents, and town type:
E = English
I = Irish
S = Scottish
M = Mixed
N = New Zealand
A = Australian
L = Elsewhere
U = Unknown*
(*For the towns, 'Unknown' = unable to be classified using census data.)

References

Abell, Marcia 1980, *A Study of Sociolinguistic Stereotyping by Fourth Form Students in Christchurch*, unpublished MA thesis, University of Canterbury, Christchurch.

Adams, Robert N. 1903, *How to Pronounce Accurately on Scientific Principles*, Dunedin: Otago Daily Times.

Akenson, Donald H. 1990, *Half the World from Home: Perspectives on the Irish in New Zealand 1860–1950*, Wellington: Victoria University Press.

Anderson, Peter M. 1987, *A Structural Atlas of the English Dialects*, London: Croom Helm.

Arnold, Rollo 1981, *The Farthest Promised Land: English Villagers, New Zealand Immigrants of the 1870s*, Wellington: Victoria University Press and Price Milburn.

1987, 'The Australian peoples and their world 1888–1915', in Sinclair 1996: 52–70.

Auer, Peter, Barden, Beate, and Grosskopf, Birgit 1998, 'Saliency in long-term dialect accommodation', *Journal of Sociolinguistics* 2.2: 163–87.

Baayen, R. Harald, Piepenbrock, Richard, and Gulikers, Leon 1995, *The CELEX Lexical Database* (CD-ROM), Philadelphia: Linguistic Data Consortium.

Bailey, Guy 2001, 'Real and apparent time', in Chambers et al. 2001: 312–32.

Bailey, Guy, Wikle, Tom, Tillery, Jan, and Sand, Lori 1991, 'The apparent time construct', *Language Variation and Change* 3: 241–64.

Bailey, Richard 1996, *Nineteenth Century English*, Ann Arbor: University of Michigan Press.

Baines, Dudley 1991, *Emigration from Europe 1815–1930*, Basingstoke: Macmillan.

Baker, Sidney J. 1941a, *A Popular Dictionary of Australian Slang*, Melbourne: Robertson & Mullens.

1941b, *New Zealand Slang: A Dictionary of Colloquialisms*, Christchurch: Whitcombe & Tombs.

1945, *The Australian Language*, Sydney: Angus & Robertson.

1947, *Australian Pronunciation: A Guide to Good Speech*, Sydney: Angus & Robertson.

1959, *The Drum: Australian Character and Slang*, Sydney: Currawong Publishing.

1986, *The Australian Language*, 2nd ed., reprinted Melbourne: Macmillan. (First published in 1966, Sydney: Currawong Publishing.)

Balota, David A. and Chumbley, James 1984, 'Are lexical decisions good measures of lexical access? The role of word frequency in the neglected decision stage', *Journal of Experimental Psychology: Human Perception and Performance* 10: 340–57.

Bartlett, Christopher 1992, 'Regional variation in New Zealand English: The case of Southland', *New Zealand English Newsletter* 6: 5–15.

2003, *The Southland Variety of New Zealand English: Postvocalic /r/ and the* BATH *vowel*, unpublished PhD thesis, University of Otago, Dunedin.

Bassett, Judith, Sinclair, Keith, and Stenson, Marcia 1985, *The Story of New Zealand*, Auckland: Reed Methuen.

Batchelor, T. 1809, *An Orthoepical Analysis of the English Language*, London: Didier & Tebbett.

Batterham, Margaret 1993, 'Attitudes to New Zealand English', *New Zealand English Newsletter* 7: 5–24.

1995, *'There is Another Type Here': Some Front Vowel Variables in New Zealand English*, unpublished PhD thesis, Latrobe University, Melbourne.

2000, 'The apparent merger of the front centring diphthongs', in Bell and Kuiper 2000: 111–45.

Bauer, Laurie 1979, 'The second great vowel shift?', *Journal of the International Phonetic Association* 9.2: 57–66.

1982, 'That vowel shift again', *Journal of the International Phonetic Association* 12.1: 48–9.

1984, Perspectives on Words, in *Views of English* 3, Wellington: Victoria University.

1985, 'Tracing phonetic change in the Received Pronunciation of British English', *Journal of Phonetics* 13: 61–81.

1986, 'Notes on New Zealand English phonetics and phonology', *English World-Wide* 7: 225–58.

1992, 'The second Great Vowel Shift revisited', *English World-Wide* 13.2: 253–68.

1994, 'English in New Zealand', in Burchfield 1994b: 382–429.

1997, 'Attempting to trace Scottish influence on New Zealand English', in Schneider, Edgar W. (ed.) *Englishes around the World*, Vol. 2, Philadelphia: John Benjamins, pp. 257–72.

1999, 'On the origins of the New Zealand English accent', *English World-Wide* 20: 287–307.

2000, 'The dialectal origins of New Zealand English', in Bell and Kuiper 2000: 40–52.

Bauer, Winifred 1995, 'The use of Maori words in English (Languages in Contact II)', *New Zealand Studies* 5.2: 19–24.

Baughen, Gregory A. K. 2002, 'Baeyertz, Charles Nader 1866–1943', *Dictionary of New Zealand Biography*, http://www.dnzb.govt.nz/dnzb/, accessed 30 September 2002.

Bayard, Donn 1985, 'Class and change in New Zealand English: a pilot study', Paper presented at the 6th New Zealand Linguistics Conference, Wellington.

1987, 'Class and change in New Zealand English: a summary report', *Te Reo* 30: 3–36.

1990a, '"God help us if we all sound like this": attitudes to New Zealand and other English accents', in Bell and Holmes 1990: 67–96.

1990b, 'Minder, Mork and Mindy? (–t) glottalisation and post-vocalic (–r) in younger New Zealand English speakers', in Bell and Holmes 1990: 149–64.

1991a, 'A taste of Kiwi: attitudes to accent, speaker gender, and perceived ethnicity across the Tasman', *Australian Journal of Linguistics* 11: 1–39.

1991b, 'Antipodean accents and the "cultural cringe": New Zealand and American attitudes towards NZE and other English accents', *Te Reo* 34: 15–52.

1991c, 'Social constraints on the phonology of New Zealand English', in Cheshire 1991: 169–86.

1995a, *Kiwitalk: Sociolinguistics and New Zealand Society*, Palmerston North: Dunmore Press.

1995b, 'Peers versus parents: a longitudinal study of rhotic-non-rhotic accommodation in an NZE-speaking child', *New Zealand English Newsletter* 9: 15–22.

2000, 'New Zealand English: origins, relationships, and prospects', *Moderna Språk* 94.1: 8–14.

Bayard, Donn and Bartlett, Christopher 1996, '"You must be from Gorrre": attitudinal effects of Southland rhotic accents and speaker gender in New Zealand English listeners and the question of New Zealand English regional variation', *Te Reo* 39: 25–45.

Bayard, Donn, Weatherall, Ann, Gallois, Cynthia, and Pittam, Jeffery 2001, 'Pax Americana? Accent attitudinal evaluations in New Zealand, Australia and America', *Journal of Sociolinguistics* 5: 22–49.

Bayley, Robert 2001, 'The quantitative paradigm', in Chambers et al. 2001: 117–42.

Beal, Joan 1993, 'Lengthening of /a/ in eighteenth-century English', in *Newcastle and Durham Working Papers in English Linguistics 1*, Newcastle upon Tyne: University of Newcastle, pp. 2–17.

Belich, James 1996, *Making Peoples*, Harmondsworth: Allen Lane.

Bell, Allan 1997a, 'The phonetics of fish and chips in New Zealand: marking national and ethnic identities', *English World-Wide* 18: 243–70.

1997b, 'Those short front vowels', *New Zealand English Journal* 11: 3–13.

2000, 'Māori and Pākeha English: a case study', in Bell and Kuiper 2000: 221–48.

Bell, Allan and Holmes, Janet (eds.) 1990, *New Zealand Ways of Speaking English*, Wellington: Victoria University Press.

1991, 'New Zealand', in Cheshire 1991: 153–68.

1992, '/H/-droppin': two sociolinguistic variables in New Zealand English', *Australian Journal of Linguistics* 12: 223–48.

Bell, Allan and Kuiper, Koenraad (eds.) 2000, *New Zealand English*, Wellington: Victoria University Press; Philadelphia: John Benjamins.

Bennett, J. A. W. 1943, 'English as it is spoken in New Zealand', *American Speech* 18: 81–95, reprinted in Ramson 1970: 69–83.

Benton, Richard A. 1985, 'Maori, English, and Maori English', in Pride, John B. (ed.) *Cross-Cultural Encounters: Communication and Mis-Communication*, Melbourne: River Seine Publications, pp. 110–20.

1991, 'Māori English: a New Zealand myth?', in Cheshire 1991: 187–99.

Bernard, John R. L. 1969, 'On the uniformity of spoken Australian English', *Orbis* 18.1: 62–73.

1970, 'Toward the acoustic specification of Australian English', *Zeitschrift für Phonetik* 23: 113–28.

Berthele, Raphael 2000, 'Divergence and convergence in a multilectal classroom: patterns of group structure and linguistic conformity', in Mattheier, K. (ed.), *Migration and its Consequences for Linguistic Convergence and Divergence*, New York: Lang, pp. 155–71.

Bloomfield, Leonard 1933, *Language*, London: Allen & Unwin.

Bod, Rens, Hay, Jennifer, and Jannedy, Stefanie (eds.) in press, *Probabilistic Linguistics*, Cambridge, MA: MIT Press.

Borrie, Wilfred D. 1987, 'The peopling of Australasia 1788–1988: the common heritage', in Sinclair 1996: 202–23.

Bradley, David 1991, '/æ/ and /aː/ in Australian English', in Cheshire 1991: 227–34.

Branford, William 1994, 'English in South Africa', in Burchfield 1994b: 430–96.

Breiman, Leo, Friedman, Jerome H., Olshen, Richard A., and Stone, Charles J. 1984, *Classification and Regression Trees*, Belmont, CA: Wadsworth.

Britain, David 1991, *Dialect and Space: A Geolinguistic Study of Speech Variables in the Fens*, PhD dissertation, University of Essex.

1992, 'Linguistic change in intonation: the use of high rising terminals in New Zealand English', *Language Variation and Change* 4: 77–104.

1997a, 'Dialect contact and phonological reallocation: "Canadian raising" in the English fens', *Language in Society* 26: 15–46.

1997b, 'Dialect contact, focusing and phonological rule complexity: the koinéisation of Fenland English', in *University of Pennsylvania Working Papers in Linguistics 4*, A selection of papers from NWAVE [New Ways of Analysing Variation] 25, Philadelphia: University of Pennsylvania, pp. 141–70.

2002, 'Diffusion, levelling, simplification and reallocation in the past tense BE in the English Fens', *Journal of Sociolinguistics* 6: 16–43.

Britain, David and Newman, John 1992, 'High rising terminals in New Zealand English', *Journal of the International Phonetic Association* 22.1/2: 1–11.

Britain, David and Sudbury, Andrea 2002, 'There's sheep and there's penguins: convergence "drift" and "slant" in New Zealand and Falkland Island English', in Jones and Esch 2002: 209–40.

Britain, David and Trudgill, Peter 1999, 'Migration, new-dialect formation and sociolinguistic refunctionalisation: reallocation as an outcome of dialect contact', *Transactions of the Philological Society* 97.2: 245–56.

Brook, George L. 1958, *A History of the English Language*, London: Andre Deutsch.

1963, *English Dialects*, London: Andre Deutsch.

Brosnahan, Leonard F. 1966, 'Notes on /l/ in New Zealand English', in *Proceedings and Papers of the 10th Australasian Universities Language and Literature Association Congress*, Auckland: AULLA, pp. 230–4.

Burchfield, Robert 1994a, 'Introduction', in Burchfield 1994b: 1–19.

1994b, *The Cambridge History of the English Language*, Vol. 5: *English in Britain and Overseas: Origins and Development*, Cambridge: Cambridge University Press.

Buzo, Alex 1994, *Kiwese: A Guide, a Ductionary, a Shearing of Unsights*, Port Melbourne, Victoria: Reed Books.

Bybee, Joan 2000, 'The phonology of the lexicon: evidence from lexical diffusion', in Barlow, Michael and Kemmer, Suzanne (eds.), *Usage-based Models of Language*, Stanford: CSLI [Center for the Study of Language and Information], pp. 65–85.

2001, *Phonology and Language Use*, Cambridge: Cambridge University Press.

Byrd, Dani M. 1994, *Articulatory Timing in English Consonant Sequences*, PhD dissertation, University of California.

Camm, Jack C. R. and McQuilton, John (eds.) 1987, *Australians: A Historical Atlas*, Sydney: Fairfax, Syme & Weldon.

Campbell, Arnold E. 1941, *Educating New Zealand*, Wellington: Department of Internal Affairs.

Campbell, Elizabeth and Gordon, Elizabeth 1996, 'What do you fink? Is New Zealand English losing its "TH"?', *New Zealand English Journal* 10: 40–6.

Campbell, Lyle and Ringen, Jon 1981, 'Teleology and the explanation of sound change', in Dressler, Wolfgang U., Pfeiffer, Oskar E., and Rennison, John R. (eds.), *Phonologica*, Innsbruck: Innsbrucker Beiträge zur Sprachwissenschaft, pp. 57–68.

Carmichael, Gordon A. (ed.) 1993, *Trans-Tasman Migration: Trends, Causes and Consequences*, Canberra: Australian Government Publishing Service.

Carter, Ian 1993, *Gadfly: The Life and Times of James Shelley*, Auckland: Auckland University Press.

Cedergren, Henrietta 1973, *The Interplay of Social and Linguistic Factors in Panama*, PhD dissertation, Cornell University.

1984, 'Panama revisited: sound change in real time', Paper presented at NWAVE [New Ways of Analysing Variation], Philadelphia, University of Pennsylvania.

Chambers, Jack K. 2001, 'Patterns of variation including change', in Chambers et al. 2001: 349–72.

2002, 'Dynamics of dialect convergence', *Journal of Sociolinguistics* 6: 117–30.

2003, *Sociolinguistic Theory: Linguistic Variation and its Social Significance*, 2nd ed., Oxford: Blackwell.

Chambers, Jack K. and Trudgill, Peter 1998, *Dialectology*, 2nd ed., Cambridge: Cambridge University Press.

Chambers, Jack K., Trudgill, Peter, and Schilling-Estes, Natalie (eds.) 2001, *The Handbook of Language Variation and Change*, Malden, MA: Blackwell.

Cheshire, Jenny (ed.) 1991, *English Around the World: Sociolinguistic Perspectives*, Cambridge University Press.

Cheshire, Jenny 2001, 'Sex and gender in variationist research', in Chambers et al. 2001: 423–43.

Clark, John E. (ed.) 1985, *The Cultivated Australian: Festschrift in Honour of Arthur Delbridge*, Hamburg: Helmut Buske.

Clark, Ross 1990, 'Pidgin English and Pidgin Maori in New Zealand', in Bell and Holmes 1990: 97–114.

Cleveland, William S. 1979, 'Robust locally weighted regression and smoothing scatterplots', *Journal of the American Statistical Association* 74: 829–36.

Coleridge, Kathleen A. 1966, *New Zealand English: A Preliminary Checklist*, Wellington: New Zealand Library School.

Connine, Cynthia M., Titone, Debra, and Wang, Jian 1993, 'Auditory word recognition: extrinsic and intrinsic effects of word frequency', *Journal of Experimental Psychology: Learning, Memory and Cognition* 19.1: 81–94.

Corbyn, Charles Adam 1970, reprint, *Sydney Revels of Bacchus, Cupid and Momus*, Sydney: Ure Smith. (First published in 1854.)

Coulmas, Florian (ed.) 1997, *The Handbook of Sociolinguistics*, Oxford: Blackwell.

Coupland, Nikolas 2001, 'Language, situation and the relational self: theorising dialect-style in sociolinguistics', in Rickford, John R. and Eckert, Penelope (eds.), *Style and Sociolinguistic Variation*, Cambridge: Cambridge University Press, pp. 185–210.

Cox, Felicity 1996, *An Acoustic Study of Vowel Variation in Australian English*, unpublished PhD thesis, Macquarie University, Sydney.

Cryer, Max 2002, *Curious Kiwi Words*, Auckland: HarperCollins.

Day, Patrick Adam 1994, *The Radio Years: A History of Broadcasting in New Zealand*, Vol. 1, Auckland: Auckland University Press.

Dell, G. 1990, 'Effects of frequency and vocabulary type on phonological speech errors', *Language and Cognitive Processes* 5.4: 313–49.

Denison, Norman 1997, 'Language change and progress: variation as it happens', in Coulmas 1997: 65–80.

Denoon, Donald, Mein-Smith, Philippa, and Wyndham, Marivic 2000, *A History of Australia, New Zealand and the Pacific*, Oxford: Blackwell.

Deser, Toni 1990, *Dialect Transmission and Variation: An Acoustic Analysis of Vowels in Six Urban Detroit Families*, PhD dissertation, Boston University.

Deterding, David 1997, 'The formants of monophthong vowels in standard Southern British English pronunciation', *Journal of the International Phonetic Association* 27: 47–55.

Deverson, Tony 1985, '"Home loans": Maori input into current New Zealand English', *English in New Zealand* 33: 4–10.

1988, 'A bibliography of writings on New Zealand English', *New Zealand English Newsletter* 2: 17–25.

1991, 'New Zealand English lexis: the Maori dimension', *English Today* 26: 18–25.

Disner, Sandra F. 1980, 'Evaluation of vowel normalisation procedures', *Journal of the Acoustical Society of America* 67: 253–61.

Domingue, Nicole 1971, *Bhojpuri and Creole in Mauritius: A Study of Linguistic Interference and its Consequences in regard to Synchronic Variation and Language Change*, PhD dissertation, University of Texas, Austin.

1981, 'Internal change in a transplanted language', *Studies in the Linguistic Sciences* 4: 151–9.

Dorian, Nancy C. 1994, 'Varieties of variation in a very small place: social homogeneity, prestige, norms, and linguistic variation', *Language* 70: 631–96.

2001, 'Review of "Language Change: Advances in Historical Sociolinguistics" (edited by Ernst Håkon Jahr)', *Anthropological Linguistics* 43.3: 387–9.

Downes, John 1998, *A Guide to Devon Dialect*, Padstow: Tabb House.

Downes, Peter and Harcourt, Peter 1976, *Voices in the Air: Radio Broadcasting in New Zealand*, Wellington: Methuen.

Downes, William 1984, *Language and Society*, London: Fontana.

Drummond, Alison and Drummond, Leo R. 1967, *At Home in New Zealand*, Auckland: Blackwood & Janet Paul.

Durkin, Mary 1972, *A Study of the Pronunciation, Oral Grammar and Vocabulary of West Coast School Children*, unpublished MA thesis, University of Canterbury, Christchurch.

Eagleson, Robert D. 1982, 'English in Australia and New Zealand,' in Bailey, Richard W. and Görlach, Manfred (eds.), *English as a World Language*, Ann Arbor: University of Michigan Press, pp. 415–38.

Eckert, Penelope 1988, 'Adolescent social structure and the spread of linguistic change', *Language in Society* 17: 83–207.

2000, *Linguistic Variation as Social Practice*, Oxford: Blackwell.

Elley, Warwick B., and Irving, James C. 1985, 'The Elley-Irving Socio-Economic Index: 1981. Census revision', *New Zealand Journal of Educational Studies* 20: 115–28.

Ellis, Alexander J. 1889, *On Early English Pronunciation*, Vol. 5, London: Trübner and Co.

Eustace, S. S. 1969, 'The meaning of the palaeotype in A. J. Ellis's "On Early English Pronunciation 1869–89"', *Transactions of the Philological Society* 67: 30–79.

Fidelholtz, James 1975, 'Word frequency and vowel reduction in English', in *Papers from the 75th meeting of the Chicago Linguistics Society*, Chicago: University of Chicago, pp. 200–13.

Foulkes, Paul and Docherty, Gerard J. (eds.) 1999, *Urban Voices: Accent Studies in the British Isles*, London: Arnold.

Fraser, Lyndon (ed.) 2000, *A Distant Shore: Irish Immigration and New Zealand Settlement*, Dunedin: Otago University Press.

Fromkin, Victoria, Rodman, Robert, Collins, Peter, and Blair, David 1984, *An Introduction to Language* (Australian Edition), Sydney: Holt, Rinehart & Winston.

Galbraith, Alisdair 2000, 'The invisible Irish? Re-discovering the Irish Protestant tradition in colonial New Zealand', in Fraser 2000: 36–54.

Gardner, William J. 1999, *Where they Lived: Studies in Local, Regional and Social History*, Christchurch: Regional Press.

Gibson, Campbell, J. 1971, *A Demographic History of New Zealand*, unpublished PhD thesis, University of California, Berkeley.

Giles, Howard 1973, 'Accent mobility: a model and some data', *Linguistic Anthropology* 15: 87–105.

1977, 'Social psychology and applied linguistics: towards an integrative approach', *ITL Review of Applied Linguistics* 35: 27–42.

Giles, Howard and Coupland, Nikolas 1991, *Language: Contexts and Consequences*, Pacific Grove, CA: Brooks/Cole.

Gimson, Alan C. 1962, *An Introduction to the Pronunciation of English*, London: Arnold.

Golla, Victor 2000, 'Language families of North America', in Renfrew, Colin (ed.), *America Past, America Present: Genes and Languages in the Americas and Beyond*, Cambridge: McDonald Institute for Archaeological Research, pp. 59–73.

Gordon, Elizabeth 1982, 'The study of New Zealand English', *Journal of the South Pacific Association for Commonwealth Literature and Language Studies* 14: 39–43.

1983a, 'New Zealand English pronunciation: an investigation into some early written records', *Te Reo* 26: 29–42.

1983b, 'The flood of impure vocalisation: a study of attitudes towards New Zealand speech', *The New Zealand Speech-Language Therapists' Journal* 38: 16–29.

1989, 'That colonial twang: New Zealand speech and New Zealand identity', in Novitz, David and Willmott, Bill (eds.), *New Zealand Culture and Identity*, Wellington: GP Books, pp. 77–90.

1991, 'Research into the origins of New Zealand speech', *New Zealand English Newsletter* 5: 11–12.

1994, 'Reconstructing the past: written and spoken evidence of early New Zealand speech', *New Zealand English Newsletter* 8: 5–10.

1998, 'The origins of New Zealand speech: the limits of recovering historical information from written records', *English World-Wide* 19: 61–85.

Gordon, Elizabeth and Abell, Marcia 1990, '"This objectionable colonial dialect": historical and contemporary attitudes to New Zealand speech', in Bell and Holmes 1990: 21–48.

Gordon, Elizabeth and Deverson, Tony 1985, *New Zealand English: An Introduction to New Zealand Speech and Usage*, Auckland: Heinemann.

1989, *Finding a New Zealand Voice: Attitudes Towards English used in New Zealand*, Auckland: New House.

1998, *New Zealand English and English in New Zealand*, Auckland: New House.
Gordon, Elizabeth and Maclagan, Margaret 1985, 'A study of the /iə/ /eə/ contrast in New Zealand English', *The New Zealand Speech-Language Therapists' Journal* 40.2: 16–26.
1989, 'Beer and bear, cheer and chair: a longitudinal study of the ear/air contrast in New Zealand English', *Australian Journal of Linguistics* 9: 203–20.
2000, '"Hear our voices": changes in spoken New Zealand English', *The Journal of the TESOL Association of Aotearoa New Zealand Journal* 8: 1–13.
2001, '"Capturing a sound change": a real time study over 15 years of the NEAR/SQUARE diphthong merger in New Zealand English', *Australian Journal of Linguistics* 21.2: 215–38.
Gordon, Elizabeth and Sudbury, Andrea 2002, 'The history of Southern Hemisphere Englishes', in Watts, Richard and Trudgill, Peter (eds.), *Alternative Histories of English*, London: Routledge, pp. 67–86.
Gordon, Elizabeth and Trudgill, Peter 1999, 'Shades of things to come: embryonic variants in New Zealand English sound changes', *English World-Wide* 20: 111–23.
Gordon, Elizabeth and Trudgill, Peter forthcoming, 'The English input to New Zealand', in Hickey forthcoming.
Gordon, Matthew J. 2001, 'Investigating chain shifts and mergers', in Chambers et al. 2001: 244–66.
Gordon, Pamela 1997, 'What New Zealanders believe about regional variation in New Zealand English: a folklinguistic investigation', *New Zealand English Journal* 11: 14–25.
Görlach, Manfred 1987, 'Colonial lag? The alleged conservative character of American English and other "colonial" varieties', *English World-Wide* 8: 41–60.
Graham, Jeanine 1992, 'Settler society', in Rice 1992: 112–40.
1996, 'The Pioneers 1840–1870', in Sinclair 1996: 49–74.
Gregersen, Frans and Pedersen, Ilse 1991, *The Copenhagen Study in Urban Sociolinguistics*, Copenhagen: C.A. Reitzels Forlag.
Grosjean, François 1980, 'Spoken word recognition processes and the gating paradigm', *Perception and Psychophysics* 45: 189–95.
Haggett, Geoff n.d., Recorded interview held in the Radio New Zealand Sound Archives, Christchurch.
Hall, John Herbert 1980, *The History of Broadcasting in New Zealand 1920–1954*, Wellington: Broadcasting Corporation of New Zealand.
Hall, Moira 1976, *An Acoustic Analysis of New Zealand Vowels*, unpublished MA thesis, University of Auckland.
Hammarström, Göran 1980, *Australian English: Its Origin and Status*, Hamburg: Helmut Buske.
Harrington, Jonathan and Cassidy, Steve 1999, *Techniques in Speech Acoustics*, Dordrecht: Kluwer.
Harrington, Jonathan, Palethorpe, Sallyanne, and Watson, Catherine I. 2000, 'Does the queen speak the Queen's English?', *Nature* 408 (December 21/28): 927.
Hawkins, Peter R. 1973a, 'A phonemic transcription system for New Zealand English', *Te Reo* 16: 15–21.
1973b, 'The sound-patterns of New Zealand English', in *Proceedings and Papers of the 15th Australasian Universities Language and Literature Association Conference*, Vol. 13, Sydney: AULLA, pp. 1–8.

Hazen, Kirk 2001, 'The Family', in Chambers et al. 2001: 500–25.

Hearn, Terry 2000, 'Irish migration to New Zealand to 1915', in Fraser 2000: 55–74.

Herz, Max 1912, *New Zealand: The Country and the People*, London: T. Werner Laurie.

Hickey, Raymond 1999, 'Ireland as a linguistic area', *Ulster Folklife* 45 (special issue, *Language in Ulster*, ed. J. P. Mallory): 36–53.

2000, 'Ebb and flow: a cautionary tale of language change', in Fanego, Teresa, Méndez-Naya, Belén, and Seoane, Elena (eds.), *Sounds, Words, Texts and Change*, Philadelphia: John Benjamins, pp. 105–28.

2002, 'How do dialects get the features they have?: On the process of new dialect formation', in Hickey, Raymond (ed.), *Motives for Language Change*, Cambridge: Cambridge University Press, pp. 213–39.

Hickey, Raymond (ed.) forthcoming, *Legacies of Colonial English: A Study in Transported Dialects*, Cambridge: Cambridge University Press.

Hill, Jane 2001, 'Language on the land: towards an anthropological dialectology', in Terrell, John E. (ed.), *Archaeology, Language, and History: Essays on Culture and Ethnicity*, Westport, CT: Bergin & Garvey, pp. 257–82.

Holmes, Janet 1994, 'New Zealand flappers: an analysis of T voicing in New Zealand English', *English World-Wide* 15: 195–224.

1995a, 'Glottal stops in New Zealand English: an analysis of word-final /t/', *Linguistics* 33: 433–63.

1995b, 'Time for /t/: initial /t/ in New Zealand English', *Australian Journal of Linguistics* 15: 127–56.

1995c, 'Two for /t/: flapping and glottal stops in New Zealand English', *Te Reo* 38: 53–72.

1996, 'Losing voice: is final /z/ devoicing a feature of Maori English?', *World Englishes* 15: 193–205.

1997a, 'Māori and Pākeha English: some New Zealand social dialect data', *Language in Society* 26: 65–101.

1997b, 'T-time in New Zealand', *English Today* 51 (13.3): 18–22.

Holmes, Janet and Ainsworth, Helen 1997, 'Unpacking the research process: investigating syllable-timing in New Zealand English', *Language Awareness* 6: 32–47.

Holmes, Janet and Bell, Allan 1990, 'Attitudes, varieties, discourse: an introduction to the sociolinguistics of New Zealand English', in Bell and Holmes 1990: 1–20.

1992, 'On shear markets and sharing sheep: The merger of EAR and AIR diphthongs in New Zealand English', *Language Variation and Change* 4: 251–73.

1994, 'Consonant cluster reduction in New Zealand English', in Holmes, Janet (ed.), *Wellington Working Papers in Linguistics 6*, Wellington: Victoria University, pp. 56–82.

1996, 'Maori English', in Wurm, Stephen A., Mühlhäusler, Peter, and Tryon, Darrell T. (eds.), *Atlas of Languages of Intercultural Communication in the Pacific, Asia and the Americas*, Berlin: Mouton de Gruyter, Vol. 2.1: 177–181.

Holmes, Janet, Bell, Allan, and Boyce, Mary 1991, *Variation and Change in New Zealand English: A Social Dialect Investigation*, Project Report to the Social Sciences Committee of the Foundation for Research, Science and Technology, Wellington: Victoria University.

Hooper, Joan B. 1976, 'Word frequency in lexical diffusion and the source of morphophonological change', in Christie, W. (ed.), *Current Progress in Historical Linguistics*, Amsterdam: North Holland, pp. 96–105.

Hornadge, Bill 1980, *The Australian Slanguage*, Sydney: Methuen.

Hornsby, David 2002, 'Dialect contact and koinéization: the case of northern France', in Jones and Esch 2002: 19–28.

Horvath, Barbara 1985, *Variation in Australian English*, Cambridge: Cambridge University Press.

1998, 'Finding a place in Sydney: migrants and language change', in Trudgill, Peter and Cheshire, Jenny (eds.), *The Sociolinguistics Reader*, Vol. 1: *Multilingualism and Variation*, New York: Arnold, pp. 90–102.

Horvath, Barbara M. and Horvath, Ronald J. 2001, 'A multilocality study of a sound change in progress: the case of /l/ vocalization in New Zealand and Australian English', *Language Variation and Change* 13: 37–57.

Hughes, Arthur and Trudgill, Peter 1995, *English Accents and Dialects*, 3rd ed., London: Edward Arnold.

Huygens, Ingrid and Vaughan, Graham M. 1983, 'Language attitudes, ethnicity and social class in New Zealand', *Journal of Multilingual and Multicultural Development* 4: 207–23.

Ihalainen, Ossi 1994, 'The dialects of England since 1776', in Burchfield 1994b: 197–274.

Jones, Charles 1989, *A History of English Phonology*, London: Longman.

Jones, Mari C. and Esch, Edith (eds.) 2002, *Language Change: The Interplay of Internal, External, and Extra-linguistic Factors*, Berlin: Mouton de Gruyter.

Jurafsky, Daniel in press, 'Probabilistic modelling in psycholinguistics: linguistic comprehension and production', in Bod et al. in press.

Jurafsky, Daniel, Bell, Alan, Gregory, Michelle, and Raymond, William D. 2001, 'Probabilistic relations between words: evidence from reduction in lexical production', in Bybee, Joan L. and Hopper, Paul (eds.), *Frequency and the Emergence of Linguistic Structure*, Philadelphia: John Benjamins, pp. 229–54.

Keating, Patricia A., Wright, Richard, and Zhang, Jie 1999, 'Word-level asymmetries in consonant articulation', *UCLA Working Papers in Phonetics* 97: 157–73.

Kelly, Louis G. 1966, 'The phonemes of New Zealand English', *Canadian Journal of Linguistics* 11.2: 79–82.

Kerswill, Paul 1995, 'Phonological convergence and dialect contact: evidence from citation forms', *Language Variation and Change* 7: 195–207.

1996, 'Children, adolescents, and language change', *Language Variation and Change* 8: 177–202.

2001, 'Koineization and accommodation', in Chambers et al. 2001: 669–702.

Kerswill, Paul and Williams, Ann 1992, 'Some principles of dialect contact: evidence from the new town of Milton Keynes', in Philippaki-Warburton, I. and Ingham, R. (eds.), *Working Papers*, Reading: University of Reading, pp. 68–90.

2000, 'Creating a new town koine: children and language change in Milton Keynes', *Language in Society* 29: 65–115.

2002, '"Salience" as an explanation factor in language change: evidence from dialect levelling in urban England', in Jones and Esch 2002: 81–110.

King, Jeanette 1993, 'Maori English: a phonological study', *New Zealand English Newsletter* 7: 33–47.

1995, 'Maori English as a solidarity marker for te reo Maori', *New Zealand Studies in Applied Linguistics* 1: 51–9.

1999, 'Talking bro: Māori English in the university setting', *Te Reo* 42: 20–38.

King, Michael 1981, *New Zealanders at War*, Auckland: Heinemann.

Krug, Manfred 1998, 'String frequency: a cognitive motivating factor in coalescence, language processing, and linguistic change', *Journal of English Linguistics* 26: 286–320.

Kuiper, Koenraad 1987, 'The study of New Zealand English: a brief position paper', *New Zealand English Newsletter* 1: 3–5.

Kurath, Hans and Lowman, Guy S. 1970, *The Dialectal Structure of Southern England*, Tuscaloosa: University of Alabama Press.

Labov, William 1963, 'The social motivation of sound change', *Word* 19: 273–309. Revised as ch. 1, pp. 1–42 in *Sociolinguistic Patterns*, Philadelphia: University of Pennsylvania Press, 1972.

1990, 'The intersection of sex and social class in the course of linguistic change', *Language Variation and Change* 2: 205–51.

1994, *Principles of Linguistic Change*. Vol. 1: *Internal Factors*, Oxford: Blackwell.

2001, *Principles of Linguistic Change*. Vol. 2: *Social Factors*, Oxford: Blackwell.

Lanham, Len W. 1978, 'South African English', in Lanham, Len W. and Prinsloo, Karel P. (eds.), *Language and Communication Studies in South Africa*, Cape Town: Oxford University Press, pp. 138–65.

Lass, Roger 1987, *The Shape of English*, London: Dent & Sons.

1990, 'Where do extraterrestrial Englishes come from? Dialect, input, and recodification in transported Englishes', in Adamson, Sylvia, Law, Vivien, Vincent, Nigel, and Wright, Susan (eds.), *Papers from the 5th International Conference on English Historical Linguistics*, Philadelphia: John Benjamins, pp. 245–80.

1997, *Historical Linguistics and Language Change*, Cambridge: Cambridge University Press.

Lass, Roger and Wright, Susan 1986, 'Endogeny vs. contact: "Afrikaans influence" on South African English', *English World-Wide* 7: 201–23.

Le Page, Robert B. and Tabouret-Keller, Andrée 1985, *Acts of Identity: Creole-based Approaches to Language and Ethnicity*, Cambridge: Cambridge University Press.

Levelt, Willem J. L. 1983, 'Monitoring and self-repair in speech', *Cognition* 14: 41–104.

Lewis, Ash 1994, Recording of interview, held in the ONZE project, Department of Linguistics, University of Canterbury, Christchurch.

Lewis, Gillian 1996, 'The origins of New Zealand English: a report on work in progress', *New Zealand English Journal* 10: 25–30.

Lindblom, Björn 1990, 'Explaining phonetic variation: a sketch of the H & H Hypothesis', in Hardcastle, William J. and Marchel, Alain (eds.), *Speech Production and Speech Modelling*, Dordrecht: Kluwer, pp. 403–9.

Lobanov, B. M. 1971, 'Classification of Russian vowels spoken by different speakers', *Journal of the Acoustical Society of America* 49: 606–8.

Macdonald, Charlotte 1990, *A Woman of Good Character: Single Women as Immigrant Settlers in Nineteenth-century New Zealand*, Wellington: Allen & Unwin.

Maclagan, David 1998, '/h/-dropping in early New Zealand English', *New Zealand English Journal* 12: 34–42.

Maclagan, Margaret 1975, 'Thoughts on New Zealand English', *The New Zealand Speech-Therapists' Journal* 30.1: 6–11.

1982, 'An acoustic study of New Zealand vowels', *The New Zealand Speech-Therapists' Journal* 37.1: 20–6.

1998, 'Diphthongisation of /e/ in NZE: a change that went nowhere?', *New Zealand English Journal* 12: 43–54.

2000, 'Where are we going in our language? New Zealand English today', *New Zealand Journal of Speech-Language Therapy* 53–54: 14–20.

Maclagan, Margaret and Gordon, Elizabeth 1996a, 'Out of the AIR and into the EAR: another view of the New Zealand diphthong merger', *Language Variation and Change* 8: 125–47.

1996b, 'Women's role in sound change: the case of two New Zealand closing diphthongs', *New Zealand English Journal* 10: 5–9.

1998, 'How *grown* grew from one syllable to two', *Australian Journal of Linguistics* 18: 5–28.

1999, 'Data for New Zealand social dialectology: the Canterbury Corpus', *New Zealand English Journal* 13: 50–8.

2000, 'The NEAR/SQUARE merger in New Zealand English', *Asia Pacific Journal of Speech, Language and Hearing* 5.3: 201–7.

Maclagan, Margaret, Gordon, Elizabeth, and Lewis, Gillian 1999, 'Women and sound change: conservative and innovative behaviour by the same speakers', *Language Variation and Change* 11: 19–41.

MacMahon, Michael K. C. 1983, 'Thomas Hallam and the study of dialect and educated speech', *Transactions of the Yorkshire Dialect Society* 83: 19–31.

1998, 'Phonology', in Romaine, Suzanne (ed.), *The Cambridge History of the English Language*, Vol. 4: *1776–1997*, Cambridge: Cambridge University Press, pp. 373–535.

Macquarie Dictionary 1981, ed., Delbridge, Arthur, Bernard, John R. L., Blair, David, Ramson, W. S., and Butler, Susan, Sydney: The Macquarie Library.

Madieson, Ian 1997, 'Phonetic universals', in Hardcastle, William J. and Laver, John (eds.), *The Handbook of Phonetic Sciences*, Oxford: Blackwell, pp. 619–39.

Mæhlum, Brit 1992, 'Dialect socialization in Longyearbyen, Svalbard (Spitsbergen): a fruitful chaos', in Jahr, Ernst Håkon (ed.), *Language Contact: Theoretical and Empirial Studies*, Berlin: Mouton de Gruyter, pp. 117–30.

1996, 'Semi-migration in the Arctic – a theoretical perspective on the dialect strategies of children on Spitsbergen', in Ureland, Sture and Clarkson, Iain (eds.), *Language Contact Across the North Atlantic*, Tübingen: Niemeyer, pp. 313–31.

Marckwardt, Albert H. 1958, *American English*, New York: Oxford University Press.

Marten, Clement 1992, *The Devonshire Dialect*, Newton Abbot: Peninsula Press.

Matthews, Richard 1981, 'The second Great Vowel Shift?', *Journal of the International Phonetic Association* 11.1: 22–6.

McAloon, Jim 1996, 'The colonial wealthy in Canterbury and Otago: no idle rich', *New Zealand Journal of History* 30: 43–60.

McBurney, Samuel 1887, 'Colonial pronunciation', *The Press* 5 October: 5.

McClure, J. Derrick 1994, 'English in Scotland', in Burchfield 1994b: 23–93.

McGeorge, Colin 1984, 'Hear our voices we entreat', *New Zealand Journal of History* 18: 3–18.

McKinnon, Malcolm (ed.) 1997, *New Zealand Historical Atlas*, Auckland: Bateman.

McLaughlin, John C. 1970, *Aspects of the History of English*, New York: Holt, Reinhart & Winston.

McLeod, Janet 1940, *Rhyming Roadways to Good Speech*, Christchurch: Simpson & Williams.

Mees, I. M. and Collins, B. 1999, 'Cardiff: a real-time study of glottalisation', in Foulkes and Docherty 1999: 185–202.

Mendoza-Denton, Norma, Hay, Jennifer, and Jannedy, Stefanie in press, 'Probabilistic sociolinguistics: beyond variable rules', in Bod et al. in press: 97–138.

Mesthrie, Rajend 1993, 'Koineization in the Bhojpuri-Hindi diaspora, with special reference to South Africa', *International Journal of the Sociology of Language* 99: 25–44.

Meyerhoff, Miriam 1987, 'A review of sex and language research in New Zealand', in Pauwels, Ann (ed.), *Women and Language in Australian and New Zealand Society*, Sydney: Australian Professional Publications, pp. 32–44.

Milroy, James 1983, 'On the sociolinguistic history of /h/-dropping in English', in Davenport, Michael, Hansen, Erik, and Nielsen, Hans Frede (eds.), *Current Topics in English Historical Linguistics*, Odense: Odense University Press, pp. 37–66.

1992, *Linguistic Variation and Change*, Oxford: Blackwell.

1993, 'On the social origins of language change', in Jones, Charles (ed.), *Historical Linguistics: Problems and Perspectives*, London: Longmans, pp. 213–36.

Milroy, James and Milroy, Lesley 1985, 'Linguistic change, social network and speaker innovation', *Journal of Linguistics* 21: 339–84.

Milroy, Lesley 1980, *Language and Social Networks*, Oxford: Blackwell.

2001, 'Social networks', in Chambers et al. 2001: 549–72.

2002, 'Introduction: mobility, contact and language change – working with contemporary speech communities', *Journal of Sociolinguistics* 6: 3–15.

Ministry for Culture and Heritage, 'A Home away from "Home": British and Irish immigration to New Zealand, 1840–1914', http://www.nzhistory.net.nz/gallery/brit-nz/, accessed 2002.

Mitchell, Alex G. 1995, 'The story of Australian English: users and environment', from a public lecture given at Macquarie University, 12 October, Dictionary Research Centre, Sydney.

Mitchell, Alex G. and Delbridge, Arthur 1965, *The Speech of Australian Adolescents*, Sydney: Angus & Robertson.

Mohan, Peggy 1978, *Trinidad Bhojpuri: A Morphological Study*, PhD dissertation, University of Michigan.

Morgan, James N. and Messenger, Robert C. 1973, *THAID: A Sequential Analysis Program for the Analysis of Nominal Scale Dependent Variables, Technical Report*, Ann Arbor: Institute for Social Research, University of Michigan.

Morgan, James N. and Sonquist, John A. 1963, 'Problems in the analysis of survey data, and a proposal', *Journal of the American Statistical Association* 58: 415–35.

Mufwene, Salikoko S. 1996, 'The Founder Principle in creole genesis', *Diachronica* 13: 81–134.

2001, *The Ecology of Language Evolution*, Cambridge: Cambridge University Press.

Mulgan, Alan 1927, *Home: A New Zealander's Adventure*, London: Longmans.

Munro, Murray, Derwing, Tracey, and Flege, James E. 1999, 'Canadians in Alabama: a perceptual study of dialect acquisition in adults', *Journal of Phonetics* 27: 385–403.

New Zealand Department of Education 1925, *Speech Training* (Special report no. 14), Wellington: New Zealand Department of Education.

New Zealand Ministry of Education 1990, 'Derivation of Elley-Irving codes from census occupations', unpublished manuscript, Wellington.

1994, *English in the New Zealand Curriculum*, Wellington: Learning Media.

1996, *Exploring Language: A Handbook for Teachers*, Wellington: Learning Media.
Northcote-Bade, James 1976, 'An introduction to New Zealand English', *Englisch* 11: 147–51.
NZhistory.net 2002 – See Ministry for Culture and Heritage.
O'Connor, Joseph D. 1973, *Phonetics*, Harmondsworth: Penguin.
Oliver William H. 1960, *The Story of New Zealand*, London: Faber & Faber.
Omdal, Helge 1977, 'Høyangermålet – en ny dialekt' [The language of Høyanger – a new dialect], *Språklig Samling* 1: 7–9.
Orsman, Harold W. 1951, 'New Zealand English', in Partridge and Clark 1951: 93–5.
1995, 'The dictionary of New Zealand English – a beginning and (almost) an end', *New Zealand English Newsletter* 9: 9–12.
Orton, Harold and Wakelin, Martyn F. 1967, *Survey of English Dialects: The Southern Counties*, Leeds: Arnold.
Orton, Harold and Tilling, Philip M. 1969, *Survey of English Dialects: The East Midland Counties and East Anglia*, Leeds: Arnold.
Owens, John M. R. 1992, 'New Zealand before annexation', in Rice 1992: 28–56.
Page, Ian W. 1956, *Relations between New Zealand and the Australian Colonies, 1850–1870*, MA thesis, University of Otago, Dunedin.
Partridge, Eric and Clark, John W. (eds.) 1951, *British and American English Since 1900*, London: Andrew Dakers.
Payne, Arvilla 1980, 'Factors controlling the acquisition of the Philadelphia dialect by out-of-state children', in Labov, William (ed.), *Locating Language in Time and Space*, New York: Academic Press, pp. 143–78.
Pei, Mario A. 1946, *The World's Chief Languages*, 3rd ed., New York: S. F. Vanni.
Phillipps Kenneth C. 1984, *Language and Class in Victorian England*, Oxford: Blackwell.
Pickens, Keith A. 1977, 'The origins of the population of nineteenth century Canterbury', *New Zealand Geographer* 33.2: 60–75.
Porter, Frances 1989, *Born to New Zealand: A Biography of Jane Maria Atkinson*, Wellington: Allen & Unwin and Port Nicholson Press.
Porter, Frances and Macdonald, Charlotte (eds.) 1996, *My Hand Will Write What My Heart Dictates*, Auckland: Auckland University Press and Bridget Williams Books.
Portney, Leslie G. and Watkins, Mary P. 2000, *Foundations of Clinical Research, Applications to Practice*, 2nd ed., Upper Saddle River, NJ: Prentice Hall Health.
Prince, Ellen 1987, 'Sarah Gorby, Yiddish folksinger: a case study of dialect shift', *International Journal of the Sociology of Language* 67: 83–116.
Ramson, William S. (ed.) 1970, *English Transported: Essays on Australasian English*, Canberra: Australian National University Press.
Rastatter, Michael P. and Jacques, Richard D. 1990, 'Formant frequency structure of the ageing male and female vocal tract', *Folia Phoniatrica et Logopaedica* 42: 312–19.
Rastatter, Michael P., McGuire, Richard A., Kalinowski, Joseph, and Stuart, Andrew 1997, 'Formant frequency characteristics of elderly speakers in contextual speech', *Folia Phoniatrica et Logopaedica* 49: 1–8.
Rice, Geoffrey W. (ed.) 1992, *The Oxford History of New Zealand*, 2nd ed., Auckland: Oxford University Press.
Rickford, John R. 1997, 'Prior creolization of African-American vernacular English? Sociohistorical and textual evidence from the 17th and 18th centuries', *Journal of Sociolinguistics* 1: 315–36.

Rickford, John R. and McNair-Knox, Faye 1994, 'Addressee- and topic-influenced style shift: a quantitative sociolinguistic study', in Biber, Douglas and Finegan, Edward (eds.), *Sociolinguistic Perspectives on Register*, Oxford: Oxford University Press, pp. 235–76.

Ritchie, William C. and Bhatia, Tej K. 1999 (eds.), *Handbook of Child Language Acquisition*, San Diego: Academic Press.

Roach, Peter 1983, *English Phonetics and Phonology: A Practical Course*, Cambridge: Cambridge University Press.

Robinson, Portia 1985, *The Hatch and Brood of Rime: A Study of the First Generation of Native-born White Australians 1788–1828*, Melbourne: Oxford University Press.

Romaine, Suzanne 1994, *Language in Society: An Introduction to Sociolinguistics*, Oxford: Oxford University Press.

Ross, Malcolm 1996, 'Contact-induced change and the comparative method: cases from Papua New Guinea', in Durie, Mark and Ross, Malcolm (eds.), *The Comparative Method Reviewed: Regularity and Irregularity in Language Change*, Oxford: Oxford University Press, pp. 180–217.

1997, 'Social networks and kinds of speech community events', in Blench, Roger and Spriggs, Matthew (eds.), *Archaeology and Language*, Vol. 1: *Theoretical and Methodological Orientations*, London: Routledge, pp. 209–61.

2001, 'Contact-induced change in Oceanic languages in North-West Melanesia', in Aikhenvald, Alexandra Y. and Dixon, R. M. W. (eds.), *Areal Diffusion and Genetic Inheritance: Problems in Comparative Linguistics*, Oxford: Oxford University Press, pp. 134–66.

Sankoff, Gillian 1980, *The Social Life of Language*, Philadelphia: University of Pennsylvania Press.

Sankoff, Gillian, Blondeau, Hélène, and Charity, Anne 2001, 'Individual roles in a real-time change: Montreal (r > R) 1947–1995', in Van de Velde, Hans and van Hout, Roeland (eds.), *'r-atics: Sociolinguistic, Phonetic and Phonological Characteristics of /r/*, Etude and Travaux 4, Brussels: ILVP, pp. 141–57.

Sapir, Edward 1921, *Language: An Introduction to the Study of Speech*, New York: Harcourt Brace & Co.

Schilling-Estes, Natalie 2002, 'On the nature of isolated and post-isolated dialects: innovation, variation, and differentiation', *Journal of Sociolinguistics* 6: 64–85.

Scholtmeijer, Harm 1992, *Het Nederlands van de IJsselmeerpolders*, Kampen: Mondiss.

Scholtmeijer, Harm 1997, 'Language in the Dutch polders: Why dialects did not mix', Paper given at the European Science Foundation Conference on the Convergence and Divergence of Dialects in a Changing Europe, Heidelberg.

Schreier, Daniel 2001, *Non-standard Grammar and Geographical Isolation: The Genesis, Development and Structure of Tristan da Cunha English*, PhD dissertation, University of Fribourg, Switzerland.

2002a, 'Past *be* in Tristan da Cunha: the rise and fall of categoriality in language change', *American Speech* 77: 70–99.

2002b, 'Terra incognita in the anglophone world: Tristan da Cunha, South Atlantic Ocean', *English World-Wide* 23.1: 1–29.

2003, *Isolation and Language Change: Contemporary and Sociohistorical Evidence from Tristan da Cunha English*, Houndmills, Basingstoke: Palgrave Macmillan.

Shorrocks, Graham 1998, *A Grammar of the Dialect of the Bolton Area, part 1: Introduction, Phonology*, Frankfurt: Lang.

Siegel, Jeff 1985, 'Koines and koineization', *Language in Society* 14: 357–78.

1993, 'Dialect contact and koineization (review of *Dialects in Contact*, by Peter Trudgill)', *International Journal of the Sociology of Language* 99: 105–21.

Simpson, Sam 1996, *Dialect Contact in Telford New Town*, unpublished BA project, University of Essex.

Simpson, Tony 1997, *The Immigrants: The Great Migration from Britain to New Zealand, 1830–1890*, Auckland: Godwit.

Sinclair, Keith 1986a, *A Destiny Apart: New Zealand's Search for National Identity*, Wellington: Allen & Unwin.

1986b, *The Native Born: The Origins of New Zealand Nationalism*, Occasional publication no. 8, Palmerston North: Massey University.

(ed.) 1987, *Tasman Relations: New Zealand and Australia, 1788–1988*, Auckland: Auckland University Press.

1991, *A History of New Zealand*, 4th ed., Auckland: Penguin.

(ed.) 1996, *The Oxford Illustrated History of New Zealand*, 2nd ed., Auckland: Oxford University Press.

Sivertsen, Eva 1960, *Cockney Phonology*, Oslo: Oslo University Press.

Soljak, Philip B. 1946, *New Zealand: Pacific Pioneer*, New York: Macmillan, excerpt reprinted in *New Zealand English Newsletter* 5, 1991: 42–4.

Stewart, Dorothy M. 1925, *Phonetics Practice Book*, 2nd ed., Christchurch: Whitcombe & Tombs.

Strang, Barbara M. H. 1970, *A History of English*, London: Methuen.

Stubbe, Maria and Holmes, Janet 2000, *Talking Maori or Pakeha in English*, in Bell and Kuiper 2000: 249–78.

Sudbury, Andrea 2000, *Dialect Contact and Koineisation in the Falkland Islands: Development of a Southern Hemisphere Variety*, unpublished PhD thesis, University of Essex.

2001, 'Falkland Islands English: a southern hemisphere variety?', *English World-Wide* 22: 55–80.

Sudbury, Andrea and Hay, Jennifer 2002, 'The fall and rise of /r/: rhoticity and /r/ sandhi in early New Zealand English', in *Working Papers in Linguistics* 8.3: Papers from NWAVE [New Ways of Analysing Variation] 30, Philadelphia: University of Pennsylvania, pp. 281–95.

Sutch, William B. 1966, *The Quest for Security in New Zealand 1840–1966*, Wellington: Oxford University Press.

Swainson, William 1859, *New Zealand and its Colonisation*, London: Smith, Elder & Co.

Sweet, Henry 1888, *A History of English Sounds from the Earliest Period, with Full Word-lists*, Oxford: Clarendon Press.

Tabouret-Keller, Andrée 1997, 'Language and identity', in Coulmas 1997: 315–26.

Thelander, Mats 1979, *Språkliga variationsmodeller tillämpade på nutida burträsktal* [Models of linguistic variation applied to the modern dialect of Burträsk], Uppsala: Acta Universitatis Upsaliensis.

Thomas, Alan 1994, 'English in Wales', in Burchfield 1994b: 94–147.

Thurston, William R. 1987, *Processes of Change in the Languages of Northwestern New Britain*, Canberra: Australian National University.

1989, 'How exoteric languages build a lexicon: esoterogeny in West New Britain', in Harlow, Ray and Hooper, Robin (eds.), *VICAL 1, Oceanic Languages: Papers from the 5th International Conference of Austronesian Linguistics*, Auckland: Linguistic Society of New Zealand, pp. 555–80.

Tollfree, Laura 1999, 'South East London English', in Foulkes and Docherty 1999: 163–84.

Treiman, Rebecca and Danis, Catalina 1998, 'Syllabification of intervocalic consonants', *Journal of Memory and Language* 27: 87–104.

Trudgill, Peter 1974, *The Social Differentiation of English in Norwich*, Cambridge: Cambridge University Press.

1986a, 'Dialect mixture and the analysis of colonial dialects: the case of Canadian raising', in Warkentyne, H. (ed.), *Methods in Dialectology 5*, Victoria, BC: University of Victoria, pp. 35–46.

1986b, *Dialects in Contact*, Oxford: Blackwell.

1988, 'On the role of dialect contact and interdialect in linguistic change', in Fisiak, Jacek (ed.), *Historical Dialectology*, Berlin: Mouton de Gruyter, pp. 547–63.

1989, 'Interlanguage, interdialect and typological change', in Gass, Susan M., Madden, Carolyn G., Preston. Denis, and Selinker, Larry (eds.), *Variation in Second Language Acquisition: Psycholinguistic Issues*, Clevedon: Multilingual Matters, pp. 244–53.

1997a, 'British vernacular dialects in the formation of American English: the case of East Anglian *do*', in Hickey, Ray and Puppel, Stanislaw (eds.), *Linguistic History and Linguistic Modelling: A Festschrift for Jacek Fisiak on his 60th Birthday*, Berlin: Mouton de Gruyter, pp. 749–58.

1997b, 'The chaos before the order: New Zealand English and the second stage of new dialect formation', in Jahr, Ernst Håkon (ed.), *Language Change: Advances in Historical Sociolinguistics*, Berlin: Mouton de Gruyter, pp. 197–207.

1999a, 'A Southern Hemisphere East Anglian: New Zealand English as a resource for the study of 19th century British English', in Carls, Uwe and Lucko, Peter (eds.), *Form, Function and Variation in English: Studies in Honour of Klaus Hansen*, Berlin: Peter Lang, pp. 169–74.

1999b, 'A window on the past: "colonial lag" and New Zealand evidence for the phonology of 19th-century English', *American Speech* 74: 227–39.

1999c, 'New-dialect formation and dedialectalization: embryonic and vestigial variants', *Journal of English Linguistics* 27.4: 319–27.

1999d, *The Dialects of England*, 2nd ed., Oxford: Blackwell.

2001, 'On the irrelevance of prestige, stigma and identity in the development of New Zealand English phonology', *New Zealand English Journal* 15: 42–6.

Trudgill, Peter, Gordon, Elizabeth, and Lewis, Gillian 1998, 'New dialect formation and Southern Hemisphere English: the New Zealand short front vowels', *Journal of Sociolinguistics* 2.1: 35–51.

Trudgill, Peter, Gordon, Elizabeth, Lewis, Gillian, and Maclagan, Margaret 2000a, 'Determinism in new-dialect formation and the genesis of New Zealand English', *Journal of Linguistics* 36: 299–318.

2000b, 'The role of drift in the formation of native-speaker Southern Hemisphere Englishes: some New Zealand evidence', *Diachronica* 17: 111–38.

Trudgill, Peter and Hannah, Jean 1982 *International English: A Guide to Varieties of Standard English* [4th ed. 2002], London: Edward Arnold.

Trudgill, Peter, Maclagan, Margaret, and Lewis, Gillian 2003, 'Linguistic archaeology: the Scottish input to New Zealand English phonology', *Journal of English Linguistics*.

Trudgill, Peter, Schreier, Daniel, Long, Daniel, and Williams, Jeffrey P. in press, 'On the reversibility of mergers: /w/, /v/ and evidence from lesser-known Englishes', *Folia Linguistica Historica*.

Turner, George W. 1960, 'On the origin of Australian vowel sounds', *Journal of the Australasian Universities Modern Language Association* 13: 33–45.

1966, *The English Language in Australia and New Zealand*, London: Longmans.

1967, 'Samuel McBurney's newspaper article on colonial pronunciation', *Journal of the Australasian Universities Modern Language Association* 27: 81–5.

1970, 'New Zealand English today', in Ramson 1970: 84–101.

1994, 'English in Australia', in Burchfield 1994b: 277–327.

United States War and Navy Department 1944, *A Short Guide to New Zealand*, Washington, DC: US Government Printing Office, reprinted in *New Zealand English Newsletter* 5, 1991: 42–4.

van Bergem, Dick R. 1993, 'Acoustic vowel reduction as a function of sentence accent, word stress and word class', *Speech Communication* 12: 1–23.

Venables, William N. and Ripley, Brian D. 1994, *Modern Applied Statistics with S-Plus*, New York: Springer-Verlag.

Wall, Arnold 1936, *The Mother Tongue in New Zealand*, Dunedin: Reed.

1939, *New Zealand English: How it Should be Spoken*, Christchurch: Whitcombe & Tombs.

1951a, 'New Zealand English', in Partridge and Clark 1951: 90–1.

1951b, 'The Way I Have Come', Radio broadcast recording held in the Radio New Zealand Sound Archives, Christchurch. Transcription by Elizabeth Gordon.

1958, *The Queen's English*, Christchurch: Pegasus Press.

1959, *New Zealand English: A Guide to the Correct Pronunciation of English, with Special Reference to New Zealand Conditions and Problems*, 3rd enlarged ed. [1939], Christchurch: Whitcombe & Tombs.

1964, *The Jeweller's Window – Some Notes and Reflections on the Ways of Words and Men*, Christchurch: Whitcombe & Tombs.

1966, 'New Zealand speech', in McLintock A. H. (ed.), *An Encyclopedia of New Zealand*, Vol. 2, Wellington: Government Printer, pp. 677–80.

Ward, A. 1952, *Some Problems in the English Orthoepists 1750–1809*, unpublished BLitt thesis, University of Oxford.

Watson, Catherine, Harrington, Jonathan, and Evans, Zoe 1998, 'An acoustic comparison between New Zealand and Australian English vowels', *Australian Journal of Linguistics* 18: 185–207.

Watson, Catherine, Maclagan, Margaret, and Harrington, Jonathan 2000, 'Acoustic evidence for vowel change in New Zealand English', *Language Variation and Change* 12: 51–68.

Wells, John C. 1982, *Accents of English*, Cambridge: Cambridge University Press.

1994, 'The Cockneyfication of RP?', in Melchers, Gunnel and Johannesson, Nils-Lennart (eds.), *Nonstandard Varieties of Language*, Stockholm: Almqvist & Wiksell International, pp. 198–205.

Whalen, Douglas 1991, 'Infrequent words are longer in duration than frequent words', *Journal of the Acoustical Society of America* 90: 2311.

Whitney, William Dwight 1904, *Language and the Study of Language: Twelve Lectures on the Principles of Language Science*, 6th ed., New York: Charles Scribner & Co.

Williams, Ann and Kerswill, Paul 1999, 'Dialect level/ing: change and continuity in Milton Keynes, Reading and Hull', in Foulkes and Docherty 1999: 141–62.

Wolfram, Walt and Beckett, Daniel 2000, 'The role of individual differences in Earlier African American Vernacular English', *American Speech* 75: 1–30.

Wolfram, Walt and Schilling-Estes, Natalie 1998, *American English: Dialects and Variation*, Malden, MA: Blackwell, pp. 94–6.

forthcoming, 'Remnant dialects in the coastal United States', in Hickey forthcoming.

Wolfram, Walt and Sellers, Jason 1999, 'Ethnolinguistic marking of past *be* in Lumbee Vernacular English', *Journal of English Linguistics* 27: 94–114.

Wolfram, Walt and Thomas, Erik R. 2002, *The Development of African American English*, Oxford: Blackwell.

Wolfram, Walt, Hazen, Kirk, and Schilling-Estes, Natalie 1999, *Dialect Change and Maintenance on the Outer Banks, American Dialect Society no. 81*, Tuscaloosa: University of Alabama Press.

Wolfram, Walt, Thomas, Erik, and Green, Elaine 2000, 'The regional context of Earlier African-American speech: evidence for reconstructing the development of AAE', *Language in Society* 29: 315–55.

Woods, Nicola 1997, 'The formation and development of New Zealand English: interaction of gender-related variation and language change', *Journal of Sociolinguistics* 1.1: 95–125.

2000a, 'Archaism and innovation in New Zealand English', *English World-Wide* 21: 109–50.

2000b, 'New Zealand English across the generations: an analysis of selected vowel and consonant variables', in Bell and Kuiper 2000: 84–110.

2001, 'Internal and external dimensions of language change: the great divide? Evidence from New Zealand English', *Linguistics* 39.5: 973–1007.

Wright, Joseph 1905, *The English Dialect Grammar*, Oxford: Oxford University Press.

Wright, Richard 1997, 'Lexical competition and reduction in speech: a preliminary report', in *Research on Spoken Language Processing, Progress report no. 21*, Bloomington: Indiana University, pp. 471–83.

Wyld, Henry Cecil 1914, *A Short History of English*, 3rd ed., reprinted 1929, London: John Murray.

1936, *History of Modern Colloquial English*, 3rd ed. [1920], Oxford: Blackwell.

Yaeger-Dror, Malcah 1994, 'Sound change in Montreal French', in Keating, Patricia (ed.), *Phonological Structure and Phonetic Form*, Papers in Laboratory Phonology 3, Cambridge: Cambridge University Press, pp. 267–92.

1996, 'Phonetic evidence for the evolution of lexical classes: the case of a Montreal French vowel shift', in Guy, Gregory, Feagin, Crawford, Baugh, John, and Schiffrin, Deborah (eds.), *Towards a Social Science of Language*, Philadelphia: John Benjamins, pp. 263–87.

Yaeger-Dror, Malach and Kemp, William 1992, 'Lexical classes in Montreal French (ᴇː)', *Language and Speech* 35.3: 251–93.

Yallop, Colin 2000, 'A. G. Mitchell and the development of Australian pronunciation', in Blair, David and Collins, Peter (eds.), *English in Australia*, Philadelphia: John Benjamins.

Yoneda, Masato 1993, ‘Survey of standardization in Tsuruoka City, Japan: Comparison of results from three surveys conducted at twenty-year intervals’, Paper presented at Methods 8: International Conference in Dialectology, University of Victoria, British Columbia.

Zelinsky, Wilbur 1992, *The Cultural Geography of the United States: A Revised Edition*, Englewood Cliffs, NJ: Prentice Hall.

Index